The HUTCHINSC
DICTIONARY OF
COMPUTING
AND THE
INTERNET
FOURTH EDITION

Helicon

Text and original illustrations © Helicon Publishing Limited 1997, 1998, 1999, 2001
First Published (as *The Hutchinson Dictionary of Computing,
Multimedia and the Internet*) 1997
Second Edition 1998
Third Edition 1999
Reprinted 1999
Fourth Edition 2001

Helicon Publishing Ltd
42 Hythe Bridge Street
Oxford OX1 3EP
e-mail: admin@helicon.co.uk
Web Site: http://www.helicon.co.uk

ISBN 1-85986-357-4

British Cataloguing in Publication Data

A catalogue record for this book is available from the British Library

Typeset by Florence Production Ltd, Stoodleigh, Devon
Printed and bound in Spain by
Mateu Cromo Atres Graficas

Acknowledgements

We would like to thank the following for screen shots of proprietory software:
Adobe (Illustrator), MegaTech Software GmbH (MegaCAD),
Microsoft Corp. (Excel, Internet Explorer, PowerPoint, Word),
Netscape (Navigator); and the following WWW pages:
AltaVista (http://www.altavista.com)
Internet Explorer (http://www.microsoft.com/windows.ie) © Microsoft Corporation
Infoseek (http://www.go.com) © 2000 Disney Enterprises, Inc. All rights reserved
Netscape (http://home.netscape.com) © Netscape Communications Corporation
Yahoo (http://www.yahoo.com) © Yahoo! Inc
Humbul Humanities Hub (http://www.humbul.ac.uk)

Contents

How to Use This Book

The articles are arranged in alphabetical order as if there were no spaces between words. Thus entries after **site** follow the order: **site, site licence, 16-bit, 64-bit, slide shows.**

Terms are usually placed under the name by which they are most widely known. If the abbreviated form of a term is so widely used that the expanded form is unlikely to be looked up, the main definition is given under the abbreviation, for example **RAM** not **random access memory**.

As well as articles, the dictionary provides feature essays by journalists whose business it is to spot recent developments, and by academics who are writing in their field. Subjects include 'Handheld Computers', 'Interactive Television', 'Electronic Books' and 'Payment over the Internet'. There are many illustrations to give visual support to the articles, and a good number of tables that help you compare like with like. In addition, the dictionary has a special 'Tips' feature whereby handy hints are displayed alongside the articles.

Finally, there is an expansive and detailed chronology at the end of the book. This gives a step-by-step guide to the developments in computer science and technology, and a distillation of the major contributors from the earliest times until the present day.

Consultant editor

Alan Stewart is a freelance business technology writer, and was formerly an information technology manager. A regular contributor to the *Financial Times* and *Internet Business*, he is also author of *The Business Impact of Network Computing* and *How to Make it in IT*.

Contributors

Charles Arthur is technical editor for the *Independent*.

Stephen Ball is a freelance author and editor, and a visiting lecturer in publishing at Oxford Brookes University.

Paul Bray is a freelance technology journalist who writes for the *Daily Telegraph*, the *Sunday Times*, and a number of computer magazines.

Wendy M Grossman is a freelance writer specializing in science and technology. She is a regular contributor to the *Daily Telegraph* and *Scientific American*, and author of *net.wars* and *From Anarchy to Power: The Net Comes of Age*.

Anne Querée is a freelance journalist and business writer.

Jonathan Rowe is a lecturer in Computer Science at Birmingham University.

Jack Schofield is a journalist and computer editor for the *Guardian*.

Trevor Clawson is a business journalist specialising in e-commerce and new media issues. He is currently working as a staff writer for *e. Business* magazine.

Alan Stewart is a freelance business technology writer, and was formerly an information technology manager. A regular contributor to the *Financial Times* and *Internet Business*, he is also author of *The Business Impact of Network Computing* and *How to Make it in IT*.

Editors

Editorial Director
Hilary McGlynn

Managing Editor
Elena Softley

Project Editor
Heather Slade

Technical Editor
Rachel Margolis

Content Editors
Tracey Auden
Claire Lishman

Production and Design

Cover Design
Mark-making Ltd

Picture Research
Sophie Evans

Production Manager
John Normansell

Production Assistant
Stacey Penny

Illustrations
Mike Ing

Features

Tables

Illustrations

Introduction to the Internet

Browsing the World Wide Web The World Wide Web was invented in 1990 by Tim Berners-Lee and Robert Caillau, researchers at CERN (European Laboratory for Particle Physics) in Geneva, Switzerland, as an easy way of accessing information on computers connected to the Internet. The Web only began to be used in a big way, however, three years later, when Mosaic, the first Web browser program for Microsoft Windows, was written by Marc Andreessen and Eric Bina of the University of Illinois's National Center for Supercomputing Applications (NCSA). The two main Web browsers in use today are Microsoft Internet Explorer and Netscape Navigator, both based on Mosaic.

By 2000, the Web had over 1.2 billion pages, containing just about anything you might possibly be interested in, and quite a lot that you would think hardly anyone would want to know about! These Web pages are grouped together into Web sites (nearly three million of them publicly accessible), each of which has a unique address, known as a uniform resource locator or URL. Most URLs begin with the letters 'www' and end in standardized suffixes that identify the type and location of the organization. For example, 'co' indicates a company, and 'uk' that its location is in the United Kingdom.

Organizations large and small have put up sites on the Web. Big corporations usually have several linked sites for different countries in their own languages, often containing video and audio clips. Vast numbers of private individuals have also created their own sites with information on different aspects of their lives, usually illustrated with photographs. Sometimes, an individual's Web site will be there to display examples of their work, but mostly it will be just for fun, perhaps containing information on a particular hobby or interest, or general information on their life.

To get to a particular Web site, you just type the address of its opening page (or home page) into the address line of the browser and press the return key, and the home page should appear on your screen. You don't have to remember lots of addresses, though, because you can store them as 'favorites' (in Explorer) or 'bookmarks' (in Navigator) and select the addresses from there next time. You can group the addresses together, so that you can easily find them again.

You can normally specify which Web site you want your browser to go to each time you open it to log on to the Internet. Your Internet Service Provider (ISP) will probably have selected its own Web site as a default, and sometimes you are not allowed to change that. Usually, the ISP's site will be a portal providing a number of services such as news, Web e-mail, shopping, and auctions.

To reach these services, or other linked Web sites, you need only click on a link, often an underlined URL on the page you're looking at. In addition, when you move the mouse pointer across the page, you'll sometimes see the pointer change to a hand and a Web address appear at the bottom of the browser screen. Again, you only have to click with your mouse and you'll be taken to the relevant site.

Choosing a modem You can't get onto the Internet without a modem (short for modulator/demodulator), which converts the digital data from your computer into analogue signals for the telephone line, and vice versa. Most home computers these days come with a modem built in. If your PC or Macintosh doesn't already have one, however, you can fairly easily add an internal modem by plugging one into your computer's main board. Adding an internal modem is not a task for the complete novice, however, as some of your computer's existing settings may have to be changed. If you're in doubt, it's best to get a dealer to do it for you.

The modem plugs into the telephone system through a standard telephone socket. Ideally, you'll be using a different telephone line for Internet access from the one you use for voice calls. If you don't want to pay for a second line, you need a small device to route your incoming calls to your phone, computer, or fax machine. Otherwise, you might find that, when someone tries to call you, your phone doesn't ring, although the caller hears a ringing tone on their phone.

A modem in a new computer should transmit at a speed of 56 Kilobits per second (Kbps) to V.90 standard, and that's what you should be looking for too. Anything slower than that will work for e-mail, but not for Web browsing, where even 56 Kbps can seem fairly slow. This is what people jokingly refer to as the 'World Wide Wait'.

Getting a faster connection The type of modem mentioned above is for standard dial-up access, using an ordinary telephone line. As this is not very fast, you may want to consider a connection using Integrated Services Digital Network (ISDN), which can transmit at a rate of 128 Kbps. Instead of a modem, ISDN uses a terminal adapter, which is more expensive, and the charges for ISDN rental and calls are likely to be higher than for a standard phone line.

For much faster broadband access, you could try Asymmetric Digital Subscriber Line (ADSL), which can provide a connection rate ranging from 512 Kbps to 6 Megabits per second (Mbps). Speeds of between 1.5 and 2.7 Mbps can be reached using a cable modem but, as with ADSL, the actual speeds obtained depend on the number of other users on the line at the time. ISDN, ADSL, and cable modems provide an 'always on' service, whereas it takes about half a minute to log on via a dial-up service.

However, even a fast connection will not remove delays that are due to 'traffic jams' on the main Internet backbone cable or satellite links, or at the other end of the connection, if a Web site is particularly popular.

Choosing an Internet service provider Once you have a modem in your computer, you need the services of an Internet Service Provider (ISP). This is a company that your computer phones up, which connects it to the Internet. If you live in a country like the UK, where even local telephone calls are metered, you can end up paying some fairly hefty phone bills, once you start logging onto the Internet regularly.

What you should be looking for is completely free, unmetered Internet access, with no charges even for your connecting phone calls. The next best thing is paying a flat fee to the ISP and getting free calls. If you don't pay any money to the ISP, but you do pay for phone calls, you still need to be careful how long you spend online. The phone calls are usually the most expensive part of the cost of Internet access.

Some ISPs merely connect you to the Internet, without providing any added value. Others, such as America Online (AOL), are better described as Online Service Providers, with a great deal of content (information and services) accessible to their subscribers alone. Before you choose whom to connect through, you need to look carefully at the competing offers available from different ISPs.

Downloading software Among the programs you're likely to want to download onto your computer are the latest versions of the Explorer or Navigator browsers. At

How to Search the World Wide Web: A Tutorial for Beginners and Non-Experts

http://204.17.98.73/midlib/tutor.htm

Extensive guide to searching the Internet. The tutorial begins with 'Basics Of Conducting A Search' and progresses onto more 'Advanced Information' such as 'Search Tool Descriptions'.

WEB LINK

Internet Detective

http://sosig.ac.uk/desire/
internet-detective.html

Interactive tutorial that teaches users how to evaluate the quality of information they find on the Internet. There are numerous hints and tips, as well as practical examples of the evaluation process. Not only does the tutorial cover standard Web sites, but also electronic journals and mailing lists.

WEB LINK

Digital Librarian

http://www.digital-
librarian.com/

Site based on a US librarian's choice of the best sites on the Web. Start from an A–Z list of first-level categories, then click on a subcategory to access a list of sites selected by the author.

WEB LINK

the Microsoft or Netscape Web sites, you will find instructions on how to download the software free of charge. How long it will take depends on the speed at which your modem operates and the size of the program you're downloading. With a 56-Kbps modem, even a very large program will only take about half an hour to transfer to your PC or Macintosh.

As well as new browser versions, you can also download free versions of other software, such as RealPlayer, which will play audio and video files. These can be either streaming (playing as you download them from the Internet) or files you already have on your PC or Macintosh. Alternatively, you may want to download new games to play on your computer, or perhaps listen to music, in which case you can first download player software such as WinAmp, and then some music files compressed in MP3 format.

There are special programs, such as WS-FTP or CuteFTP, that use File Transfer Protocol (FTP) to enable you to download from (and upload to) Web sites, but you can do basic downloads over the Web using a browser.

Searching for information A big problem with the Internet is that, although there are all those millions of Web sites, it can be very difficult to find the information you want. To make this easier, there are a number of sites that feature what is known as a search engine. You enter a description of the information you want to find (for example 'online banking'), and the search engine will list all the Web pages containing these words. The trouble is that you're more likely to find half a million than half a dozen sites. The best search engines, however, such as Google and AltaVista, list the most relevant sites first.

Shopping and banking online Nowadays, there are a great many Web sites where you can buy things. The most popular items are books, compact discs, videos, and airline tickets, because you don't need to see them before you buy. You can also buy all kinds of other goods online, and even do your weekly grocery shopping at various supermarkets on the Web.

The usual method of payment is by credit card, and people often worry about sending their credit card details over the Internet. They're quite right to be concerned, as there have been some high-profile cases of Web sites, including banks, not having in place the tight security they ought to.

You shouldn't send sensitive information such as credit card details over the Internet unless the site you're sending them to allows you to do so over a secure connection. Your information will then be encrypted (scrambled) before it is transmitted, so that, even if other people managed to intercept it, they wouldn't be able to read it.

As well as shopping online, you can also bank over the Internet, and in some countries this is very popular. It is certainly very convenient to be able to check your account balance from home or work, and to be able to pay bills online, transfer money, or look at your credit card statement. You can also download information from your bank account to a financial software package on your PC, such as Intuit Quicken or Microsoft Money.

Sending electronic mail Despite the growth of the World Wide Web, sending electronic mail (e-mail) is still the biggest use of the Internet. E-mail programs such as Microsoft Outlook Express, Netscape Messenger, Eudora, and Pegasus allow you to compose messages offline, and queue them up, before sending them to their respective destination e-mail addresses. When you send e-mail to private individuals, it only reaches their computers once these people have linked to their ISP's mail server and downloaded any messages waiting for them.

Internet for Beginners

http://learnthenet.com

Includes links for
exploring the World Wide
Web, information on
creating your own Web
pages, time-saving tips and
tricks, and a weekly
newsletter to help you get
the most out of the
Internet.

WEB LINK

**Parents' Guide to the
Internet**

http://www.ed.gov/pubs/pa
rents/internet

Useful electronic booklet
aiming to bridge the gap
between children's and
parents' knowledge of the
Internet. The site
introduces the main
features of the 'information
superhighway' and argues
for the benefits of getting
connected to the Internet
at home.

WEB LINK

Because of the way messages are sent and retrieved, you need to spend very little time online, making e-mail an extremely cheap (and fast) method of sending information. As well as the actual message itself, you can send any sort of file as an attachment. Don't forget, though, that these files can take a long time to download at the other end.

While an e-mail message cannot contain a virus, an attachment can – although the virus will not have any effect unless the attachment file is opened or run. It is therefore important to treat attachments with great care, not opening any files you're not expecting. Some programs, such as Outlook Express, can be set to open attachments automatically, so make sure that this facility is switched off.

Using online discussion groups Usenet is a collection of over 25,000 online discussion groups, known as newsgroups, where you can post messages and get replies from people all over the world. The topics under discussion cover everything you might possibly wish for, and quite a few that you might not! Newsgroups usually contain a list of Frequently Asked Questions (FAQs), to avoid everyone new to the group taking up space and time by asking the same questions about the purpose of the group, and so on.

Newsgroups can be particularly useful if you're having a problem with a piece of software or hardware. Sometimes you won't even need to post a message, if you're lucky. You may find that the problem is quite common, and that there's already a discussion going on. Messages are held online for only a few days, but you can find an index to all previous Usenet postings at the Deja.com Web site (formerly known as Deja News). To access the newsgroups, you need a program such as Microsoft Outlook Express, Netscape Collabra, Agent, or Newswatcher (for the Macintosh).

Chatting online E-mail may be quick, but using it to have a conversation is still like sending letters backwards and forwards. For instant communication, you need Internet Relay Chat, using programs such as mIRC, or Homer (for the Macintosh), where your messages will be read and can be replied to immediately. You can use either public or private channels or chatrooms. Public discussion can be about specific topics, but a lot of it is just general talk. After all, this is chat!

You do have to be careful with IRC, however, as people are not necessarily who or what they say they are. So don't go arranging to meet anyone without observing the usual sensible dating precautions: don't give your full name, postal address, telephone number, or e-mail address to someone who is really a total stranger. If you do arrange to meet, do it in a public place, make sure someone knows where you're going, and make sure the person you're meeting is aware of that.

Accessing the Internet without a computer You can also access the Internet via a television set connected to a digital set-top box. Interactive television providers, as well as the Microsoft-owned WebTV, are providing Web access and e-mail, plus home shopping, banking, and travel services in competition with Web sites.

In addition, WAP-enabled mobile phones can access information on what is billed as the 'mobile Internet'. In reality, services are text-based and slow (9.6 Kbps) at present, and limited to data from a few WAP-enabled Web sites and some new location-based services. The number of services available will no doubt mushroom in the next few years, particularly with the arrival of WAP's Japanese competitor i-Mode (from NTT DoCoMo), and also new third-generation mobile phones with colour screens and small keyboards.

Alan Stewart
March 2001

A

absolute (of a value) real and unchanging. For example, an absolute address is a location in memory and an absolute cell reference is a single fixed cell in a spreadsheet display. The opposite of absolute is ⤳ relative.

Accelerated Graphics Port *AGP*, dedicated port that links the graphics controller on a personal computer directly to the computer's memory, instead of data having to be fetched via the expansion bus. AGP can handle at least twice the throughput of a standard ⤳ PCI bus. The AGP was developed by Intel, and AGP support was added to later versions of Microsoft Windows 95.

accelerator board type of ⤳ expansion board that makes a computer run faster. It usually contains an additional processor (see ⤳ central processing unit).

acceptable use set of rules enforced by a service provider or backbone network restricting the use to which their facilities may be put. Every organization on the Internet has its own acceptable use policy (AUP); schools, for example, may ban the use of their facilities to find or download pornography from the Internet.

Originally, when the Internet was publicly funded, acceptable use banned advertising, and although funding is moving to private enterprise and advertising has now become commonplace, some service providers still do not allow commercial exploitation. The US National Science Foundation's NSFnet, for example, imposes a strict AUP to prohibit commercial organizations from using the network.

access way in which ⤳ file access is provided so that the data can be stored, retrieved, or updated by the computer.

access privilege in networking, authorized access to files. The ability to authorize or restrict access selectively to files or directories, including separate privileges such as reading, writing, or changing data, is a key element in computer security systems. This kind of system ensures that, for example, a company's employees cannot read its personnel files or alter payroll data unless they work for the appropriate departments, or that freelance or temporary staff can be given access to some areas of the computer system but not others.

Certain types of restrictions may be applied by users themselves to files on their own desktop machines, such as private e-mail; others may be granted only by the system administrator.

On all client–server systems, all data, even private e-mail and personal letters, can be accessed by the system administrator, who needs system-wide privileges in order to manage the network properly. Data which is encrypted, however, will not be readable unless the system administrator knows the user's individual password.

The privacy of employee e-mail is a contentious issue, as many employees assume their e-mail is private, while many companies presume ownership of all data stored on company systems.

access provider another term for ↝ Internet Service Provider.

access time or *reaction time*, time taken by a computer, after an instruction has been given, to read from or write to ↝ memory.

account on a network, a ↝ user-ID issued to a specific individual to enable access to the system for purposes of billing, administration, or private messaging. The existence of accounts allows system administrators to assign ↝ access privileges to specific individuals (which in turn enables those individuals to receive private messages such as e-mail) and also to track the use of the computer system and its resources.

On commercial systems such as CompuServe or America Online, users are given an account when they dial up the system and give the number of a credit card to which usage may be billed. On other types of systems, accounts are typically issued by the system administrator. In all cases, accounts are protected by a password, which should be carefully chosen.

accumulator special register, or memory location, in the ↝ arithmetic and logic unit of the computer processor. It is used to hold the result of a calculation temporarily or to store data that is being transferred.

ack radio-derived term for 'acknowledge'. It is used on the Internet as a brief way of indicating agreement with or receipt of a message or instruction. It is used by network protocols as a brief way of indicating agreement with or receipt of a message.

ACM abbreviation for the US ↝ Association for Computing Machinery.

Acorn UK computer manufacturer. In the early 1980s, Acorn produced a series of home microcomputers, including the Electron and the Atom. Its most successful computer, the ↝ BBC Microcomputer, was produced in conjunction with the BBC. Subsequent computers (the Master and the ↝ Archimedes) were less successful. Acorn was rescued by the Italian company Olivetti in 1985 but it has since sold off its majority shareholding.

In 1999, Acorn was bought by US investment bank Morgan Stanley and broken up. Acorn's successful spin-off ↝ ARM continues to thrive, however.

Acrobat program developed by Adobe to allow users of different types of computers to view the same documents complete with graphics and layout. Launched in 1993, Acrobat was designed to get around the limitations of existing systems when transferring data between different types of computers, which typically required all formatting to be stripped from the documents. The program to generate the code that makes the documents transferable with formatting intact must be bought, but the program for reading the documents is available free of charge. One of Acrobat's strengths is its ability to include hyperlinks within the document. As a hypertext development tool it rivalled early developments on the World Wide Web.

By 1996 Acrobat was in common use on the World Wide Web for distributing certain types of company documents, and the program had been enhanced to integrate with Web ⟿ browsers.

Acrobat coding was designed to turn computers into information distributors that would allow personal computer users to view a document in its original form. It can be generated directly from ⟿ PostScript files.

acronym abbreviation that can be pronounced as a word, for example RISC (Reduced Instruction Set Computer) and MUD (multi-user dungeon). People in the computer industry often incorrectly refer to all abbreviations as acronyms. Both are frequently used as industry jargon and as shorthand to save typing on the Net.

Active Desktop optional feature of Microsoft Windows that changes the desktop into the equivalent of a Web page. This feature enables programs to be run with a single click of the mouse instead of the usual double-clicking.

Acronym/ Abbreviation	Meaning	Acronym/ Abbreviation	Meaning
AFAICT	As Far As I Can Tell	ISTR	I Seem To Recall/ Remember
AFAIK	As Far As I Know		
AFAIR	As Far As I Recall/ Remember	ISWYM	I See What You Mean
		IYKWIM	If You Know What I Mean
AIUI	As I Understand It	JAM	Just A Minute
ATM	At The Moment	LCW	Loud, Confident, and Wrong
B4	Before		
BCNU	Be Seeing You	LOL	Lots Of Luck/Laughing Out Loud
BTDT	Been There Done That		
BTW	By The Way	NAFAIK	Not As Far As I Know
CUL	See You Later	NALOPKT	Not A Lot Of People Know That
DQM	Don't Quote Me		
FAQ	Frequently Asked Question	OIC	Oh I See
		OTOH	On The Other Hand
FOAF	Friend Of A Friend	OTT	Over The Top
FOC	Free Of Charge	PD	Public Domain
FOCL	Falls Off Chair Laughing	PMFJI	Pardon Me For Jumping In
F2F	Face To Face		
FUD	Fear, Uncertainty, and Doubt	POV	Point Of View
		ROTFL	Rolling On The Floor Laughing
FWIW	For What It's Worth		
FYI	For Your Information	TIC	Tongue In Cheek
GIGO	Garbage In Garbage Out	TPTB	The Powers That Be
HTH	Hope That Helps	TTBOMK	To The Best of My Knowledge
IIRC	If I Recall/Remember Correctly		
		TTFN	Ta Ta For Now
IKWYM	I Know What You Mean	TTYL	Talk To You Later
IME	In My Experience	TYVM	Thank You Very Much
IMHO	In My Humble Opinion	WRT	With Respect To
IMNSHO	In My Not So Humble Opinion	WYSIWYG	What You See Is What You Get
IMO	In My Opinion	YHM	You Have Mail
IOW	In Other Words	YKWIM	You Know What I Mean
ISTM	It Seems To Me		

acronym
A selection of acronyms and abbreviations in use online

Active Desktop was introduced with Microsoft's Internet Explorer 4 Web browser for Windows. It is an integral component of Windows 2000.

active matrix LCD or *TFT (thin film transistor) display*, type of colour ⤳ liquid crystal display (LCD) commonly used in laptop computers. Active matrix displays are made by sandwiching a film containing tiny transistors between two plates of glass. They achieve high contrast and brightness by applying voltage across the horizontal and vertical wires between the two glass plates, balanced by using a small transistor inside each ⤳ pixel to amplify the voltage when so instructed.

To create ⤳ VGA colour, each pixel must also integrate colour filters; essentially, each logical pixel is made up of three physical pixels, one for each of red, blue, and green, the primary colours of light. The consequence of this – and the reason active matrix screens are such expensive options – is that a VGA display requires approximately a billion transistors, and even minute imperfections render the screens useless for computing purposes. A high refresh rate means that the screens are extremely responsive, so the cursor does not disappear as a mouse is moved quickly across the screen.

Active Server Pages *ASP*, Web pages generated using Microsoft's progamming tools and ⤳ scripting languages, either VB Script (Visual Basic Script) or JScript (Microsoft's version of ⤳ JavaScript), instead of with ⤳ CGI scripts written in ⤳ Perl, for example. Active Server Pages have the file extension .asp instead of .html.

active window on graphical operating systems, the ⤳ window containing the program actually in use at any given time. Usually active windows are easily identified by the use of colour schemes which assign a different colour to the window's title bar (a thin strip along the top of each window bearing the name of the window's specific program or function) from that of the title bars of inactive windows.

On a true ⤳ multitasking system, each window may represent an active program, but the active window is the one into which the user may enter data. A user might, for example, be typing a document into a word processor in the active window while in the background other programs back up files or sort data in a database. In some windowing systems the active window is also referred to as the window in, or with, focus.

ActiveX Microsoft's umbrella name for a collection of technologies used to create applications that run on the World Wide Web or on ⤳ intranets.

ActiveX is based on DCOM (Microsoft's Distributed Component Object Model) and uses ActiveX Controls, which are a lightweight version of OLE (⤳ object linking and embedding) Custom Controls or OCXs. It also includes scripting languages such as JavaScript and VB Script (Visual Basic Script), and a ⤳ Java Virtual Machine (JVM).

ActiveX was announced in 1996, and later that year was handed to the ⮑ Open Group to manage its development and turn it into a cross-platform industry standard.

Ada high-level computer-programming language, developed and owned by the US Department of Defense, designed for use in situations in which a computer directly controls a process or machine, such as a military aircraft. The language took more than five years to specify, and became commercially available only in the late 1980s. It is named after English mathematician Ada Augusta ⮑ Byron.

ADC abbreviation for ⮑ analogue-to-digital converter.

adder electronic circuit in a computer or calculator that carries out the process of adding two binary numbers. A separate adder is needed for each pair of binary ⮑ bits to be added. Such circuits are essential components of a computer's ⮑ arithmetic and logic unit (ALU).

addiction obsession with working with computers; the inability to stop interferes with and is damaging to the rest of the addict's life. Many computer users describe themselves as being 'addicted' to computers or online systems, but the percentage of users who have serious problems as a result seems to be small, although research continues.

Addiction has been used as a defence in ⮑ hacking cases, including one of the early arrests of US hacker Kevin Mitnick and the 1993 trial of British hacker Paul Bedworth, who was the first to be prosecuted under the ⮑ Computer Misuse Act.

add-on small program written to extend the features of a larger one. The earliest successful add-on for personal computer users in the UK was a small routine which allowed the original version of the spreadsheet Lotus 1-2-3 to print out a pound sign (£), something the program's US developers had thought unnecessary.

address in a computer memory, a number indicating a specific location. At each address, a single piece of data can be stored. For microcomputers, this normally amounts to one ⮑ byte (enough to represent a single character, such as a letter or digit).

The maximum capacity of a computer memory depends on how many memory addresses it can have. This is normally measured in units of 1,024 bytes (known as kilobytes, or K).

address means of specifying either a computer or a person for the purpose of directing messages or other data across a network. Addressing e-mail to a person across the Internet involves typing in a string of characters such as 'userID@machine.system.type.country'. To send mail to Jane Doe, for example, whose user ID is 'janed' and who works at a company called Anyco in the UK, a user would type in 'janed@anyco.co.uk'.

Computers do not, however, use these named addresses in routing data. The portion after the address is known as a domain, and the domain name is an easy-to-remember alias for a numbered address that is understandable to a computer. This numbered address, which takes a form similar to 127.0.0.1, is known as an IP (Internet protocol) address. Both the numbered IP addresses and domain names are assigned by registrars accredited by ⮝ ICANN.

At the lowest level is the address associated with the computers network interface card (NIC). The MAC address, as it is sometimes called, is built into the NIC when it is manufactured. Every NIC made for a particular networking standard, for example Ethernet, has a unique MAC address.

TIP

address book

Always keep a backup of your address book in case of mishaps.

address book facility in most e-mail software that allows the storage and retrieval of e-mail addresses. Address books remove the problem of trying to remember a particular user's exact e-mail address – and it must be exact, as computers are unable to correct human errors. The best address-book software allows a user to type in just the correspondent's name and fills in the rest automatically.

address bus electrical pathway or ⮝ bus used to select the route for any particular data item as it is moved from one part of a computer to another.

Adobe US company specializing in graphics and desktop publishing software. Founded in 1982 by former Xerox PARC researchers John Warnock and Chuck Geschke, Adobe was the inventor of ⮝ PostScript and is the publisher of ⮝ Acrobat and Pagemaker. Adobe's enduring contribution to the computer industry is that it facilitated the use of computers to produce the fancy fonts without which desktop publishing would not have been possible.

Adobe Type Manager program from Adobe that manages fonts under Microsoft Windows and allows the printing and display of ⮝ PostScript fonts.

ADSL abbreviation for *asymmetric digital subscriber line, loop, or link,* standard for transmitting data through existing copper telephone wires. ADSL was developed by US telephone companies as a way of competing with cable television companies in delivering both TV and phone services. By 1996 it was developing into a possible alternative means for high-speed Internet access. ADSL is one of several types of digital subscriber loops (DSLs) in use.

An ADSL service was introduced by British Telecommunications plc (BT) in July 2000, aimed at both business and the consumer.

Advanced Technology Attachment Packet Interface enhancement to integrated drive electronics (IDE), usually abbreviated to ⮝ ATAPI.

advertising practice of paying to place information about a company's services or products in front of consumers. The earliest advertisers on the Net used to distribute their information as widely as possible in a practice quickly dubbed 'spamming'. By 1996 the practice of advertising on the World Wide Web was becoming commonplace.

ALGORITHM   7

Much Web advertising is sold in the same way as advertising in traditional media such as the print and broadcasting industries. Advertisers pay to place a small graphic known as an 'advertising banner' on a particular Web page in a spot (usually the top) where users are expected to see it clearly and click on it to follow the link to the advertiser's own site for more information. More sophisticated systems are under development which allow an advertising agency to track users' interests by watching which Web sites they visit and using that information to choose banners to insert which match those users' interests.

agent software that mimics intelligence by automating tasks according to user-defined rules. The most visible agent on the Internet in 1995 was Firefly, which recommends music that users might like based on information they have already given about their favourite artists. Agents might also select news stories of interest, arrange scheduling with other agents, and filter out unwanted junk e-mail.

Much research on agents is proceeding at the ⬄ MIT Media Lab, where Pattie Maes directs the group studying the capability and potential of autonomous agents. See also ⬄ crawler and ⬄ bot.

AGP abbreviation for ⬄ Accelerated Graphics Port.

AI abbreviation for ⬄ artificial intelligence.

Aiken, Howard Hathaway (1900–1973) US mathematician and computer pioneer. In 1939, in conjunction with engineers from ⬄ IBM, he started work on the design of an automatic calculator using standard business-machine components. In 1944 the team completed one of the first computers, the Automatic Sequence Controlled Calculator (known as the Harvard Mark I), a programmable computer controlled by punched paper tape and using punched cards.

The Harvard Mark I was principally a mechanical device, although it had a few electronic features; it was 15 m/49 ft long and 2.5 m/8 ft high, and weighed more than 30 tonnes. Addition took 0.3 sec, multiplication 4 sec. It was able to manipulate numbers of up to 23 decimal places and to store 72 of them. The Mark II, completed in 1947, was a fully electronic machine, requiring only 0.2 sec for addition and 0.7 sec for multiplication. It could store 100 ten-digit figures and their signs.

ALGOL *contraction of algorithmic language*, early high-level programming language, developed in the 1950s and 1960s for scientific applications. A general-purpose language, ALGOL is best suited to mathematical work and has an algebraic style. Although no longer in common use, it has greatly influenced more recent languages, such as Ada and Pascal.

algorithm procedure or series of steps that can be used to solve a problem.
In computer science, it describes the logical sequence of operations to be

---

agent

http://agentswww.media. mit.edu/groups/agents/

An overview of agent-related resources is available on the Web.

WEB LINK

performed by a program. A ↝ flow chart is a visual representation of an algorithm.

The word derives from the name of 9th-century Arab mathematician Muhammad ibn-Mūsā al-Khwārizmī.

alias name representing a particular user or group of users in e-mail systems. This feature, which is not available on all systems, is a matter of convenience as it allows a user to substitute shorter or easier-to-remember real names for e-mail addresses. In 1995 CompuServe announced a system of named aliases for its long, numbered addresses.

aliasing or *jaggies*, effect seen on computer screen or printer output, when smooth curves appear to be made up of steps because the resolution is not high enough. The steps are caused by clumps of pixels that become visible when the monitor's definition is lower than that of the image that it is trying to show. ↝ Anti-aliasing is a software technique that reduces this effect by using intermediate shades of colour to create an apparently smoother curve.

ALife contraction of ↝ artificial life.

Allen, Paul (1953–) US entrepreneur and computer programmer, co-founder of ↝ Microsoft 1975. Allen and Bill ↝ Gates became friends at Lakeside School near Seattle, Washington, where they developed their first computer software business, Traf-O-Data. Allen took a job at aircraft electronics group, Honeywell International, in Massachusetts while Gates was at Harvard, and in 1975, bought a copy of the *Popular Electronics* magazine that featured the MITS Altair as the 'world's first minicomputer kit to rival commercial models'. Gates and Allen created a version of ↝ BASIC for the Altair, moved to Albuquerque, New Mexico, to be close to MITS, and founded Microsoft.

In 1982, Allen was diagnosed as having Hodgkin's disease, and the following year, he left Microsoft to travel and think about what he wanted to do. The huge increase in the price of Microsoft stock in the 1980s and 1990s made Allen one of the world's richest men, and instead of returning to Microsoft, he spent his time making a wide range of investments and enjoying his unexpected wealth.

alligator clip small metal clip wired to other similar clips to allow temporary connections. Today's modular phone jacks generally make it easy to hook up modems and telephones. However, in some situations, such as a hotel room where a telephone is hard-wired to the wall or in a foreign country where a visitor's modem plug is incompatible with the local telephone network, the only answer is to take the phone apart and hook the modem directly to the phone line using these small clips.

alpha first version of a new software program. Developing modern software requires much testing and many versions before the definitive product is achieved. The first versions of any new product are typically full of ↝ bugs, and are tested by the developers and their assistants. Later versions, known as ⤳ beta versions, are given to outside users to test.

alpha channel in ⤳ 24-bit colour, a channel for controlling colour information. Describing colour for a computer display requires three channels of information per ⤳ pixel, one for each of the primary colours of light: red, blue, and green. A 24-bit graphics adapter with a 32-bit ⤳ bus can use the remaining 8 bits to send control information for the remaining 24 bits.

alphanumeric data data made up of any of the letters of the alphabet and any digit from 0 to 9. The classification of data according to the type or types of character contained enables computer ⤳ validation systems to check the accuracy of data: a computer can be programmed to reject entries that contain the wrong type of character. For example, a person's name would be rejected if it contained any numeric data, and a bank-account number would be rejected if it contained any alphabetic data. A car's registration number, by comparison, would be expected to contain alphanumeric data but no punctuation marks.

AltaVista search engine on the World Wide Web, originally set up by Digital Equipment, and now run by CMCOI. AltaVista runs an automated program to index all the pages it can find on the Web, enabling visitors to enter search terms such as a name or subject and quickly retrieve a list of pages to visit to look for specific information. It has a similar indexing program for Usenet. AltaVista has 250 million pages in its index, including 50 million images and video and audio clips. The index is updated at least every 28 days.

In 2000, AltaVista introduced an ⤳ Internet Service Provider service in the UK with a flat fee and no charges for telephone connection. AltaVista was reported to be the most popular Internet search engine in five of the fastest growing markets in 2000: Germany, France, the UK, Australia, and Canada. The rankings, compiled by the Media Metrix company which gathers Internet information in several countries, found that 900,000 Internet users in Germany, France, the UK, and Australia visited AltaVista each month.

alt hierarchy on Usenet, the 'alternative' set of ⤳ newsgroups, set up so that anyone can start a newsgroup on any topic. Most areas of Usenet, such as the ⤳ Big Seven hierarchies, allow the creation of newsgroups only after structured discussion and a vote to demonstrate that demand for the newsgroup exists. The alt hierarchy was created to allow users to bypass this process.

Many of the most active newsgroups are alt groups, such as alt.flame and alt.sex.

ALU abbreviation for ⤳ arithmetic and logic unit.

Amazon.com online shop launched in July 1995 by Jeff ⤳ Bezos, originally selling only books, but since extended to offer also CDs, videos, DVDs, toys and games, electronic items, and even furniture. Although by 2000 Amazon

AltaVista

http://www.altavista.com/.
http://www.altavista.co.uk/

Main Web site and UK site.

WEB LINK

TIP

alt hierarchy

More information about starting an alt group is available on the Net in the Start Your Own Newsgroup FAQ.

claimed 17 million customers in over 160 countries, and was one of the world's most visited Web sites, the company had yet to make a profit, and its losses continued to mount.

As well as local UK and German sites (each selling over 1 million book titles), the Amazon.com family of Web sites also includes the Internet Movie Database (with information on more than 150,000 films), LiveBid.com (a provider of live auctions on the Internet), and PlanetAll.com (a Web-based address book, calendar, and reminder service).

Amdahl, Gene (1922–   ) US computer engineer and hardware designer. Amdahl designed his first computer as part of his PhD dissertation, and then worked for International Business Machines (IBM) where he led the design of the IBM 704 in the 1950s, and the S/360 series of computers in the early 1960s which came to dominate the world of mainframes. In 1970, he founded Amdahl Corporation, then the largest manufacturer of IBM-compatible computers, to develop the first 'plug compatible' computers that would run the same software as IBM's machines. In 1980, he formed Trilogy to build large computers.

American National Standards Institute *ANSI*, US national standards body. It sets official procedures in (among other areas) computing and electronics. The ANSI ↝ character set is the standard set of characters used by Windows-based computers.

ANSI C is a version of the C language that has been approved by the ANSI committee. In theory, all ANSI C compilers, regardless of which company produces them, should behave in the same way.

America Online *AOL*, US market-leading commercial information service. America Online was launched in 1986 with a bright, colourful graphical interface and a marketing campaign that issued free disks on almost every US magazine cover. In 1995 it out-performed the then market leader, CompuServe, and in 1997 it took over this rival service. America Online combined with the German publishing conglomerate Bertelsmann to launch a UK and Continental version of the service, known as AOL Europe, in early 1996. It quickly became the UK's largest online service, until the arrival of ↝ Freeserve. In July 1999 AOL announced that its AOLEurope division would offer a free Internet service, Netscape Online. In January 2000 AOL announced that it would acquire Time Warner for $160 billion in stock, making it the largest merger in history, bringing together the largest Internet provider and the leading media company. As Bertelsmann was a competitor of Time Warner, it bought out Bertelsmann's share of AOL Europe to take direct control of its subsidiary.

AOL teamed up with General Motors at the beginning of 2000, in a deal to market cars over the Internet and to provide in-car Internet access. America Online grew from 500,000 subscribers in 1993 to 5 million in 1996, and passed 15 million in 1998. Each subscription provides five screen names with different mailboxes which can be used by, for example, different members of the same family.

Because a number of America Online users, many of them using temporary accounts set up from the many free disks, acted in breach of ↝ netiquette when America Online opened its Internet ↝ gateway in 1994, America Online users were held in contempt by many parts of the Net.

Amiga microcomputer produced by US company Commodore in 1985 to succeed the Commodore C64 home computer. The original Amiga was based on the Motorola 68000 microprocessor and achieved significant success in the domestic market.

Despite a failure to sell to the general business market, the latest versions of the Amiga were widely used in the film and video industries, where the Amiga's specialized graphics capabilities were used to create a variety of visual effects.

analogue (of a quantity or device) changing continuously; by contrast, a ↝ digital quantity or device varies in a series of distinct steps. For example, an analogue clock measures time by means of a continuous movement of hands around a dial, whereas a digital clock measures time with a numerical display that changes in a series of discrete steps.

Most computers are digital devices. Therefore, any signals and data from an analogue device must be passed through a suitable ↝ analogue-to-digital converter before they can be received and processed by computer. Similarly, output signals from digital computers must be passed through a ↝ digital-to-analogue converter before they can be received by an analogue device.

analogue computer computing device that performs calculations through the interaction of continuously varying physical quantities, such as voltages (as distinct from the more common ↝ digital computer, which works with discrete quantities). An analogue computer is said to operate in real time (corresponding to time in the real world), and can therefore be used to monitor and control other events as they happen.

Although common in engineering since the 1920s, analogue computers are not general-purpose computers, but specialize in solving differential calculus and similar mathematical problems. The earliest analogue computing device is thought to be the flat, or planispheric, astrolabe, which originated in about the 8th century.

analogue-to-digital converter *ADC*, electronic circuit that converts an analogue signal into a digital one. Such a circuit is needed to convert the signal from an analogue device into a digital signal for input into a computer. For example, many ↝ sensors designed to measure physical quantities, such as temperature and pressure, produce an analogue signal in the form of voltage and this must be passed through an ADC before computer input and processing. A ↝ digital-to-analogue converter performs the opposite process.

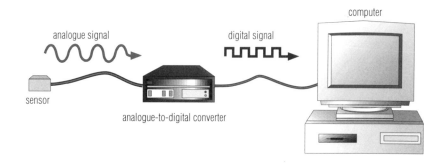

analogue-to-digital converter
An analogue-to-digital converter, or ADC, converts a continuous analogue signal produced by a sensor to a digital ('off and on') signal for computer processing.

analytical engine programmable computing device designed by English mathematician Charles ↪ Babbage in 1833.

It was based on the ↪ difference engine but was intended to automate the whole process of calculation. It introduced many of the concepts of the digital computer but, because of limitations in manufacturing processes, was never built.

Among the concepts introduced were input and output, an arithmetic unit, memory, sequential operation, and the ability to make decisions based on data. It would have required at least 50,000 moving parts. The design was largely forgotten until some of Babbage's writings were rediscovered in 1937.

anamorphic projection technique used in film and in ↪ virtual reality to squeeze wide-frame images so that they fit into the dimensions of a 35-mm frame of film. In film projection, the projector has a complementary lens which reverses the process. In virtual reality, the computer must calculate the amount of deformation and reverse it.

anchor an HTML (hypertext markup language) tag that turns ordinary text into a ↪ hyperlink. Anchors are used to enable easy navigation within a single large document or to link to remote documents on distant computers. On the World Wide Web, anchor text is usually underlined, coloured differently, or surrounded by a dotted line in order to mark it out from normal text.

AND gate in electronics, a type of ↪ logic gate.

Andreessen, Marc (1972–) US systems developer and co-author of the first widely available graphical ↪ browser for the World Wide Web, ↪ Mosaic.

Andreessen wrote Mosaic with fellow researcher Eric Bina while working at the National Center for Supercomputing Applications (NCSA), based at the University of Illinois. In 1994 both moved to the start-up company ↪ Netscape Communications Corporation to work on the next generation of browser software. This included Netscape Navigator, which was made freely available on the Internet and contributed to the explosive growth of the World Wide Web in the mid-1990s.

Andreessen became chief technology officer at ⌐ America Online, when it bought Netscape in March 1999. Six months later, however, he left to found ⌐ Web hosting company Loudcloud, of which he is chairman.

angle brackets <>, in documentation, brackets that indicate places where the user should input information of the type described between the brackets. Angle brackets are also used in online services and on the Internet to indicate that the name used is a user-ID rather than a real name, and on CompuServe as part of certain ⌐ emoticons.

animation, computer computer-generated graphics that appear to move across the screen. Traditional animation involves a great deal of drudgery in creating the 24 frames per second needed to deceive the human eye into seeing a moving picture on film. In computer-generated animation, while humans still create the key frames that specify the starting and ending points of a particular sequence – a character running through a landscape, for example – computers are faster and more accurate at calculating the in-between positions and generating the frames.

The first completely computer-generated character to appear in a major motion picture was the sea-water creature in James Cameron's film *The Abyss* (1990), developed at the leading special effects shop ⌐ Industrial Light & Magic. The first entirely computer-animated full-length feature film was ⌐ Pixar's *Toy Story* (1995), which was the first film ever to achieve independent motion of characters and backgrounds in the same sequence.

annotate to add one's own comments to Web pages or graphical computerized documents such as stored faxes.

anonymous FTP abbreviation for *anonymous file transfer protocol,* method of retrieving a file from a remote computer without having an account on that computer. Many organizations, such as universities and software companies, maintain publicly accessible archives of files that may be retrieved across the Internet via ⌐ FTP. An ordinary user who is not affiliated to the organization may retrieve files by entering the FTP address and then typing in either 'anonymous' or 'ftp' when asked for a user-ID or log-in name, followed by the user's e-mail address in place of a password. These users are typically offered ⌐ access privileges to only a small part of the company's stored files, and the rest may be cordoned off from access by a ⌐ firewall.

anonymous remailer service that allows Internet users to post to Usenet and send e-mail without revealing their true identity or e-mail address. To send an anonymous message, a user first sends the message to the remailer, which strips all identifying information from the message before sending it on to its specified destination, identified only as coming from the anonymous server.

The ability to post anonymously also removes user accountability, and so these servers are controversial. However, they provide a useful function on the Net in support groups and other areas where the ability to post anonymously allows people to speak freely about confidential matters without the risk of being identified by friends, family, or anyone else.

The best-known anonymous server, the Finnish anon.penet.fi was closed down in August 1996 as it could no longer guarantee anonymity following a court case ordering the operator to reveal a user's name. The more elaborate servers use encryption to make the message even more difficult to trace.

anorak term used interchangeably with geek, techie, or nerd. It derives from the stereotype that all technical people resemble the stereotypical anorak-wearing trainspotter; in other words, that they are obsessive, slightly antisocial, and overly knowledgeable about matters that interest very few other people.

ANSI acronym ⤳ American National Standards Institute, a US national standards body.

anti-aliasing in computer graphics, a software technique for diminishing ⤳ aliasing ('jaggies') – steplike lines that should be smooth. Jaggies occur because the output device, the monitor or printer, does not have a high enough resolution to represent a smooth line. Anti-aliasing reduces the prominence of jaggies by surrounding the steps with intermediate shades of grey (for grey-scaling devices) or colour (for colour devices). Although this reduces the jagged appearance of the lines, it also makes them fuzzier.

TIP

antivirus software

Antivirus software must be updated regularly, as new viruses are written and released all the time.

antivirus software software that detects ⤳ viruses and/or cleans viruses from an infected computer system. There are many types of antivirus software. Scanners check a computer system and detect viruses; these must be updated regularly, as new viruses are written and released. Other utilities allow a user to edit the data on hard and floppy disks directly or repair system damage. Still other types, which may come with specialized hardware, function by detecting and blocking changes to files or system activities which are typical of how viruses behave.

AOL abbreviation for ⤳ America Online.

Apache most popular Web server software on the Internet because it is both good and free. Like the Mosaic Web browser, Apache was written at America's National Center for Supercomputing Applications (NCSA) at the University of Illinois. It is now being maintained and developed by the Apache Group, an ad hoc group of programmers and users who – as with the ⤳ Linux operating system – have open access to the source code. The Apache name puns on the fact that the code has been patched up, making it a patchy server.

API abbreviation for ⤳ Applications Program Interface, standard environment in which computer programs are written.

Apple US computer company, manufacturer of the Macintosh range of computers.

The success of PCs running Microsoft's Windows 3, launched in 1990, put pressure on Apple and the arrival of Windows 95 started Apple's decline. Apple's annual revenues peaked at $11.1 billion in 1995, and by 1998 had slumped to $5.9 billion. For comparison, Compaq, the market-leading PC supplier, increased its sales from $10.9 billion in 1995 to $18.1 billion in 1997. In 1997, however, Microsoft invested heavily in Apple, and, in October 1998, Apple announced its first profit (£182 million) in three years. This was largely due to the success of the iMac computer.

In 1977, Apple's founders Steve ⤳ Jobs and Steve ⤳ Wozniak received backing from a rich venture capitalist, Mike Markkula, who backed the production of the Apple II. Apple's early market lead in personal computing was destroyed by the entry of the computer industry's behemoth, ⤳ IBM in 1981. Unfortunately Apple's imaginative response – the Macintosh, launched 1984 – was a proprietary design and was never able to gain enough market share to compete with thousands of firms making computers compatible with IBM's PCs. In 1994 Apple licensed the Macintosh for the first time, thus enabling other manufacturers to make cheaper machines, the first appearing in 1996. Unfortunately Apple proved unable to compete and reversed its licensing strategy, buying its license back from Power Computing, and leading Motorola to leave the clone business in 1997. Apple's long-term future is not assured. However, the Macintosh still has a very strong following in the creative world, particularly in the publishing and the multimedia industries, thanks to its ease of use and the availability of the most popular software for these applications. In 1997 Microsoft invested $150 million in Apple.

applet

http://java.sun.com/applets/

Information about ready-to-use applets can be found on Sun's Web site.

WEB LINK

applet mini-software application. Examples of applets include Microsoft WordPad, the simple word processor in Microsoft Windows or the single-purpose applications that in 1996 were beginning to appear on the World Wide Web, written in Java. These include animations such as a moving ticker tape of stock prices.

Today Java is the most common programming language used to create applets for the World Wide Web, though early enthusiasm for its potential has died down. Development of a number of high-profile Web-applet based applications has been stopped because of problems with performance and compatibility.

application program or job designed for the benefit of the end user. Examples of general purpose application programs include ⤳ word processors, ⤳ desktop publishing programs, ⤳ databases, ⤳ spreadsheet packages, and ⤳ graphics programs (see ⤳ CAD and ⤳ CAM). Application-specific programs include payroll and stock control systems. Applications may also be custom designed to solve a specific problem, not catered for in other types of application.

The term is used to distinguish such programs from those that control the computer (⤳ systems programs) or assist the programmer, such as a ⤳ compiler.

application service provider *ASP*, company providing access to computer ⮢ applications via the Internet. By renting applications through an ASP, companies can avoid the task of procuring and implementing complex systems themselves, and, in some cases, cut down considerably on their in-house ⮢ information technology infrastructure.

applications package set of programs and related documentation (such as instruction manuals) used in a particular application. For example, a typical payroll applications package would consist of separate programs for the entry of data, updating the master files, and printing the pay slips, plus documentation in the form of program details and instructions for use.

Applications Program Interface *API*, standard environment, including tools, protocols, and other routines, in which programs can be written. An API ensures that all applications are consistent with the operating system and have a similar ⮢ user interface.

Archimedes microcomputer introduced by ⮢ Acorn in 1987. It was based on a ⮢ RISC microprocessor called the ⮢ ARM, and was intended to be the successor to Acorn's BBC Microcomputer. Despite its technically advanced design, it did not prove commercially successful.

architecture overall design of a computer system, encompassing both hardware and software. The architecture of a particular system includes the specifications of individual components and the ways they interact. Because the operating system defines how these elements interact with each other and with application software, it is also included in the term.

archive collection of computer files. The term is commonly used to refer to the files created by ⮢ data compression programs, such as the popular PKZIP, which contain one or more files. On the Internet it is also used to refer to a large store of files from which visitors can select the ones they want.

argument value on which a ⮢ function operates. For example, if the argument 16 is operated on by the function 'square root', the answer 4 is produced.

arithmetic and logic unit *ALU*, in a computer, the part of the ⮢ central processing unit (CPU) that performs the basic arithmetic and logic operations on data.

ARM acronym for *Advanced RISC Machine*, microprocessor developed by Acorn in 1985 for use in the ⮢ Archimedes microcomputer. In 1990 the company Advanced RISC Machines was formed to develop the ARM microprocessor. The ARM is the microprocessor in Apple's ⮢ Newton.

ARM's fortunes increased dramatically recently in 1999, as they were awarded a contract to supply the microprocessors for digital television set-top boxes.

ARPANET acronym for *Advanced Research Projects Agency Network*, early US network that forms the basis of the ➴ Internet. It was set up in 1969 by ARPA to provide services to US academic institutions and commercial organizations conducting computer science research. ARPANET pioneered many of today's networking techniques.

It was renamed DARPANET when ARPA changed its name to Defense Advanced Research Projects Agency. In 1975 responsibility for DARPANET was passed on to the Defense Communication Agency.

array in computer programming, a list of values that can all be referred to by a single ➴ variable name. Separate values are distinguished by using a subscript with each variable name.

Arrays are useful because they allow programmers to write general routines that can process long lists of data. For example, if every price stored in an accounting program used a different variable name, separate program instructions would be needed to process each price. However, if all the prices were stored in an array, a general routine could be written to process, say, 'price$_{(J)}$', and, by allowing J to take different values, could then process any individual price.

For example, consider this list of highest daily temperatures: day 1 – 22°C; day 2 – 23°C; day 3 – 19°C; day 4 – 21°C. This array might be stored with the single variable name 'temp'. Separate elements of the array would then be identified with subscripts. So, for example, the array element 'temp$_{(1)}$' would store the value '22', and the array element 'temp$_{(3)}$' would store the value '19'.

article or posting, on Usenet, individual public message.

artificial intelligence *AI*, branch of science concerned with creating computer programs that can perform actions comparable with those of an intelligent human. Current AI research covers such areas as planning (for robot behaviour), language understanding, pattern recognition, and knowledge representation.

The possibility of artificial intelligence was first proposed by the English mathematician Alan ➴ Turing in 1950. Early AI programs, developed in the 1960s, attempted simulations of human intelligence or were aimed at general problem-solving techniques. By the mid-1990s, scientists were concluding that AI was more difficult to create than they had imagined. It is now thought that intelligent behaviour depends as much on the knowledge a system possesses as on its reasoning power. Present emphasis is on ➴ knowledge-based systems, such as ➴ expert systems, while research projects focus on ➴ neural networks, which attempt to mimic the structure of the human brain.

On the ➴ Internet, small bits of software that automate common routines or attempt to predict human likes or behaviour based on past experience are called intelligent agents or bots.

Technosphere III

http://www.technosphere.org.uk/

Innovative Web site that allows you to create an artificial life form, and then monitor its progress in 'Technosphere', the environment in which these creatures live. You will receive e-mails from your creation, and can communicate with it as it grows, evolves, and finally dies in its 3-D environment.

WEB LINK

ASCII Chart and Other Resources

http://www.jimprice.com/jim-asc.htm

Features a brief introduction to ASCII, a series of related questions and answers, and numerous other ASCII resources.

WEB LINK

artificial life contracted to *ALife*, area of scientific research that attempts to simulate biological phenomena via computer programs. See *Artificial Life* feature essay

ASCII acronym for *American Standard Code for Information Interchange*, coding system in which numbers are assigned to letters, digits, and punctuation symbols. Although computers work in code based on the ↝ binary number system, ASCII numbers are usually quoted as decimal or ↝ hexadecimal numbers. For example, the decimal number 45 (binary 0101101) represents a hyphen, and 65 (binary 1000001) a capital A. The first 32 codes are used for control functions, such as carriage return and backspace.

Strictly speaking, ASCII is a 7-bit binary code, allowing 128 different characters to be represented, but an eighth bit is often used to provide ↝ parity or to allow for extra characters. The system is widely used for the storage of text and for the transmission of data between computers.

ASCII art pictures or fancy graphics created entirely out of ↝ ASCII characters such as letters of the alphabet or punctuation marks. ASCII art has existed since the invention of computers. Today it is found in Usenet ↝ signatures (.sigs), special ↝ newsgroups such as alt.art.ascii, and occasionally in messages, both public and private.

ASIC abbreviation for *application-specific integrated circuit*, integrated circuit built for a specific application.

ASP abbreviation for ↝ Active Server Pages or ↝ application service provider.

assembler program that translates a program written in an assembly language into a complete ↝ machine code program that can be executed by a computer.

assembly language low-level computer-programming language closely related to a computer's internal codes. It consists chiefly of a set of short sequences of letters (mnemonics), which are translated, by a program called an assembler, into ↝ machine code for the computer's ↝ central processing unit (CPU) to follow directly. In assembly language, for example, 'JMP' means 'jump' and 'LDA' means 'load accumulator'. Assembly code is used by programmers who need to write very fast or efficient programs.

Because they are much easier to use, high-level languages are normally used in preference to assembly languages. An assembly language may still be used in some cases, however, particularly when no suitable high-level language exists or where a very efficient machine-code program is required.

Association for Computing Machinery *ACM*, US organization made up of computer professionals of all types. Its monthly journal, the *Communications of the Association for Computing Machinery*, is peer-reviewed. Its subsidiary special interest groups, or SIGs, focus on areas such as graphics and

Artificial Life

Machines mimicking life Artificial life is a new research area which encompasses biology and computer science. By trying to understand the fundamental processes of biology, researchers aim to create new life forms by simulating these processes on a computer. It is hoped that this will put nature into a context of life as it might be. The evolution of life on this planet has been the result of many chance happenings and accidents. It is interesting to speculate what might have evolved if these events had happened differently. We can use computers to simulate these processes and see what alternative forms of life might have looked like.

One of the fundamental processes of life is replication. Parents produce children that are in many ways similar to themselves. This process was studied in the computer program Tierra, by Tom Ray. Tierra starts with a single individual, which is a computer program that, when it runs, makes copies of itself. Sometimes it makes errors in the copying process which leads to mutant programs. These can evolve into different programs that can themselves replicate. All the programs in Tierra compete with each other for space in the memory of the computer, and for processing time in the CPU. In this way, more and more efficient programs evolve. Sometimes, parasite programs will evolve. These are short programs that attach themselves to other ones and get copied along with them. Many other biological phenomena have been discovered in the Tierra system as it evolves.

Patterns Another aspect of artificial life research is to study the shapes and forms that living things grow into. The biologist Richard Dawkins has written a program called the Blind Watchmaker that grows insect-like shapes. The shapes are determined by a set of growth instructions which form a kind of genetic code for the creatures. The program starts with a population of simple shapes. The user can select some of these shapes which then reproduce by making copies of their genetic code. Again, some errors may occur in the copying process, which gives rise to a collection of slightly different shapes. By continuing to select shapes with certain properties and allowing them to reproduce, many lifelike shapes can be evolved.

Behaviour Whenever there is a population of creatures (like in Tierra, the Blind Watchmaker, and in nature itself), they will interact with each other. Animals may compete for resources. Predators will hunt prey. Some creatures will work together to create societies (for example, humans, ants, and wasps). Sometimes one species will cooperate with another. For example, there is a certain species of fish that make their living cleaning the teeth of sharks. The sharks do not eat them and offer protection from other predators. These kinds of interactions can be simulated on a computer. Individual creatures can be represented by short, self-contained computer programs called agents. Agents can interact with each other. They can either be nice and help each other, or be nasty and hinder each other. When agents are nice to each other they are collectively more successful. However, a nasty agent can exploit the goodwill of a nice agent. The nasty agent will benefit and the nice one will suffer. However, two nasty agents refuse to help each other and both do badly. In this kind of society, how do nice agents ever evolve? As soon as any agent tries to be nice, it will be exploited by the nasty agents. By simulating this agent model on a computer, you can study the conditions under which nice, cooperative behaviour evolves. Robert Axelrod discovered that one condition is that agents have to interact with each other many times. If you know you are going to do business with someone again, then it is worth being nice. However, if this encounter is the only one you are likely to have, then you might as well be nasty. Be aware, though, that the other agent is likely to be nasty too!

Processes A basic feature of all artificial life programs is the idea of emergent systems. These are systems that are made up of lots of components that interact with each other, but no one is in charge. Control is said to be de-centralized. In biology this happens at a number of levels. For example, all the cells in your body live, operate, and die according to their own rules. No individual cell is in charge. And yet through

Artificial Life (continued)

their shared genetic code they cooperate with each other to form a coordinated body. At a different level, individual birds in a flock act independently and yet they fly together as a coordinated group. This kind of behaviour, that is visible at the group level but not the individual level, is what is meant by emergent behaviour. The complex actions of the group emerge from the simple interactions of the individuals.

Behaviour and structure at the group level often exhibit what is called recursive structure. This means that high-level, general features are made up of more detailed features which have a similar structure. This is seen most clearly in fractal pictures. These are images that look the same no matter what scale you are looking at. This property has been used to generate computer pictures which are very lifelike. Przemysław Prusinkiewicz has used this technique to create images of plants (both real and artificial). It works because the growth of a plant often has a recursive structure. For example, a tree is made up of a trunk that splits into branches. Each branch in turn splits into smaller branches. And so on, until you reach the smallest twigs. The process is the same at each level.

The future The field of artificial life was started by Chris Langton, a researcher at the Los Alamos Laboratories in New Mexico. He subsequently founded the artificial life research group at the Santa Fe Institute. You can look at their Web page http://alife.org for an extensive set of resources. Chris Langton has now gone on to the Swarm Corporation (http://www.swarm.com) which seeks to apply the ideas of artificial life to modelling complex systems commercially.

Jonathan Rowe

human-computer interaction. Several of these run major conferences for their areas such as SIGGRAPH (graphics) and SIGCHI (human-computer interaction).

The equivalent UK organization is the ↝ British Computer Society (BCS).

asterisk *; or star, wild card character standing for multiple characters in most operating systems. It allows a user to specify a group of files for mass handling. Typing 'dir *.bat' in DOS, for example, will return a list of all files with the extension .BAT in the current directory. On Usenet, * is used to denote a group of ↝ newsgroups; the phrase 'alt.music.*' means all the newsgroups in the alt.music hierarchy, such as alt.music.pop, alt.music.jazz, and so on. On the Internet, an asterisk before and after a word is a way of indicating emphasis.

asymmetric digital subscriber loop standard for transmitting video data; see ↝ ADSL.

asynchronous irregular or not synchronized. In computer communications, the term is usually applied to data transmitted irregularly rather than as a steady stream. Asynchronous communication uses ↝ start bits and ↝ stop bits to indicate the beginning and end of each piece of data. Most personal computer communications are asynchronous, including connections across the Internet.

asynchronous transfer mode *ATM*, high-speed computer ↝ networking standard suitable for all types of data, including voice and video, that can be

Character	Binary (base 2)	Decimal (base 10)	Hexadecimal (base 16)	Character	Binary (base 2)	Decimal (base 10)	Hexadecimal (base 16)
Space	00100000	32	20	P	01010000	80	50
!	00100001	33	21	Q	01010001	81	51
'	00100010	34	22	R	01010010	82	52
#	00100011	35	23	S	01010011	83	53
$	00100100	36	24	T	01010100	84	54
%	00100101	37	25	U	01010101	85	55
&	00100110	38	26	V	01010110	86	56
`	00100111	39	27	W	01010111	87	57
(	00101000	40	28	X	01011000	88	58
)	00101001	41	29	Y	01011001	89	59
*	00101010	42	2A	Z	01011010	90	5A
+	00101011	43	2B	[	01011011	91	5B
,	00101100	44	2C	\	01011100	92	5C
-	00101101	45	2D	]	01011101	93	5D
.	00101110	46	2E	^	01011110	94	5E
/	00101111	47	2F	_	01011111	95	5F
0	00110000	48	30	`	01100000	96	60
1	00110001	49	31	a	01100001	97	61
2	00110010	50	32	b	01100010	98	62
3	00110011	51	33	c	01100011	99	63
4	00110100	52	34	d	01100100	100	64
5	00110101	53	35	e	01100101	101	65
6	00110110	54	36	f	01100110	102	66
7	00110111	55	37	g	01100111	103	67
8	00111000	56	38	h	01101000	104	68
9	00111001	57	39	i	01101001	105	69
:	00111010	58	3A	j	01101010	106	6A
;	00111011	59	3B	k	01101011	107	6B
<	00111100	60	3C	l	01101100	108	6C
=	00111101	61	3D	m	01101101	109	6D
>	00111110	62	3E	n	01101110	110	6E
?	00111111	63	3F	o	01101111	111	6F
@	01000000	64	40	p	01110000	112	70
A	01000001	65	41	q	01110001	113	71
B	01000010	66	42	r	01110010	114	72
C	01000011	67	43	s	01110011	115	73
D	01000100	68	44	t	01110100	116	74
E	01000101	69	45	u	01110101	117	75
F	01000110	70	46	v	01110110	118	76
G	01000111	71	47	w	01110111	119	77
H	01001000	72	48	x	01111000	120	78
I	01001001	73	49	y	01111001	121	79
J	01001010	74	4A	z	01111010	122	7A
K	01001011	75	4B	{	01111011	123	7B
L	01001100	76	4C			01111100	124	7C
M	01001101	77	4D	}	01111101	125	7D
N	01001110	78	4E	~	01111110	126	7E
O	01001111	79	4F	Delete	01111111	127	7F

ASCII Codes
ASCII codes for character and letters of the alphabet

used on both private and public networks. ATM is used mainly on the core 'backbones' of large communications networks and in wide-area networks.

The basic technology was developed as part of the Cambridge Ring in the late 1970s, and is now being adopted by companies such as IBM and AT&T.

Atanasoff, John Vincent (1903–1995) US physicist and computer engineer, and co-developer of the ABC (Atanasoff–Berry Calculator). Atanasoff, a professor of mathematics at Iowa State College, became interested in computing in the 1930s, and in 1939 he started to build a binary calculating machine with Clifford ⌐ Berry, a graduate student in electrical engineering. He was visited by Dr John ⌐ Mauchly, co-developer of ENIAC, in 1941, and explained the workings of his machine. Partly as a result of this, a US judge disallowed patents on the ENIAC in 1973.

ATAPI abbreviation for *Advanced Technology Attachment Packet Interface*, enhancement to integrated drive electronics (IDE) that allows easier installation and support of CD-ROM drives and other devices. Part of the Enhanced IDE standard introduced by hard disk manufacturer Western Digital in 1994, ATAPI uses a standard software device driver and does away with the need for older, proprietary interfaces.

AT command set abbreviation for *attention command set*, set of standard commands allowing a ⌐ modem to be controlled via software. These commands are used via special communications software to control a modem's actions from the computer console. The most common are ATZ to reset the modem and ATH to hang the modem up at the end of a call. The set was invented by Hayes Computer Products for its earliest modems.

ATM abbreviation for ⌐ asynchronous transfer mode, automated teller machine, or ⌐ Adobe Type Manager, depending on context.

attachment way of incorporating a file into an e-mail message for transmission. Within a single system, such as a corporate local area network (LAN) or a commercial online service, ⌐ binary files can be sent intact. Over the Internet, attached files must be encoded into ⌐ ASCII characters and then decoded by the receiver. See ⌐ MIME.

audio file computer file that encodes sounds which can be played back using the appropriate software and hardware. On the World Wide Web, the latest types of audio files can be played on the user's computer system in real time while they are being downloaded. Apple Macintosh computers have sound capabilities built in, as do multimedia personal computers (MPCs). Older PCs need to have a ⌐ sound card installed in order to achieve good playback quality.

Audio–Video Interleave ⌐ file format for video clips.

audit trail record of computer operations, showing what has been done and, if available, who has done it. The term is taken from accountancy, but audit trails are now widely used to check many aspects of computer security, in addition to use in accounts programs.

augmented reality use of computer systems and data to overlay video or other real-life representations. For example, a video of a car engine with the mechanical drawings overlaid.

AUP abbreviation for *acceptable use policy*; see ↝ acceptable use.

authentication system for certifying the origin of an electronic communication. In the real world, a handwritten signature authenticates a document, for example a contract, as coming from a particular person. In the electronic world, encryption systems provide the same function via ↝ digital signatures and other techniques.

In ↝ public-key cryptography, for example, the ability to decrypt a message with a particular user's public key authenticates the message as coming from that user and no one else. Authentication is an essential requirement for electronic commerce.

authoring development of multimedia presentations. Authoring includes pulling together the necessary audio, video, graphics, and text files and formatting them for display.

authoring tool software that allows developers to create multimedia presentations or World Wide Web pages. Typically, these tools automate some of the more difficult parts of generating program source codes so that developers can work on a higher, more abstract level. Popular authoring tools for the World Wide Web include Hot Metal and HTML Assistant, both available in ↝ shareware versions.

authorization permission to access a particular system. Unauthorized access to private computer systems was made illegal in many countries during the late 1980s.

Software	Manufacturer	Description
3D WebMaster	Superscape	interactive 3D authoring tool for creating 3D Web sites
Aesthetic World Visions	Aesthetic Solutions	component-based Virtual Reality authoring tool
Authorware Attain	Macromedia	visual-rich-media authoring tool for online learning
Director	Macromedia	powerful multimedia and Web authoring tool
HoTMetaL	SoftQuad	HTML authoring and publishing tool for Web site development
PageMill	Adobe	easy-to-use Web page creation software
Premiere	Adobe	a powerful tool for professional digital video editing

authoring
The main features of some major authoring programs

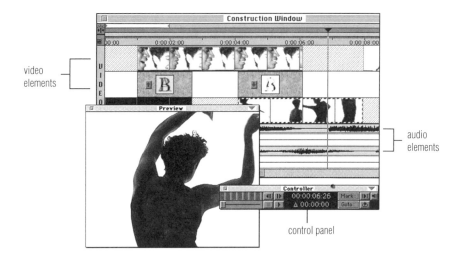

video elements

audio elements

control panel

authoring tool
A typical authoring tool,
which is used to combine
audio and video to create
multimedia presentations
or pages for the World
Wide Web.

TIP

autoresponder

If you subscribe to any mailing lists, make sure you cancel or suspend your subscription before you go off on holiday leaving an autoresponder turned on, so that the autoresponder does not flood the list with useless messages.

AutoCAD leading computer-aided design (CAD) software package. It is published by the specialist US company AutoDesk (founded 1982). Users include engineers, architects, and designers.

autoexec.bat file in the ⤳ MS-DOS operating system that is automatically run when the computer is ⤳ booted.

automatic fallback feature allowing ⤳ modems to drop to a slower speed if conditions such as line noise make it necessary. Modem speeds are typically rated according to one or another ⤳ CCITT standard (known as a V number). All modems rated for a specific standard are ⤳ backwards compatible.

autoresponder on the Internet, a ⤳ server that responds automatically to specific messages or input. A common use for autoresponders is to automate the dispatch of sales information via e-mail. A user requesting such information typically sends a message with specified words such as 'send info' in the subject line or the body of the message. The words trigger the autoresponder to send the prepared information file.

Autoresponders are also used in e-mail systems which can be configured to notify correspondents that the user is on holiday.

avatar computer-generated character that represents a human in on-screen interaction. In the mid-1990s, avatars were primarily used in computer games, but because they take up much less memory or bandwidth than full video, companies such as British Telecom were researching the possibility of building multiparty videoconferencing systems using this technology.

In 1999, 3D avatars of 'virtual newsreaders' were created. The Press Association's Ananova is not based on any one person, but bears a strong resemblance to pop singer Kylie Minogue. Channel 5's Vandrea, however, is based on the channel's real-life newsreader Andrea Catherwood.

AVI abbreviation for *Audio-Visual Interleave*, file format capable of storing moving images (such as video) with accompanying sound. AVI files can be replayed by any multimedia PC with Microsoft ↪ Windows and a ↪ sound card. AVI files are frequently very large (around 50 Mbyte for a five-minute rock video, for example), so they are usually stored on ↪ CD-ROM.

Babbage, Charles (1792–1871) English mathematician who devised a precursor of the computer. He designed an ⇝ analytical engine, a general-purpose mechanical computing device for performing different calculations according to a program input on punched cards (an idea borrowed from the ⇝ Jacquard loom). This device was never built, but it embodied many of the principles on which digital computers are based.

Babbage was born in Totnes, Devon. As a student at Cambridge, he assisted John Herschel with his astronomical calculations and thought they could be better done by machines. His mechanical calculator, or ⇝ difference engine, begun in 1822, which could compute squares to six places of decimals, got him a commission from the British Admiralty for an expanded version. But this project was abandoned in favour of the analytical engine, on which he worked for the rest of his life. The difference engine could perform only one function, once it was set up. The analytical engine was intended to perform many functions; it was to store numbers and be capable of working to a program. The first computer printer, also designed but never built by Charles Babbage, was completed and put on show at London's Science Museum in April 2000.

Babbage was a founder member of the Royal Astronomical Society, the British Association, the Cambridge Philosophical Society, and the Statistical Society of London. He was elected Fellow of the Royal Society in 1816. His book *On the Economy of Machinery and Manufactures* (1832) is an analysis of industrial production systems and their economics.

In 1991, the British Science Museum completed Babbage's second difference engine (to demonstrate that it would have been possible with the materials then available). It evaluates polynomials up to the seventh power, with 30-figure accuracy.

backbone in networking, a high-⇝ bandwidth trunk to which smaller networks connect. The original backbone of the Internet was NSFnet, funded by the US National Science Foundation, which linked together the five regional supercomputing centres.

In Britain, SuperJANET is the high-speed backbone that connects universities, colleges, and research centres.

backing storage memory outside the ⇝ central processing unit used to store programs and data that are not in current use. Backing storage must be nonvolatile – that is, its contents must not be lost when the power supply to the computer system is disconnected.

Backing storage uses either direct or serial access methods. Direct access means that particular files can be found without the need to read through all of the data, as with serial access. Data may be stored on (or written to) ⇝ CD-ROM, ⇝ floppy disk (both direct access), or ⇝ magnetic tape (serial access).

backup copy file that is transferred to another medium, usually a ⇝ floppy disk or tape. The purpose of this is to have available a copy of a file that can be restored in case of a fault in the system or the file itself. Backup files are also created by many applications (with the extension .BAC or .BAK); a version is therefore available of the original file before it was modified by the current application.

backup system duplicate computer system that can take over the operation of a main computer system in the event of equipment failure. A large interactive system, such as an airline's ticket-booking system, cannot be out of action for even a few hours without causing considerable disruption. In such cases a complete duplicate computer system may be provided to take over and run the system should the main computer develop a fault or need maintenance.

Backup systems include incremental backup and full backup.

backwards compatible term describing a product that is designed to be compatible with its predecessors. In software, a word processor is backwards compatible if it can read and write the files of earlier versions of the same software, and an operating system is backwards compatible if it can run programs designed for earlier versions of the operating system. Similarly, all modems are compatible with all the standards (V numbers) which precede the fastest one they can handle.

balloon help small cartoon-style bubble which pops up in a graphical computer system to convey ↪ online help. In many new products, balloon help is activated by holding the mouse over an icon or other type of control for a few seconds. Such help is context-sensitive.

bandwidth in communications, the rate of data transmission, measured in ↪ bits per second (bps).

bang in Unix, exclamation mark (!). It appears in some older types of Internet addresses and is used in dictating the commands necessary to run Unix systems.

bang path list of routing that appears in the header of a message sent across the Internet, showing how it travelled from the sender to its destination. It is named after the ↪ bangs separating the sites in the list.

banner advertisement on a World Wide Web page, usually but not always in the form of a horizontal rectangle. Clicking on a banner usually takes the user to the advertised Web site. Noncommercial sites display one another's banners via organizations like LinkExchange and BannerExchange.

bar code pattern of bars and spaces that can be read by a computer. Bar codes are widely used in retailing, industrial distribution, and libraries. The code is read by a scanning device; the computer determines the code from the widths of the bars and spaces.

The technique was patented in 1949 but became popular only in 1973, when the food industry in North America adopted the Universal Product Code system.

Bardeen, John (1908–1991) US physicist. He was awarded the Nobel Prize for Physics in 1956, with Walter Brattain and William Shockley, for the development of the transistor in 1948 and he became the first double winner of the Nobel Prize for Physics in 1972 (with Leon Cooper and Robert Schrieffer) for his work on superconductivity.

At the Bell Telephone laboratory, New Jersey, 1945-51, in a team with Shockley and Brattain, Bardeen studied semiconductors, especially germanium, used in radar receivers in the same way that crystals had been used in the earliest radio sets. The work led to the development of the transistor in 1956. The second Nobel prize was won for explaining superconductivity, the total loss of electrical resistance by some metals when cooled within a few degrees of absolute zero. The theory developed in 1957 by Bardeen, Schrieffer, and Cooper states that superconductivity arises when electrons travelling through a metal interact with the vibrating atoms of the metal.

baseband type of ⮁ network that transmits a computer signal without modulation (conversion of ⮁ digital signals to ⮁ analogue). To be able to send a computer's signal over the analogue telephone network, a ⮁ modem is required to convert – or modulate – the signal. On baseband networks, which include the most popular standards such as ⮁ Ethernet, the signal can be sent directly, without such processing.

BASIC acronym for *beginner's all-purpose symbolic instruction code*, high-level computer-programming language, developed in 1964, originally designed to take advantage of ⮁ multiuser systems (which can be used by many people at the same time). The language is relatively easy to learn and is popular among microcomputer users.

Most versions make use of an ⮁ interpreter, which translates BASIC into ⮁ machine code and allows programs to be entered and run with no intermediate translation. Some more recent versions of BASIC allow a ⮁ compiler to be used for this process.

batch file file that runs a group (batch) of commands. The most commonly used batch file is the ⮁ DOS start-up file ⮁ AUTOEXEC.BAT.

batch processing system for processing data with little or no operator intervention. Batches of data are prepared in advance to be processed during regular 'runs' (for example, each night). This allows efficient use of the computer and is well suited to applications of a repetitive nature, such as a company payroll, or the production of utility bills.

In ⮁ interactive computing, by contrast, data and instructions are entered while the processing program is running.

baud in engineering, a unit of electrical signalling speed equal to one pulse per second, measuring the rate at which signals are sent between electronic devices such as telegraphs and computers.

Bauds were used as a measure to identify the speed of ⮁ modems until the early 1990s because at the lower modem speeds available then the baud rate

BASIC Archives

http://www.fys.ruu.nl/ ~bergmann/basic.html

Detailed guide to BASIC. This site includes an informative 'Frequently Asked Questions' section, giving tips on such topics as 'how to print graphics with BASIC', 'how to display a BMP or GIF file', and 'how to make an EXE file'. There is also a brief history of the development of BASIC and a number of links to related sites.

WEB LINK

generally equalled the rate of transmission measured in ⮫ bps (bits per second). At higher speeds, this is not the case, and modem speeds now are generally quoted in bps.

Baudot code five-bit code developed in France by engineer Emil Baudot (1845–1903) in the 1870s. It is still in use for telex.

BBC Microcomputer microcomputer developed in 1982 in the UK by ⮫ Acorn for use in a BBC computer literacy project. The BBC Model B followed on from the Acorn Atom, and was widely adopted in the UK education market, though a cut-down home computer version, the Electron, was not a success. The BBC B was followed by an upgraded version, the BBC Master, and replaced by the Acorn Archimedes.

The computer was also the beneficiary of UK government funding to schools, which were able to buy the BBC Micro at reduced prices. As a result, it became the dominant microcomputer in British schools.

The BBC Micro was a highly advanced microcomputer for its time, with full support for disk drives and network connection. Its immediate successor, the BBC Master, also sold well to schools, but was too expensive for home use and unsuccessful in the business market.

BBS abbreviation for ⮫ bulletin board system.

benchmark measure of the performance of a piece of equipment or software, usually consisting of a standard program or suite of programs. Benchmarks can indicate whether a computer is powerful enough to perform a particular task, and so enable machines to be compared. However, they provide only a very rough guide to practical performance, and may lead manufacturers to design systems that get high scores with the artificial benchmark programs but do not necessarily perform well with day-to-day programs or data.

Benchmark measures include Whetstones, Dhrystones, SPECmarks, and TPC. SPECmarks are based on ten programs adopted by the Systems Performance Evaluation Cooperative for benchmarking workstations; the Transaction Processing Performance Council's TPC-B benchmark is used to test databases and online systems in banking (debit/credit) environments.

BeOS computer ⮫ operating system developed by Be Inc, a company founded in the USA in 1990 by French-born Jean-Louis Gassée, head of research and development and manufacturing at ⮫ Apple from 1985 to 1990. The BeOS, launched in October 1995, was originally intended to run on the BeBox (Be's microcomputer designed for video and audio applications), without the need to be backwards-compatible like the Windows PC.

Before Apple bought ⮫ NeXTStep to use as the basis for its new generation of operating systems, it considered using the BeOS. Like ⮫ NeXT Technology Inc before it, Be decided to drop its own hardware in January 1997, and the BeOS now runs on both the Apple Macintosh and the Windows PC. In 2000, Be launched BeIA, an operating system for Internet appliances, based on the BeOS.

Berners-Lee, Timothy (1955–) English inventor of the World Wide Web in 1990. He developed the Web whilst working as a consultant at CERN. He currently serves as director of the ↝ W3 Consortium, a neutral body that manages the Web. In 1996, the British Computing Society (BCS) gave him a Distinguished Fellow award.

Berners-Lee was born and brought up in London and his parents, both mathematicians, worked on England's first commercial computer, the Ferranti Mark 1, in the 1950s. He graduated from Oxford University with a degree in physics.

Berry, Clifford (1918–1963) US scientist and co-developer of the ABC (Atanasoff–Berry Calculator). Berry, a graduate student at the University of Iowa, combined with John ↝ Atanasoff to build one of the first electronic binary calculating machines. Later he gained an international reputation in the field of mass spectrometry.

beta pre-release version of a new software program still in development, which is handed out to users for testing. The worst ↝ bugs are usually eliminated at the earlier alpha stage of development. Beta testers use the software to do real work and report any bugs or badly implemented features they find to the developers, who incorporate this information in refining the product for release. Companies that assist with such testing are known as beta sites.

beta version pre-release version of ↝ software or an ↝ application program, usually distributed to a limited number of expert users (and often reviewers). Distribution of beta versions allows user testing and feedback to the developer, so that any necessary modifications can be made before release.

Bézier curve curved line invented by Pierre Bézier that connects a series of points (or 'nodes') in the smoothest possible way. The shape of the curve is governed by a series of complex mathematical formulae. They are used in ↝ computer graphics and ↝ CAD.

Bezos, Jeff (1964–) US computer entrepreneur. Bezos founded ↝ Amazon.com, of which he is chairman and chief executive, in July 1995, with an initial investment of $300,000. In May 2000, Bezos's wealth was estimated by the US financial magazine *Forbes* at $6.1 billion. His wealth is, however, dependent on the share price of Amazon, which fluctuates considerably.

After graduating with honours from Princeton University, where he had studied electrical engineering and computer science, Bezos joined Fitel, a high-tech start-up company in New York. Two years later, in April 1988, he went to work for Bankers Trust Company in New York, leading the development of the company's computer systems and becoming its youngest vice-president in February 1990.

In December 1990, Bezos moved to DE Shaw & Co in New York, where he worked until June 1994. There he helped to build one of the most technically sophisticated quantitative hedge funds on Wall Street. From being a self-proclaimed 'in-house geek', Bezos turned into a money manager, and became the firm's youngest senior vice-president in 1992.

Big Blue popular name for ➥ IBM, derived from the company's size and its blue logo.

Big Seven hierarchies on Usenet, the original seven ➥ hierarchies of ➥ newsgroups. They are: comp (computing), misc (miscellaneous), news, rec (recreation), sci (science), soc (social issues), and talk (debate). These categories of newsgroups are managed according to specific rules which govern the creation of new groups, in contrast to the ➥ alt hierarchy.

binary file any file that is not plain text. Program (.EXE or .COM), sound, video, and graphics files are all types of binary files. Such files require special treatment for inclusion in e-mail sent across the Internet, which can transmit only ➥ ASCII text and imposes a size limit of 64Kb per message. Several programs have been developed to code binary files into ASCII for transmission, splitting them into smaller parts as necessary. The most commonly used such program is ➥ UUencode, but there are others including base64 and BinHex. See also ➥ MIME.

binary large object *BLOB*, any large single block of data stored in a database, such as a picture or sound file. A BLOB does not include record fields, and so cannot be directly searched by the database's search engine.

binary newsgroup any Usenet ➥ newsgroup set up for the transmission of picture and other nontext files. The binary newsgroups have their own sub-hierarchy, alt.binaries, and include groups such as alt.binaries.pictures.fine-art.digitized and alt.binaries.pictures.erotica.

Because newsgroups are subject to the same restrictions as Internet e-mail for the transmission of ➥ binary files, pictures, programs, and other files posted to these newsgroups are ➥ UUencoded and split into sections. To view the pictures, all the parts must be downloaded and then UUdecoded and stitched back together to form the original file, which can then be viewed using the appropriate graphics program.

Other binary newsgroups distribute sound files (alt.binaries.sound.*) or user-contributed new levels for games such as *Doom* (alt.binaries.doom). These newsgroups take up a lot of ➥ bandwidth and therefore not all sites elect to carry them; blocking software typically bars access to many of these groups.

binary number system system of numbers to base two, using combinations of the digits 1 and 0. Codes based on binary numbers are used to represent

---

TIP

binary newsgroup

It is considered a breach of netiquette to post binary files to nonbinary newsgroups.

---

binary number system
The capital letter A
represented in binary form.

data	A
binary code	0 1 0 0 0 0 0 1
digital signal in the computer	

instructions and data in all modern digital computers, the values of the binary digits (contracted to 'bits') being stored or transmitted as, for example, open/closed switches, magnetized/unmagnetized disks and tapes, and high/low voltages in circuits.

The value of any position in a binary number increases by powers of 2 (doubles) with each move from right to left (1, 2, 4, 8, 16, and so on). For example, 1011 in the binary number system represents $(1 \times 8) + (0 \times 4) + (1 \times 2) + (1 \times 1)$, which adds up to 11 in the decimal system.

The value of any position in a normal decimal, or base-10, number increases by powers of 10 with each move from right to left (1, 10, 100, 1,000, 10,000, and so on). For example, the decimal number 2,567 stands for:

$(2 \times 1,000) + (5 \times 100) + (6 \times 10) + (7 \times 1)$

Decimal Number System (base 10)

In the decimal number system numbers can be seen as written under columns based on the number 10.

1000s	100s	10s	1s
(10^3)	(10^2)	(10^1)	(10^0)
2	5	6	7

Binary Number System (base 2)

In the binary number system numbers can be seen as written under columns based on the number 2. The binary number 1101 corresponds to the decimal number 13.

8s	4s	2s	1s
(2^3)	(2^2)	(2^1)	(2^0)
1	1	0	1

Octal Number System (base 8)

In the octal number system numbers can be seen as written under columns based on the number 8. The octal number 2164 corresponds to the decimal number 1140.

512s	64s	8s	1s
(8^3)	(8^2)	(8^1)	(8^0)
2	1	6	4

Hexadecimal Number System (base 16)

In the hexadecimal number system numbers can be seen as written under columns based on the number 16. Since digits up to a value of decimal 15 are permitted, the letters A to F are used to represent digits corresponding to decimal 10 to 15. The hexadecimal number 23BF corresponds to the decimal number 9151.

4096s	256s	16s	1s
(16^3)	(16^2)	(16^1)	(16^0)
2	3	B	F

binary number system
The table illustrates the difference between the binary and other number systems.

BinHex program for coding ↝ binary files into ↝ ASCII for transmission over the Internet via e-mail.

biometrics term applied loosely to the measurement of biological (human) data, usually for security purposes, rather than the statistical analysis of biological data. For example, when someone wants to enter a building or cash a cheque, their finger or eyeball may be scanned and compared with a fingerprint or eyeball scan stored earlier. Biometrics saves people from having to remember PINs (personal identification numbers) and passwords.

BIOS acronym for basic input/output system, part of a computer's operating system which handles the basic input and output operation for standard computer ᔟ hardware. For example, the BIOS reads the keystrokes from the keyboard, puts information on the display, and sends information to the printer. The small computer programs within the BIOS that carry out these tasks are called device drivers.

bistable circuit or *flip-flop*, simple electronic circuit that remains in one of two stable states until it receives a pulse (logic 1 signal) through one of its inputs, upon which it switches, or 'flips', over to the other state. Because it is a two-state device, it can be used to store binary digits and is widely used in the ᔟ integrated circuits used to build computers.

bit contraction of *binary digit*, single binary digit, either 0 or 1. A bit is the smallest unit of data stored in a computer; all other data must be coded into a pattern of individual bits. A ᔟ byte represents sufficient computer memory to store a single ᔟ character of data, and usually contains eight bits. For example, in the ᔟ ASCII code system used by most microcomputers the capital letter A would be stored in a single byte of memory as the bit pattern 01000001.

The maximum number of bits that a computer can normally process at once is called a word. Microcomputers are often described according to how many bits of information they can handle at once. For instance, the first micro-processor, the Intel 4004 (launched in 1971), was a 4-bit device. In the 1970s several different 8-bit computers, many based on the Zilog Z80 or Rockwell 6502 processors, came into common use. In 1981, the IBM Personal Computer (PC) was introduced, using the Intel 8088 processor, which combined a 16-bit processor with an 8-bit ᔟ data bus. Business micros of the later 1980s began to use 32-bit processors such as the Intel 80386 and Motorola 68030. Machines based on the first 64-bit microprocessor appeared in 1993.

The higher the number of bits a computer can process simultaneously, the more powerful the computer is said to be. However, other factors influence the overall speed of a computer system, such as the ᔟ clock rate of the processor and the amount of ᔟ RAM available. Tasks that require a high pro-cessing speed include sorting a database or doing long, complex calculations in spreadsheets. A system running slowly with a ᔟ graphical user interface may benefit more from the addition of extra RAM than from a faster processor.

In the PC industry, new hardware is most readily adopted when it is compatible with old software, which slows the adoption of new software. For example, most people were still using Microsoft's 16-bit Windows 3 program with 16-bit applications in 1995–96, a decade after 32-bit processors like Intel's

80386 became widely available. This was true even though 32-bit operating systems – Unix, IBM's OS/2, and Microsoft's Windows NT – had been available for some years.

bit map pattern of ⌖ bits used to describe the organization of data. Bit maps are used to store typefaces or graphic images (bit-mapped or ⌖ raster graphics), with 1 representing black (or a colour) and 0 white.

Bit maps may be used to store a typeface or ⌖ font, but a separate set of bit maps is required for each typesize. A vector font, by contrast, can be held as one set of data and scaled as required. Bit-mapped graphics are not recommended for images that require scaling (compare ⌖ vector graphics – those stored in the form of geometric formulas).

bit map
The difference in close-up between a bit-mapped and vector font. As separate sets of bit maps are required for each different type size, scaleable vector graphics (outline) is the preferred medium for fonts.

vector font

bit-mapped font

bit-mapped font ⌖ font held in computer memory as sets of bit maps.

bit pad computer input device; see ⌖ graphics tablet.

bits per second *bps*, commonly used measure of the speed of transmission of a ⌖ modem. In 2000 the fastest modems were rated at 56,600 bps. Modem speeds should conform to standards, known as ⌖ V numbers, laid down by the ⌖ Comité Consultatif International Téléphonique et Télégraphique (CCITT) so that modems from different manufacturers can connect to each other. Many modems transfer data much faster than their nominal speeds via techniques such as ⌖ data compression.

blind carbon copy e-mail message sent to multiple recipients who do not know each other's identities. The facility for blind carbon copies is built into some e-mail software, and is useful in eliminating long lists of recipients which clutter up a mass-distribution message; it also protects the confidentiality of a particular user's contact list.

blind signature encryption technique that authenticates a message without revealing any information about the sender. Blind signatures are one element in the attempt to develop technology that protects individual privacy as more and more transactions take place over public networks where users' activities can be tracked.

blink in communications, to ➥ log on using an offline reader or other software that uses automated ➥ scripts. Blinking saves on communications and telephone charges, but it changes the nature of online interaction because users cannot use chat facilities. Blinking also encourages repetition, since users replying off-line are unlikely to realize they are echoing each others' comments. On America Online, a blink is called a flashsession.

BLOB acronym for ➥ binary large object.

block group of records treated as a complete unit for transfer to or from ➥ backing storage. For example, many disk drives transfer data in 512-byte blocks.

blocking software any of various software programs that work on the World Wide Web to block access to categories of information considered offensive or dangerous. Typically used by parents or teachers to ensure that children do not see pornographic or other adult material, some blocking products additionally allow the blocking of personal information such as home addresses and telephone numbers; some people regard this as censorship.

Blocking software became even more controversial in mid-1996 when Washington, DC-based reporters Brock Meeks and Declan McCullagh revealed that the list of banned sites in some popular products included political material and that some sites were blocked indiscriminately.

Popular blocking software products include Net Nanny, SurfWatch, CyberPatrol, and CyberSitter.

blue-ribbon campaign campaign for free speech on the Internet. It was launched to protest against various international moves towards censorship on the Internet, especially the ➥ Communications Decency Act in 1996. Participation in the campaign is indicated by the small graphic of a looped blue ribbon displayed on many sites on the World Wide Web and available from the campaign's Web site http://www.eff.org/blueribbon.html.

Bluetooth short-range radio communications system designed to connect personal computers, printers, mobile phones, cameras, and similar devices, thus avoiding the need for cables. Bluetooth was announced in 1998 and is being developed by Ericsson, IBM, Intel, Nokia, and Toshiba. It will operate in the licence-free 2.45GHz band. When available, it should be more convenient than today's ➥ IrDA infrared connections as ➥ WIDs (wireless information devices) do not need to be kept within line-of-sight to operate.

BMP in Windows, a file extension indicating a graphics file in ➥ bit-map format. Bit-mapped files are commonly used for icons and wallpaper.

Bolero consortium launched in September 1999 to introduce an electronic paperless environment for international trading finance. Bolero was created by the world's logistics and banking communities. The aim was to remove the inefficiencies of international trade by moving it onto the Internet, allowing documents and data to be exchanged online.

By June 2000, 32 companies had signed up to Bolero, including the US commodities trading house Cargill, Mitsui of Japan, and the German firm Otto Versand (the world's largest mail order company). Users also included seven of the world's top ten banks, including Chase Manhattan, HSBC, ABN Amro, and Citibank, as well as carriers such as K Line, Cosco, and Evergreen.

bookmark facility for marking a specific place in electronic documentation to enable easy return to it. It is used in several types of software, including electronic help files and tutorials. Bookmarks are especially important on the World Wide Web, where it can be difficult to remember a uniform resource locator (⤳ URL) in order to return to it. Most Web browsers therefore have built-in bookmark facilities, whereby the browser stores the URL with the page name attached. To return directly to the site, the user picks the page name from the list of saved bookmarks.

Boole, George (1815–1864) English mathematician. His work *The Mathematical Analysis of Logic* (1847) established the basis of modern mathematical logic, and his Boolean algebra can be used in designing computers.

Boole's system is essentially two-valued. By subdividing objects into separate classes, each with a given property, his algebra makes it possible to treat different classes according to the presence or absence of the same property. Hence it involves just two numbers, 0 and 1 – the binary system used in the computer.

Boole was born in Lincoln and was largely self-taught. In 1849 he was appointed professor of mathematics at Queen's College in Cork, Ireland.

Boolean algebra set of algebraic rules, named after English mathematician George Boole, in which TRUE and FALSE are equated to 0 and 1. Boolean algebra includes a series of operators (AND, OR, NOT, NAND (NOT AND), NOR, and XOR (exclusive OR)), which can be used to manipulate TRUE and FALSE values (see ⤳ truth table). It is the basis of computer logic because the truth values can be directly associated with ⤳ bits.

These rules are used in searching databases either locally or across the ⤳ Internet via services like AltaVista to limit the number of hits to those which most closely match a user's requirements. A search instruction such as 'tennis NOT table' would retrieve articles about tennis and reject those about ping-pong.

boot or *bootstrap*, process of starting up a computer. Most computers have a small, built-in boot program that starts automatically when the computer is switched on – its only task is to load a slightly larger program, usually from a hard disk, which in turn loads the main ⤳ operating system.

TIP

boot

Some boot programs can be customized so that, for example, the computer, when switched on, always loads and runs a program from a particular backing store or always adopts a particular mode of screen display.

TIP

boot disk

Always have a boot disk to hand and keep it up-to-date; before using it to restart your computer after a virus attack, make sure it is write-protected.

TIP

bounce

If e-mail bounces, check that the address is correct and try sending it again; if it bounces a second time, try sending an e-mail message with the user ID replaced with the word postmaster, asking if the user ID is valid.

boot disk or *emergency disk*, floppy disk containing the necessary files to ↪ boot a computer without needing to access its hard disk. Boot disks are vital in recovering from virus attacks, when it is not known which files on a computer's hard disk may be infected; in recovering from a system crash which has corrupted existing files; or in correcting mistakes introduced into files necessary for starting up the computer by newly installed software programs.

'bot short for robot, on the Internet, automated piece of software that performs specific tasks. 'Bots are commonly found on multi-user dungeons (↪ MUDs) and other multi-user role-playing game sites, where they maintain a constant level of activity even when few human users are logged on. On the World Wide Web, 'bots automate maintenance tasks such as indexing Web pages and tracing broken links.

bounce system by which an electronic mail message that cannot be delivered to its addressee is returned ('bounced back') to the sender, with a note advising of its failure to reach its destination. Failed delivery is usually due to an incorrect e-mail address or a network problem.

bps abbreviation for *bits per second*, measure used in specifying data transmission rates.

bridge device that connects two similar local area networks (LANs). Bridges transfer data in packets between the two networks, without making any changes or interpreting the data in any way. See also ↪ router and ↪ brouter.

British Computer Society *BCS*, main professional body for those working in the field of ↪ information technology in the UK. Founded in 1957, the BCS was granted a royal charter in 1984. The society is also an Engineering Institution, fully licensed by the Engineering Council to nominate Chartered and Incorporated Engineers and to accredit university courses and training schemes.

The equivalent US organization is the ↪ Association for Computing Machinery (ACM).

broadband type of data transmission in which a single circuit can carry several channels at once, used for example in cable television. Broadband networking is one way of supplying much greater Internet ↪ bandwidth over the existing telephone system. See also ↪ ADSL.

brouter device for connecting computer networks that incorporates the facilities of both a ↪ bridge and a ↪ router. Brouters usually offer routing over a limited number of ↪ protocols, operating by routing where possible and bridging the remaining protocols.

browse to explore a computer system or network for particular files or information. To browse in Windows is to search for a particular file to open or run. On the World Wide Web, browsing is the activity of moving from site to site to view information. This is sometimes also called 'surfing'.

browser any program that allows the user to search for and view data. Browsers are usually limited to a particular type of data, so, for example, a graphics browser will display graphics files stored in many different file formats. Browsers usually do not permit the user to edit data, but are sometimes able to convert data from one file format to another.

Web browsers allow access to the ⮑ World Wide Web. ⮑ Netscape Navigator and Microsoft's Internet Explorer were the leading Web browsers in 2000. They act as a graphical interface to information available on the Internet – they read ⮑ HTML (hypertext markup language) documents and display them as graphical documents which may include images, video, sound, and ⮑ hypertext links to other documents.

browser
Two popular World Wide Web browsers, Netscape Navigator and Microsoft Internet Explorer, which provide the user with a straightforward method of accessing information online.

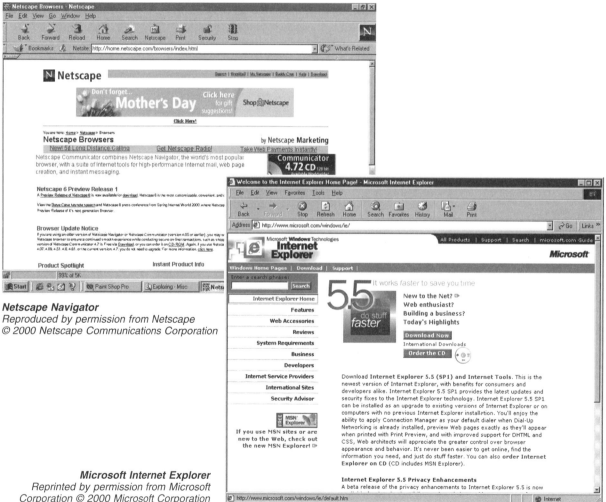

Netscape Navigator
Reproduced by permission from Netscape © 2000 Netscape Communications Corporation

Microsoft Internet Explorer
Reprinted by permission from Microsoft Corporation © 2000 Microsoft Corporation

The first widespread browser for personal computers (PCs) was the text-based program Lynx, which is still used via ∽ gateways from text-based online systems such as Delphi and CIX. Browsers using ∽ graphical user interfaces became widely available from 1993 with the release of ∽ Mosaic, written by Marc ∽ Andreessen and Eric Bina.

Some Web sites contain special pages that might contain animation, 3D scenes, or a particular kind of audio. The basic browser technology needs to be enhanced using plug-in technology if these kind of effects are to be seen or heard. An example of a browser plug-in is the Macromedia Flash plug-in, which can display sophisticated animations and multimedia effects.

BT formerly *British Telecom*, British telecommunications company. Its principal activity is the supply of local, long-distance, and international telecommunications services and equipment in the UK, serving 27 million exchange lines. BT also offers an international direct-dialled telephone service to more than 200 countries and other overseas territories – covering 99% of the world's 800 million telephones.

In September 1999 British Telecom and AT&T announced their plans to form an international cellular phone network called Advance to attract business customers. The two companies had annual sales of $12 billion and served 41 million mobile phone customers in 17 countries.

In 2000, BT's UK fixed network business was separated into wholesale and retail divisions. The company's other assets in the UK, Europe, and elsewhere were regrouped by market sector rather than geography. Four new businesses were created: Ignite, a ∽ broadband business for corporate and wholesale markets; BTopenworld, a mass-market Internet business including broadband services; BTWireless (formely BT Cellnet), an international cellular operator; and Yell (formerly Yellow Pages), an international directories and ∽ electronic commerce business.

BT deals with 103 million local and international calls a day. It is now a prominent Internet service provider, and also provides Campus, the educational and training network. BT is the second-largest shareholder in INTELSAT and operates satellite stations at London Docklands, Goonhille Downs, Cornwall, in Hereford, and at Aberdeen.

bubble-jet printer ∽ ink-jet printer in which the ink is heated to boiling point so that it forms a bubble at the end of a nozzle. When the bubble bursts, the ink is transferred to the paper.

bubble memory memory device based on the creation of small 'bubbles' on a magnetic surface. Bubble memories typically store up to 4 megabits (4 million ∽ bits) of information. They are not sensitive to shock and vibration, unlike other memory devices such as disk drives, yet, like magnetic disks, they are nonvolatile and do not lose their information when the computer is switched off.

bubble sort technique for ∽ sorting data. Adjacent items are continually exchanged until the data are in sequence.

buddy list list of friends made by users of the ⏗America Online service. Users who are online are automatically notified when their friends are also online, or on the Web, so that they can chat or exchange instant messages. Mirabilis Ltd's ⏗ICQ provides the same facility for Internet users. Both parties must use the same buddy list system for this to work.

buffer part of the ⏗memory used to store data temporarily while it is waiting to be used. For example, a program might store data in a printer buffer until the printer is ready to print it.

bug ⏗error in a program. It can be an error in the logical structure of a program or a syntax error, such as a spelling mistake. Some bugs cause a program to fail immediately; others remain dormant, causing problems only when a particular combination of events occurs. The process of finding and removing errors from a program is called debugging.

bulletin board centre for the electronic storage of messages, usually accessed over the telephone network via a ⏗modem but also sometimes accessed via ⏗Telnet across the Internet. Bulletin board systems (often abbreviated to BBSs) are usually dedicated to specific interest groups, and may carry public and private messages, notices, and programs.

bus electrical pathway through which a computer processor communicates with some of its parts and/or peripherals. Physically, a bus is a set of parallel tracks that can carry digital signals; it may take the form of copper tracks laid down on the computer's ⏗printed circuit boards (PCBs), or of an external cable or connection.

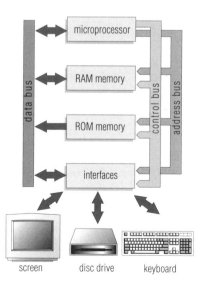

bus
The communication path used between
the component parts of a computer

A computer typically has three internal buses laid down on its main circuit board: a *data bus*, which carries data between the components of the computer; an *address bus*, which selects the route to be followed by any particular data item travelling along the data bus; and a *control bus*, which is used to decide whether data is written to or read from the data bus. An external expansion bus is used for linking the computer processor to peripheral devices, such as modems and printers.

Bushnell, Nolan (1943–) US entrepreneur and founder of Atari and the video games business. Bushnell completed BSc in electrical engineering at the University of Utah and has been involved with a large number of ventures, from robotic pets to chains of pizza restaurants. He has been called 'the P T Barnum of Silicon Valley'. Bushnell and Al Alcorn developed one of the first coin-operated arcade games, which ran a primitive version of table tennis (no net) called Pong. In 1972, he founded Atari with $250 and by 1982 – years after Bushnell had sold out to Warner Brothers – its sales reached $2 billion a year.

Byron, (Augusta) Ada, Countess of Lovelace (1815–1852) English mathematician, a pioneer in writing programs for Charles ↪ Babbage's analytical engine. In 1983 a new, high-level computer language, Ada, was named after her.

She was the daughter of the poet Lord Byron.

byte sufficient computer memory to store a single ↪ character of data. The character is stored in the byte of memory as a pattern of ↪ bits (binary digits), using a code such as ↪ ASCII. A byte usually contains eight bits – for example, the capital letter F can be stored as the bit pattern 01000110.

A single byte can specify 256 values, such as the decimal numbers from 0 to 255; in the case of a single-byte ↪ pixel (picture element), it can specify 256 different colours. Three bytes (24 bits) can specify 16,777,216 values. Computer memory size is measured in kilobytes (1,024 bytes) or megabytes (1,024 kilobytes).

C high-level, general-purpose programming language popular on minicomputers and microcomputers. Developed in the early 1970s from an earlier language called BCPL, C was first used as the language of the operating system ↝ Unix, though it has since become widespread beyond Unix. It is useful for writing fast and efficient systems programs, such as operating systems (which control the operations of the computer).

C++ high-level programming language used in ↝ object-oriented applications. It is derived from the language C.

cable modem box supplied by cable companies to provide television and telephone services, including Internet. The advantages of cable modems over traditional ↝ modems, which operate over standard telephone lines, are greatly increased speed of communications as well as the ability to transmit video and two-way audio, and lower costs.

cache memory reserved area of the ↝ immediate access memory used to increase the running speed of a computer program.

The cache memory may be constructed from ↝ SRAM, which is faster but more expensive than the normal ↝ DRAM. Most programs access the same instructions or data repeatedly. If these frequently used instructions and data are stored in a fast-access SRAM memory cache, the program will run more quickly. In other cases, the memory cache is normal DRAM, but is used to store frequently used instructions and data that would normally be accessed from ↝ backing storage. Access to DRAM is faster than access to backing storage so, again, the program runs more quickly. This type of cache memory is often called a disk cache.

Read cache is used to store copies of data and instructions that are retrieved from main memory or mass storage. If the central processing unit (CPU) needs to access the same data or instructions again, it can use the copy in read cache. This is much faster than going back to main memory or mass storage again. Write cache is a temporary store for data that needs to be written to main memory or mass storage. The CPU can move the data into cache very quickly, and then continue executing instructions. The data is subsequently moved to its permanent location by the cache controller, a process that takes more time because main memory and mass storage devices are much slower to access than cache memory.

There are different levels of cache. Level one cache is the fastest and most expensive, and is positioned the closest to the CPU. Level two cache is slower, but cheaper, and usually found in larger quantities. Modern PCs are technically capable of having level three cache. This is slower and cheaper than level one or two.

CAD acronym for *computer-aided design*, use of computers in creating and editing design drawings. CAD also allows such things as automatic testing of designs and multiple or animated three-dimensional views of designs. CAD systems are widely used in architecture, electronics, and engineering, for

Neil's C++ Stuff

http://www.cyclone7.com/cpp/

Features a number of tutorials on the programming language C++, covering topics such as 'Loops', 'Classes', and 'Arrays'. The information is presented clearly, and there is also a glossary and list of FAQs should you get stuck.

WEB LINK

example in the motor-vehicle industry, where cars designed with the assistance of computers are now commonplace. With a CAD system, picture components are accurately positioned using grid lines. Pictures can be resized, rotated, or mirrored without loss of quality or proportion.

A related development is ↝ CAM (computer-aided manufacturing).

CAL acronym for *computer-assisted learning*, use of computers in education and training: the computer displays instructional material to a student and asks questions about the information given; the student's answers determine the sequence of the lessons.

calculator pocket-sized electronic computing device for performing numerical calculations. It can add, subtract, multiply, and divide; many calculators also compute squares and roots and have advanced trigonometric and statistical functions. Input is by a small keyboard and results are shown on a one-line computer screen, typically a ↝ liquid-crystal display (LCD) or a light-emitting diode (LED). The first electronic calculator was manufactured by the Bell Punch Company in the USA in 1963.

call for votes on ↝ Usenet, process by which the nature and scope of a new ↝ newsgroup is determined. Calls for votes are posted to news.announce. newgroups. In the case of the ↝ Big Seven hierarchies, the call for votes is a requirement; it is recommended but not compulsory for ↝ alt hierarchy groups. The point is to ensure that newsgroup names follow a consistent pattern and that new newsgroups are formed in response to genuine interest.

CAM acronym for *computer-aided manufacturing*, use of computers to control production processes; in particular, the control of machine tools and robots in factories. In some factories, the whole design and production system has been automated by linking ↝ CAD (computer-aided design) to CAM.

Linking flexible CAD/CAM manufacturing to computer-based sales and distribution methods makes it possible to produce semicustomized goods cheaply and in large numbers.

campus-wide information system *CWIS*, computerized information service used on US university campuses, often hooked to the Internet. These systems typically include local events listings, general campus information, access to the library catalogue, weather reports, directories, and even ↝ bulletin-board and messaging services.

One of the first such systems was Cornell University's CUINFO, developed by a team led by technical administrator Steve Worona in 1982. The development of ↝ Gopher servers in 1991 made these systems much easier to navigate, and many systems were redesigned to take advantage of the new technology. In the mid-1990s these systems began moving to the World Wide Web.

cancelbot automated software program (see ↝ bot) that cancels messages on Usenet. The arrival of ↝ spamming (advertising) on the Net prompted the development of technology to use features built into Usenet to cancel messages. While single messages are easily cancelled manually, an automated routine is needed to handle mass postings, which may go out to more than 14,000 newsgroups. Cancelbot is activated by the ↬ CancelMoose.

CancelMoose anonymous individual who fires off the ↬ cancelbot. The CancelMoose (usually written as 'CancelMoose [TM]' on the Net) monitors newsgroups such as alt.current-events.net-abuse and news.admin.net-abuse for complaints about ↬ spamming (advertising), usually defined as messages posted to more than 25 newsgroups of widely varying content. The CancelMoose's identity is kept secret for reasons of personal safety.

Capstone long-term US government project to develop a set of standards for publicly available ↬ cryptography as authorized by the Computer Security Act 1987. The initiative has four elements: a data encryption ↬ algorithm (Skipjack), a ↬ hash function, a key exchange protocol, and a ↬ digital signature algorithm (DSS).

The project is managed primarily by the National Security Agency (NSA) and the National Institute of Standards and Technology (NIST).

capture saving of user actions as digital data that can be read by a computer. In real-time data communications, it refers to using software to log a session so that the session can be saved to a file. The term is also used with reference to screens, where the graphical material displayed on a computer screen may be saved as a picture file. In the study of ↬ human–computer interaction, the data captured are user keystrokes, mouse movements, and even facial expressions and muttered complaints so that developers can replay the session to help them design better ↬ user interfaces.

carbon copy in e-mail, a duplicate copy of a message sent to multiple recipients; a nod to traditional office systems. It is often abbreviated in software and on line to 'cc'.

carriage return *CR*, special code (↬ ASCII value 13) that moves the screen cursor or a print head to the beginning of the current line. Most word processors and the ↬ MS-DOS operating system use a combination of CR and line feed (LF – ASCII value 10) to represent a hard return. The ↬ Unix system, however, uses only LF and therefore files transferred between MS-DOS and Unix require a conversion program.

cascading style sheets *CSS*, feature of ↬ HTML that enables Web programmers to define a style that can be applied to any number of pages. More than one style sheet can be applied to a page. For example, a Webmaster can define an overall style for a Web site, then use different style sheets for different sections, and add further sheets for pages lower down the hierarchy: hence cascading. CSS has been developed under the auspices of the ↬ W3C.

The standard definition of CSS has been available for several years. However, the companies that design Web browsers do not always implement the design properly, or in its entirety. This causes problems for Web page designers because their pages may appear differently from one browser to another.

case-sensitive term describing a system that distinguishes between capitals and lower-case letters. Domain names and Internet addresses are typically not case-sensitive; however, a particular system may be case-sensitive for user IDs.

CCD abbreviation for ⇝ charge coupled device.

CCITT abbreviation for ⇝ Comité Consultatif International Téléphonique et Télégraphique.

CD-I or *CD*-i; abbreviation for *compact disc-interactive*, compact disc developed by Philips for storing a combination of video, audio, text, and pictures. It was intended principally for the consumer market to be used in systems using a combination of computer and television. It flopped as a consumer system but is still used in education and training.

CD-quality sound digitized sound at 44.1 KHz and 16 bits, the standard defined in ISO 10149, known as the Red Book. CD-quality sound was designed to be the minimum standard required to reproduce every sound the human ear can hear. Most audio CDs are recorded to this level.

CD-R abbreviation for *compact disc-recordable*, compact disc on which data can be recorded (compare ⇝ CD-ROM).

The blank disc has a very fine groove that forms a large spiral, starting from the centre of the disc and finishing on the edge. Visible to the laser at the bottom of this groove is a layer of organic dye. During the recording process the laser switches to a higher power and 'burns' a mark in the dye. These marks in the dye are like the pits found on CD-ROM discs, and can be read by the laser operating at a lower power.

CD-ROM acronym for *compact-disc read-only memory*, computer storage device developed from the technology of the audio compact disc. It consists of a plastic-coated metal disk, on which binary digital information is etched in the form of microscopic pits. This can then be read optically by passing a laser beam over the disk. CD-ROMs typically hold over 600 ⇝ megabytes of data, and are used in distributing large amounts of text, graphics, audio, and video, such as encyclopedias, catalogues, technical manuals, and games.

Standard CD-ROMs cannot have information written onto them by computer, but must be manufactured from a master, although recordable CDs, called CD-R disks, have been developed for use as computer disks. A compact disc, CD-RW, that can be overwritten repeatedly by a computer has also been developed. The compact disc, with its enormous storage capability, may eventually replace the magnetic disk as the most common form of backing store for computers.

The technology is being developed rapidly: a standard CD-ROM disk spins at between 240–1170 rpm, but faster disks have been introduced which speed up data retrieval to many times the standard speed. Research is being conducted

---

into high-density CDs capable of storing many ⤳ gigabytes of data, made possible by using multiple layers on the surface of the disk, and by using double-sided disks. The first commercial examples of this research include DVD players and DVD-ROM computer disks launched in 1997.

PhotoCD, developed by Kodak and released in 1992, transfers ordinary still photographs onto CD-ROM disks.

CD-ROM drive disk drive for reading CD-ROMs. The vast majority of CD-ROM drives conform to the Yellow Book standard, defined by Philips and Sony. Because of this, all drives are essentially interchangeable. CD-ROM drives are available either as stand-alone or built-in units with a variety of interfaces (connections) and access times.

Drives are usually described as being times some number, ×4 for example. This refers to how much faster the disc is moving past the read head in comparison to a standard music CD. Modern drives are sometimes quoted as being ×44 or higher. However, this will only be true for data retrieved from certain areas of the disc surface, not the whole disc.

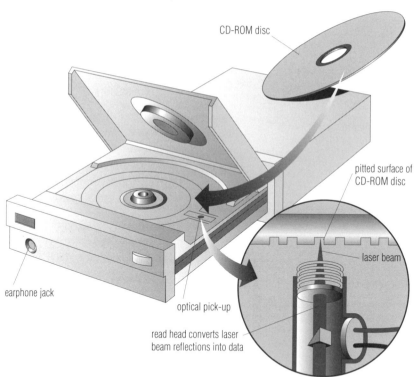

CD-ROM disc

pitted surface of CD-ROM disc

laser beam

earphone jack

optical pick-up

read head converts laser beam reflections into data

CD-ROM drive
Data is obtained by the CD-ROM drive by converting the reflections from a disk's surface into digital form.

CD-ROM XA abbreviation for *CD-ROM extended architecture*, set of standards for storing multimedia information on CD-ROM. Developed by Philips, Sony, and Microsoft, it is a partial development of the ⤳ CD-I standard. It interleaves data (as in CD-I) so that blocks of audio data are sandwiched between blocks of text, graphics, or video. This allows parallel streams of data to be handled, so that information can be seen and heard simultaneously.

CD-RW abbreviation for *compact disc-rewritable*, compact disc on which data can be recorded (compare ⇒ CD-ROM, compact disc read-only memory); unlike ⇒ CD-R recordable disks, CD-RW disks can be reused.

CD-RW drives can read CD-ROM disks but CD-RW disks cannot be read in standard CD-ROM drives.

Data is recorded onto a CD-RW disc by changing the properties of a special metal alloy at points corresponding to the pits on a CD-ROM. This change is made by a laser operating at its highest power. By pointing the laser at the same spot, but on medium power, the properties of the metal alloy revert to their original state, and the data is effectively erased. The data can be read because the laser-affected points of the alloy reflect light much less well than the parts of the alloy not changed by the laser.

CE Microsoft operating system for palm-sized and handheld computers, in-car PCs, set-top boxes, and similar devices. CE originally stood for *Consumer Electronics*, though it is now aimed at a broader market. Windows CE is not a cut-down version of Windows 95 but a different operating system that runs on a wide range of processors. It is often used in handheld computers based on ⇒ RISC processors from Hitachi and Mips. In 2000, the operating system was revamped and renamed PocketPC. See also ⇒ Windows.

Ceefax ('see facts') one of Britain's two ⇒ teletext systems (the other is Teletext), or 'magazines of the air', developed by the BBC and first broadcast on television in 1973.

In 1995 the BBC began testing a scheme to allow Ceefax (repackaged in HTML, hypertext markup language, to enable it to behave like Web pages) to be viewed on a PC by connecting a DAB (digital audio broadcasting) radio to the PC like a modem.

Celeron brand name of a type of Intel Pentium II processor designed for use in low cost personal computers. When launched in 1998, Celeron chips were not well received, as their lack of ⇒ cache memory made them relatively slow. Intel soon added on-chip cache memory which enabled them to perform as well as standard Pentium II chips. The equivalent Intel product designed for use in servers and workstations is the ⇒ Xeon.

cellular modem type of ⇒ modem that connects to a cellular phone for the wireless transmission of data.

cellular phone wireless phone that operates over radio frequencies and links calls to the public telephone system via a base station; the area covered by each base station is called a cell. Unlike phones connected up by telephone lines, cellular phones allow mobility, as calls can be made while moving from one radio cell to another. A network of connected base stations and exchanges connects the cellular calls to the public telephone system.

In the UK, the four main networks are Cellnet, One 2 One, Orange, and Vodafone, all covering more than 90% of the country. Vodafone Air-Touch was, in 2000, the world's largest cellular phone company, with a value of $259

Electronic Frontier Foundation

http://www.eff.org/

US-based non-profit organization that aims to protect free speech on the Internet. This site includes a lot of technical legal jargon and the full text of Supreme Court decisions relating to their campaigns.

WEB LINK

billion. Older analogue cellular phones are easily tapped via commonly available scanners. Although this practice is illegal, in the early 1990s transcriptions of several phone calls made to or from members of the British royal family found their way into newspapers around the world. Newer digital phones use encryption to protect the confidentiality of phone conversations.

In Europe, the newer digital standard, GSM (Global System for Mobiles), has been adopted by many countries, enabling travellers to use a single phone throughout Europe.

In September 1999, the US company Bell Atlantic bought the $15 billion mobile phone network of Vodafone Air-Touch. Vodafone acquired a 45% stake in the new company. The union allowed customers of both companies to call from almost anywhere out of their usual area in the country without paying an extra 'roaming' charge.

In February 2000, Vodafone bought the German mobile-operator Mannesmann for £113 billion. As part of the deal, Vodafone had to sell off the Orange network, which had been bought by Mannesmann. Orange was bought by France Telecom in June 2000 for $46 billion, and was to be combined with France Telecom's other mobile companies in France, Belgium, and the Netherlands, with a total of 21 million subscribers (compared to Vodafone Air-Touch's 38 million).

CE Marking abbreviation for *Conformité Européene* Marking, mark which must be affixed to certain products, such as personal computers, to show that they conform to legislation required by 18 countries in the European Community. CE Marking acts as a 'passport' which allows a manufacturer to distribute products within the European marketplace.

censorship banning of certain types of information from public access. Concerns over the ready availability of material such as bomb recipes and pornography have led a number of countries to pass laws attempting to censor the Internet. The best known of these is the US ⤳ Communications Decency Act 1996, but initiatives have been taken in other countries, for example Singapore, which announced in 1996 new regulations bringing the Internet under the Singapore Broadcasting Authority and requiring all access providers and users to be registered and licensed. Less formal pressures have been applied against ⤳ Internet Service Providers in Germany and the UK to block specific types of material.

In 2000, a survey by US organization Freedom House found that 63% of countries restrict print and electronic journalists. The French monitoring service Reporters sans Frontieres states that the following countries totally or largely restrict Internet access: Azerbaijan, Belarus, Burma, China, Cuba, Iran, Iraq, Kazakhstan, Kyrgystan, Libya, North Korea, Saudi Arabia, Sierra Leone, Sudan, Syria, Tajikistan, Tunisia, Turkmenistan, Uzbekistan, and Vietnam. See also ⤳ Regulation of Investigatory Powers Act.

central processing unit *CPU*, main component of a computer, the part that executes individual program instructions and controls the operation of other parts. It is sometimes called the central processor or, when contained on a single integrated circuit, a microprocessor.

---

censorship

http://www.eff.org/pub/
Censorship/

More information about censorship on the Internet is available from the Censorship and Free Expression archive and from the Electronic Frontier Foundation.

WEB LINK

The CPU has three main components: the arithmetic and logic unit (ALU), where all calculations and logical operations are carried out; a control unit, which decodes, synchronizes, and executes program instructions; and the immediate access memory, which stores the data and programs on which the computer is currently working. All these components contain ⬂ registers, which are memory locations reserved for specific purposes.

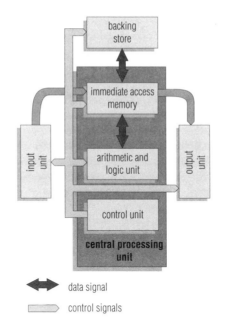

central processing unit
The relationship between the three main areas of a computer's central processing unit. The arithmetic and logic unit (ALU) does the arithmetic, using the registers to store intermediate results, supervised by the control unit. Input and output circuits connect the ALU to external memory, input, and output devices.

data signal
control signals

Centronics interface standard type of computer ⬂ interface, used to connect computers to ⬂ parallel devices, usually printers. (Centronics was an important printer manufacturer in the early days of microcomputing.)

Cerf, Vinton (1943–   ) US inventor of part of the ⬂ TCP/IP protocols on which the Internet is based. Known throughout the industry as the 'Father of the Internet', Cerf was president of the ⬂ Internet Society from 1992 to 1995 and was a principal developer of the ⬂ ARPANET.

Formerly assistant professor of electrical engineering and computer science at Stanford University, Cerf is senior vice-president of data architecture for MCI WorldCom's Data Services Division in Reston, Virginia. He was awarded the US National Medal of Technology in 1997.

Cerf sits on the boards of around a dozen companies and organizations. He is chairman of the Internet Societal Task Force, which aims to make the Internet accessible to everyone and analyzes international, national, and local policies surrounding its use.

CERT abbreviation for ⬂ Computer Emergency Response Team.

CGA abbreviation for *colour graphics adapter*, first colour display system for IBM PCs and compatible machines. It has been superseded by ⬂ EGA, ⬂ VGA, ⬂ SVGA, and ⬂ XGA.

CGI abbreviation for ⬂ common gateway interface.

channel on a Web site, a directory of selected Web resources about a particular topic such as personal finance, sport, or entertainment. Many ⬂ search engines and ⬂ portals also offer a selection of channels. Unlike directories, channels are not intended to be comprehensive but may be programmed to suit a particular kind of user. Some companies may charge to include Web sites in their channels.

character one of the symbols that can be represented in a computer. Characters include letters, numbers, spaces, punctuation marks, and special symbols.

character printer computer ☞ printer that prints one character at a time.

character set complete set of symbols that can be used in a program or recognized by a computer. It may include letters, digits, spaces, punctuation marks, and special symbols.

character type check ☞ validation check to ensure that an input data item does not contain invalid characters. For example, an input name may be checked to ensure that it contains only letters of the alphabet or an input six-figure date may be checked to ensure it contains only numbers.

charge-coupled device *CCD*, device for forming images electronically, using a layer of silicon that releases electrons when struck by incoming light. The electrons are stored in ☞ pixels and read off into a computer at the end of the exposure. CCDs are used in digital cameras, and have now almost entirely replaced photographic film for applications such as astrophotography where extreme sensitivity to light is paramount.

chat real-time exchange of messages between users of a particular system. Chat allows people who are geographically far apart to type messages to each other which are sent and received instantly. On a system like ☞ America Online, users may chat while playing competitive games or while reading messages, as well as joining public or private 'rooms' to talk with a variety of other users. The biggest chat system is Internet Relay Chat (IRC), which is used for the exchange of information and software as well as for social interaction.

check box small, square box used as a control in ☞ dialog boxes. Check boxes ☞ toggle functions and are operated by moving the cursor over the box and clicking the mouse button to check or clear the box.

check digit digit attached to an important code number as a ☞ validation check.

checksum ☞ control total of specific items of data. A checksum is used as a check that data have been input or transmitted correctly. It is used in communications and in, for example, accounts programs. See also ☞ validation.

chip or *silicon chip*, another name for an ☞ integrated circuit, a complete electronic circuit on a slice of silicon (or other semiconductor) crystal only a few millimetres square.

chip-set group of ☞ chips that work together to perform a particular set of functions. Standard chip-sets, for example, manage graphics or form the working parts of a modem.

cholestric LCD screen type of ☞ liquid-crystal display developed by Kent Display Systems with technology from Kent State University, Ohio, USA. The screen has been created for use in ☞ electronic book readers and ☞ personal digital assistants.

The screen uses a form of cholesterol to create an opaque background of any colour and a foreground ⏤ resolution of 100 dpi (sharper than on a PC), requiring no backlight. Cholestric screens require no power to hold a static image, and are completely glass-free and consequently much lighter than conventional glass screens.

chroma key in television, technique for substituting backgrounds. For example, the empty studio behind a newscaster may be replaced with an outdoor scene or a frame of video footage. This technique is commonly used on news programmes and other shows that feature 'talking heads'.

A computer analyses the image of the newscaster, who is placed in front of a plain background, usually blue, to identify the exact ⏤ pixels where the talking figure begins and ends. It can then substitute a new image for just the area specified. The technique allows broadcasters to add visual interest while keeping costs down.

CinePak software method of compressing and decompressing ⏤ QuickTime 'movies', also called a software codec. CinePak takes a recorded QuickTime file and reduces it in size, frame by frame. This is a slow process, but the result is a file that can be played back efficiently by computers with QuickTime installed.

CIS or *CI$*, abbreviations for *CompuServe Information Service*; see ⏤ CompuServe.

CISC acronym for *complex instruction-set computer*, term referring to the design of the CPU and its instruction set. CISC computers are characterized by having large numbers of instructions, varying a lot in size and complexity. Usually, the various stages of instruction execution are followed, and only when all the stages have been finished can a new instruction start to be executed. RISC CPUs, by comparison, usually have few instructions in the instruction set, and the instructions are smaller and simpler. Complex problems are solved by executing several of the smaller instructions.

RISC CPUs often outperform CISC designs because the instructions are executed in a pipeline, which is analogous to a factory assembly line. The pipeline enables the execution of instructions to be overlapped, with the first stages of instruction taking place before the final stages of the previous instruction have been completed.

Citrix US-based software house that pioneered the use of WBTs (⏤ Windows-Based Terminals) as a way of running Microsoft Windows applications remotely from a server. Microsoft has a shareholding in Citrix.

CIX abbreviation for ⏤ Commercial Internet eXchange; ⏤ Compulink Information eXchange.

ClariNet commercial news service distributed via Usenet. It is not available on all sites since companies must pay to receive ClariNet, which is owned by

ClariNet

http://www.clarinet.com

Public access is available via the World Wide Web.

WEB LINK

Clarinet Communications Corp. Under the service's terms and conditions, professional media personnel are banned from using ClariNet news as a source in their work.

Clark, Jim (James) US founder of ⤳ Silicon Graphics Inc in 1982 and the ⤳ Netscape Communications Corporation in 1994. As an associate professor at Stanford University, California, he and a team of graduate students developed the initial technology upon which Silicon Graphics' first products were built. He resigned as chair of Silicon Graphics in early 1994 to start up Netscape, of which he is chair.

cleartext or *plaintext*, in encryption, the original, unencrypted message.

ClearType font technology developed by ⤳ Microsoft in 1998 for use in ⤳ electronic book readers and ⤳ personal digital assistants, and first used on PocketPC devices in 2000. By addressing an area smaller than a ⤳ pixel, ClearType makes screen type easier to read, especially on the ⤳ liquid-crystal displays found on ⤳ laptop computers.

CLI abbreviation for ⤳ command-line interface.

click to press down and then immediately release a button on a ⤳ mouse. The phrase 'to click on' means to select an ⤳ icon on a computer screen by moving the mouse cursor to the icon's position and clicking a mouse button. See also ⤳ double click.

clickstream unedited log of mouse-clicks that records visitor actions on a site on the World Wide Web. This data is analysed to create feedback for advertisers, enabling them to check whether their strategies are successful in attracting user attention.

client in ⤳ client-server architecture, software that enables a user to access a store of data or programs on a ⤳ server. On the Internet, client software is the software that users need to run on home computers in order to be able to use services such as the World Wide Web.

client–server architecture system in which the mechanics of looking after data are separated from the programs that use the data. For example, the 'server' might be a central database, typically located on a large computer that is reserved for this purpose. The 'client' would be an ordinary program that requests data from the server as needed.

Most Internet services are examples of client–server applications, including the World Wide Web, FTP, Telnet, and Gopher.

clip art small graphics used to liven up documents and presentations. Many software packages such as word processors and presentation graphics packages come with a selection of clip art.

TIP

clip art
Always check the copyright status before distributing widely.

clipboard temporary file or memory area where data can be stored before being copied into an application file. It is used, for example, in cut-and-paste operations.

Clipper chip controversial encryption hardware system that contains built-in facilities to allow authorized third parties access to the encrypted data. Adopted as a US government standard in 1994, the Clipper chip was a chip that used ➷ public-key cryptography and a proprietary ➷ algorithm called Skipjack, and could be built into any communications device, such as a telephone or modem. It was developed by the US National Security Agency as part of its ➷ Capstone project.

Clipper was instantly unpopular on the Net because of privacy concerns: it contained a system for depositing a copy of the user's private key in escrow (see ➷ key escrow), from where it could be obtained by law enforcement officials equipped with an appropriate court order.

Clipper suffered further defeat when Matt Blaze, a researcher at AT&T Bell Labs, cracked the technology in 1995. In 1996, the US government proposed the development of a network of trusted third parties to hold keys in escrow; the initiative was dubbed 'Clipper III'.

clock interrupt ➷ interrupt signal generated by the computer's internal electronic clock.

clock rate frequency of a computer's internal electronic clock. Every computer contains an electronic clock, which produces a sequence of regular electrical pulses used by the control unit to synchronize the components of the computer and regulate the ➷ fetch–execute cycle by which program instructions are processed.

A fixed number of time pulses is required in order to execute each particular instruction. The speed at which a computer can process instructions therefore depends on the clock rate: increasing the clock rate will decrease the time required to complete each particular instruction.

Clock rates are measured in megahertz (MHz), or millions of pulses a second. Microcomputers commonly have a clock rate of 8–50 MHz.

clone copy of hardware or software that may not be identical to the original design but provides the same functions. All personal computers (PCs) are to some extent clones of the original IBM PC and PC AT launched by IBM in 1981 and 1984, respectively – including IBM's current machines. Clones typically compete by being cheaper and are sometimes less well made than the branded product, but this is not always the case. Compaq, for example, competed with IBM by producing the first portable PC and by building better desktop machines, while Dell competed by building PCs to individual orders and supplying customers direct.

Cloning a disk drive or workstation, however, means making an exact copy of all the files or software so that the new drive or machine functions identically to the original one.

cluster several computers joined together by a high-speed network or ⤻ backbone, and presented to users as one unit. Building clusters of computers improves the system's overall tolerance to faults and availability to users. If one computer in the cluster fails, its programs and users are transferred to another computer in the cluster with minimal interruption.

CMOS abbreviation for *complementary metal-oxide semiconductor*, family of integrated circuits (chips) widely used in building electronic systems.

CMYK abbreviation for *cyan–magenta–yellow–black*, four-colour separation used in most (subtractive) colour printing processes. Representation on computer screens normally uses the additive ⤻ RGB method and so conversion is usually necessary on output for printing either on colour printers or as separations.

CNC abbreviation for ⤻ computer numerical control.

COBOL acronym for *common business-oriented language*, high-level computer-programming language, designed in the late 1950s for commercial data-processing problems; it has become the major language in this field. COBOL features powerful facilities for file handling and business arithmetic. Program instructions written in this language make extensive use of words and look very much like English sentences. This makes COBOL one of the easiest languages to learn and understand.

code expression of an ⤻ algorithm in a ⤻ programming language. The term is also used as a verb, to describe the act of programming.

codec contraction of *coder/decoder*, device that codes and decodes an ⤻ analogue stream to or from ⤻ digital data. It is used in applications such as remote broadcast-quality voiceovers recorded in a remote studio and transmitted via codecs and ⤻ Integrated Services Digital Network (ISDN) lines to a central studio for final mixing. Codecs are also used to compress and decompress digital audio and video for multimedia presentations, especially when delivered over the Internet using ⤻ streaming technology.

collapsed backbone method by which network ⤻ backbone cables are replaced with powerful network routers or network switches that effectively collapse the backbone network cable into one 'black box'. All of the devices that used to plug onto the backbone cable then plug into the router or switch. Significant improvements in performance can be achieved using this technique, and it provides a more manageable solution. The disadvantage of using this technique is that it introduces a single point of failure into the network, so if the collapsed backbone device fails, the whole network fails.

collision detection in ⤻ virtual reality, the ability of software to detect when two on-screen objects make contact.

Colossus arguably the world's first stored program computer, built at Bletchley Park, Buckinghamshire, in 1943. Designed to help decode enemy communications during World War II, Colossus was built by Dr Thomas Flowers, a research engineer. The design of Colossus is attributed to Max Newman, a mathematician, but it also drew heavily on Alan ↝ Turing's concept of the universal machine. At the end of the war, Flowers was ordered to destroy all the blueprints for Colossus, and the computer was broken up and stored away. The existence of Colossus was kept an official secret for many years. Because of this secrecy, history has recorded that the first computer was ENIAC, built in the USA at the University of Pennsylvania in 1945. One of the ten Colossus Mk 2s built after D-day has now been rebuilt in its original room at Bletchley Park.

colour depth maximum number of colours that can be displayed simultaneously in an image by a particular computer system.
    The most common modes are 16, 256, 32K, 64K, and 16.7 million (true colour). The greater the colour depth, the larger the size of the picture file but the more detailed and realistic the quality of the picture.

com abbreviation for *commercial*, in the Internet's ↝ domain name system (DNS), one of the top-level domains, along with net, gov, org, edu, and mil. US-based companies typically have Internet addresses of the form name.com; the UK equivalent is name.co.uk.

COM acronym for ↝ Component Object Model; ↝ computer output on microfilm/microfiche.

Comité Consultatif International Téléphonique et Télégraphique *CCITT* international organization that determines international communications standards and protocols for data communications, including ↝ fax. It was subsumed into the International Telecommunications Union (ITU) in 1993.

command language set of commands and the rules governing their use, by which users control a program. For example, an ↝ operating system may have commands such as SAVE and DELETE, or a payroll program may have commands for adding and amending staff records.

command line interface *CLI*, character-based interface in which a prompt is displayed on the screen at which the user types a command, followed by ↝ carriage return, at which point the command, if valid, is executed. Additional options may be used after the command in a line; these are known as command line parameters.
    A typical example of a command line interface is the DOS prompt.

Commercial Internet eXchange *CIX*, US-based international nonprofit-making organization of ↝ Internet Service Providers and other data network suppliers. It is part of the Internet's US ↝ backbone funded by commercial service providers.

CGI for the Total Non-Programmer

http://www.webteacher.
com/cgi/index.html

Guide to programming
Common Gateway
Interfaces (CGIs) with
Perl on a Unix platform.
The guide is intended for
beginners with no
experience of CGI, Perl,
or Unix.

WEB LINK

common gateway interface *CGI*, on the World Wide Web, a facility for adding scripts to handle user input. It allows a Web ⮿ server to communicate with other programs running on the same server in order to process data input by visitors to the Web site. CGI scripts 'parse' the input data, identifying each element and feeding it to the correct program for action, normally a ⮿ search engine or e-mail program. The results are then fed back to the user in the form of search results or sent by e-mail. The CGI also describes how CGI applications should present their output, so that it can be displayed properly by the Web browser.

comms program contraction of ⮿ communications program.

communications see ⮿ data communications.

Communications Decency Act 1996 rider (supplement) to the US Telecommunications Bill seeking to prohibit the transmission of indecent material to minors via the Internet.

Within hours of the bill's passage into law on 8 February 1996, suits were filed by 46 plaintiffs including the American Civil Liberties Union, Voter Telecom Watch, the Electronic Frontier Foundation, and the Center for Democracy and Technology to block the law's enforcement. On 12 June the Philadelphia federal court struck the law down with a judgement that read in part: 'Just as the strength of the Internet is chaos, so the strength of our liberty depends upon the chaos and cacophony of the unfettered speech the First Amendment (to the US Constitution) protects'. A second judgement from a New York court agreed. The government was expected to appeal both rulings to the Supreme Court.

Communications Electronics Security Group *CESG*, part of GCHQ (Government Communications Headquarters), the UK government's security monitoring service. CESG is the UK government's national technical authority for ⮿ cryptography, information security, and ⮿ public key infrastructure.

The group's main customers are Civil Service departments and the armed forces, as well as other public sector organizations and private companies with a role in the UK's critical information technology infrastructure (such as power, water, and telecommunications companies).

communications program or *comms program*, general-purpose program for accessing older ⮿ online systems and ⮿ bulletin board systems which use a ⮿ command-line interface; also known as a terminal emulator.

Most operating systems include a trimmed-down comms program, but full-featured programs include facilities to store phone numbers and settings for frequently called services, address books, and the ability to write scripts to automate logging on. Popular comms programs include ProComm, Smartcom, Qmodem, and Odyssey.

compiler computer program that translates programs written in a ⮿ high-level language into machine code (the form in which they can be run by the

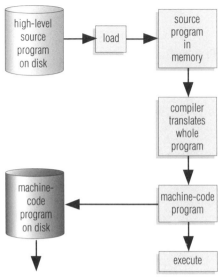

compiler
The process of compilation; a program written in a high-level language is translated into a program that can be run without the original source being present.

computer). The compiler translates each high-level instruction into several machine-code instructions – in a process called compilation – and produces a complete independent program that can be run by the computer as often as required, without the original source program being present. Different compilers are needed for different high-level languages and for different computers. In contrast to using an ➷ interpreter, using a compiler adds slightly to the time needed to develop a new program because the machine-code program must be recompiled after each change or correction. Once compiled, however, the machine-code program will run much faster than an interpreted program.

complementary metal-oxide semiconductor *CMOS*, in electronics, a particular way of manufacturing integrated circuits (chips). The main advantage of CMOS chips is their low power requirement and heat dissipation, which enables them to be used in electronic watches and portable microcomputers. However, CMOS circuits are expensive to manufacture and have lower operating speeds than have circuits of the ➷ transistor–transistor logic (TTL) family.

Component Object Model *COM*, Microsoft's framework for creating object-oriented software, and a rival to the industry standard ➷ Corba. COM is the underlying foundation for Microsoft's ➷ ActiveX.

TIP

COM port

In Windows, the mouse must be on COM1 or COM2.

COM port contraction of *communication port*, on a personal computer (PC), one of the serial ➷ ports through which ➷ data communications take place. PCs may have up to four COM ports. However, these cannot all be used simultaneously as COM1 and COM3 share an ➷ interrupt, as do COM2 and COM4. A modem added to a machine with a mouse on COM1 must be attached to COM2 or COM4.

compound document in Windows, a document containing elements that have been created using other programs. Usually managed through a word processor, such a document might include a table created in a spreadsheet and pictures created in a drawing program. These items may be linked using ➷ object linking and embedding (OLE), so that any changes made to the table in the word processor will also be made to the original table developed in the spreadsheet.

Compressed Serial Line Internet Protocol protocol usually abbreviated to ⮑ CSLIP.

compression see ⮑ data compression.

Compulink Information eXchange *CIX*, London-based electronic conferencing system founded in 1987. CIX is the oldest and largest native British conferencing system. In 1996 it had approximately 16,000 users, including most of the country's technology journalists.

CompuServe large (US-based) public online information service. It is widely used for ⮑ electronic mail and ⮑ bulletin boards, as well as ⮑ gateway access to large periodical databases.

CompuServe was established in 1979. It is easier to use than the Internet and most computer hardware and software suppliers provide support for their products on CompuServe. Worldwide subscribers to CompuServe have risen from half a million in 1988 to about 5.2 million in 1997. CompuServe started moving some of its services to the ⮑ World Wide Web in 1996 and was taken over by rival ⮑ America Online in 1997.

There were 400,000 members in the UK in 1997.

computer programmable electronic device that processes data and performs calculations and other symbol-manipulation tasks. There are three types: the ⮑ digital computer, which manipulates information coded as binary numbers (see ⮑ binary number system); the ⮑ analogue computer, which works with continuously varying quantities; and the hybrid computer, which has characteristics of both analogue and digital computers.

There are four types of digital computer, corresponding roughly to their size and intended use. Microcomputers are the smallest and most common, used in small businesses, at home, and in schools. They are usually single-user machines. Minicomputers (or mid-range computers) are found in medium-sized businesses and university departments. They may support from around 10 to 200 users at once. Mainframes (or enterprise servers), which can often service several hundred users simultaneously, are found in large organizations, such as national companies and government departments. Supercomputers are mostly used for highly complex scientific tasks, such as analysing the results of nuclear physics experiments and weather forecasting.

Microcomputers now come in a range of sizes, from battery-powered pocket personal computers (PCs) and electronic organizers, notebook and laptop PCs, to floor-standing tower systems that may serve local area ⮑ networks or work as minicomputers. Most minicomputers are now built using low-cost micro-processors, and large-scale computers built out of multiple microprocessors are starting to challenge traditional mainframe and supercomputer designs.

A based on the binary number system is used to represent instructions and data in all modern digital computers – for example, in the ⮑ ASCII code system used by most microcomputers, the capital letter A is represented by the binary number 01000001.

Computer Museum

http://www. computerhistory.org/

Well-designed interactive museum, examining the history, development, and future of computer technology.

WEB LINK

FOLDOC: Free Online Dictionary of Computing

http://www.foldoc.org/

Authoritative source of definitions of acronyms and jargon in computing and Internet use. Not only useful for computing terms, this one-stop source provides links to other resources on the Web and also covers related areas, such as communications.

WEB LINK

Main Events in Computing History

http://www.bozdoc.f2s. com/history.htm

From 1937 to the present day, these chronologies of computing and computer-aided design cover all the major developments. Learn about the inventions and products that have driven the computer and Internet revolution.

WEB LINK

Because binary numbers use only the digits 0 and 1, they can be represented by any device that can exist in two different states. In a digital computer several different two-state devices are used to store or transmit binary number codes – for example, circuits, which may or may not carry a voltage; disks or tapes, parts of which may or may not be magnetized; and switches, which may be open or closed. Digital computers are designed in this way for two reasons. Firstly, it is much easier and cheaper to construct two-state devices than devices that can exist in more than two states. Secondly, communication between two-state devices is very reliable because only two different signals, 0 or 1 (on or off), need to be recognized.

At the heart of a computer is the central processing unit (CPU), which executes individual program instructions and controls the operation of other parts. The CPU has three main components: the arithmetic and logic unit (ALU), where all calculations and logical operations are carried out; a control unit, which decodes, synchronizes, and executes program instructions; and the immediate access memory, which stores the data and programs on which the computer is currently working. All these components contain ↝ registers, which are memory locations reserved for specific purposes. A main power supply is needed and, for a mainframe or minicomputer, a cooling system. The computer's 'device driver' circuits control the peripheral devices that can be attached. These will normally be keyboards and ↝ VDUs (visual display units) for user input and output, disk drive units for mass memory storage, and printers.

Computers are only one of the many kinds of ↝ computing device. The first mechanical computer was conceived by Charles ↝ Babbage in 1835. He

computer
A mainframe computer. Functionally, it has the same component parts as a microcomputer, but on a much larger scale. The central processing unit is at the hub, and controls all the attached devices.

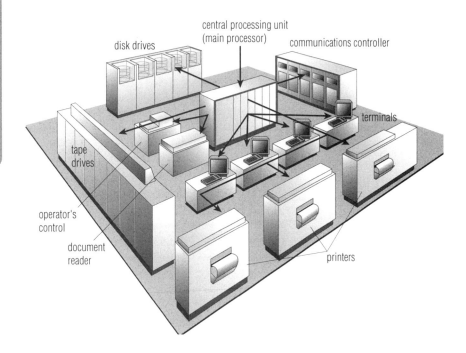

designed an ⤳ analytical engine, a general-purpose mechanical computing device for performing different calculations according to a program input on punched cards (an idea borrowed from the ⤳ Jacquard loom). This device was never built, but it embodied many of the principles on which digital computers are based.

The US inventor Herman ⤳ Hollerith devised the first device for high-volume data processing, a mechanical tabulating machine. Hollerith's tabulator was widely publicized after being successfully used in the 1890 census. The firm he established, the Tabulating Machine Company, was later one of the founding companies of ⤳ IBM.

In 1943, more than a century after Babbage's analytical engine, Thomas Flowers (1905–98) built Colossus, the first electronic computer. Working with him at the time was Alan ⤳ Turing, a mathematician who seven years earlier had published a paper on the theory of computing machines that had a major impact on subsequent developments. John ⤳ Von Neumann's computer, EDVAC, built in 1949, was the first to use binary arithmetic and to store its operating instructions internally. This design still forms the basis of today's computers.

computer-aided design use of computers to create and modify design drawings; see ⤳ CAD.

computer-aided manufacturing use of computers to regulate production processes in industry; see ⤳ CAM.

computer art art produced with the help of a computer. Since the 1950s the aesthetic use of computers has been increasingly evident in most artistic disciplines, including film animation, architecture, and music.

⤳ Computer graphics has been the most developed area, with the 'paint-box' computer liberating artists from the confines of the canvas. It is now also possible to program computers in advance to generate graphics, music, and sculpture, according to 'instructions' which may include a preprogrammed element of unpredictability. In this last function, computer technology has been seen as a way of challenging the elitist nature of art by putting artistic creativity within relatively easy reach of anyone owning a computer.

computer-assisted learning use of computers in education and training; see ⤳ CAL.

computer-assisted reporting use of computers to do journalistic research. At its simplest, computer-assisted reporting involves searching an online database for basic information such as addresses and phone numbers. At their most sophisticated, computer systems allow journalists to sift through large quantities of data to find patterns of behaviour or connections that would not be visible by other means.

computer crime broad term applying to any type of crime committed via a computer, including unauthorized access to files. Most computer crime is committed by disgruntled former employees or subcontractors. Examples include the releasing of ☞ viruses, ☞ hacking, and computer fraud. Many countries, including the USA and the UK, have specialized law enforcement units to supply the technical knowledge needed to investigate computer crime.

Computer Emergency Response Team *CERT*, team of engineers based at Carnegie Mellon University in Pittsburgh, Pennsylvania, USA, that issues security advice and helps resolve emergencies on the Internet by providing technical expertise.

In 1996 the US government announced the formation of a national emergency response team.

computer engineer job classification for ☞ computer personnel. A computer engineer repairs and maintains computer hardware.

computer game or *video game*, any computer-controlled game in which the computer (sometimes) opposes the human player. Computer games typically employ fast, animated graphics on a ☞ VDU (visual display unit) and synthesized sound.

Commercial computer games became possible with the advent of the ☞ microprocessor in the mid-1970s and rapidly became popular as amusement-arcade games, using dedicated chips. Available games range from chess to fighter-plane simulations.

Some of the most popular computer games in the early 1990s were id Software's *Wolfenstein 3D*, *Doom*, and *Quake*, which were designed to be played across networks including the Internet. A whole subculture built up around those particular games, as users took advantage of id's help to create their own additions to the games.

The computer games industry has been criticized for releasing many violent games with little intellectual content.

computer generation any of the five broad groups into which computers may be classified: first generation – the earliest computers, developed in the 1940s and 1950s, made from valves and wire circuits; second generation from the early 1960s, based on transistors and printed circuits; third generation from the late 1960s, using integrated circuits and often sold as families of computers, such as the IBM 360 series; fourth generation using ☞ microprocessors, large-scale integration (LSI), and sophisticated programming languages, still in use in the 1990s; and fifth generation based on parallel processing and very large-scale integration, currently under development.

computer graphics use of computers to display and manipulate information in pictorial form. Input may be achieved by scanning an image, by drawing with a mouse or stylus on a graphics tablet, or by drawing directly on the screen with a light pen.

The output may be as simple as a pie chart, or as complex as an animated sequence in a science fiction film, or a seemingly three-dimensional engineering

Exploratories Project

http://www.cs.brown.edu/exploratory/

Brown University project that introduces visitors to research into Web-based education. The Exploratories use two- and three-dimensional explorable worlds to offer learning experiences not attainable with conventional educational methods. Aimed at teachers and researchers, the site offers guided tours of subjects such as computer graphics, and links to sites of educational interest.

WEB LINK

blueprint. The drawing is stored in the computer as raster graphics or vector graphics.

Vector graphics are stored in the computer memory by using geometric formulas. They can be transformed (enlarged, rotated, stretched, and so on) without loss of picture resolution. It is also possible to select and transform any of the components of a vector-graphics display because each is separately defined in the computer memory. In these respects vector graphics are superior to raster graphics. They are typically used for drawing applications, allowing the user to create and modify technical diagrams such as designs for houses or cars.

Raster graphics are stored in the computer memory by using a map to record data (such as colour and intensity) for every ↩ pixel that makes up the image. When transformed (enlarged, rotated, stretched, and so on), raster graphics become ragged and suffer loss of picture resolution, unlike vector graphics. They are typically used for painting applications, which allow the user to create artwork on a computer screen much as if they were painting on paper or canvas.

Software	Manufacturer	Description
Adobe Illustrator	Adobe	industry-standard illustration software
Adobe Photoshop	Adobe	professional standard photo design and production tool
AutoCAD	AutoDesk	industry-standard CAD software; powerful 2D drawing and editing tool
ClarisDraw	Claris	integrates painting and image-editing effects, advanced text handling, presentation features, and drawing tools
CorelDRAW	Corel	graphics suite that includes applications for page layout and illustration, photo editing and bitmap creation, and 3D modelling and rendering
DesignCAD	ViaGrafix	powerful CAD system that includes solid modelling, true 3D texture mapping, animation, and anti-aliasing
FreeHand	Macromedia	established design tool; create and publish professional layouts, designs, and illustrations for print and the Web
Painter	MetaCreations	comprehensive set of image-editing features allowing you to paint like the great masters, collage photographs, or design with mosaic tiles
Paint Shop Pro	JASC	popular, easy-to-use image-editing and drawing program; versions available as shareware
Visual Reality	Visual Software	create 3D graphics, 3D animations, and complete 3D VRML worlds

computer graphics
The main features of some major graphics and design programs

3-D design created with CAD software

3-D model   shape menu

graphics and text combined

in illustration program

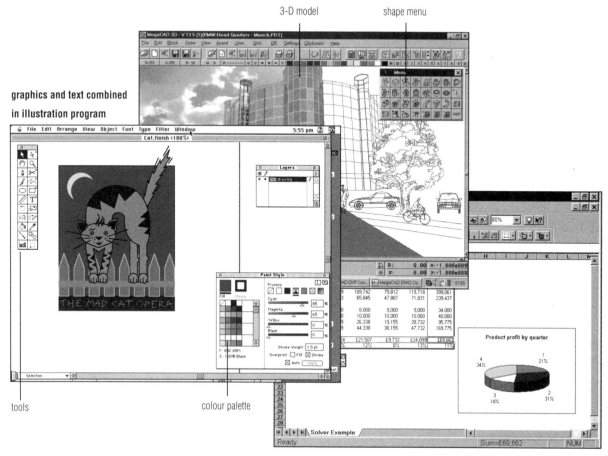

tools   colour palette

simple pie chart generarated by spreadsheet program

computer graphics
Some examples of the
kinds of graphic design that
can be achieved using
computers. Text and
graphics may be combined
within an illustration
package, and sophisticated
three-dimensional drawings
can be created using a
computer-aided design
(CAD) system.

Computer graphics are increasingly used in computer-aided design (↝ CAD), and to generate models and simulations in engineering, meteorology, medicine and surgery, and other fields of science.

Recent developments in software mean that designers on opposite sides of the world will soon be able to work on complex three-dimensional computer models using ordinary personal computers (PCs) linked by telephone lines rather then powerful graphics workstations.

computer language see ↝ programming language.

computer-mediated communication umbrella term for all types of communication via computers, such as ↝ electronic conferencing and chat.

Computer Misuse Act British law passed in 1990 which makes it illegal to hack into computers (see ↝ hacking). The first prosecution under the Act was that of British hacker Paul Bedworth, who in 1993 was acquitted on the grounds that he was addicted to computing.

The law was inspired by the Law Lords' acquittal on appeal of Robert Schifreen and Steve Gold, two journalists who had hacked into Prince Philip's mailbox in 1984 on the British Telecom service Prestel. The Lords ruled that the Forgery Act did not cover deceiving a computer.

computer numerical control control of machine tools, most often milling machines, by a computer. The pattern of work for the machine to follow, which often involves performing repeated sequences of actions, is described using a special-purpose programming language.

computer operator job classification for ↝ computer personnel. Computer operators work directly with the computer, running the programs, changing disks and tapes, loading paper into printers, and ensuring all ↝ data security procedures are followed.

computer output on microfilm/microfiche *COM*, technique for producing computer output in very compact, photographically reduced, form (↝ microform).

computer personnel people who work with or are associated with computers. In a large computer department the staff may work under the direction of an information technology (IT) manager, who supervises and coordinates the work performed. Computer personnel can be broadly divided into two categories: those who run and maintain existing ↝ applications programs (programs that perform a task for the benefit of the user) and those who develop new applications.

Personnel who run existing applications programs: systems programmers look after the systems software: operating systems, database management systems, physical and logical computer security, and so on; computer operators work directly with computers, running the programs, changing disks and tapes, loading paper into printers, and ensuring that all ↝ data security procedures are followed; computer engineers repair and maintain computer hardware; file librarians, or media librarians, store and issue the data files used by the department; an operations manager coordinates all the day-to-day activities of these staff. Personnel who develop new applications: systems analysts carry out the analysis of an existing system (see ↝ systems analysis), whether already computerized or not, and prepare proposals for a new system; programmers write the software needed for new systems. Web sites are created by Web developers. The entire development effort is controlled by a systems development manager.

Computer Professionals for Social Responsibility *CPSR*, US organization advocating the responsible use of computers. Based in Washington, DC, it was one of the first organizations to oppose President Reagan's Strategic Defense

Initiative on the grounds that the many billions of lines of code it would take to program it could never be debugged successfully.

computer program coded instructions for a computer; see ➷ program.

computer simulation representation of a real-life situation in a computer program. For example, the program might simulate the flow of customers arriving at a bank. The user can alter variables, such as the number of cashiers on duty, and see the effect.

More complex simulations can model the behaviour of chemical reactions or even nuclear explosions. The behaviour of solids and liquids at high temperatures can be simulated using quantum simulation. Computers also control the actions of machines – for example, a ➷ flight simulator models the behaviour of real aircraft and allows training to take place in safety. Computer simulations are very useful when it is too dangerous, time consuming, or simply impossible to carry out a real experiment or test.

computer-supported collaborative work *CSCW*, work undertaken by individuals who, using computers, are able to function together as a group on a project despite being geographically separated. The technology to facilitate CSCW is still under development. Early initiatives include video and data conferencing so that two users can talk on the telephone while simultaneously viewing a document in progress. Changes made by either participant affect both participants' displays.

computer terminal device whereby the operator communicates with the computer; see ➷ terminal.

Computer Underground Digest widely distributed ➷ e-zine covering such issues as ➷ hacking, freedom of speech, and security risks.

computing device any device built to perform or help perform computations, such as the abacus, slide rule, or ➷ computer.

The earliest known example is the abacus. Mechanical devices with sliding scales (similar to the slide rule) date from ancient Greece. In 1642, French mathematician Blaise Pascal built a mechanical adding machine and in 1672–74 German mathematician Gottfried Leibniz produced a machine to carry out multiplication. The first mechanical computer, the ➷ analytical engine, was designed by British mathematician Charles Babbage in 1835. For the subsequent history of computing, see ➷ computer.

config.sys ➷ configuration file used by the MS-DOS and OS/2 ➷ operating systems. It is read when the system is ➷ booted. It is used to load device drivers and set certain parameters used by the operating system.

configuration way in which a system, whether it be ➷ hardware and/or ➷ software, is set up. A minimum configuration is often referred to for a particular application, and this will usually include a specification of processor, disk and memory size, and peripherals required.

console combination of keyboard and screen (also described as a terminal). For a multiuser system, such as ↝ Unix, there is only one system console from which the system can be administered, while there may be many user terminals. See also ↝ games console.

content provider organization or individual who creates intellectual property, such as information databases, which may be distributed via traditional media or via the World Wide Web.

context-sensitive help type of help built into software that displays information related to the particular function in use.

contouring in ↝ computer graphics, a technique for enhancing the outline of a particular shape. This technique is used in applications such as mapping (see ↝ animation, computer), where a computer following the contours of an object ↝ pixel by pixel can be much more precise than a human.

control bus electrical pathway, or ↝ bus, used to communicate control signals.

control character any character produced by depressing the control key (Ctrl) on a keyboard at the same time as another (usually alphabetical) key. The control characters form the first 32 ↝ ASCII characters and most have specific meanings according to the operating system used. They are also used in combination to provide formatting control in many word processors, although the user may not enter them explicitly.

control total ↝ validation check in which an arithmetic total of a specific field from a group of records is calculated. This total is input together with the data to which it refers. The program recalculates the control total and compares it with the one entered to ensure that no entry errors have been made.

control unit component of the ↝ central processing unit that decodes, synchronizes, and executes program instructions.

cookie on the World Wide Web, a short piece of text that a Web site stores in a Cookies folder or a cookie.txt file on the user's computer, either for tracking or configuration purposes, for example, to improve the targeting of banner advertisements. Cookies can also store user preferences and passwords. Special instructions are issued to the browser by the server when data held in a cookie is required.

Cookies are derived from 'magic cookies', the identification tokens used by some Unix systems.

Originally, a cookie was an aphorism or short, witty saying obtained by typing 'cookie' at a computer's main system prompt. A cookie was then chosen at random – like a 'fortune cookie' – from a database called a 'cookie file'.

coprocessor additional ↝ processor that works with the main ↝ central processing unit to carry out a specific function. The two most common coprocessors are the mathematical coprocessor, used to speed up calculations, and the graphic coprocessor, used to improve the handling of graphics.

copy protection techniques used to prevent illegal copying of computer programs. Copy protection is not as common as it used to be because it also prevents legal copying (for backup purposes). Alternative techniques to prevent illegal use include dongles, passwords and the need to uninstall a program before it can be installed on another machine.

Corba acronym for *common object request broker architecture*, agreed specification that enables software components or 'objects' from different suppliers running on different computers using different operating systems to interoperate with one another. Corba has been extended via the Internet Inter-Orb Protocol (IIOP) to work over the Internet. Corba is promulgated as a standard by the Object Management Group (OMG).

Corel Canadian software company founded in 1985 by British citizen Michael Cowpland. Its drawing program CorelDRAW led the market from its first release in 1989, and has now sold over 10 million copies. Corel bought the desktop publishing package Ventura Publisher in 1995 and then the word processor WordPerfect in 1996.

corruption of data introduction or presence of errors in data. Most computers use a range of ↝ verification and ↝ validation routines to prevent corrupt data from entering the computer system or detect corrupt data that are already present.

CoSy contraction of *conferencing system*, ↝ command-line interface electronic conferencing software developed at the University of Guelph in the Canadian province of Ontario. It is used on London's ↝ Compulink Information eXchange (CIX) service and for the Open University's conferencing, as well as many others worldwide.

CP/M abbreviation for *control program/monitor* or *control program for microcomputers*, one of the earliest ↝ operating systems for microcomputers. It was written by Gary Kildall, who founded Digital Research. In the 1970s it became a standard for microcomputers based on the Intel 8080 and Zilog Z80 8-bit microprocessors. In the 1980s it was superseded by Microsoft's ↝ MS-DOS, written for Intel's 16-bit 8086/88 microprocessors.

CPSR abbreviation for ↝ Computer Professionals for Social Responsibility.

CPU abbreviation for ↝ central processing unit.

cracker hacker (see ↝ hacking); the term distinguishes criminal hacking ('cracking') from those who explore to satisfy their intellectual curiosity. The term is used much less than most hackers would like.

crawler on the World Wide Web, automated indexing software that scours the Web for new or updated sites. See also ⤳ 'bot, ⤳ spider, and ⤳ agent.

Cray, Seymour Roger (1925–1996) US computer scientist and pioneer in the field of supercomputing. He designed one of the earliest computers to contain transistors in 1960. In 1972 he formed Cray Research to build the first popular ⤳ supercomputer, the Cray-1, released in 1976. Its success led to the production of further supercomputers, including the Cray-2 1985, the Cray Y-MP, a multiprocessor design in 1988, and the Cray-3 in 1989.

Creative Labs name of the US and British subsidiaries of the parent computing company Creative Technology, which was founded in Singapore in 1981. Creative Labs manufactures the leading ⤳ sound card, the SoundBlaster, which it markets alongside the Internet telephony, video, and multimedia products that make up the company's product range.

By 1997 the company claimed 50 million users of its products and had 5,000 staff worldwide, 400 of them in research and development.

critical path analysis procedure used in the management of complex projects to minimize the amount of time taken. The analysis shows which subprojects can run in parallel with each other, and which have to be completed before other subprojects can follow on.

By identifying the time required for each separate subproject and the relationship between the subprojects, it is possible to produce a planning schedule showing when each subproject should be started and finished in order to complete the whole project most efficiently. Complex projects may involve hundreds of subprojects, and computer ⤳ applications packages for critical path analysis are widely used to help reduce the time and effort involved in their analysis.

crop to cut away unwanted portions of a picture. The term comes from traditional manual methods of layout and paste-up; in computing, cropping is an option made available via photo-finishing and graphics software.

cross-posting on Usenet, the practice of sending a message to more than one ⤳ newsgroup. A small amount of cross-posting is acceptable if the message is on a topic that is relevant to more than one newsgroup. For example, a message about top tennis player André Agassi's personal life might be posted to both rec.sport.tennis and alt.showbiz.gossip.

cryptography science of creating and reading codes, for example, those produced by the German Enigma machine used in World War II, those used in the secure transmission of credit card details over the Internet, and those used to ensure the privacy of e-mail messages. Unencoded text (known as plaintext) is converted to an unreadable form (known as cyphertext) by the process of encryption. The recipient must then decrypt the message before it can be read. The breaking of such codes is known as cryptanalysis. No encryption method is completely unbreakable, but cryptanalysis of a strongly encrypted message can be so time-consuming and complex as to be almost impossible.

The growth of the Internet and online commerce has brought an increasing demand for good cryptography. Most Internet cryptography systems involve the use of digital 'keys' to encrypt and decrypt messages. In ⇌ symmetric-key cryptography, both sender and recipient use the same key. An example of this is the ⇌ Data Encryption Standard (DES), used by the US government. In ⇌ public-key cryptography, each party has both a freely-available public key (used by anyone to encrypt messages) and a private key (used to decrypt received messages). The program ⇌ Pretty Good Privacy (PGP) is a popular and effective (and free for non-commercial use) implementation of public-key cryptography. Encrypted messages may be further protected by concealing them within large graphics, audio, or video files – a technique known as ⇌ steganography.

Many governments consider strong cryptography a threat to national security, as it makes 'wiretapping' (monitoring private messages) practically impossible. In the USA, strong encryption software is classified as a weapon under the ⇌ International Traffic in Arms Regulations and its export is illegal. In addition, the ⇌ Clipper chip system, introduced in 1994, and used to provide encryption in devices such as mobile phones, requires that the keys required to decrypt messages are made available to law enforcement officials.

In 2000, the UK government passed a ⇌ Regulation of Investigatory Powers Act, under which holders of data encryption keys could be forced to hand these over to the police or security services.

CSCW abbreviation for ⇌ computer-supported collaborative work.

CSLIP abbreviation for *Compressed Serial Line Internet Protocol*, newer version of ⇌ SLIP allowing slightly faster dial-up connections to the Internet.

CSS abbreviation for ⇌ Cascading Style Sheets.

CTS/RTS abbreviation for *Clear To Send/Ready To Send*, hardware handshaking (see ⇌ handshake) used in high-speed modems. In most communications software this is an option that can be ⇌ toggled on or off. The alternative, software handshaking, is considered less reliable at high speeds.

CUA abbreviation for *common user access*, standard designed by ⇌ Microsoft to ensure that identical actions, such as saving a file or accessing help, can be carried out using the same keystrokes in any piece of software. For example, in programs written to the CUA standard, help is always summoned by pressing the F1 function key. New programs should be easier to use because users will not have to learn new commands to perform standard tasks.

current directory in a computer's file system, the ⇌ directory in which the user is positioned. As users move around a computer system, opening, reading, writing, and storing files, they navigate through that computer's directory structure. Most file commands are assumed to apply to the files in the current directory.

In DOS, adding the command 'prompt pg' to the ↝ autoexec.bat file sets the computer to display the name and path of the current directory at the system prompt. On an FTP (file transfer protocol) site, the command 'pwd' will print the name of the current directory on the remote machine.

cursor on a computer screen, the symbol that indicates the current entry position (where the next character will appear). It usually consists of a solid rectangle or underline character, flashing on and off.

CU-SeeMe software that enables ↝ videoconferencing across the Internet. Developed by US computer scientist Richard Cogger, CU-SeeMe was bought in 1996 by US videoconferencing specialist White Pine Software of Nashua, New Hampshire, and is now a commercial product.

Early experiments with CU-SeeMe included broadcasts by the National Aeronautics and Space Administration (NASA) of live and prerecorded video footage of shuttle missions, New Year parties held at cybercafés around the world, and live hook-ups between schools.

customer relationship management *CRM*, computer systems covering the consolidation of sales force, call centre, field service, help desk, and marketing automation ↝ applications. CRM systems allow companies to measure the value of their customers.

In 2000, the principal suppliers of CRM systems were Siebel, Trilogy, Clarify, and Oracle. Software companies supplying ↝ enterprise resource planning (ERP) systems have either written their own CRM modules (as SAP and Oracle have done), or acquired CRM software suppliers (as PeopleSoft and Baan have done).

CWIS abbreviation for ↝ campus-wide information service.

cybercafé coffeehouse equipped with public-access Internet terminals. Typically, users pay a small sum to use the terminals for short periods. Cafés usually supply brief tutorials for newcomers.

There were more than 1,200 cybercafés in 78 countries by the end of 1997. In developing countries they are often the only way that ordinary people can get access to the Internet.

Britain's first cybercafé was Cyberia, set up in Whitfield Street, London in 1994.

CyberCash one of several schemes for electronic money that can be used to trade on the Internet. Founded in 1994, CyberCash uses the RSA encryption ↝ algorithm to protect customer financial information in transit.

The system stores customers' payment information, such as credit card numbers, in an electronic wallet, software which is downloaded from the company's site on the World Wide Web. When a customer wishes to buy something at a commercial Web site, the site generates a payment request, the customer adds a payment method, and the CyberCash server authenticates the transaction. By 2000, over 20,000 electronic commerce sites were using

CyberCash

http://www.cybercash.com.

The CyberCash World Wide Web site.

WEB LINK

CyberCash services. Future plans are to add electronic cheques and cash or debit cards to the choice of payment instruments.

cyberlaw relatively new field of Internet and computer law. Still being defined, the field includes new areas such as the responsibility of ⮑ Internet Service Providers and ⮑ bulletin-board system operators for the material that passes through or is stored on their systems and the framework for international electronic commerce, and a new look at traditional areas such as intellectual property rights and copyright and censorship.

cybernetics study of how communication and control mechanisms in machines can be made to imitate those of human beings.

cyberpunk term coined by US science fiction writer and editor Gardner Dozois for a particular type of modern science fiction that combines high-technology landscapes with countercultural social and political ideas. Leading writers in this genre include William Gibson, Bruce Sterling, Pat Cadigan, Greg Bear, and Rudy Rucker.

cybersex online sexual fantasy spun by two or more participants via live, online chat. Futurists hypothesize about a future where 'virtual' sex will take place in ⮑ virtual reality via body suits and other hardware input devices. In 1996, however, cybersex is limited to text-based systems such as IRC (⮑ Internet Relay Chat) or the shared worlds created in ⮑ MUDs (Multiuser dungeons) and ⮑ MOOs (MUD, object-oriented), both shared role-playing game worlds.

cyberspace imaginary, interactive 'worlds' created by networked computers; often used interchangeably with 'virtual world'. The invention of the word 'cyberspace' is generally credited to US science fiction writer William Gibson (1948–   ) in his novel *Neuromancer* (1984).

As well as meaning the interactive environment encountered in a virtual reality system, cyberspace is 'where' the global community of computer-linked individuals and groups lives. From the mid-1980s, the development of computer networks and telecommunications, both international (such as the ⮑ Internet) and local (such as the services known as 'bulletin board' or conferencing systems), made possible the instant exchange of messages using ⮑ electronic mail and electronic conferencing systems directly from the individual's own home.

cylinder combination of the tracks on all the platters making up a hard drive or fixed disk that can be accessed without moving the read/write heads.

cypherpunk contraction of '*cipher*' and '*cyberpunk*', passionate believer in the importance of free access to strong encryption on the Net, in the interests of guarding privacy and free speech.

24 Hours in Cyberspace

http://www.cyber24.com/htm3/toc.htm?about

Inspiring 'cyberstories' and hundreds of accompanying photos collected by photojournalists from around the world.

WEB LINK

DAC abbreviation for ⇀ digital-to-analogue converter.

DARPANET early US computer network. See ⇀ ARPANET.

data singular *datum*, facts, figures, and symbols, especially as stored in computers. The term is often used to mean raw, unprocessed facts, as distinct from information, to which a meaning or interpretation has been applied.

Continuous data are data that can take any of an infinite number of values between whole numbers and so may not be measured completely accurately. This type of data contrasts with discrete data, in which the variable can only take one of a finite set of values. For example, the sizes of apples on a tree form continuous data, whereas the numbers of apples form discrete data.

database structured collection of data, which may be manipulated to select and sort desired items of information. For example, an accounting system might be built around a database containing details of customers and suppliers. In larger computers, the database makes data available to the various programs that need it, without the need for those programs to be aware of how the data are stored. The term is also sometimes used for simple record-keeping systems, such as mailing lists, in which there are facilities for searching, sorting, and producing records.

There are four main types (or 'models') of database: relational, object oriented, hierarchical, and network, of which relational is the most widely used. Object oriented databases have become more popular for certain types of application, and hybrids like object-relational are also available. In a relational database data are viewed as a collection of linked tables. A free-text database is one that holds the unstructured text of articles or books in a form that permits rapid searching. A telephone directory stored as a database might allow all the people whose names start with the letter B to be selected by one program, and all those living in Chicago by another.

A collection of databases is known as a databank. A database-management system (DBMS) is software that ensures that the integrity of the data is maintained by controlling the degree of access of the ⇀ applications programs using the data.

Databases are usually created using a database tool that enables a user to define the database structure by selecting the number of fields, naming those fields, and allocating the type and amount of data that are valid for each field. To sort records within a database, one or more sort fields may be selected, so that when the data are sorted, it is ordered according to the contents of these fields. A key field is used to give a unique identifier to a particular record. Data programs also determine how data can be viewed on screen or extracted into files.

data bus electrical pathway, or ⇀ bus, used to carry data between the components of the computer.

data capture collecting information for computer processing and analysis. Examples of automated data capture include using a ⇀ sensor that continuously

Software	Manufacturer	Description
Access	Microsoft	desktop relational database which features wizards and macros; included in Microsoft Office Professional for Windows
Approach	Lotus	desktop relational database, easy to learn and includes programming capabilities
Filemaker Pro	FileMaker	versatile and easy-to-use desktop relational database software for Windows or Mac
FoxPro	Microsoft	high-level professional relational database management system for Windows, DOS, or Unix
Oracle	Oracle Software	powerful, scalable relational database management system that includes point-and-click GUI tools that speed and simplify database management
SQL Server	Microsoft	powerful, scalable relational database management system designed specifically for distributed client/server computing

database
The features of some major database programs

monitors physical conditions such as temperature, or scanning bar codes to produce detailed receipts at a shop check-out (↝ point-of-sale terminal). Manual data capture methods include reading electricity meters, or filling in a form or questionnaire.

Forms and questionnaires designed for data capture should be laid out in a clear and attractive manner, and should be straightforward to follow and complete. Particularly with questionnaires, using check boxes (for yes/no answers or multiple-choice questions) enables the data to be clearly categorized for processing.

datacentre computer centre used for the storage of data. Purpose-built datacentres have been opened in the last few years by a number of major ↝ Web hosting services. These typically have a temperature-controlled environment, with fire-suppression systems, an ↝ uninterruptible power supply, and a back-up diesel generator.

data communications sending and receiving data via any communications medium, such as a telephone line. The term usually implies that the data are digital (such as computer data) rather than analogue (such as voice messages). However, in the ISDN (↝ Integrated Services Digital Network) system, all data – including voices and video images – are transmitted digitally.

data compression techniques for reducing the amount of storage needed for a given amount of data. They include word tokenization (in which frequently used words are stored as shorter codes), variable bit lengths (in which common characters are represented by fewer ↝ bits than less common ones), and run-length encoding (in which a repeated value is stored once along with a count).

database table
containing customer details

data format
options

database containing customer details

database
An example of the type of information that may be stored on a database. The information may be stored in various formats, enabling it to be sorted and output to other software programs.

In lossless compression the original file is retrieved unchanged after decompression. Some types of data (sound and pictures) can be stored by lossy compression where some detail is lost during compression, but the loss is not noticeable. Lossy compression allows a greater level of compression. The most popular compression program is ➥ PKZIP, widely available as ➥ shareware.

Compression is necessary for the many applications imagined for the future of the Internet, such as ➥ video on demand. Compressed files take up less storage space and can be transmitted across the Internet much faster. Most modems include facilities for compressing data while in transmission. New standards of compression have been developed for audio and video, such as DVI (➥ digital video interactive) and MPEG.

data dictionary file that holds data about data – for example, lists of files, number of records in each file, and types of fields. Data dictionaries are used by database software to enable access to the data; they are not normally accessible to the user.

Data Encryption Standard *DES*, widely used US government standard for encryption, adopted in 1977 and recertified for five more years in 1993. DES was developed by IBM and adopted as a government standard by the National Security Agency. It is a private-key system, so that the sender and recipient encrypt and decrypt the message using the same key.

This means that a secure way has to be found to send the key from one party to the other; any third party who has the key can decrypt the encoded transmissions. Concerns over the long-term security of DES in the face of increasingly available cheap hardware have been somewhat mitigated by new techniques such as triply encrypted DES.

data flow chart diagram illustrating the possible routes that data can take through a system or program; see ⮑ flow chart.

DataGlove in ⮑ virtual reality, a glove wired to the computer that allows it to take input from a user's hand gestures. Sensors in the glove detect the wearer's hand movements, and transmit these to the computer in a digital format which the computer can interpret.

DataGlove is a trademark of VPL Research; the general term for such devices is ⮑ wired glove.

data logging process, usually automatic, of capturing and recording a sequence of values for later processing and analysis by computer. For example, the level in a water-storage tank might be automatically logged every hour over a seven-day period, so that a computer could produce an analysis of water use. The monitoring is carried out through ⮑ sensors or similar instruments, connected to the computer via an ⮑ interface.

The computer logging the data samples the readings at regular time intervals. Data is analysed either continuously (displayed on a changing screen display or as a graph on a ⮑ plotter) or at the end of the logging period.

data mining analysis of computer data to determine trends. It is used by retailers to find out those items often purchased together. For example, one supermarket chain found that purchases of nappies and beer were linked, and so increased sales by putting beer next to nappies. Store 'loyalty cards' enable retailers to profile customers' week-by-week shopping against their age, sex, and address.

data preparation preparing data for computer input by transferring it to a machine-readable medium. This usually involves typing the data at a keyboard (or at a ⮑ key-to-disk or key-to-tape station) so that it can be transferred directly to tapes or disks. Various methods of direct data capture, such as ⮑ bar codes, ⮑ optical mark recognition (OMR), and ⮑ optical character recognition (OCR), have been developed to reduce or eliminate lengthy data preparation before computer input.

data processing *DP*, or *electronic data processing*, *EDP*, use of computers for performing clerical tasks such as stock control, payroll, and dealing with orders. DP systems are typically ⮑ batch systems, running on mainframe computers.

For data to be processed the following cycle of operations must be undergone: data are collected, then input into a computer where they are processed to produce the output. As the output may also be the input of a subsequent process the process is deemed cyclical. Whilst being processed, data may undergo other operations such as storage and ⮑ validation.

A large organization usually has a special department to support its DP activities, which might include the writing and maintenance of software (programs), control and operation of the computers, and an analysis of the organization's information requirements. See also ↝ computer personnel.

The term 'data processing' has now been superseded by 'information technology'.

data protection safeguarding of information about individuals stored on computers, to protect privacy.

The Council of Europe adopted, in 1981, a Data Protection Convention, which led in the UK to the Data Protection Act 1984. This requires computer databases containing personal information to be registered, and users to process only accurate information and to retain the information only for a necessary period and for specified purposes. Subject to certain exemptions, individuals have a right of access to their personal data and to have any errors corrected.

The Data Protection Act 1998 replaced the 1984 act, giving effect in UK law to European Commission Directive 95/46/EC. The new act, which came into force on 1 March 2000, extends data protection law beyond electronic records to cover paper-based records too. It brings tighter controls over data security and the use of data, and gives individuals the right to know for what their data is being used and to whom it is being passed. Individuals can also claim compensation for damage caused by a breach of the act.

data recovery any of several possible procedures for restoring a computer system and its data after a system crash, burglary, or other damage. The first line of defence in any computer system is ↝ backups.

Every system fails at some point, and typically the data on the system is more valuable than the hardware on which it resides. The best course of action depends on the cause of the damage, which may be due to an outside agent, such as a virus, or a simple mistake, such as accidentally deleting important files. Some antivirus software comes with tools to assist users to clean up their systems; for deleted files, utility software such as Norton Utilities may be able to restore ('undelete') the data. In worse cases, specialists may still be able to restore the information by reading the hard disk's platters directly.

data security precautions taken to prevent the loss or misuse of data, whether accidental or deliberate. These include measures that ensure that only authorized personnel can gain entry to a computer system or file, and regular procedures for storing and 'backing up' data, which enable files to be retrieved or recreated in the event of loss, theft, or damage.

A number of ↝ verification and ↝ validation techniques may also be used to prevent data from being lost or corrupted by misprocessing.

Encryption involves the translation of data into a form that is meaningless to unauthorized users who do not have the necessary decoding software.

TIP

data recovery

If files on your hard drive are missing or corrupted, **do not** install any new software onto the hard drive as it will probably overwrite the data you are trying to recover. Run a program like Norton Utilities from a floppy disk. If the damage is too serious for Norton (or your technical ability), call a specialist for advice. Do not let anyone install software on that disk – even reinstalling existing software – until a specialist has agreed the data is irretrievable.

Passwords can be chosen by, or issued to, individual users. These secret words (or combinations of alphanumeric characters) may have to be entered each time a user logs on to a computer system or attempts to access a particular protected file within the system.

Physical access to the computer facilities can be restricted by locking entry doors and storage cabinets.

Master files (files that are updated periodically) can be protected by storing successive versions, or generations, of these files and of the transaction files used to update them. The most recent version of the master file may then be recreated, if necessary, from a previous generation. It is common practice to store the three most recent versions of a master file (often called the grandfather, father, and son generations).

Direct-access files are protected by making regular dumps, or back-up copies. Because the individual records in direct-access files are constantly being accessed and updated, specific generations of these files cannot be said to exist. The files are therefore dumped at fixed time intervals onto a secure form of backing store. A record, or log, is also kept of all the changes made to a file between security dumps.

Fireproof safes are used to store file generations or sets of security dumps, so that the system can be restarted on a new computer in the event of a fire in the computer department.

Write-protect mechanisms on disks or tapes allow data to be read but not deleted, altered, or overwritten. For example, the protective case of a 3½-inch floppy disk has a write-protect tab that can be slid back with the tip of a pencil or pen to protect the disk's contents.

data terminator or *rogue value*, special value used to mark the end of a list of input data items. The computer must be able to detect that the data terminator is different from the input data in some way – for instance, a negative number might be used to signal the end of a list of positive numbers, or 'XXX' might be used to terminate the entry of a list of names. This is now considered to be very bad programming technique. A lot of old programs used data terminators, and many programmers used 00 as a year data terminator, leading to problems in the year 2000.

daughterboard small printed circuit board that plugs into a ↝ motherboard to give it new capabilities.

dBASE family of microcomputer programs used for manipulating large quantities of data; also, a related ↝ fourth-generation language. The first version, dBASE II, was published by Ashton-Tate in 1981; it has since become the basis for a recognized standard for database applications, known as xBase.

DBS abbreviation for ↝ direct broadcast system.

DCOM abbreviation for *Distributed Component Object Model*, the network version of Microsoft's ↝ Component Object Model.

DDE abbreviation for ↝ dynamic data exchange, a form of communication between processes used in Microsoft Windows.

debugging finding and removing errors, or ↝ bugs, from a computer program or system.

DEC acronym for *Digital Equipment Corporation*, US computer manufacturer. DEC was founded by US computer engineers Kenneth Olsen and Harlan Anderson, and was the first ↝ minicomputer manufacturer. It became the world's second-largest computer manufacturer, after ↝ IBM, but made huge losses in the early 1990s before being taken over by Compaq Computer in 1998. DEC's most successful computers were the PDP-11 and the VAX (Virtual Address eXtension). The former was used in the creation of the ↝ Unix operating system.

DEC's original aim was to make the first small computers for engineering and departmental use, and the PDP (Programmed Data Processor) range became known as minicomputers to contrast them with giant mainframes. In the 1990s DEC developed new businesses, such as the ↝ AltaVista search engine, and sold off many of its old ones. The company has had success in recent years because of the design of its computers that use the DEC Alpha microprocessor. The Alpha chip is a very advanced ↝ RISC design, and has one of the fastest clock speeds of any chip in its class.

decimal number system or *denary number system*, most commonly used number system, to the base ten. Decimal numbers do not necessarily contain a decimal point; 563, 5.63, and –563 are all decimal numbers. Other systems are mainly used in computing and include the ↝ binary number system, ↝ octal number system, and ↝ hexadecimal number system.

Decimal numbers may be thought of as written under column headings based on the number ten. For example, the number 2,567 stands for 2 thousands, 5 hundreds, 6 tens, and 7 ones. Large decimal numbers may also be expressed in ↝ floating-point notation.

decision table method of describing a procedure for a program to follow, based on comparing possible decisions and their consequences. It is often used as an aid in systems design.

The top part of the table contains the conditions for making decisions (for example, if a number is negative rather than positive and is less than 1), and the bottom part describes the outcomes when those conditions are met. The program either ends or repeats the operation.

declarative programming computer programming that does not describe how to solve a problem, but rather describes the logical structure of the problem. It is used in the programming language PROLOG. Running such a program is more like proving an assertion than following a ↝ procedure.

decoder electronic circuit used to select one of several possible data pathways. Decoders are, for example, used to direct data to individual memory locations within a computer's immediate access memory.

dedicated computer computer built into another device for the purpose of controlling or supplying information to it. Its use has increased dramatically since the advent of the ↪ microprocessor: washing machines, digital watches, cars, and video recorders all now have their own processors.

A dedicated system is a general-purpose computer system confined to performing only one function for reasons of efficiency or convenience. A word processor is an example.

Deep Blue name given to the IBM chess-playing computer that first defeated a human grandmaster, the Russian Garry Kasparov, in 1996. This was the first match of a six-match series that Kasparov went on to win 4–2, but in 1997 Deep Blue won a rematch series 3.5–2.5, fuelling debate about the possibilities of artificial intelligence.

The architect and principal designer of Deep Blue is Feng-Hsiung Hsu, who joined IBM in 1989. Deep Blue's award-winning precursor, Deep Thought, was developed by Hsu and other graduate students at Carnegie Mellon University in Pittsburgh. In 1988 it was the first computer to achieve a grandmaster rating.

default factory setting for user-configurable options. Default settings appear in all areas of computing, from the on-screen colour scheme in a ↪ graphical user interface to the directories where software programs store data.

defragmentation program or *disk optimiser*, program that rearranges data on disk so that files are not scattered in many small sections. See also ↪ fragmentation.

Deja News Web site that allows users to search messages posted in ↪ Usenet Newsgroups. The author feature provides a list of the newsgroups to which a particular user has posted, and the number of posts. The site has now expanded to become a general portal under the name Deja.com.

delete to remove or erase. In computing, the deletion of a character removes it from the file; the deletion of a file normally means removing its directory entry, rather than actually deleting it from the disk. Many systems now have an ↪ undelete facility that allows the restoration of the directory entry. While deleted files may not have been removed from the disk, they can be overwritten.

Dell, Michael (1964–) US computer entrepreneur, who founded the PC manufacturing company Dell Computer, of which he is chief executive, in 1984 with $1,000. Dell, who began customizing PCs as a student at the University of Texas, Austin, aimed with his new company to cut out the middleman and sell custom-built PCs direct to end-users.

When he was 12 years old, Dell made $2,000 from a mail-order stamp trading business. At age 16, he was making $18,000 from selling newspaper subscriptions. By 2000, Dell Computer's sales had reached $27 billion a year, and in May of that year, Michael Dell's personal wealth was estimated by the US financial magazine *Forbes* at $17.8 billion.

TIP

default

To make it easier to back up important data, change the default settings so that programs store data in a common directory or directory tree of your own choosing.

TIP

delete

While deleted files may not have been removed from the disk, they can be overwritten.

Delphi text-based UK and US national online information service. In 1992, Delphi was the first national US service to open a ⬿ gateway to the Internet. Founded in 1982 as the world's first online encyclopedia, Delphi was bought by News International in 1993, and launched its UK service in 1994. In 1996 the US arm of Delphi was sold back to one of its original owners. The UK service continues in the hands of News International.

demo or *demonstration software*, preview version of software that allows users to try out the main features of a particular program before buying it. Especially common among ⬿ shareware producers, demo software usually blocks some features of the full version, so that a demo database might be able to handle only a small number of records.

The word 'demo' is also used to refer to fancy graphics and sound routines which are created by young programmers to demonstrate their skills to friends, admirers, and potential employers such as computer game publishers.

Demon Internet Britain's first and largest mass-market ⬿ Internet Service Provider. Founded in 1992 by English hardware salesman Cliff Stanford with 200 founding subscribers who each paid £120 in advance for a year's service, Demon set the price (£10 a month plus VAT) for Internet access in the UK. The number of Demon users grew to 65,000 in 1996 and 250,000 in 1998, when the company was taken over by Scottish Telecom.

demonstration software see ⬿ demo.

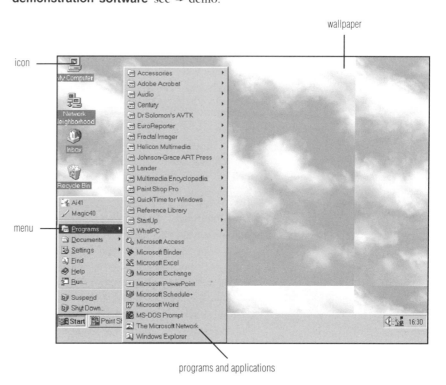

desktop
A typical graphical desktop, showing the menu system, icons, programs, and applications available to the user.

DES abbreviation for ⮑ Data Encryption Standard.

desktop graphical representation of file systems, in which applications and files are represented by pictures (icons), which can be triggered by a single or double click with a ⮑ mouse button. Such a ⮑ graphical user interface can be compared with the ⮑ command line interface, which is character-based.

desktop publishing *DTP*, use of microcomputers for small-scale typesetting and page makeup. DTP systems are capable of producing camera-ready pages (pages ready for photographing and printing), made up of text and graphics, with text set in different typefaces and sizes. The page can be previewed on the screen before final printing on a laser printer.

A DTP program is able to import text and graphics from other packages; run text as columns, over pages, and around artwork and other insertions; enable a wide range of ⮑ fonts; and allow accurate positioning of all elements required to make a page.

desktop publishing
The features of some major desktop publishing programs

Software	Manufacturer	Description
FrameMaker	Adobe	powerful; strong on technical reports and book production
PageMaker	Adobe	powerful professional tool; strong layout and colour capabilities for both printed and online pages
PagePlus	Serif	good value, low-level tool; aimed mainly at marketing and home use
Publisher	Microsoft	low-level for beginners; provides wizards and clip art gallery
QuarkXPress	Quark	industry standard; expert type, layout, colour, and graphics handling

desktop video ⮑ videoconferencing system that can be used by an individual from a desktop computer. A desktop conferencing system needs a computer, an attached video camera, microphone, and speakers, and a telephone or network connection. Desktop video is becoming increasingly common. The latest range of Apple Macintosh computers come with video cameras and microphones built in, and come with all the software necessary for videophone communications.

Early videoconferencing systems required such expensive equipment that participants had to gather in the room where the equipment was kept. Systems introduced in the mid-1990s, however, made videoconferencing as convenient, private, and easy to use as ordinary telephone calls.

The first desktop videoconferencing system on the Internet was ⮑ CU-SeeMe.

destination page page designated by a ⮑ hypertext link.

developer designer of a computer system, most commonly used to mean a software developer.

Device Bay standardized slot or drive bay for hard disk drives, CD-ROM drives, tape back-up units, and other devices. Device Bay should make personal computers easier to upgrade, and should allow devices to be swapped easily between different machines. Devices are connected either via a ↝ USB port or a ↝ 1394 port built into the bay. The Device Bay format was agreed by Compaq, Intel, and Microsoft in 1997.

device driver small piece of software required to tell the operating system how to interact with a particular input or output device or peripheral.

Much work has been done to standardize devices and their interfaces to eliminate the need for individual device drivers. Peripherals such as CD-ROM drives, for example, work with a single standard device driver (in Microsoft Windows, MSCDEX.EXE). Other devices, such as modems and printers, still need an individual driver tailored to work with that specific model.

dialler element of an Internet software package that makes the connection to the ↝ online service or ↝ Internet Service Provider. In Windows systems, this is usually the WINSOCK.DLL file, with or without a front end (part of the program that interacts with the user) to make configuration easier.

dialog box in ↝ graphical user interfaces, a small on-screen window with blanks for user input.

dial-up connection connection to an ↝ online system or ↝ Internet Service Provider made by dialling via a ↝ modem over a telephone line.

DIANE acronym for *direct information access network for Europe*, collection of information suppliers, or 'hosts', for the European computer network.

difference engine mechanical calculating machine designed (and partly built in 1822) by the British mathematician Charles ↝ Babbage to produce reliable tables of life expectancy. A precursor of the ↝ analytical engine, it was to calculate mathematical functions by solving the differences between values given to variables within equations. Babbage designed the calculator so that once the initial values for the variables were set it would produce the next few thousand values without error.

Diffie-Hellman key exchange system basis of ↝ public-key cryptography, proposed by researchers Whitfield Diffie and Martin Hellman in 1976.

digit any of the numbers from 0 to 9 in the decimal system. Different bases have different ranges of digits. For example, the ↝ hexadecimal system has digits 0 to 9 and A to F, whereas the binary system has two digits (or ↝ bits), 0 and 1.

Quality in a Digital Age

Listening When compact disc began to oust the vinyl record from its pre-eminent position in music reproduction, hi-fi buffs warned that something special was being lost. Music broken into tiny digital steps has subliminal effects on listeners, they claimed. Music lovers risked forfeiting the musical fidelity and dynamic range of the system that had served them well for some 30 years. In its place they would find only a showy substitute – something that sounded good on a first encounter, but that would soon prove 'harsh' and a source of digital 'fatigue' for its listeners.

Enthusiasts aside, most people were unaware of this debate. For them, the CD was much tougher than scratch- and dust-prone vinyl, and the sound was cleaner and clearer. Who was right? Perhaps they both were. Hi-fi enthusiasts were thinking in terms of their expensive turntables, arms, cartridges, amplifiers, and other equipment that partly overcame the inherent disadvantages of vinyl records and their ever-diminishing spiral grooves. Everybody else played their vinyl disks on music centres or cheaper record players. For a comparable outlay, they could buy a CD system and experience a quantum leap in quality. A minority saw quality drop, but the majority saw it rise.

What happened to music reproduction is symptomatic of the 'digital effect' in other media: most people see digitization as a clear benefit, and enjoy its products, but smaller groups cry out that there is a quality 'down side'. These groups often include established media professionals. For each medium, the key question is whether this down side matters – and to whom – and what its effects will be in the longer term.

Watching It's worth mentioning that there are instances of digital techniques stopping the quality rot. Think of television cartoons. In the 1950s and 1960s, the demand for children's media 'product' spawned a mass of cheap cartoon programming in the USA. The resulting 'limited animation' shorts, with their two-dimensional feel and feeble backgrounds, were a far cry from lush, labour-intensive Hollywood cartoon features, or even the frantic shorts of Warner Brothers and others. Computer animation techniques came to the rescue, so that today's stock TV cartoons enjoy a better animation quality than many of their conventionally produced forebears. Whether the programme content of these cartoons is any better is a moot point.

It's sometimes said that digitization has removed the very bottom and very top of the quality spectrum. The very worst has gone, but the very best is often unattainable – it has disappeared along with the highly skilled people who produced it. What is left ranges from the mediocre to the near-excellent, though it is probably true that the upper reaches of this middle band are more affordable than they were in analogue days. One of the great benefits of the digital world is that it offers greatly increased accessibility to relatively high-quality media.

Reading Print media have already proved extremely susceptible to digital inroads. 'Quality' in relation to print has several dimensions, notably in judging typesetting and printing, typographical and graphic design, and the complex web of values associated with the 'text' itself.

Of course, there is more than digitization at work here – other gains in technology, and in particular in IT, have moved everything forwards. For example, it is not simply digitization that allowed us to use laser printers and photocopiers for our routine stationery. Commercial interests had to develop new, efficient implementations of xerographic technology. But digitization is the engine of modern technology, and of media technology in particular.

At first sight, everything in the world of print seems to have changed for the better. Authors can create and endlessly refine their masterpieces using powerful wordprocessors, then send the digital output by disk or wire to the publisher. Or they can self-publish in print, or via the print-analogues of the Web-page and electronic document formats such as Acrobat or Envoy. Publishers large and small – indeed, anybody with a PC and the right software – can appropriate the generations of composing and printing expertise that is allegedly built into their software to produce 'professional' leaflets, newsletters and newspapers, flyers, magazines, journals, books . . .

Admittedly, some higher-end print products still need to call on commercial printing and manufacturing services, but the increase in the accessibility of good quality print media has been vast. And from the professional end of print media (let's not forget that digitization has radically affected professional practitioners too) there is often a higher, if superficial, 'look and feel' quality than was possible two or three decades ago.

So where is the down side? Once again, the voices of the few sound a warning to the enthusiastic many: designers and typographers can argue that increased accessibility, though a 'good thing' in itself, has put typesetting and printing capabilities into the hands of people who don't know how to use them. Much of today's printed matter is poorly designed to the point of being chaotic. And the flood of cheap typefaces available to the PC-user has severely eroded typographical discipline, aiding and accelerating the advertising-driven move away from legibility towards mere impact.

Writing Writing has changed too: entering text into a wordprocessor is significantly different from longhand writing, or bashing the keys of a finger-crunching manual typewriter. The wordprocessor has brought substantial change: authors are not just doing the same thing with a different tool, but many new and different things.

Accessible IT kicks aside quality thresholds – it's as though anybody with a wordprocessor can write, and anybody with a DTP package or Web editor can design pages. A less conspicuous but extremely important problem is the fate of editing and proofreading. Commercial publishing has good reason to be nervous here. Editorial expertise is leaking out of mainstream publishing at an alarming rate. New editors often lack basic training in editorial intervention, or even an awareness of its potential and importance.

Add commercial pressures that attempt to trim or sidestep editorial fixed costs, and the ease of editor-less self-publishing, and you have a recipe that threatens the long-term survival of publishing enterprises in their present form. To survive, publishers need to sell visibly added value to authors and readers; editorial input scales has always been a prime component of that added value.

'Quality' is not a single, measurable dimension. There are complex value-related and economic issues at stake. Whose quality standards for sound, text, design, animation . . . are at issue, and how are these standards justified?

Quality costs money Who cares? Market-minded economists would say that media consumers reveal their own quality standards whenever they buy media products. On these grounds, suppliers can claim that their standards are *good enough*. Quality costs money – this is as true now as it was in analogue days. Marginal quality improvements – however these are defined – will occur only if media consumers are willing to pay for them.

The immense drive of digital progress does lower the cost of products. This will certainly help to increase physical quality – scanner and imagesetter resolution, say, or transmission bandwiths and video compression techniques – but it's highly unlikely to improve the deeper quality of text and programme contents. Are we losing sight of this 'greyer' aspect of quality – hedged round as it is with subjectivity, multiple viewpoints, and vested interests?

Stephen Ball

digital in electronics, a term meaning 'coded as numbers'. A digital system uses two-state, either on/off or high/low voltage pulses, to encode, receive, and transmit information. A digital display shows discrete values as numbers (as opposed to an analogue signal, such as the continuous sweep of a pointer on a dial).

Digital electronics is the technology that underlies digital techniques. Low-power, miniature, integrated circuits (chips) provide the means for the coding, storage, transmission, processing, and reconstruction of information of all kinds.

digital camera camera that uses a ⤳ charge-coupled device (CCD) to take pictures that are stored as digital data rather than on film. The output from digital cameras can be downloaded onto a computer for retouching or storage, and can be readily distributed as computer files. Leading manufacturers of digital cameras include Canon and Kodak.

The late 1990s saw an explosion in the number of digital cameras being produced. Many people now buy digital cameras in preference to conventional cameras. By 2000 digital cameras were produced with the ability to capture over 3 million pixels of information.

digital certificate ⤳ public key certificate issued by a certification authority (CA) to guarantee that a user's identities and keys are valid and trustworthy. Digital certificates include the user's name, the public key of the user, the period over which the certificate is valid, and whether the key is to be used for data ⤳ encryption, verification of ⤳ digital signatures, or both. See ⤳ public key infrastructure and ⤳ trusted third party.

digital city area in ⤳ cyberspace, either text-based or graphical, that uses the model of a city to make it easy for visitors and residents to find specific types of information.

digital composition or *compositing*, computerized film editing. Some film special effects require shots to be cut together – composited. A sequence showing an actor hanging off the edge of a skyscraper, for example, may be put together out of footage of the actor in a safe location inserted into a shot looking down the side of the skyscraper, which may itself be a model. Traditional techniques for creating such a shot involved photographing the foreground shot with the background shot playing behind it, with an inevitable degradation of quality in the background material. In digital compositing, the same footage is digitized, and the work of merging the two sequences is done by manipulating computer files. The composite image is then transferred back onto film with no loss of quality.

digital computer computing device that operates on a two-state system, using symbols that are internally coded as binary numbers (numbers made up of combinations of the digits 0 and 1); see ⤳ computer.

digital data transmission way of sending data by converting all signals (whether pictures, sounds, or words) into numeric (normally binary) codes before transmission, then reconverting them on receipt. This virtually eliminates any distortion or degradation of the signal during transmission, storage, or processing.

digital monitor display ⤳ monitor using standard cathode-ray tube technology that converts a ⤳ digital signal from the computer into an ⤳ analogue signal for display.

digital city

http://www.arenanet.fi/
english/virtuality/html

One of the best-known digital cities is a mirror of Helsinki, in Finland.

WEB LINK

Digital monitors are unable to display the continuously variable range of colours offered by analogue monitors.

Digital Nervous System Microsoft's way of describing how information technology – particularly its own software products – can help companies to operate more efficiently. Digital Nervous System is used to market Microsoft's ideas to people considered not technical enough to understand ⤳ DNA, its Distributed interNetwork Applications architecture.

digital recording technique whereby the pressure of sound waves is sampled more than 30,000 times a second and the values converted by computer into precise numerical values. These are recorded and, during playback, are reconverted to sound waves.

This technique gives very high-quality reproduction. The numerical values converted by computer represent the original sound-wave form exactly and are recorded on compact disc. When this is played back by laser, the exact values are retrieved.

When the signal is fed via an amplifier to a loudspeaker, sound waves exactly like the original ones are reproduced.

digital retouching technique for touching up digital photographs, similar to airbrushing in the analogue world. It is commonly used in the film industry to remove scratches or to cover up filming mistakes.

The retoucher points out the error to the computer and the computer calculates new colour values for the affected ⤳ pixels from the colours of neighbouring pixels.

digital signal processor *DSP*, special-purpose integrated circuit that handles voice. DSPs are used in voice modems, which add answering machine facilities to a personal computer, and also in computer dictation systems.

digital signature method of using encryption to certify the source and integrity of a particular electronic document. Because all ⤳ ASCII characters look the same no matter who types them, methods have to be found to certify the origins of particular messages if they are to be legally binding for electronic commerce or other transactions. One type of digital signature commonly seen on the Net is generated by the program ⤳ Pretty Good Privacy (PGP), which adds a digest of the message to the signature.

digital television *DTV*, system of transmitting television programmes in digital code. Until the late 1980s it was considered impossible to convert a TV signal into digital code because of the amount of information needed to represent a visual image. However, the developement of ⤳ data compression techniques made it possible to develop a digital technology in the 1990s that offered sharper and wider pictures with superior image quality. A common world standard for DTV, the MPEG-2, was agreed in April 1993 at a meeting of engineers representing manufacturers and broadcasters from 18 countries.

Although a number of channels had already been broadcasting in the digital mode, 1 November 1998 was recognized as the birth of the DTV era in the UK and saw several new channels launched in digital form. The advent of DTV constitutes a revolutionary overhaul of television, making a wider variety of programming available and improving the quality of image and sound. It is expected that DTV will have superseded the analogue television system by 2006. By this time, industry experts hope, 'multiplexing' (where more than one television programme can share the same bandwidth) of both HDTV and SDTV (standard definition) programmes will have been widely adopted, as will the broadcast of nontelevision data, such as Web content and stock-market information.

digital-to-analogue converter electronic circuit that converts a digital signal into an ⌐ analogue (continuously varying) signal. Such a circuit is used to convert the digital output from a computer into the analogue voltage required to produce sound from a conventional loudspeaker.

digital versatile disk or *digital video disk* (DVD), disk format for storing digital information. DVDs can hold 14 times the data stored on current CDs. Pre-recorded DVDs have a storage capacity of 4.7 gigabytes and can hold a full-length feature film. As with CDs, information is etched in the form of microscopic pits onto a plastic disk (though the pits are half the size), which is then coated with aluminium. DVDs may have two pitted surfaces per side whereas CDs have only one. The data is read optically using a laser as the disk rotates. A double-layer disk can hold four hours of video. The Japanese company TDK produced the rewriteable DVD-RAM, capable of holding 2.6 gigabytes, in 1996. The DVD-RW, the rival rewritable format to DVD-RAM, is being developed by Sony and Philips (1998), and can hold 4.7 gigabytes.

DVD now comes as standard on many new PCs. DVD-RAM has become the standard of choice in the rewriteable market. The latest DVD-RAM drives are capable of storing 6 gigabytes of data (3 gigabytes on each side). DVD players for home entertainment are now common, and before long DVD-RAM machines for home entertainment use will become affordable, which could mean the beginning of the end for video cassette technology.

digital versatile disk
Comparison of DVD and CD-ROM

Features	DVD	CD
pit diameter (microns)	0.4	0.83
distance between data tracks (microns)	0.74	1.6
data spiral length (km/mi)	11/6.8	5/3
type of laser	red	infrared
laser wavelength (nanometres)	635–650	780
data capacity	8.5 gigabytes	680 megabytes

digital versatile disk
A DVD player can be connected to a television or a computer, in order to play digital versatile disks. DVD players are becoming increasingly popular as a means of playing feature films, in place of video cassette recorders.

digital video interactive powerful compression system used for storing video images on computer; see ⇨ DVI.

digitize to turn ⇨ analogue signals into the binary data a computer can read. Any type of analogue signal can be digitized, including pictures, sound, video, or film. The result is files that can be manipulated, stored, or transmitted by computers. See ⇨ analogue-to-digital converter.

DVD player

digitizer device that converts an analogue video signal into a digital format so that video images can be input, stored, displayed, and manipulated by a computer. The term is sometimes used to refer to a ⇨ graphics tablet.

dingbat non-alphanumeric character, such as a star, bullet, or arrow. Dingbats have been combined into ⇨ PostScript and ⇨ TrueType fonts for use with word processors and graphics programs.

DIP abbreviation for ⇨ document image processing.

DIP switch abbreviation for *dual in-line package switch*, tiny switch that controls settings on devices such as printers and modems. The owner's manual will usually specify how DIP switches should be set.

On printers, these switches are typically used to specify which emulation to use; on modems, they set the modem to match the ⇨ COM port to which it is connected. They should not need to be changed once the device has been installed and is working properly.

direct access or *random access*, type of ⮑ file access. A direct-access file contains records that can be accessed by the computer directly because each record has its own address on the storage disk. Direct access storage mediums include CD-ROMs and magnetic disks (such as floppy disks).

direct broadcast system *DBS*, combination of a small satellite dish and receiver which allows consumers to receive television and radio broadcasts from a satellite rather than via terrestrial broadcasting towers and repeaters.

The most common systems in the UK are those that work with the four Astra satellites, which carry a group of channels from British Sky Broadcasting (BSkyB), among others. New plans announced in the UK in 1996 include a move to digital direct broadcast systems, which besides allowing the transmission of many more channels will also allow fast access to data from the most popular sites on the World Wide Web.

direct connection connection between two computers via cable to transfer files without the intermediary of a network or online service. Each computer must be running communications software using the same protocols for file transfers. If the computers are in the same room, they can be connected using a special type of serial cable known as a null modem cable; if they are connected via telephone lines each must have a modem so that one can dial the other.

There are several software packages designed for this purpose; the market leader is Laplink.

direct memory access *DMA*, technique used for transferring data to and from external devices without going through the ⮑ central processing unit (CPU) and thus speeding up transfer rates. DMA is used for devices such as ⮑ scanners.

direct memory access channel channel used for the fast transfer of data; usually abbreviated as ⮑ DMA channel.

Director multimedia software ⮑ authoring tool published by Macromedia, a company of multimedia software specialists based in San Francisco, USA.

directory list of file names, together with information that enables a computer to retrieve those files from ⮑ backing storage. The computer operating system will usually store and update a directory on the backing storage to which it refers. So, for example, on each ⮑ disk used by a computer a directory file will be created listing the disk's contents.

The term is also used to refer to the area on a disk where files are stored; the main area, the root directory, is at the top-most level, and may contain several separate sub-directories.

directory tree collective name for a ⇨ directory and all its subdirectories.

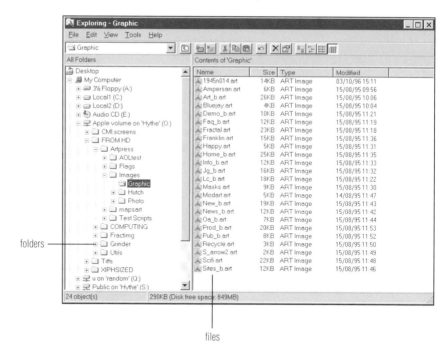

folders

files

DirectX programming interface developed by Microsoft to simplify the problem of writing programs to use the wide variety of graphics hardware – particularly the number of different 3-D graphics cards – found in personal computers. Programmers can write to the DirectX software layer, which in effect converts these general instructions into the commands required by specific pieces of hardware.

Discman Sony trademark for a portable compact-disc player; the equivalent of a Walkman, it also comes in a model with a liquid-crystal display for data disks.

disk common medium for storing large volumes of data (an alternative is ⇨ magnetic tape). A magnetic disk is rotated at high speed in a disk-drive unit as a read/write (playback or record) head passes over its surfaces to record or read the magnetic variations that encode the data. Recently, optical disks, such as ⇨ CD-ROM (compact-disc read-only memory) and ⇨ WORM (write once, read many times), have been used to store computer data. Data are recorded on the disk surface as etched microscopic pits and are read by a laser-scanning device.

Optical disks have an enormous capacity – ranging from 650 megabytes for CD-ROM to 2.6 gigabytes for magneto-optical drives.

Magnetic disks come in several forms: fixed hard disks are built into the disk-drive unit, occasionally stacked on top of one another. A fixed disk cannot be removed: once it is full, data must be deleted in order to free space or a complete new disk drive must be added to the computer system in order to increase storage capacity. Hard disks can now store up to 22 gigabytes, and the smallest hard disk it is possible to buy is 4 gigabytes. Arrays of such disks were also used to store minicomputer and mainframe data in RAID storage systems, replacing large fixed disks and removable hard disks.

Removable hard disks are still found in minicomputer and mainframe systems. The disks are contained, individually or as stacks (disk packs), in a protective plastic case, and can be taken out of the drive unit and kept for later use. By swapping such disks around, a single hard-disk drive can be made to provide a potentially infinite storage capacity. However, access speeds and capacities tend to be lower that those associated with large, fixed hard disks. A floppy disk (or diskette) is the most common form of backing store for microcomputers. It is much smaller in size and capacity than a hard disk, normally holding 0.5–2 megabytes of data. The floppy disk is so called because it is manufactured from thin flexible plastic coated with a magnetic material. The earliest form of floppy disk was packaged in a card case and was easily damaged; more recent versions are contained in a smaller, rigid plastic case and are much more robust. All floppy disks can be removed from the drive unit.

disk compression technique, based on ⇝ data compression, that makes hard disks and floppy disks appear to have more storage capacity than is normally

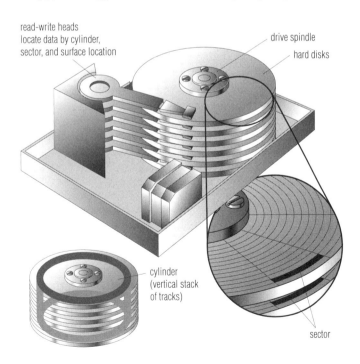

read-write heads
locate data by cylinder,
sector, and surface location

drive spindle

hard disks

cylinder
(vertical stack
of tracks)

sector

disk
A hard disk. Data is stored in sectors within cylinders and is read by a head which passes over the spinning surface of each disk.

TIP

disk compression

Several commercial disk compression products are available, for example DoubleSpace in MS-DOS 6.0 and Stacker.

available. If the data stored on a disk can be compressed to occupy half the original amount of disk space, it will appear that the disk is twice its original size. The processes of compression (to store data) and decompression (so that data can be used) are hidden from the user by the software.

disk drive mechanical device that reads data from, and writes data to, a magnetic ➷ disk.

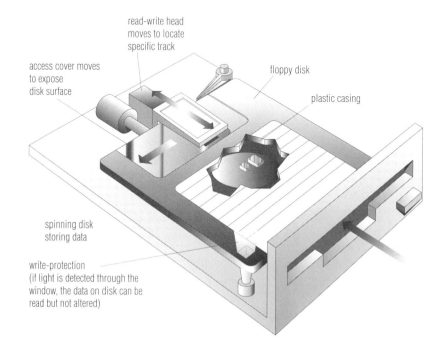

read-write head
moves to locate
specific track

access cover moves
to expose
disk surface

floppy disk

plastic casing

spinning disk
storing data

write-protection
(if light is detected through the
window, the data on disk can be
read but not altered)

disk drive
A floppy disk drive. As the disk is inserted into the drive, its surface is exposed to the read-write head, which moves over the spinning disk surface to locate a specific track.

disk formatting preparing a blank magnetic disk in order that data can be stored on it. Data are recorded on a disk's surface on circular tracks, each of which is divided into a number of sectors. In formatting a disk, the computer's operating system adds control information such as track and sector numbers, which enables the data stored to be accessed correctly by the disk-drive unit.

Some floppy disks, called hard-sectored disks, are sold already formatted. However, because different makes of computer use different disk formats, disks are also sold unformatted, or soft-sectored, and computers are provided with the necessary ➷ utility program to format these disks correctly before they are used.

disk optimizer another name for a ➷ defragmentation program, a program that gathers together files that have become fragmented for storage on different areas of a disk. See also ➷ fragmentation.

display ↝ output device that looks like a television set and displays commands to the computer and their results.

display control interface standard developed by Microsoft and Intel for the ↝ device drivers that control ↝ graphics cards.

distance learning form of education using technology to teach pupils who are dispersed geographically. The UK's Open University, founded in 1969, is the oldest and most successful distance-learning institution in Europe, using a mixture of postal mail, television, electronic conferencing, and the Internet to offer degree courses to students all over the world. Experiments in the 1990s used ↝ videoconferencing and other multimedia techniques to widen the university's range.

distributed processing computer processing that uses more than one computer to run an application. ↝ Local area networks, ↝ client–server architecture, and ↝ parallel processing involve distributed processing.

dithering in computer graphics, a technique for varying the patterns of dots in an image in order to give the impression of shades of grey. Each dot, however, is of the same size and the same intensity, unlike grey scaling (where each dot can have a different shade) and photographically reproduced half-tones (where the dot size varies).

DLL abbreviation for ↝ dynamic link library.

DMA channel abbreviation for *direct memory access channel*, type of channel used for the fast transfer of data between a computer and peripherals such as CD-ROM drives. Most ISA (industry standard architecture) personal computers (PCs) have eight DMA channels, of which typically six are available for use by add-on peripherals, most of which require dedicated channels.

DNA abbreviation for *Distributed interNetwork Applications*, Microsoft's marketing name for a software architecture announced in 1997 and designed to extend the use of Microsoft's PC-based client/server products and standards – including ↝ COM and ↝ ActiveX – onto and across the Internet. One of the aims is to enable programmers used to working on personal computers in local area networks to use the same tools on the Internet instead of having to learn the Internet's way of doing things. One example is ↝ Active Server Pages (ASP).

DNS abbreviation for domain ↝ name server.

document data associated with a particular application. For example, a text document might be produced by a ↝ word processor and a graphics document might be produced with a ↝ CAD package. An ↝ OMR or ↝ OCR document is a paper document containing data that can be directly input to the computer using a ↝ document reader.

TIP

DMA channel

Keep a log book for your PC listing each peripheral you have installed with a note of the DMA channel number, interrupt request (IRQ) lines, and memory address assigned to it, to make installing additional devices easier.

documentation written information associated with a computer program or ⌐ applications package. Documentation is usually divided into two categories: program documentation and user documentation.

Program documentation is the complete technical description of a program, drawn up as the software is written and intended to support any later maintenance or development of that program. It typically includes details of when, where, and by whom the software was written; a general description of the purpose of the software, including recommended input, output, and storage methods; a detailed description of the way the software functions, including full program listings and ⌐ flow charts; and details of software testing, including sets of ⌐ test data with expected results. User documentation explains how to operate the software. It typically includes a nontechnical explanation of the purpose of the software; instructions for loading, running, and using the software; instructions for preparing any necessary input data; instructions for requesting and interpreting output data; and explanations of any error messages that the program may produce.

document image processing *DIP*, scanning documents for storage on ⌐ CD-ROM. The scanned images are indexed electronically, which provides much faster access than is possible with either paper or ⌐ microform. See also ⌐ optical character recognition.

Document Object Model *DOM*, specification of a standard framework for creating object-oriented documents devised by the ⌐ W3C. DOM allows a Web page – a document – to be treated as a *container* for holding a number of *objects*. Each object is seen as a node in a tree, with each document having a *parent* or root node and any number of *child* nodes. An object might be a comment, a processing instruction (PI), a piece of text, or any other item. In an ⌐ HTML or ⌐ XML version of this dictionary, for example, the book would be the parent, headwords are child nodes, and definitions are child nodes of headwords. A processing instruction might be used to display all headwords in bold type. The hope is that DOM will provide a structure for the Web, which is, at the moment, just tens of millions of words of barely connected text. In any event, it is much easier to use ⌐ scripting languages and intelligent software to manipulate containers of named objects than to do everything using ⌐ tags.

document reader input device that reads marks or characters, usually on pre-prepared forms and documents. Such devices are used to capture data by ⌐ optical mark recognition (OMR), ⌐ optical character recognition (OCR), and ⌐ mark sensing.

DOM acronym for ⌐ Document Object Model.

domain on the Internet, segment of an address that specifies an organization, its type, or its country of origin. Domain names are read backwards, starting at the end. All countries except the USA use a final two-letter code such as ca

Generic Top-Level Domains

.com	commercial business
.edu	academic
.gov	government
.int	organization established by international treaty
.mil	military
.net	Internet network
.org	non-commercial business

UK Domains

.ac.uk	academic
.co.uk	commercial business
.gov.uk	government
.lea.sch.uk	Local Education Authority
.ltd.uk	limited company
.mod.uk	Ministry of Defence
.net.uk	Internet network
.nhs.uk	National Health Service
.org.uk	non-commercial business
.plc.uk	public limited company

Selected Other Country Domains

.au	Australia
.ca	Canada
.cn	China
.de	Germany
.fr	France
.jp	Japan
.nl	Netherlands
.us	USA

domain
Common Internet
domain names

Doomgate – Where it all Begins

http://www.gamers.org/doomgate/

Wealth of information on the computer game *Doom*. Frequently updated, it contains advice, a 'Frequently Asked Questions' section, technical details about graphics and specifications, add-on utilities, and links to the large number of *Doom* newsgroups.

WEB LINK

for Canada and uk for the UK. US addresses end in one of seven 'top-level' domains, which specify the type of organization: com (commercial), mil (military), org (usually a nonprofit-making organization), and so on. In July 1999 there were 60 million domain names registered on the Internet.

The domain names are for the benefit of humans; to enable mail and other messages to be sorted by machine, computers use IP (Internet protocol) numbers. To route a message, the computer looks up the domain name on a domain name server (DNS), which tells the computer the number.

In 1999, the US Government handed over responsibility for the top-level domain names com, org, and net from the private company Network Solutions Inc (NSI) to the non-commerical organization ⮑ ICANN.

domain name server see ⮑ name server.

Doom popular computer game released in 1994. It is one of a series of games from the Texas-based company id Software, which specializes in 3-D graphics, alien monsters, and complex mazes which players must navigate to find secret treasures and hidden keys along the way. *Doom* can be played competitively over a network as well as on a single computer.

Because the company has encouraged players to create their own additional levels for *Doom* (and its other games) by releasing the necessary source code, a whole culture has grown up around *Doom* and id's other games.

Computer Games

From simple to 'real' Computer and video games have come a long way since Atari's *Pong* first appeared in 1972. That was a simplistic version of table tennis (ping pong) without a table or a net. Today's tennis games, like Codemasters' *Sampras' Extreme Tennis* for the Sony PlayStation and PC CD-ROM, and Virtua Tennis for the Sega Dreamcast, show huge advances in realism. The programmers of the Sampras game used motion capture to turn video footage into realistic computer graphics, and even the crowd in the game reacts to events on the court.

Simulation Simulation – creating computer versions of real-life games – has always been one of the driving forces of the genre. Flight simulators and driving games (*Pole Position, Formula 1 Grand Prix*) have long been popular, but all sorts of sports have been simulated including angling, golf, ice hockey, and even swimming. Martial arts are the basis of many popular fighting games, including *Mortal Kombat*. There have also been computer versions of card and board games such as bridge, backgammon, chess, Monopoly, Risk, and Trivial Pursuit. With a computer, you always have someone to play.

Simulations can be cerebral as well as physical. Management games allow fans to enjoy managing a football or motor racing team through several seasons, or run a railway, a theme park, or a chain of pizza parlours. You can even start with a small tribe of settlers and build a whole civilization, or start with a single space ship and rule the universe. Finish such a game by one means and you can then try others – a flexibility that keeps players coming back for more.

Games to win Simulations tend to be open-ended, but in other computer games, the player has to solve problems set by the programmers. Examples include puzzle games, adventure games, and so-called platform games like the famous Super Mario and Sonic games. These can take days or months to finish, and once finished, are rarely played again.

Adventures – where you guide a character or 'persona' on an adventure – started as text-based games, where players typed in things like 'kill troll with spear'. Good adventures created imaginary worlds, like good science fiction and fantasy novels. Today, text is being replaced by three-dimensional graphics, and the persona by an avatar. Some of these role-playing games (RPGs), such as Nintendo's Zelda series and Square's Final Fantasy series, are among the most popular entertainment products available. Final Fantasy IX shipped more than 2 million copies on its first day on sale in Japan.

Unseen opponents Many games can be played by more than one person, and some can be played on networks or via online services. In football and tennis simulations and martial arts games, for example, each side can be controlled by a different player. Adventure games are also played online, usually in the form of MUDs (Multi-User Dungeons). Often the human interaction between personae is more fun than the nominal aims such as killing trolls and finding treasure. In some MUDs, players are able to create their own areas or 'rooms', and their online characters may have 'virtual sex' with or even marry other personae. All this is done by typing in text, but in the future, graphics-based and 'virtual reality' games may raise this idea to a new level of interest.

Shoot 'em-up Computer gaming is still strongly associated with 'shoot'em-ups': games that involve death and destruction, and that test the player's speed of reaction. The first really popular game, *Space Invaders*, was one example, but today's titles are much more realistic and contain far more gore. Examples include id Software's series, *Wolfenstein 3D*, *Doom*, and *Quake*, all of which reached huge audiences by being offered as shareware. Networked and online versions of these games are now very popular worldwide, especially *Quake 3 Arena* and *Half-Life Counterstrike*. The best players play in professional gamers leagues and teams sometimes represent their countries in international tournaments. It has even been proposed that gaming should become an Olympic sport.

Whether violent games are beneficial (in being cathartic) or harmful (in being brutalizing) is open to argument, but only the ignorant think all computer games are the same.

Jack Schofield

DOS acronym for *disk operating system*, computer ⤳ operating system specifically designed for use with disk storage; also used as an alternative name for a particular operating system, ⤳ MS-DOS.

dot full stop that separates ⤳ IP addresses, sections of domain names, and the hierarchies in ⤳ newsgroup names, as well as file names and their extensions.

dotcom company conducting ⤳ electronic commerce only over the ⤳ World Wide Web, with no bricks and mortar stores. The term comes from the Internet ⤳ domain name suffix '.com' for commercial organizations.

dot pitch distance between the dots which make up the picture on a computer monitor. The smaller the dot pitch, the better and finer-grained the picture.

double click to click (press and release a ⤳ mouse button) twice in quick succession. Double clicking on an ⤳ icon shown on a ⤳ graphical user interface (GUI) is used to start an application. In most GUIs it is possible to set the maximum time interval between the two clicks.

double precision type of floating-point notation that has higher precision, that is, more significant decimal places. The term 'double' is not strictly correct, deriving from such numbers using twice as many ⤳ bits as standard floating-point notation.

downtime time when a computer system is unavailable for use, due to maintenance or a system crash. Some downtime is inevitable on almost all systems.

dpi abbreviation for *dots per inch*, measure of the ⤳ resolution of images produced by computer screens and printers.

drag and drop in ⤳ graphical user interfaces, feature that allows users to select a file name or icon using a mouse and move it to the name or icon representing a program so that the computer runs the program using that file as input data.

This method is convenient for computer users, as it eliminates unnecessary typing. Moving the name of a text file, for example, to a copy of a word processor will start up the word processor with that file loaded and ready for editing.

DRAM acronym for *dynamic random-access memory*, computer memory device in the form of a silicon chip commonly used to provide the ⤳ immediate-access memory of microcomputers. DRAM loses its contents unless they are read and rewritten every 2 milliseconds or so. This process is called refreshing the memory. DRAM is slower but cheaper than ⤳ SRAM, an alternative form of silicon-chip memory.

TIP

drive bay

Having a spare drive bay in a personal computer allows room for expansion when you run out of hard drive space.

drawing program software that allows a user to draw freehand and create complex graphics. Additional features may include special ⤳ fonts, ⤳ clip art, or painting facilities that allow a user to simulate on the computer the drawing characteristics of specific real-world implements such as charcoal, watercolours, or pastels. The market-leading drawing package is CorelDRAW.

drive bay slot in a computer designed to hold a disk drive such as a hard drive, floppy drive, or CD-ROM drive. Like most computer components, disk drives have decreased in size. Older drives were 5¼ inches in size, but most newer drives are 3½ inches. Kits to fit a 3½ inch drive into a 5¼ inch bay are readily available.

driver program that controls a peripheral device. Every device connected to the computer needs a driver program.

The driver ensures that communication between the computer and the device is successful.

For example, it is often possible to connect many different types of printer, each with its own special operating codes, to the same type of computer. This is because driver programs are supplied to translate the computer's standard printing commands into the special commands needed for each printer.

drop-down list in a ⤳ graphical user interface, a list of options that hangs down from a blank space in a ⤳ dialog box or other on-screen form when a computer awaits user input.

To select one of the choices, highlight it and click. The list will disappear and the selected item will appear in the blank. If the list is longer than the space available, small arrows and a scroll bar will appear on the right-hand side.

DSL abbreviation for *Digital Subscriber Loop* (or Line). Examples include ⤳ ADSL, ZDSL and, generically, xDSL.

DSP abbreviation for ⤳ digital signal processor.

DTP abbreviation for ⤳ desktop publishing.

Dual In-line Memory Module *DIMM*, small printed circuit board carrying several ⤳ memory chips. The chips are located on both sides of the board, with independent electrical contacts on either side.

dumb terminal ⤳ terminal that has no processing capacity of its own. It works purely as a means of access to a main ⤳ central processing unit. Compare with a ⤳ personal computer used as an intelligent terminal – for example in ⤳ client–server architecture.

dump process of rapidly transferring data to external memory or to a printer. It is usually done to help with debugging (see ⤳ bug) or as part of an error-recovery procedure designed to provide ⤳ data security. A ⤳ screen dump makes a printed copy of the current screen display.

duplex or *echo*, in printing, the ability to print on both sides of the page; in computer communications, setting that ⮑ toggles the ability to send and receive signals simultaneously. Full duplex means two-way communication is enabled; half duplex means it is disabled.

DVD abbreviation for ⮑ digital versatile disk or digital video disk.

CD-ROM Future

The rise of CD-ROM Over the past decade, the growing size of popular computer programs has made the CD-ROM (compact-disc read-only memory) the distribution medium of choice for software. In the future, that process looks like being extended with the adoption of DVD (digital versatile disk), which is an enhanced version of the CD format.

CD-ROM's advantage is that a single disk can hold more than 600 megabytes of data, the equivalent of more than 400 standard 3.5 in floppy disks. Thanks to high-volume production of audio CDs, CD-ROMs are also very cheap to produce, and it is not unusual to find them given away free with computer magazines. The CD-ROM has thus become the standard format for operating systems (Microsoft Windows and Apple's Mac OS), for suites of programs (Microsoft Office, Corel Office), for large books and encyclopedias (*The Oxford English Dictionary*, *Encyclopaedia Britannica*), and for computer games, where the CD-based Sony PlayStation and CD-based personal computers have become the largest formats.

The development of DVD CD-ROM's disadvantage is that a single disk cannot hold a full-length Hollywood movie. This has helped to prompt the development of DVD, which has enough storage capacity to hold four films on a single disk. DVD works exactly like CD-ROM but packs more data bits into the same area. It then doubles this enhanced capacity by putting two layers of data on the disk, one on top of the other. The storage capacity can then be doubled again by the simple expedient of using both sides of the disk.

DVD's first use was for playing back movies (originally the name stood for digital video disk), but it is now being adopted by the computer industry. Applications that require more than one CD – and some games have been produced with up to eight disks – can be put on one or two DVDs.

Hybrids The disadvantage of mass-produced CDs and DVDs is that they can't be changed. A CD-ROM encyclopedia that is correct when published may become 'wrong' as events unfold. At best it will be incomplete. The solution is to produce hybrids, where the bulk of the data is delivered on disk and then updated via an online communications system such as the Internet.

Even operating systems such as Microsoft Windows are hybrids: most of the code usually comes on a CD, but updates and new versions of software drivers must be downloaded from bulletin boards or World Wide Web sites.

Hybrids are now becoming popular in the games world. CD-based titles are bought and played in the usual way on a single computer or games console, but many can also be played in multi-user mode by connecting to other users via an online system such as BT's WirePlay. Often, the program code for three-dimensional virtual worlds like 3DO's *Meridian 59* will be delivered on CD-ROM to avoid the costs and time-delays of downloading many megabytes of data, but the game is played over the Internet.

Here for now, at least In an ideal world, every computer would be permanently connected to a network that could deliver tens of megabytes of data per second; hard drives and CD-ROMs would then be unnecessary. However, outside of large corporations, most people have very slow dial-up connections via modems and ordinary phone lines, and they have to pay for every second they spend online. Under these circumstances, hybrid CD-ROMs and DVDs have a useful part to play, and seem unlikely to disappear in the near future.

Jack Schofield

DVI abbreviation for digital video interactive, powerful compression and decompression system for digital video and audio. DVI enables 72 minutes of full-screen, full-motion video and its audio track to be stored on a CD-ROM. Originally developed by the US firm RCA, DVI is now owned by Intel and has active support from IBM and Microsoft. It can be used on the hard disk of a PC as well as on a CD-ROM.

Dvorak keyboard alternative keyboard layout to the normal typewriter keyboard layout (↝ QWERTY). In the Dvorak layout the most commonly used keys are situated in the centre, so that keying is faster.

DWANGO acronym for Dial-up Wide Area Network Game Operation, server that enables computer users with modems to play each other at action games such as *Doom*, *Duke Nuken 3D*, and *Monster Truck Madness* without the variable delays involved in moving data over the Internet.

dynamic data exchange *DDE*, form of interprocess communication used in Microsoft ↝ Windows, providing exchange of commands and data between two applications. DDE was used principally to include live data from one application in another – for example, spreadsheet data in a word-processed report. After Windows 3.1 DDE was replaced by ↝ object linking and embedding.

DDE links between files rely on the files remaining in the same locations in the computer's directory.

Dynamic Host Configuration Protocol method for supplying computers with certain network ↝ configuration information when they start up. It is commonly used for supplying computers with the configuration information they need to connect to the Internet.

Dynamic HTML fourth version of hypertext markup language (↝ HTML), the language used to create Web pages. It is called Dynamic HTML because it enables dynamic effects to be incorporated in pages without the delays involved in downloading Java ↝ applets and without referring back to the server.

dynamic IP address temporary ↝ IP address assigned from a pool of available addresses by an ↝ Internet Service Provider when a customer logs on to begin an online session.

Companies and other organizations which have their own networks typically have their own permanent IP addresses. Customers of a dial-up service provider, however, only need addresses for the length of time that they are actually on line. This method allows the finite number of available IP addresses to be used most efficiently.

dynamic link library *DLL*, files of executable functions that can be loaded on demand in Microsoft ↝ Windows and linked at run time. Windows itself uses DLL files for handling international keyboards, for example, and Windows word-processing programs use DLL files for functions such as spelling and hyphenation checks, and thesaurus.

Dynamic HTML Zone

http://www.dhtmlzone.
com/alt.html

Dedicated to Dynamic HTML, an advanced programming language for the Internet, this site offers a Dynamic HTML tutorial, a selection of articles, a number of demonstrations, and a discussion group.

WEB LINK

eBay online auction house launched in September 1995 by Pierre Omidyar, ostensibly to assist his wife in collecting Pez candy dispensers and interacting with other collectors over the Internet. By 2000, more than 4,320 categories of goods (from cars to coins) were being bought and sold on eBay's Web sites, which provide over 4 million new auctions and 450,000 new items every day.

EBCDIC abbreviation for *extended binary-coded decimal interchange code*, code used for storing and communicating alphabetic and numeric characters. It is an 8-bit code, capable of holding 256 different characters, although only 85 of these are defined in the standard version. It is still used in many mainframe computers, but almost all mini- and microcomputers now use ↝ ASCII code.

e-cash contraction of *electronic cash*, generic name for new electronic money systems such as Mondex, ↝ CyberCash, and DigiCash.

echo user input that is printed to the screen so the user can read it.

Eckert, J(ohn) Presper (1919–1995) US electronics engineer and mathematician who collaborated with John ↝ Mauchly on the development of the early ENIAC (1946) and UNIVAC 1 (1951) computers.

Eckert was born in Philadelphia, Pennsylvania, and studied at the University of Pennsylvania. During World War II he worked on radar ranging systems and then turned to the design of calculating devices, building the Electronic Numerical Integrator and Calculator (ENIAC) with Mauchly. The Eckert–Mauchly Computer Corporation, formed in 1947, was incorporated into Remington Rand in 1950 and subsequently came under the control of the Sperry Rand Corporation.

The ENIAC weighed many tonnes and lacked a memory, but could store a limited amount of information and perform mathematical functions. It was used for calculating ballistic firing tables and for meteorological and research problems.

ENIAC was superseded by BINAC, also designed in part by Eckert, and in the early 1950s, Eckert's group began to produce computers for the commercial market with the construction of the UNIVAC 1. Its chief advance was the capacity to store programs.

ECMA abbreviation for *European Computer Manufacturers' Association*.

e-commerce contraction of ↝ electronic commerce.

EcoNet one of several international computer networks dedicated to environmental issues.

edge connector electrical connection formed by taking some of the metallic tracks on a ↝ printed circuit board to the edge of the board and using them to plug directly into a matching socket.

Edge connectors are often used to connect the computer's main circuit board, or motherboard, to the expansion boards that provide the computer with extra memory or other facilities.

Payment over the Internet

Paying for goods and services online The credit card is still the principal method of paying for goods and services ordered over the Internet. Its advantages for the Web world are many: it can be used remotely; it works in any currency; leading brands are universally accepted; and credit card companies provide the consumer with some protection against non-delivery or non-performance of goods.

Defeating fraud on the Web But credit card fraud is a significant problem on the Internet, and one that threatens to inhibit the growth of e-commerce. Cardholders fear large-scale misuse of their credentials, for example when lists of credit card numbers and names are accidentally or intentionally published on the Web. (An August 2000 survey by the UK's National Consumer Council found that 54% of UK Internet users have concerns about releasing credit card and personal details online.) But it is the merchants who bear the burden of online credit card fraud and disputes, since, if a cardholder disputes a remote transaction, the seller usually carries the loss.

The technology exists to prevent much of this fraud. So-called 'smart' cards contain a microprocessor that can store a digital certificate and other details about the card holder and his or her spending patterns. When used in conjunction with a personal identification number (PIN) or password and data encryption, these cards provide both physical security and authentication of the user. However, although a global standard for such cards, Secure Electronic Transaction (SET), was agreed some years ago, implementation has been slow. Only now are large-scale roll-outs of the necessary cards and card readers beginning and server-side authentication solutions starting to emerge that should make the implementation of SET more flexible.

Other payment methods But even if credit cards can be made close to 100% secure for online use, they do not meet all the requirements of e-commerce. Some consumer groups, such as children and those on very low incomes, do not have access to them. And in the business-to-business environment, e-commerce must accommodate established invoicing, settlement, and accounting procedures.

A range of solutions is available from a large number of software companies to provide the interface between Web sites and the payment mechanisms available in the physical world, such as debit card payments, account-to-account transfers, and direct debits. Many of these solutions provide a customized wallet, or a 'pay it button' at the customer end, and middleware between the Web server and the banks' legacy systems at the back end. Some offer the different levels of authorization needed for business procurement, and incorporate digital certificates for additional authentication of payers. Solutions exist that allow parents to set up online pocket money accounts for their children, and even to specify sites where the money may be spent.

The Internet is also creating a need for new types of payment. For example, business-to-business online auctions may result in high-value transactions between counterparties in different jurisdictions and with no previous knowledge of each other. In these circumstances, online escrow accounts, where the buyer can deposit funds with a neutral third party, such as a bank, against satisfactory fulfilment of the contract, can be useful.

Another requirement is for immediate, low-cost account-to-account transfers, enabling merchants to receive cleared funds on the same day an order is made. In the UK, the Association of Payment and Clearing Services (an association of major banks and building societies) is working to introduce such a payment mechanism by mid-2001.

The Internet has presented the payments industry with a particular challenge through the new opportunities for purchases of small amounts of digital information or services, such as video clips, online games, music, and information downloads. The need for so-called 'micropayments' has spawned some innovative solutions, including a number of online currencies and e-purses (smart cards that hold actual monetary value which can be spent and replenished like cash). But these solutions have so far found very limited success online.

It may well be that, as the Internet becomes accessible through a variety of

Payment over the Internet (continued)

mobile and home entertainment devices, the phone and cable companies are best placed to capture these low-value transactions. They are past masters of the art of metered billing, and have already built mass-market customer relationships.

Electronic bill presentment and payment A sub-industry is springing up to deliver the bills that need to be paid. Electronic bill presentment and payment services are designed to make it easy, even pleasant, for customers to pay their bills online. Consolidators group individuals' accounts with a number of service providers on one site for convenience. Push services also exist, to notify customers by e-mail or on their mobile phone when a bill is ready for payment. Other services provide analysis tools to enable customers to work out the most cost-effective tariffs, based on their actual usage.

The current proliferation of new online payment solutions is fascinating to observe, but a problem for those needing to decide which options to make available to their customers. Expect a shake-out as e-commerce matures.

Anne Querée

EDI abbreviation for ↝ electronic data interchange.

EDIFACT acronym for *electronic data interchange for administration, commerce, and trade*, ISO and ANSI standard system for handling EDI transactions.

editing act of creating, changing, and formatting word processor documents or pages for distribution on the World Wide Web.

EDO RAM abbreviation for *extended data out random-access memory*, faster type of ↝ RAM introduced in the mid-1990s.

edu abbreviation for *educational*, in the Internet's ↝ domain name system (DNS), one of the top-level domains, along with net, gov, org, com, and mil. US-based colleges and universities typically have Internet addresses of the form name.edu.

Educational Resources Information Center database of resources for education available on the Internet. See ↝ ERIC.

edutainment contraction of *education and entertainment*, ↝ multimedia-related term, used to describe computer software that is both educational and entertaining. Examples include educational software for children that teaches them to spell or count while playing games, and ↝ CD-ROMs about machines that contain animations showing how the machines work. Compare ↝ infotainment.

e-envoy UK government post created in 1999 to fulfil the prime minister Tony Blair's promise that Britain would become the best country in the world in which to carry out ↝ electronic commerce, and also to ensure that business leaders understand its importance to their businesses.

The first e-envoy was Alex Allen, formerly UK High Commissioner to Australia, who had worked as a computer consultant before joining the Civil

Service. Allen took up the post in January 2000, responsible directly to the prime minister, but reporting on a day-to-day basis through both the e-minister and the minister for e-government.

EEPROM acronym for *electrically erasable programmable read-only memory*, computer memory that can record data and retain it indefinitely. The data can be erased with an electrical charge and new data recorded.

Some EEPROM must be removed from the computer and erased and reprogrammed using a special device. Other EEPROM, called flash memory, can be erased and reprogrammed without removal from the computer.

EFF abbreviation for ↝ Electronic Frontier Foundation.

EFTPOS acronym for *electronic funds transfer at point of sale*, a form of electronic funds transfer.

EGA abbreviation for *enhanced graphics array*, computer colour display system superior to ↝ CGA (colour graphics adapter), providing 16 colours on screen and a resolution of 640 x 350, but not as good as ↝ VGA.

egg online bank launched in the UK by Prudential plc in October 1998 as an Internet-only bank, offering low-interest-rate savings accounts, mortgages, and personal loans. In September 1999, egg launched a credit card with a very low interest rate, which offered 2% cashback on purchases made over the Internet.

EIS abbreviation for *executive information systems*, software applications that extract information from an organization's computer applications and data files and present the data in a form required by management.

EISA abbreviation for *extended industry standard architecture*, one of several types of ↝ data bus created to improve on the original ISA (industry standard architecture) design introduced with the IBM PC AT microcomputer in 1984. The EISA bus adds speed and capacity because it is a 32-bit bus (ISA is a 16-bit bus), although it can still accept ISA-compatible expansion cards.

The EISA bus was developed by a consortium of PC manufacturers to counter IBM's proprietary MCA (micro channel architecture) bus in 1987, but it has since been superseded by the ↝ PCI (peripheral component interconnect) bus designed by Intel. See also ↝ local bus.

electronic banking system whereby a user can execute banking transactions via a modem, either directly or through an online service or the Internet.

The first bank to offer modem access in the UK was the Royal Bank of Scotland. In 1995, the TSB announced a limited service via CompuServe allowing customers 24-hour access to account statements and current balances.

electronic book or *e-book*, software with or without specialized hardware that provides the equivalent of a book's worth of information. The term is used generally to apply even to simple text files created by scanning printed books or manuals such as those created and archived by ↝ Project Gutenberg.

---

electronic book

http://www.cs.indiana.edu/
metastuff/bookfaq.html

A selection of electronic book available on line.

WEB LINK

Electronic Books

A book by any other name Electronic books, or e-books, are an idea whose time appears to have come at last. For many years, people have toyed with the idea of making books available in electronic form. Indeed, many hundreds of out-of-copyright classics have been collected by the University of Illionis's Project Gutenberg and made available over the Internet. The problem has been that reading books on a PC screen is hard on the eye, while printing out hundreds of pages of text in A4 format is also far from ideal.

In the last few years, however, several companies in the USA have announced plans for handheld e-book readers. NuvoMedia launched its Rocket eBook in late 1998, with SoftBook Press following shortly afterwards with its SoftBook reader. Both Glassbook and Librius, who had originally planned to release their own readers, decided instead to concentrate on software for existing handheld computers, such as those using the Palm and PocketPC operating systems.

The pros and cons of e-books Conventional wisdom is that no-one is going to prefer an e-book to a 'real' book. In fact, electronic books are already with us in the form of encyclopedias on CD-ROM or DVD. The *Encyclopedia Britannica* is no longer available as 32 heavy and bulky volumes: instead, all of its 73,000 articles fit onto one CD-ROM. (Entries can also be viewed free of charge via the Web.) Academic textbooks are another ready market for books in electronic form. WizeUp Digital Textbooks announced in 2000 that it would be offering over 75 digital textbooks in Windows or Macintosh format to more than 50 US universities.

The main advantages of dedicated e-book readers are that many books can be contained in one device, and that the books can be downloaded over the Internet. Against this, the screens of handheld computers are not as easy on the eye as paper pages, although this is being remedied. The devices are not yet light enough or cheap enough, while electronic books themselves are generally still much more expensive than would seem justified with no printing, and low distribution costs. Despite efforts by the Open eBook Forum to develop a standard format for e-books, proprietary formats are still the order of the day.

Dedicated e-book readers In January 2000, both manufacturers of dedicated e-book readers (NuvoMedia and Soft-Book Press) were acquired by Gemstar, a provider of electronic programming guide services for television. In July 2000, Gemstar took over TV Guide, publishers of the USA's best-selling TV programme schedules magazine. In September 2000, Thomson Multimedia was set to introduce its RCA-brand dedicated e-book readers, with both colour and monochrome screens. These second-generation devices incorporate technology licensed from Gemstar-TV Guide.

Although NuvoMedia and SoftBook Press had both signed up to the Open eBook standard format, backed by Microsoft and leading publishers, each company had produced a reader with its own proprietary format for e-books. The two companies had also signed agreements to distribute *Bloomberg News*, *Time*, *Newsweek*, *Fortune*, *Money*, *The New York Times*, *Wall Street Journal*, and the *Washington Post* in electronic form.

Adobe's Portable Document Format In 1993, software supplier Adobe launched its Acrobat program, which generated documents in Portable Document Format (PDF), allowing them to be viewed electronically in their original printed layout. The Acrobat Reader is available free of charge via the Web, through which many PDF documents are available.

At the end of August 2000, Adobe purchased Glassbook, whose Glassbook Reader (also available free of charge) could already read PDF documents. The Glassbook Reader technology will be incorporated into future versions of Acrobat Reader, providing a better user interface, annotation and dictionary look-up features, and a two-page spread. The Glassbook Reader runs under Windows 95/98, NT 4.0, and 2000, the last of these also providing text-to-speech facilities.

Microsoft Reader Microsoft launched its free e-book Reader in May 2000 for the PocketPC operating system and in August 2000 for Windows 95 and higher. The Microsoft Reader includes the company's ClearType technology, which improves the appearance of text on a screen. ClearType is aimed in particular at improving the clarity of text on a liquid-crystal display (LCD) screen.

Barnes & Noble's Web site carries e-books (some free of charge) for the Microsoft and Glassbook Readers, as well as for NuvoMedia's Rocket eBook. Amazon.com announced at the end of August 2000 that it too would set up a special store on its site to sell e-books in the Microsoft Reader format, while Microsoft promised a special version of its Reader that would connect directly to Amazon's new store.

Librius Reader software from Librius at its Books2Read Web site is available for handheld devices running the Palm and PocketPC operating systems, with versions for Windows, Epoc/Symbian, MacOS, and Linux planned. The Librius Reader is also available free of charge.

Better screen displays Microsoft's ClearType font technology is already available, offering a better display for LCD screens. Adobe plans to include its similar CoolType in future releases of its Acrobat Reader. Kent Display Systems have been developing cholesteric LCD screens, which it is claimed will be as easy to read in bright sunlight as paper is. A similar technology is Xerox's 'electronic paper', which Xerox announced mid-1999 would be manufactured by 3M.

Publishing issues The major publishing conglomerates Random House, Penguin Putnam, Time Warner, HarperCollins, and Simon & Schuster are keen to embrace electronic publishing, and are members of the Open eBook Forum. This is hardly surprising, as publishers' costs will decrease substantially when the e-book format becomes more popular. In 2000, horror writer Stephen King self-published from his own Web site chapters from a novel, *The Plant*, bypassing his publisher and conventional booksellers. Thriller writer Frederick Forsyth followed suit later in the year with 'The Veteran', the first in a series of five new short stories released exclusively on the Internet by e-book publisher Online Originals.

It seems unlikely, however, that the majority of authors will be able to manage without a publisher or some sales via bricks-and-mortar booksellers. Although many authors are self-publishing books on the Web, these are generally books that have failed to find a conventional publisher, and the standard of their content is therefore likely to fall well below that of paper books. Also, just as new Web sites need considerable marketing to stand out from the millions of others, so Web users will not be aware of new e-books by unknown authors.

Although e-books may not completely replace paper books for some time, there can be no doubt that sales of conventional books will be affected considerably. Some commentators liken the arrival of e-books to that of television, which did not mean the end of films, radio, or newspapers. Nevertheless, television did considerably reduce the importance of the other three media.

Television was a completely new medium, however, and it might therefore be relevant to look at the case of recorded music, where 78-rpm discs were replaced by 45-rpm singles and 33-rpm albums in vinyl. These were in turn replaced by cassette tapes and compact discs (CDs), which may eventually be superseded by a combination of digital versatile discs (DVDs), mini discs, and MP3-encoded tracks on a PC's hard disk. Similarly, e-books are not a new medium, but rather the latest means of distribution. After all, printed books were preceded by manuscripts, which superseded clay tablets.

Alan Stewart

In October 1998, US company NuvoMedia launched a handheld reader for electronic books, which could store around ten novels. This was followed by a similar device from SoftBook Press. To avoid a standards war, these companies, many leading publishers, Microsoft, Adobe, and others formed a working party to develop an ↪ Open eBook standard.

Electronic Book Exchange *EBX*, standard for copyright protection for ↪ electronic books, based on the ↪ World Intellectual Property Organization copyright treaty. The driving force behind EBX is Glassbook, a US electronic book software company. Members and associates of the group include ↪ Adobe, HarperCollins, Houghton Mifflin, ↪ Microsoft, and Philips Electronics.

electronic business or *e-business*, integration of the Internet into all aspects of an organization's business, thus transforming it. E-business should not be confused with ↪ electronic commerce. ↪ IBM was one of the first companies to make wide use of the term e-business.

electronic cash see ↪ e-cash.

electronic commerce business-to-business use of networks such as the Internet to handle legally binding transactions. Traditionally, electronic commerce has required expensive membership of an electronic data interchange (EDI) service. In the mid-1990s, electronic commerce began to shift to the Internet to take advantage of its global reach and inexpensive connections. Many legal issues remain to be resolved, including taxation and encryption.

Electronic Communications Privacy Act US law passed in 1986 that protects the privacy of e-mail and other electronic communications.

electronic conferencing public discussions conducted on an online service or via ↪ Usenet; any participant may log in at any time and read the collected messages and add new ones.

Because of its time-independent, many-to-many nature, electronic conferencing can be used to provide some of the same functions as real-life meetings, classrooms, and unstructured socializing without requiring the participants to meet face-to-face. While electronic conferencing is no substitute for live interaction, it does allow people who are widely geographically separated or who might otherwise never meet to exchange ideas.

electronic data interchange *EDI*, system for managing business-to-business transactions such as invoicing and ordering to eliminate the wastefulness of paper-based transaction systems.

Traditionally, most EDI systems relied on proprietary protocols and private data networks, with the disadvantages that individual systems were incompatible. The growth of the Internet is now opening the way for the rapid adoption of global electronic commerce.

Electronic Frontier Foundation *EFF*, US organization that lobbies for the extension of civil liberties and constitutional rights into ↪ cyberspace. It was founded by former Grateful Dead lyricist John Perry Barlow and Lotus founder Mitchell ↪ Kapor in 1991 after a series of US raids on suspected computer hackers. Its offices are in San Francisco.

E-Commerce

Introduction The Internet has the potential to be the biggest revolution in world commerce since the invention of money. There are more than half a billion companies out there, trying to sell us everything from cars to garden gnomes. Beside the Internet, the advent of the credit card, the supermarket, and the single European currency may be no more than footnotes on the balance sheet of history. It is difficult not to lapse into hyperbole when discussing Internet commerce (otherwise known as electronic commerce, or e-commerce for short). Sober-suited business analysts make amazing predictions. Mighty corporations jostle for our attention on the World Wide Web with animated gimmicks and unbeatable offers. Politicians hold high-level powwows and pretend to understand it all (though really they are trying to work out how to tax it).

A brief history A few years ago the Internet was all promise and hot air. Early attempts at virtual shopping malls attracted much interest from the chattering classes, but sold virtually nothing. The few enterprising souls who did try to buy online were often disappointed, finding that choice was limited, or that they had to log off and place their orders by phone or fax. More recently, things appeared to be looking up. Virtual bookstores opened, offering lower prices and more stock than conventional shops; they even claimed to get to know their customers and to lead them to titles that they thought would interest them. Personal computer (PC) manufacturers allowed people to design their own PCs online and have them delivered to their door within days. Banks let customers check account balances and transfer funds from the comfort of their home PCs. But it emerged that many Internet start-up firms made no profits, and that many PC buyers were window shopping on the Internet but ordering by phone. And the queues at the banks did not get much shorter, since only a minority of customers had logged on to virtual branches. According to the research firm Verdict, British consumers spent just £581 million via e-commerce in 1999. The most popular purchases included books, music, videos, and computer software. Consumer sales are projected to rise to £7.4 billion a year by 2004. This sounds impressive, but it would only represent about 3% of the UK's total retail sales. None of this is very surprising. Telephones had been around for generations before they carried significant amounts of trade. Hole-in-the-wall cash machines were largely ignored for a decade, until customers came to trust them. It would be naive to expect people suddenly to part with billions of pounds via a medium many of them had never even heard of five years ago.

Drawbacks of e-commerce The potential drawbacks of buying and selling on the Internet are obvious to all but its most diehard adherents. Customers cannot handle the goods, as they can in a shop. They must pay for the privilege in telephone charges, whereas catalogues are (usually) free. They may have to trust that a company they have never heard of, possibly overseas, will supply the goods they have ordered within a reasonable time and in good condition; that it will offer after-sales support if necessary, or take goods back if unwanted or damaged; and that it will take good care of their credit card number, not misusing it or allowing it to be intercepted by fraudsters.

Advantages of 'click' businesses And yet e-commerce makes good economic sense. A distinction is increasingly being drawn in commerce between 'click' and 'brick' businesses. Conventional brick businesses rely on physical shops, offices, and so on to reach their customers and house their staff. Click businesses (the term is derived from clicking with a computer mouse) operate mostly online, often with small or no physical premises. In their most extreme form, they contract out all their physical processes, including making, storing, and despatching the actual products, leaving little more than a Web site and a PO box number. A click business could literally be run from a spare bedroom. Click businesses incur only a fraction of the costs involved in maintaining and stocking conventional retail outlets. They can sell to markets, overseas or within their own countries that they would otherwise lack the resources to reach. They can establish relationships with customers by soliciting personal information and observing buying

E-Commerce (continued)

patterns, which would be much more difficult in a big store. Customers benefit by being able to shop, bank, or renew their insurance from home or the office, day or night. They can compare prices and garner product information without tramping from shop to shop. They can consult impartial buying advice, from magazines, user groups, and the like. And they can often benefit from lower prices and a wider choice, as electronic traders strive to differentiate themselves from more established competitors, and intermediaries such as eBay, QXL, and Priceline run online auctions or invite consumers to name their own price. Even the weekly trudge round the supermarket can be replaced by Internet ordering, as customers send in their shopping list via the Internet and have the goods delivered for a small additional charge.

Security concerns Concerns about security are understandable, but largely unfounded. Quoting your credit card number online may be no more risky than giving it over the telephone, or handing your card to a waiter in a restaurant. UK consumer credit laws also apply online, so holders of personal credit cards are given some protection by the credit card company if the goods are faulty or fail to arrive, as long as the transaction is worth more than a certain amount and takes place in the UK. It is important that the vendor uses an appropriate 'encryption' (encoding) standard, and no one should buy online without ensuring that this is the case – for example by checking that the vendor uses the Secure Electronic Transactions (SET) system or a secure intermediary, such as NetBanx, or that it displays the logo of an independent vetting service such as WebTrust.

The wider business picture E-commerce is not just about physical goods. In fact, as a virtual medium it is better suited to 'virtual' products like insurance policies, share trading, or information services – not to mention pornography, one of the early success stories of e-commerce. Airlines can sell 'tickets' without issuing pieces of paper, by instead giving the passenger an authorization code that can be quoted at the check-in desk. Music publishers can sell tracks or whole albums without manufacturing CDs, by allowing customers to download them from Web sites for a fee. Nor is the Web just about consumer sales. There are even bigger opportunities in business-to-business sales. Large corporations such as General Electric, Cisco, and Microsoft are already making big savings in time and money by procuring raw materials, manufactured goods, or services via the Web – either seeking out the best deals around the world, or inviting tenders.

Effects of e-commerce E-commerce will have a profound effect on us all. Some of us will lose our jobs or see our shareholdings dwindle as some firms miss the electronic boat. Others will strike it rich as start-up businesses can compete on equal terms with multinationals. Some of us will see our lifestyles change as we have access to an undreamed-of variety of goods and services. We will all become the targets of 'micromarketing' campaigns – a carefully personalized mix of offers and e-mails designed to appeal to our individual tastes, as revealed by our previous purchases or even the products we have glanced at on the vendor's Web site. Nobody knows when e-commerce will hit the big time – two years, five years, ten years maybe. But when it does, the impetus of a market with limited costs and limitless reach – what *Business Week* magazine described as 'frictionless capitalism' – will be almost impossible to stop.

Paul Bray

electronic mail or *e-mail*, messages sent electronically from computer to computer via network connections such as ⟿ Ethernet or the ⟿ Internet, or via telephone lines to a host system. Messages once sent are stored on the network or by the host system until the recipient picks them up. As well as text, messages may contain enclosed text files, artwork, or multimedia clips.

Subscribers to an electronic mail system type messages in ordinary letter form on a word processor, or microcomputer, and 'drop' the letters into a central computer's memory bank by means of a computer/telephone connector (a ⌐ modem). The recipient 'collects' the letter by calling up the central computer and feeding a unique password into the system. Due to the high speed of delivery electronic mail is cheaper than an equivalent telephone call or fax.

The US Supreme Court ruled in April 1999 that a federal law criminalizing the transmission of e-mails that are 'obscene, lewd, or indecent' did not compromise the right to free speech.

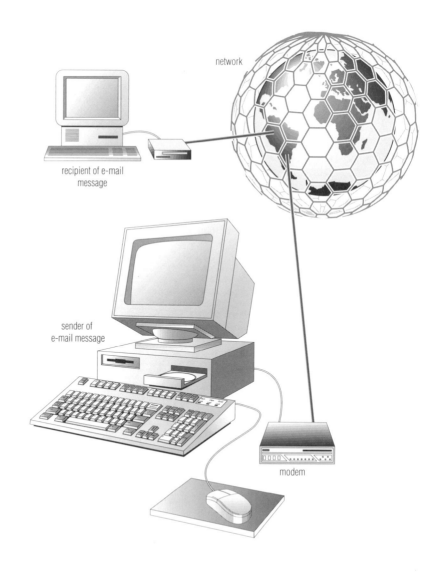

network

recipient of e-mail
message

sender of
e-mail message

modem

e-mail system
The basic structure of an electronic mail system. A message is sent via a telephone line and stored in a central computer. The message remains there until the recipient calls up the central computer and collects the message.

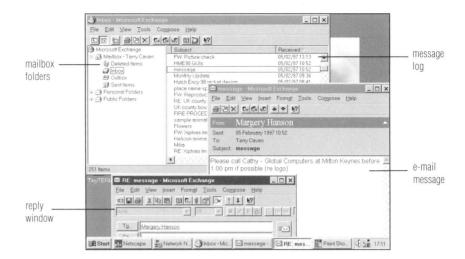

mailbox folders

message log

reply window

e-mail message

e-mail
A typical e-mail user interface. Because messages can be created 'off-line' and are sent at high speed, line connection time, and therefore costs, can be kept to a minimum.

electronic marketplace or *e-marketplace*, business-to-business ⤳ electronic commerce site. E-marketplaces are often closed communities or industry trading groups, such as AutoXchange (set up by car manufacturers Ford, General Motors, and Chrysler) and GlobalNetXchange (set up by major retailers Sears of the USA, Sainsbury of the UK, Metro of Germany, and Carrefour of France).

electronic publishing distribution of information using computer-based media such as ⤳ multimedia and ⤳ hypertext in the creation of electronic 'books'. Critical technologies in the development of electronic publishing were ⤳ CD-ROM, with its massive yet compact storage capabilities, and the advent of computer networking with its ability to deliver information instantaneously anywhere in the world.

Ellison, Larry (Lawrence) (1944–) US computer entrepreneur, who founded ⤳ Oracle, of which he is chairman and chief executive, in 1977. Ellison also sits on the boards of ⤳ Apple (a company he once considered taking over along with his friend Steve ⤳ Jobs) and the Dian Fossey Gorilla Fund.

Ellison has received many awards and honours, including Entrepreneur of the Year from the Harvard Business School. In May 2000, Ellison's wealth was estimated by the US financial magazine *Forbes* at $47 billion, making him the second richest person in the world, after his arch-rival Bill ⤳ Gates.

In addition to his business success, Ellison is a world sailing champion, but was almost killed by a hurricane during the Sydney-to-Hobart race in December 1998. He also pilots a private jet.

EMACS or, more properly, *GNU EMACS*, heavyweight ⤳ text editor used mainly by Unix hackers. The name is derived from Editing Macros, but is humorously, and recursively, said to stand for EMACS Makes A Computer Slow. EMACS was written by Richard Stallman at the MIT AI Lab and is published as public-domain software; EMACS was created by the US ⮑ Free Software Foundation.

e-mail abbreviation for ⮑ electronic mail.

emoticon contraction of emotion and icon, symbol composed of punctuation marks designed to express some form of emotion in the form of a human face. Emoticons were invented by ⮑ e-mail users to overcome the fact that communication using text only cannot convey nonverbal information (body language or vocal intonation) used in ordinary speech.

The following examples should be viewed sideways:

:-) smiling
:-O shouting
:-(glum
8-) wearing glasses and smiling.

EMS abbreviation for ⮑ expanded memory specification.

emulator item of software or firmware that allows one device to imitate the functioning of another. Emulator software is commonly used to allow one make of computer to run programs written for a different make of computer. This allows a user to select from a wider range of ⮑ applications programs, and perhaps to save money by running programs designed for an expensive computer on a cheaper model.

Many printers contain emulator firmware that enables them to imitate Hewlett Packard and Epson printers, because so much software is written to work with these widely used machines.

encapsulate term used to describe the technique that uses one ⮑ protocol as an envelope for another for transmission across a network.

encapsulated PostScript *EPS*, computer graphics file format used by the ⮑ PostScript page-description language. It is essentially a PostScript file with a special structure designed for use by other applications.

encryption encoding a message so that it can only be read by the intended recipient. See ⮑ cryptography.

end user user of a computer program; in particular, someone who uses a program to perform a task (such as accounting or playing a computer game), rather than someone who writes programs (a programmer).

Energy Star US programme requiring all computer equipment to conserve electrical power. Key features of Energy Star-compliant hardware include a built-in function to put the computer and monitor into suspended animation after a specified period of disuse and limits on the amount of power computers and printers can draw.

Energy Star

http://www.epa.gov/
appdstar/estar/
products.html

A list of Energy Star-compliant products is available at their Web site.

WEB LINK

Emoticon	Interpretation
:-)	happy
:)	
:->	
: >	
:-(	sad
: (	
:-<	
: <	
;-)	winking
;)	
;->	
; >	
:-t	cross, angry
~:-(	
:-I	indifferent
:-o	surprised, amazed, shocked
8-0	
:-D	laughing
:,-(	crying
:'-(	
;-(	
8-I	in suspense
I-I	asleep (bored)
:-&	tongue-tied
:-#	lips are sealed
:-x	
:-\	undecided
:-/	sceptical
:-P	poking tongue out
$-)	greedy
>:-)	devilish
>:->	
>;-)	
>;->	
0:-)	angelic
<:-)	dunce (stupid question?)
<:-#	smiling with beard
8-)	smiling with glasses
8)	
8->	
8 >	
(-:	left-handed, Australian
:-*	kiss
:-X	
(8(I)	Homer Simpson
@ @ @ @8 (I)	Marge Simpson

Electronic Communications: Emoticons
An emoticon or 'smiley' is a symbol designed to communicate emotion in text using punctuation marks and other symbols. Most emoticons take the form of a human face and should be viewed sideways. Below is a selection of some of the growing number of emoticons now in use online.

Engelbart, Douglas C (1925–) US computer engineer. He invented the mouse and created the first two-dimensional editing system. He was also the first to demonstrate the use of mixed text-graphics and shared-screen viewing and founded the Bootstrap Project at Stanford University.

Born in Portland, Oregon, Engelbart served in the US Navy during World War II, and later studied and taught at the University of California at Berkeley. In 1956 he moved to the Stanford Research Institute where he launched the SRI Augmentation Research Centre. In 1968 he gave a demonstration of a mouse-operated hypertext system that inspired later research at Xerox's PARC (Palo Alto Research Centre). Xerox's work led on to the Apple Macintosh and Microsoft's Windows interface.

engine core piece of software around which other features and functions are built. A database ⇝ search engine, for example, accepts user input and handles the processing necessary to find matches between the user input and the database records.

In a computer game, the term 'engine' is also used to refer to the core software that allows users to move around the game's levels and pick up weapons and treasure.

enterprise computing trade jargon for the market represented by large corporations, especially the ones with mainframe data centres. Enterprise computing strategies, which deal with hundreds of servers and thousands of personal computers and terminals, have to consider questions of reliability and ⇝ scalability that do not concern personal computer users and small businesses.

enterprise resource planning *ERP*, integrated ⇝ database and ⇝ applications, covering accounting and billing, production scheduling, logistics, human resources, and customer services.

Software companies providing ERP systems include the Dutch firm Baan, SAP of Germany, and the US companies Oracle, J D Edwards, and PeopleSoft. As well as Web-enabling their systems, ERP vendors are extending them into ⇝ customer relationship management and supply chain planning, in some cases through partnerships with suppliers in those areas.

EPOC operating system designed for use in electronic organizers such as the Psion Series 3 and Series 5 handheld computers, in mobile phones, and in other ⇝ wireless information devices. EPOC is licensed by Symbian, a company founded in 1998 by Psion and mobile telephony suppliers Nokia and Ericsson.

EPROM acronym for *erasable programmable read-only memory*, computer memory device in the form of an ⇝ integrated circuit (chip) that can record data and retain it indefinitely. The data can be erased by exposure to ultraviolet light, and new data recorded. Other kinds of computer memory chips are ⇝ ROM (read-only memory), ⇝ PROM (programmable read-only memory), and ⇝ RAM (random-access memory).

EPS abbreviation for ⇝ encapsulated PostScript.

erasable optical disk another name for a ⇝ floptical disk.

TIP

ergonomics

Ergonomics advice: maintain good posture and a straight wrist level at your computer; and take regular breaks from your screen – ideally every 30 minutes.

ergonomics study of the relationship between people and the furniture, tools, and machinery they use at work. The object is to improve work performance by removing sources of muscular stress and general fatigue: for example, by presenting data and control panels in easy-to-view form, making office furniture comfortable, and creating a generally pleasant environment.

Good ergonomic design makes computer systems easier to use and minimizes the health hazards and physical stresses of working with computers for many hours a day: it helps data entry workers to avoid conditions like ↝ repetitive strain injury (RSI), eyestrain, and back and muscle aches.

In Europe, many measures intended to protect workers were introduced in the 1992 Ergonomics Directive, which in Britain is enforced by the Health and Safety Executive.

ERIC abbreviation for *Educational Resources Information Center*, database of resources for education available on the Internet. Established in 1966, ERIC is a federally funded network of educational information. Sixteen clearing houses index educational materials for the database, which is housed at the University of Saskatchewan, Canada. The database is distributed in a variety of formats including printed books, CD-ROM, and microfiche.

ERNIE acronym for *electronic random number indicator*, machine designed and produced by the UK Post Office Research Station to select a series of random 9-figure numbers to indicate prizewinners among Premium Bond holders.

error fault or mistake, either in the software or on the part of the user, that causes a program to stop running (crash) or produce unexpected results. Program errors, or bugs, are largely eliminated in the course of the programmer's initial testing procedure, but some will remain in most programs. All computer operating systems are designed to produce an error message (on the display screen, or in an error file or printout) whenever an error is detected, reporting that an error has taken place and, wherever possible, diagnosing its cause.

Errors can be categorized into several types:

syntax errors are caused by the incorrect use of the programming language, and include spelling and keying mistakes. These errors are detected when the ↝ compiler or ↝ interpreter fails to translate the program into machine code (instructions that a computer can understand directly); *logical errors* are faults in the program design – for example, in the order of instructions. They may cause a program to respond incorrectly to the user's requests or to crash completely; *execution errors*, or *run-time errors*, are caused by combinations of data that the programmer did not anticipate. A typical execution error is caused by attempting to divide a number by zero. This is impossible, and so the program stops running at this point. Execution errors occur only when a program is running, and cannot be detected by a compiler or interpreter.

Computers are designed to deal with a set range of numbers to a given range of accuracy. Many errors are caused by these limitations: *overflow error* occurs when a number is too large for the computer to deal with; an *underflow error* occurs when a number is too small; *rounding* and *truncation errors* are caused by the need to round off decimal numbers, or to cut them off (truncate them) after the maximum number of decimal places allowed by the computer's level of accuracy.

error detection techniques that enable a program to detect incorrect data. A common method is to add a check digit to important codes, such as account numbers and product codes. The digit is chosen so that the code conforms to a rule that the program can verify. Another technique involves calculating the sum (called the ↪ hash total) of each instance of a particular item of data, and storing it at the end of the data.

error message message produced by a computer to inform the user that an error has occurred.

escape sequence string of characters sent to a ↪ modem to switch it from sending data to a state in which it can accept and act upon commands.

Most modems use the escape sequence patented by Hayes, which consists of three plus signs (+++) with a brief pause on either side to distinguish the characters from data.

ESPRIT abbreviation for *European Strategic Programme for Research and Development in Information Technology*, European Union programme that funds technology research at an early stage of development. ESPRIT's goals include encouraging the development of international standards and cooperation between European companies, universities, and research centres in order to develop the infrastructure necessary for Europe to be able to compete with Japan and the USA.

Ethernet most popular protocol for ↪ local area networks. Ethernet was developed principally by the Xerox Corporation, but can now be used on most computers. It normally allows data transfer at rates of up to 10 Mbps, but 100-Mbps Fast Ethernet – often called 100Base-T – is already in widespread use while the first product versions are now available of 1,000-Mbps Gigabit Ethernet.

Ethernet, Fast Ethernet, and Gigabit Ethernet are all IEEE standards.

Eudora popular program for handling and receiving Internet e-mail. Published by the Californian company Qualcomm, Eudora uses ↪ POP3, and by the mid-1990s was one of the most commonly used e-mail programs on the Net.

European Strategic Programme for Research and Development in Information Technology full name for ↪ ESPRIT.

event-driven computer system that does not do anything until events are detected, such as mouse-clicks. Microsoft Windows is an event-driven operating environment.

Gigabit Ethernet Alliance

http://www.gigabit-ethernet.org/

This site, aimed at technical readers, describes the technology and developments behind the world's fastest Internet networking tool, the Gigabit Ethernet.

WEB LINK

Excel ↝ spreadsheet program produced by ↝ Microsoft in 1985. Versions are available for PC-compatibles running ↝ Windows and for the Apple Macintosh. Excel pioneered many advanced features in the ease of use of spreadsheets, and has displaced ↝ Lotus 1-2-3 as the standard spreadsheet program.

executable file file – always a program of some kind – that can be run by the computer directly. The file will have been generated from a ↝ source program by an ↝ assembler or ↝ compiler. It will therefore not be coded in ↝ ASCII and will not be readable as text. On ↝ MS-DOS systems executable files have an .EXE or .COM extension.

expanded memory additional memory in an ↝ MS-DOS-based computer, usually installed on an expanded-memory board. Expanded memory requires an expanded-memory manager, which gives access to a limited amount of memory at any one time, and is slower to use than ↝ extended memory. Software is available under both MS-DOS and ↝ Windows to simulate expanded memory for those applications that require it.

expansion board or *expansion card*, printed circuit board that can be inserted into a computer in order to enhance its capabilities (for example, to increase its memory) or to add facilities (such as graphics).

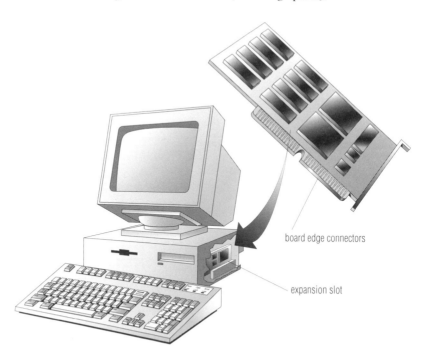

board edge connectors

expansion slot

expansion board
An expansion board may be fitted into any free expansion slot in a computer to provide additional facilities or functionality.

expert system computer program for giving advice (such as diagnosing an illness or interpreting the law) that incorporates knowledge derived from human expertise. A kind of ↝ knowledge-based system, it contains rules that can be applied to find the solution to a problem. It is a form of ◞ artificial intelligence.

expire function for removing old Usenet articles from an off-line reader program. Sometimes also called 'prune' or 'purge', this function is necessary to make room for new articles.

export file file stored by the computer in a standard format so that it can be accessed by other programs, possibly running on different makes of computer.

For example, a word-processing program running on an Apple ◞ Macintosh computer may have a facility to save a file on a floppy disk in a format that can be read by a word-processing program running on an IBM PC-compatible computer. When the file is being read by the second program or computer, it is often referred to as an import file.

extended character set in PC-based computing, the set of 254 characters stored in ◞ ROM. Besides the 128 ◞ ASCII characters, the set includes block graphics and foreign language characters.

extended memory memory in an ◞ MS-DOS-based system that exceeds the 1 Mbyte that DOS supports. Extended memory is not accessible to the ◞ operating system and requires an extended memory manager.

external modem ◞ modem that is a self-contained unit sitting outside a personal computer (PC) and connected to it by a cable. There are two main types of external modem: mains-powered desktop modems and credit-card sized modems that fit the PCMCIA slots in notebook and handheld computers.

External modems have the advantage over internal ones in that they are easy to move from computer to computer as needed. However, high-speed modems outstrip the capabilities of the serial ports on older and cheaper PCs by taking in data too fast for the computer to be able to read it.

extranet corporate ◞ intranet that has been extended beyond the usual company boundaries to include major customers or suppliers.

extruded shape in computer graphics, a three-dimensional shape created by extending a two-dimensional shape along a third dimension.

e-zine contraction of *electronic magazine*, periodical sent by ◞ e-mail. E-zines can be produced very cheaply, as there are no production costs for design and layout, and minimal costs for distribution. Like printed magazines, e-zines typically have multiple contributors and an editor responsible for selecting content.

One of the best-known e-zines is the ◞ *Computer Underground Digest*, which tracks battles over freedom of speech online and issues concerning hacking and computer crime.

TIP

external modem

Before attaching a high-speed modem to a PC, check that it has a 16550 UART; if it does not, consider getting an internal modem with one built in, or install an expansion card with a high-speed serial port on it.

F1 on personal computers (PCs), the key to access ⮑ online help.

FAQ abbreviation for *frequently asked questions*, file of answers to commonly asked questions on any topic. First used on Usenet, where regular posters to ⮑ newsgroups got tired of answering the same questions over and over and wrote these information files to end the repetition. By 1996 FAQ was a common term for any information file, on line or off line.

FAT abbreviation for ⮑ file allocation table.

fault tolerance general term given to technologies or techniques employed to make a computer system more tolerant of faults. Typically, fault tolerant computers will have some of their ⮑ hardware duplicated, so that if one component fails, the duplicate can take over straight away without the computer having to be shut down. Computers that are highly fault tolerant are very expensive and difficult to design, but are necessary for systems like nuclear power station control systems, and aircraft control systems, where safety is crucial.

favourites menu option on Microsoft's Internet Explorer Web browser that allows users to go quickly to sites that have been bookmarked, as with the ⮑ bookmarks feature in Netscape Navigator. The access software for the AOL and CompuServe online services uses Favourite Places to provide the same feature.

fax or *facsimile transmission* or *telefax*, transmission of images over a telecommunications link, usually the telephone network. When placed on a fax machine, the original image is scanned by a transmitting device and converted into coded signals, which travel via the telephone lines to the receiving fax machine, where an image is created that is a copy of the original. Photographs as well as printed text and drawings can be sent. The standard transmission takes place at 4,800 or 9,600 bits of information per second.

The world's first fax machine, the *pantélégraphe*, was invented by Italian physicist Giovanni Caselli in 1866, over a century before the first electronic model came on the market. Standing over 2 m/6.5 ft high, it transmitted by telegraph nearly 5,000 handwritten documents and drawings between Paris and Lyon in its first year.

fax modem ⮑ modem capable of transmitting and receiving data in the form of a fax.

A normal fax machine sends data in binary form down a telephone line, in a similar way to a modem. A modem can therefore act as a fax machine, given suitable software. This means a document does not need to be printed before faxing and an incoming fax can be viewed before printing out on a plain-paper printer. However, the computer must be permanently turned on in order to receive faxes.

A separate ⮑ scanner is needed to fax information created outside the computer (such as a picture).

FAQs about FAQs

http://www.faqs.org/faqs/faqs/about-faqs/

'Frequently Asked Questions' (FAQ) are part of many Web sites and consist of a series of questions and answers. This FAQ answers questions about FAQs themselves and contains information on what FAQs are, how to write one, and how to put it on the Internet.

WEB LINK

How Can I Send a Fax From the Internet?

http://www.savetz.com/fax/

Tutorial for sending faxes from the Internet. It clearly explains the requirements for sending faxes, and points you to Web sites that allow you to fax over the Internet for free.

WEB LINK

FDDI abbreviation for *fibre-optic digital device interface*, series of network protocols, developed by the ⮎ American National Standards Institute, concerned with high-speed networks using ⮎ fibre optic cable.

FDDI supports data transmission rates of up to 100 Mb per second and is being introduced in many sites as a replacement for ⮎ Ethernet. FDDI not only makes possible transmission of large amounts of data, for example colour pictures, but also allows the transmission of voice and video data. See also ⮎ optical fibres.

feedback general principle whereby the results produced in an ongoing reaction become factors in modifying or changing the reaction; it is the principle used in self-regulating control systems, from a simple thermostat and steam-engine governor to automatic computer-controlled machine tools. A fully computerized control system, in which there is no operator intervention, is called a closed-loop feedback system. A system that also responds to control signals from an operator is called an open-loop feedback system.

In self-regulating systems, information about what *is* happening in a system (such as level of temperature, engine speed, or size of workpiece) is fed back to a controlling device, which compares it with what *should* be happening. If the two are different, the device takes suitable action (such as switching on a heater, allowing more steam to the engine, or resetting the tools). The idea that the Earth is a self-regulating system, with feedback operating to keep nature in balance, is a central feature of the Gaia hypothesis.

fetch-execute cycle or *processing cycle*, two-phase cycle used by the computer's central processing unit to process the instructions in a program. During the fetch phase, the next program instruction is transferred from the computer's immediate-access memory to the instruction register (memory location used to hold the instruction while it is being executed). During the execute phase, the instruction is decoded and obeyed. The process is repeated in a continuous loop.

fibre channel high-speed serial communications system designed to enable computers to be connected to other computers or to high-capacity storage devices using fibreoptic cable. The most common version, Fibre Channel Arbitrated Loop (FC-AL), is expected to replace ⮎ SCSI. Fibre channel has also been adapted for use over copper cables.

fibre optics branch of physics dealing with the transmission of light and images through glass or plastic fibres known as ⮎ optical fibres.

field specific item of data. A field is usually part of a record, which in turn is part of a ⮎ file.

field-length check ⮎ validation check in which the characters in an input field are counted to ensure that the correct number of characters have been entered. For example, a six-figure date field may be checked to ensure that it does contain exactly six digits.

Fibre Optic Chronology

http://www.sff.net/people/ Jeff.Hecht/Chron.html

Timeline of the history of fibre optics. Starting with the discovery of glass in around 2500 BC and leading up to the late 1970s, this site details every discovery relevant to the history of the fibre optic cables which, among other things, make the Internet possible.

WEB LINK

fifth-generation computer anticipated new type of computer based on emerging microelectronic technologies with high computing speeds and ⌣ parallel processing. The development of very large-scale integration (⌣ VLSI) technology, which can put many more circuits on to an integrated circuit (chip) than is currently possible, and developments in computer hardware and software design may produce computers far more powerful than those in current use.

It has been predicted that such a computer will be able to communicate in natural spoken language with its user; store vast knowledge databases; search rapidly through these databases, making intelligent inferences and drawing logical conclusions; and process images and 'see' objects in the way that humans do.

In 1981 Japan's Ministry of International Trade and Industry launched a ten-year project to build the first fifth-generation computer, the 'parallel inference machine', consisting of over a thousand microprocessors operating in parallel with each other. By 1992, however, the project was behind schedule and had only produced 256-processor modules. It has since been suggested that research into other technologies, such as ⌣ neural networks, may present more promising approaches to artificial intelligence. Compare earlier ⌣ computer generations.

file collection of data or a program stored in a computer's external memory (for example, on ⌣ disk). It might include anything from information on a company's employees to a program for an adventure game. Serial (or sequential) access files hold information as a sequence of characters, so that, to read any particular item of data, the program must read all those that precede it. Random-access (or direct access) files allow the required data to be reached directly. Files are usually located via a ⌣ directory.

⌣ Database files usually consist of a set of records, each having a number of fields for specific items of data. For example, the data file for a class of schoolchildren might have a record for each child, with five fields of data in each record, storing: (1) family name; (2) first name; (3) house name or number; (4) street name; (5) town. To find out, for example, which children live in the same street, one would look in field 4.

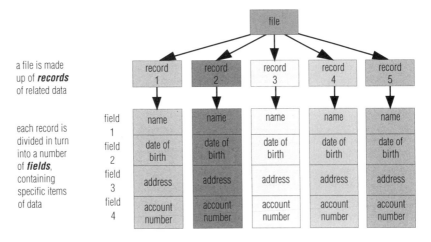

a file is made up of **records** of related data

each record is divided in turn into a number of **fields**, containing specific items of data

file
The file structure of a simple accounting system which stores the name, date of birth, address, and account number of each client.

file access way in which the records in a file are stored, retrieved, or updated by computer. There are four main types of file organization, each of which allows a different form of access to the records.

Records in a *serial file* are not stored in any particular order, so a specific record can be accessed only by reading through all the previous records.

Records in a *sequential file* are sorted by reference to a key field (see ⤳ sorting) and the computer can use a searching technique, such as a binary search, to access a specific record.

An *indexed sequential file* possesses an index that records the position of each block of records and is created and updated with that file. By consulting the index, the computer can obtain the address of the block containing the required record, and search just that block rather than the whole file.

A *direct-access* or *random-access file* contains records that can be accessed directly by the computer.

file allocation table *FAT*, table used by the operating system to record the physical arrangement of files on disk. As a result of ⤳ fragmentation, files can be split into many parts sited at different places on the disk.

file extension last three letters of a file name in DOS or Windows, which indicate the type of data the file contains. Extensions in common use include .TXT for 'text', .GIF for 'graphics interchange format', and .EXE for 'executable'.

In Windows, the operating system may be configured to associate specific file extensions with specific programs, so that double-clicking on a file name starts the right program and opens the file for editing.

file format specific way data is stored in a file. Most computer programs use proprietary file formats which cannot be read by other programs. As this is inconvenient for users, in recent years software publishers have developed filters which convert older file formats into the ones the program in use can read.

Often ⤳ file extensions are used to indicate which program was used to create a particular file. Some formats, such as ⤳ GIF (graphics interchange format), have become so popular and widely used that they are supported by many programs.

Before transmitting data over a public network to another user, it is important to check that the receiving user can read the format the data is in. For this purpose, the most commonly readable format is plain ⤳ ASCII for text and either GIF or ⤳ JPEG (Joint Photographic Experts Group) for graphics.

file generation specific version of a file. When ⤳ file updating takes place, a new generation of the file is created, containing accurate, up-to-date information. The old generation of the file will often be stored to provide ⤳ data security in the event that the new generation of the file is lost or damaged.

Extension	Type of data	Extension	Type of data
AI	Adobe Illustrator vector graphics	JPG	Joint Photographic Experts Group bitmap image
ANI	animation (various packages)	LIB	library file
ASM	assembly source code	MAC	MacPaint bitmap graphics
ASP	Active Server Page	MDB	Access database
AVI	Audio Video Interleaved animation	MID	MIDI audio
		MOV	QuickTime movie
BAK	backup file	MPG, MPEG	MPEG movie
BAS	BASIC source code	PAS	PASCAL source code
BAT	DOS batch file	PCX	Paintbrush bitmap image
BMP	Windows bitmap image	PIC	bitmap image (various packages)
C	C source code		
CDR	CorelDraw graphics	PL	Perl source code
CGI	Common Gateway Interface script	PNG	Portable Network Graphics bitmap image
COB	COBOL source code	PPT	Microsoft PowerPoint presentation
CLP	Windows clipboard		
COM	Executable program	PS	PostScript text/graphics
CPP	C++ source code	PUB	Microsoft Publisher page template
CSV	comma-separated text		
CUR	cursor	RA, RAM	RealAudio sound
DAT	data	RTF	Rich Text Format text
DIR	Macromedia Director movie	SGM(L)	Standard Generalized Markup Language document
DLL	dynamic link library		
DOC	word-processed document	SIT	STUFFIT compressed file for Macintosh
DOT	Microsoft Word document template		
		SYS	system file
DRV	device driver	TAR	compressed file
DTD	Document Type Definition for SGML document	TGA	Targa bitmap image
		TIF(F)	Tagged Image File Format bitmap image
EPS	Encapsulated PostScript		
EXE	Executable program	TMP	temporary file
FNT	Windows font	TXT	ASCII text
GIF	Graphics Interchange Format bitmap image	WAV	Windows sound file
		WK3, WK4, WKS	Lotus 1–2–3 spreadsheet
H	header file		
HLP	help information	WP, WP5, WPD	WordPerfect document
HTM(L)	HyperText Markup Language document		
		XLS	Microsoft Excel spreadsheet
ICO	Windows icon	XML	eXtensible Markup Language document
INI	initialization or configuration file	ZIP	PKZIP compressed file

file extension
common computer file extensions

file librarian or *media librarian*, job classification for ⇌ computer personnel. A file librarian stores and issues the data files used by the computer department.

file merging combining two or more sequentially ordered files into a single sequentially ordered file.

file searching ⇌ searching a computer memory (usually ⇌ backing storage) for a file.

file server computer on a ⇌ network that handles (and usually stores) the data used by other computers on the network. See also ⇌ client–server architecture.

file sorting arranging files in sequence; see ↝ sorting.

file transfer transmission of a file (data stored on disk, for example) from one machine to another. Both machines must be physically linked (for example, by a telephone line via a ↝ modem or acoustic coupler) and both must be running appropriate communications software.

file updating reviewing and altering the records in a file to ensure that the information they contain is accurate and up-to-date. Three basic processes are involved: adding new records, deleting existing records, and amending existing records.

The updating of a direct-access file is a continuous process because records can be accessed individually and changed at any time. This type of updating is typical of large interactive database systems, such as airline ticket-booking systems. Each time a ticket is booked, files are immediately updated so that double booking is impossible.

In large commercial applications, however, millions of customer records may be held in a large sequentially ordered file, called the master file. Each time the records in the master file are to be updated (for example, when quarterly bills are being drawn up), a transaction file must be prepared. This will contain all the additions, deletions, and amendments required to update the master file. The transaction file is sorted into the same order as the master file, and then the computer reads both files and produces a new updated generation of the master file, which will be stored until the next file updating takes place.

filter program that transforms data. Filters are often used when data output from one ↝ application program is input into a different program, which requires a different data format. For example files transferred between two different word-processing programs are run through either an output filter supplied with the first program or an input filter supplied with the second program.

Filters are also used to expand coding structures, which have been simplified for keyboard input, into the often more verbose form required by such standards as SGML (↝ Standard Generalized Markup Language).

finger software utility that retrieves information about a user from another computer, perhaps across the Internet. Fingering an e-mail address may, where permitted, reveal the user's real name and any other details stored in a profile or resumé, such as company, position, or telephone number. Finger first appeared in ↝ Unix but is also provided in other operating systems such as Microsoft Windows.

firewall security system built to block access to a particular computer or network while still allowing some types of data to flow in and out onto the Internet.

A firewall allows a company's employees to access sites on the World Wide Web or exchange e-mail while at the same time preventing hackers from gaining access to the company's data.

FireWire Apple's implementation of the IEEE ⤳ 1394 serial connection system.

firmware computer program held permanently in a computer's ⤳ ROM (read-only memory) chips, as opposed to a program that is read in from external memory as it is needed.

First Amendment amendment to the US Constitution that guarantees freedom of religion, of speech, of assembly, and of the press. Adopted in 1791, the First Amendment is often quoted on the Internet, even by non-US citizens, in arguments over international attempts at censorship.

First Virtual Bank joint project with the bank FirstUSA which allows shoppers on the World Wide Web to open a central account using credit cards. Shoppers use their account numbers to make purchases at any of a number of participating merchants.

fixed font ⤳ font that uses fixed, rather than proportional, spacing. It is a necessary option in off-line reader software and e-mail programs, since some ASCII art and tables do not display correctly without it.

fixed-point notation system in which numbers are represented using a set of digits with the decimal point always in its correct position. For very large and very small numbers this requires a lot of digits. In computing, the size of the numbers that can be handled in this way is limited by the capacity of the computer, and so the slower ⤳ floating-point notation is often preferred.

flag indicator that can be set or unset in order to signal whether a particular condition is true – for example, whether the end of a file has been reached, or whether an overflow error has occurred. The indicator usually takes the form of a single binary digit, or bit (either 0 or 1).

flame angry public or private ⤳ electronic mail message. Users of the ⤳ Internet use flames to express disapproval of breaches of ⤳ netiquette or the voicing of an unpopular opinion. An offensive message posted to, for example, a ⤳ Usenet ⤳ newsgroup, will cause those offended to flame the culprit. Such flames maintain a level of discipline among the Internet's users.

flash memory type of ⤳ EEPROM memory that can be erased and reprogrammed without removal from the computer.

FlashPix ⤳ file format for digital imaging intended as a universal standard for both individual multimedia applications and external communications over online services. It was developed collaboratively by Kodak, Hewlett-Packard, Live Picture, and Microsoft in 1996.

flash upgrade technique for upgrading firmware by updating the software embedded in it. It is used particularly for modems and ⤳ EPROMs.

flat screen type of display suitable for portable computers such as LCD (⤳ liquid crystal display) or gas plasma screens (see ⤳ plasma display).

Flat-screen, or flat-panel, displays are compact and lightweight compared to traditional cathode-ray tube monitors and TV sets.

It is predicted that eventually all TV screens will be made using this type of technology.

flight simulator computer-controlled pilot-training device, consisting of an artificial cockpit mounted on hydraulic legs, that simulates the experience of flying a real aircraft. Inside the cockpit, the trainee pilot views a screen showing a computer-controlled projection of the view from a real aircraft, and makes appropriate adjustments to the controls. The computer monitors these adjustments, changes both the alignment of the cockpit on its hydraulic legs, and the projected view seen by the pilot. In this way a trainee pilot can progress to quite an advanced stage of training without leaving the ground.

flip-flop another name for a ⇝ bistable circuit.

floating-point notation system in which numbers are represented by means of a decimal fraction and an exponent. For example, in floating-point notation, $123,000,000,000$ would be represented as 0.123×10^{12}, where 0.123 is the fraction, or mantissa, and 12 the exponent. The exponent is the power of 10 by which the fraction must be multiplied in order to obtain the true value of the number.

In computing, floating-point notation enables programs to work with very large and very small numbers using only a few digits; however, it is slower than ⇝ fixed-point notation and suffers from small rounding errors.

floppy disk storage device consisting of a light, flexible disk enclosed in a cardboard or plastic jacket. The disk is placed in a disk drive, where it rotates at high speed. Data are recorded magnetically on one or both surfaces.

Floppy disks were invented by IBM in 1971 as a means of loading programs into the computer. They were originally 20 cm/8 in in diameter and typically held about 240 ⇝ kilobytes of data. Present-day floppy disks, widely used on ⇝ microcomputers, are 8.8 cm/3.5 in in diameter, and generally hold up to 2 ⇝ megabytes, depending on the disk formatting.

Floppy disks are inexpensive, and light enough to send through the post, but have slower access speeds and are more fragile than hard disks. (See also ⇝ disk).

FLOPS acronym for *floating point operations per second*, measure of the speed at which a computer program can be run.

floptical disk or *erasable optical disk*, type of optical disk that can be erased and loaded with new data, just like a magnetic disk. By contrast, most optical disks are read-only. A single optical disk can hold as much as 1,000 megabytes of data, about 800 times more than a typical floppy disk. Floptical disks need a special disk drive, but some such drives are also capable of accepting standard 3.5 inch floppy disks.

flow chart diagram, often used in computing, to show the possible paths that data can take through a system or program.

A system flow chart, or data flow chart, is used to describe the flow of data through a complete data-processing system. Different graphic symbols represent the clerical operations involved and the different input, storage, and output equipment required. Although the flow chart may indicate the specific programs used, no details are given of how the programs process the data.

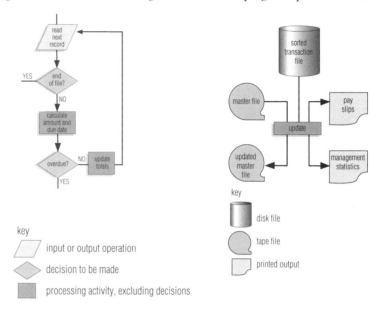

flow chart

A program flow chart shows the sequence of operations needed to achieve a task, in this case reading customer accounts and calculating the amount due for each customer. After an account has been processed, the program loops back to process the next one.

A system flow chart describes the flow of data through a data-processing system. This chart shows the data flow in a basic accounting system.

A program flow chart is used to describe the flow of data through a particular computer program, showing the exact sequence of operations performed by that program in order to process the data. Different graphic symbols are used to represent data input and output, decisions, branches, and ↝ subroutines.

flow control in data communications, hardware or software signals that control the flow of data to ensure that it is not transmitted too quickly for the receiving computer to handle.

flythrough in ↝ virtual reality, animation allowing users to view a model of a proposed or actual site as if they were inside it and moving through it.

For the 1996 Olympics in Atlanta, USA, flythroughs assisted site planners to identify areas in the main stadium where camera positions would be blocked by the audience, allowing solutions to be found in advance of construction.

FM synthesizer abbreviation for *frequency modulation synthesizer*, method for generating synthetic sounds based on techniques used to transmit FM radio signals.

FMV abbreviation for ⇨ full-motion video.

folder name for a computer directory in Microsoft Windows and on the Macintosh operating system.

follow-up post publicly posted reply to a Usenet message; unlike a personal e-mail reply, follow-up post can be read by anyone.

Full-featured ⇨ newsreaders include a facility for setting the names of the newsgroups to which follow-ups should be posted. If, for example, an original message was posted to a number of groups, several of which were inappropriate, the person posting the follow-up might want to restrict further replies to only those groups where the message actually belongs.

font or *fount*, complete set of printed or display characters of the same typeface, size, and style (bold, italic, underlined, and so on).

Fonts used in computer settings are of two main types: bit-mapped and outline. Bit-mapped fonts are stored in the computer memory as the exact arrangement of ⇨ pixels or printed dots required to produce the characters in a particular size on a screen or printer. Outline fonts are stored in the computer memory as a set of instructions for drawing the circles, straight lines, and curves that make up the outline of each character. They require a powerful computer because each character is separately generated from a set of instructions and this requires considerable computation. Bit-mapped fonts become very ragged in appearance if they are enlarged, and so a separate set of bit maps is required for each font size. In contrast, outline fonts can be scaled to any size and maintain exactly the same appearance.

In the UK, font sizes are measured in points, a point being approximately 0.3 mm.

This is Courier 10 point
This is Times italic 12 point
This is Brush Script bold 14 point
This is Kino 15 point
This is Univers bold 16 point
This is Kabel ultra 17 point

font
An example of different font typefaces and sizes.

footprint area on the desk or floor required by a computer or other peripheral device.

force feedback in ⇨ virtual reality, realistic simulation of the physical sense of touch. This is an area of active research, as many applications of virtual reality are useless or impossible without it.

For example, force feedback is essential in medical training systems to teach the students how hard to press with a scalpel in delicate areas of the human body. Even simulated games need force feedback in order to allow objects to respond realistically to falling or being hit.

In the second half of the 1990s, force feedback became popular in joysticks, hand-held controllers, and steering wheels used with computer games on personal computers and game consoles.

forensic computing recovering information from computer systems for use in criminal investigations. The use of computers by criminals to commit crimes or to support their criminal activities is increasing. The more organized computer criminals will take sophisticated steps to try to hide the information on their computers, and it is the work of forensic computer scientists, working with the police, to recover evidence.

forgery art of falsifying either the contents or the origins of a message. On the Internet, where a person's identity is shaped by his/her words as sent out via e-mail or public conferencing systems such as Usenet, sending out a forged message in another person's name can seriously damage them. Forged messages are, however, used by the ↝ CancelMoose to manage ↝ spamming and keep it from spreading.

formatting short for ↝ disk formatting.

forms on the World Wide Web, facility for accepting structured user input and inserting it into a program such as a database. Most newer graphical Web browsers can handle forms, as can the older, text-based browser Lynx. Forms are needed to manage database queries at sites such as ↝ AltaVista, and to fill out registration forms for those sites that require them.

Web page designers implement forms by using a special set of hypertext markup language (HTML) tags and attaching a ↝ script, which parses the data and feeds it to the program specified in a form the program can use. The results, such as a user name and password or a list of matches, are sent back to the user.

FORTRAN or *fortran*; contraction of *formula translation*, high-level computer-programming language suited to mathematical and scientific computations. Developed by John Backus at IBM in 1956, it is one of the earliest computer languages still in use. A recent version, Fortran 90, is now being used on advanced parallel computers. ↝ BASIC was strongly influenced by FORTRAN and is similar in many ways. Fortran 2000 is being developed and is expected to become an ISO standard in 2002.

fourth-generation language type of programming language designed for the rapid programming of ↝ applications but often lacking the ability to control the individual parts of the computer. Such a language typically provides easy ways of designing screens and reports, and of using databases. Other 'generations' (the term implies a class of language rather than a chronological sequence) are ↝ machine code (first generation); ↝ assembly languages, or low-level languages (second); and conventional high-level languages such as ↝ BASIC and ↝ Pascal (third).

fragmentation breaking up of files into many smaller sections stored on different parts of a disk. The computer ⮑ operating system stores files in this way so that maximum use can be made of disk space. Each section contains a pointer to where the next section is stored. The ⮑ file allocation table keeps a record of this.

Fragmentation slows down access to files. It is possible to defragment a disk by copying files. In addition, ⮑ defragmentation programs, or disk optimizers, allow disks to be defragmented without the need for files to be copied to a second storage device.

frame single photograph in a sequence representing motion, or movement, on film; in a ⮑ network, a unit of data; in word processing or desktop publishing, a marked-out area on a page that can contain text or graphics.

What appears to be motion on a cinema or TV screen is actually a rapid sequence of single shots. Because of limitations in the human eye – known as the Phi phenomenon – those individual shots, if played in sequence at a rate of 24 to 30 frames per second, make the motion thus captured appear continuous.

frame buffer ⮑ buffer used to store a screen image.

frame relay in ⮑ wide-area networks, a standard for the transmission of data that is optimized for high speeds up to about 1.5 Mbits/second.

Freeserve first free ⮑ Internet Service Provider (ISP), launched in September 1998 by the UK high-street electrical store chain Dixons. Freeserve is an implementation of ISP Planet Online's Connect & Go generic service, provided in conjunction with its parent, energy and telecommunications company Energis.

Although there are no registration or set-up fees and no monthly subscription charges to pay, Freeserve users do have to pay for the local-rate telephone calls required to access the service.

Freeserve soon became the UK's most popular ISP, and its business model was copied by many other European ISPs. The company encountered serious competition in 2000, however, when firms such as search engine company ⮑ AltaVista and cable operator ⮑ ntl introduced Internet access with no charge for telephone calls but, in some cases, a flat monthly or annual fee.

Free Software Foundation *FSF*, US organization, based in Boston, which creates and distributes good-quality free software and utilities. FSF is the publisher of the ⮑ GNU software, which includes compilers, operating systems, utilities, editors, databases, and PostScript viewers. All the software is free of licensing fees and restrictions.

The FSF was founded in 1983 by US artificial intelligence specialist Richard Stallman as a way of bringing back the cooperative spirit of the computing community's early days that had vanished by the early 1980s with the advent of widely sold proprietary software. The project's ultimate goal is to make commercial software obsolete by providing free software to do everything computer users want to do.

Free Software Foundation

ftp://prep.ai.mit.edu ; login: anonymous ; cd pub/gnu.

An archive of GNU software.

WEB LINK

freeware free software which may or may not be in the public domain. One of the best-known examples of freeware is the encryption program ↝ Pretty Good Privacy (PGP). This is still available free of charge for personal, non-commercial use.

frequently asked questions expansion of the abbreviation ↝ FAQ.

front-end processor small computer used to coordinate and control the communications between a large mainframe computer and its input and output devices.

FrontPage Web ↝ authoring tool developed by ↝ Microsoft. FrontPage 2000 shares common ↝ toolbars, ↝ menus, ↝ shortcuts, tools, ↝ HTML help, and background spell-checking with the Microsoft Office 2000 ↝ office suite. FrontPage also offers more than 60 pre-designed, business-ready 'themes', to provide consistency of appearance for individual ↝ Web pages or an entire ↝ Web site.

FSF abbreviation for the ↝ Free Software Foundation.

FTP abbreviation for *File Transfer Protocol*, rules for transferring files between computers on the ↝ Internet. The use of FTP avoids incompatibility between individual computers. To use FTP over the Internet, a user must have an Internet connection, an FTP client or World Wide Web ↝ browser, and an account on the system holding the files. Many commercial and noncommercial systems allow anonymous FTP either to distribute new versions of software products or as a public service.

FTPmail ↝ FTP server that can be operated by e-mail. This service is useful for people with only limited access to the Internet.

full duplex modem setting which means that two-way communication is enabled, so that everything you type is echoed back to the screen. See ↝ duplex.

full-motion video *FMV*, video system that can display continuous motion. Some slow-speed CD-ROM drives and low-bandwidth networks are unable to handle the mass of data required for full-motion video, so video playback tends to jerk unevenly.

function small part of a program that supplies a specific value – for example, the square root of a specified number, or the current date. Most programming languages incorporate a number of built-in functions; some allow programmers to write their own. A function may have one or more arguments (the values on which the function operates). A function key on a keyboard is one that, when pressed, performs a designated task, such as ending a program.

functional programming computer programming based largely on the definition of ↝ functions. There are very few functional programming languages, HOPE and ML being the most widely used, though many more conventional languages (for example, C) make extensive use of functions.

function key key on a keyboard that, when pressed, performs a designated task, such as ending a computer program.

FurryMUCK popular ⇌ MUD site where the players take on the imaginary shapes and characters of furry, anthropomorphic animals.

fuzzy logic form of knowledge representation suitable for notions (such as 'hot' or 'loud') that cannot be defined precisely but depend on their context. For example, a jug of water may be described as too hot or too cold, depending on whether it is to be used to wash one's face or to make tea.

The central idea of fuzzy logic is probability of set membership. For instance, referring to someone 175 cm/5 ft 9 in tall, the statement 'this person is tall' (or 'this person is a member of the set of tall people') might be about 70% true if that person is a man, and about 85% true if that person is a woman.

The term 'fuzzy logic' was coined in 1965 by Iranian computer scientist Lofti Zadeh of the University of California at Berkeley, although the core concepts go back to the work of Polish mathematician Jan Lukasiewicz in the 1920s. It has been largely ignored in Europe and the USA, but was taken up by Japanese manufacturers in the mid-1980s and has since been applied to hundreds of electronic goods and industrial machines. For example, a vacuum cleaner launched in 1992 by Matsushita uses fuzzy logic to adjust its sucking power in response to messages from its sensors about the type of dirt on the floor, its distribution, and its depth. Fuzzy logic enables computerized devices to reason more like humans, responding effectively to complex messages from their control panels and sensors.

gain in audio, the volume control.

games console computer capable only of playing games, which are supplied as cartridges or CD-ROM disks that slot directly into the console. The best known console manufacturer in the late 1970s was Atari; Nintendo and Sega dominated the market in the early 1990s with the Sony ⮑ PlayStation becoming the marketleader in 1996.

Usually, the price of the console is quite low, while the price of the game cartridges is high. The disadvantages of consoles include the narrow range of software and the incompatibility of one console with another.

The competition between the three major players in the market intensified in late 1999, as Sega launched its Dreamcast console. Sony planned for the release of the PlayStation2 and Nintendo was developing the Dolphin console, both due for release in 2000. Microsoft also unveiled in 1999 that it planned to enter the market, which is worth an estimated $6 billion a year. In 2000 it announced that its new console would be called X-Box, based on the Windows operating system technology with a hard drive, the first console to contain a hard drive. The new generation of consoles contain 128-bit chip technology and Internet connectivity as standard, and it is expected they will bring the Internet into a large number of homes which did not previously have access to it, due to the low cost of the consoles.

gate, logic see ⮑ logic gate.

Gates, Bill (William) Henry, III (1955–   ) US businessman and computer programmer. He co-founded ⮑ Microsoft Corporation in 1975 with school friend Paul ⮑ Allen. Together they adapted the computer language ⮑ BASIC, traditionally used on large computers, for use on personal computers. They licensed the BASIC language and the operating system ⮑ MS-DOS to ⮑ IBM for use in the IBM personal computer (PC), which was first marketed in 1981. Microsoft began to develop computer ⮑ software, and in 1990 introduced the operating system ⮑ Windows, which made computers more user-friendly by operating with on-screen symbols ('icons') and pull-down menus which are activated by a ⮑ mouse. In 1999 Gates' personal wealth and assets were estimated at $90 billion/£56 billion, and despite a reduction in his wealth 1999–2000, he remains the world's richest man with a fortune of $60 billion/£38 billion. He is the chairman and chief software architect of Microsoft, having stepped down as chief executive in January 2000, in order to devote his time to building new, Internet-based software for the future.

Gates's interests stretch beyond the Microsoft Corporation. In 1994 he invested $10 million into a biotechnology company, Darwin Molecular, with Microsoft co-founder Paul Allen. Although he has been criticized for his great wealth, his home page on the Microsoft Web site details his commitment to charitable donations: 'my wife, Melinda, and I are supporting causes that are

Gates, Bill

http://www.pathfinder.
com/time/time100/builder/
profile/gates.html

Part of a larger archive from *Time* exploring the most influential people of the 20th century, this article highlights the life and work of the US businessman and computer programmer Bill Gates. The profile also features a timeline.

WEB LINK

important to us – in our own community and around the world'. Their beneficiaries have included the International AIDS Vaccine Initiative (IAVI) in New York, the non-profit Gates Library Foundation whose aim is to provide computers and software to public libraries in the USA and Canada, and the William H Gates Foundation, which has granted multi-million dollar awards to the Cambridge University Development Office in America. In 2000 they gave a further $133 million towards vaccines, including $25 million to develop new tuberculosis drugs.

gateway point of contact between two ⤳ wide-area networks.

geek stereotypical exceptionally bright, obsessive computer user or programmer. See also ⤳ anorak and ⤳ nerd.

general MIDI abbreviation for *musical instrument digital interface*; or *GM*, standard set of 96 instrument and percussion 'voices' that can be used to encode musical tracks which can be reproduced on any GM-compatible synthesizer, or ⤳ MIDI.

general protection fault computing error message; see ⤳ GPF.

generation stage of development in computer electronics (see ⤳ computer generation) or a class of programming language (see ⤳ fourth-generation language).

geographical information system *GIS*, software that makes possible the visualization and manipulation of spatial data, and links such data with other information such as customer records.

gesture recognition technique whereby a computer accepts human gestures transmitted via hardware such as a ⤳ DataGlove as meaningful input to which it can respond. Gesture recognition is a key technology needed in the development of ⤳ virtual reality systems if they are to allow humans to interact fully and naturally with objects in computerized worlds.

GIF acronym for *Graphics Interchange Format*, popular and economical picture file format developed by CompuServe. GIF (pronounced with a hard 'g') is one of the two most commonly used file formats for pictures on the World Wide Web (the other is ⤳ JPEG) because pictures saved in this format take up a relatively small amount of space. The term is often used simply to mean 'pictures'. However, GIF uses ⤳ LZW compression, which has prompted moves to replace it with a different format such as Portable Network Graphics (PNG).

gigabyte measure of ⤳ memory capacity, equal to 1,024 ⤳ megabytes. It is also used, less precisely, to mean 1,000 billion ⤳ bytes.

GIGO acronym for *garbage in, garbage out*, expression used in computing to emphasize that inaccurate input data will result in inaccurate output data.

GII abbreviation for the ↝ Global Information Infrastructure.

GIS abbreviation for ↝ geographical information system.

Global Information Infrastructure *GII*, planned worldwide high-bandwidth network. US vice-president Al Gore proposed the GII in a 1994 speech to the International Telecommunications Union, saying that it would promote the functioning of democracy, help nations to cooperate with each other, and be the key to economic growth for national and international economies.

Global Network Navigator *GNN*, subscription-based online service for the World Wide Web, pioneered by US book publishers O'Reilly & Associates and bought by ↝ America Online in 1995. Its Virtual Places software, released in 1996, allows users to interact with each other using avatars and live messages at any Virtual Places-enabled site on the Web. GNN also offers news and resource listings.

global variable ↝ variable that can be accessed by any program instruction. See also ↝ local variable.

GM synthesizer synthesizer standard; see ↝ general MIDI.

GNN abbreviation for ↝ Global Network Navigator.

GNU suite of free Unix-like software distributed by the ↝ Free Software Foundation. The software includes operating systems, compilers, text editors (such as ↝ EMACS), and other useful utilities.
    An archive of GNU software is kept at `ftp://prep.ai.mit.edu/pub/gnu`.

Gopher derived from 'go for'; alternatively, named for the mascot of the University of Minnesota, where it was invented, menu-based server on the ↝ Internet that indexes resources and retrieves them according to user choice via any one of several built-in methods such as ↝ FTP or ↝ Telnet. Gopher servers can also be accessed via the World Wide Web and searched via special servers called Veronica. Gopher has now been eclipsed by the Web.

Gouraud shading in computer animation, technique for calculating the correct colours and intensity of lighting playing on an on-screen three-dimensional object.
    Gouraud shading works by measuring the colour and brightness at the vertices of the polygons that make up the object and mixing these to get values for the areas inside the polygons. Specialized hardware makes this process relatively fast. The technique is named after its inventor, Henri Gouraud, and was developed in 1973.

TIP

GPF

When you get a GPF, save all data, close all programs, and reboot the computer.

GPF abbreviation for *general protection fault*, in Windows 3.1, error message returned by a computer when it crashes. A GPF is the same as a UAE (unexpected application error) in Windows 3.0. It often indicates that one application has tried to use memory reserved for another.

GPRS abbreviation for *General Packet Radio Service*, implementation of ↝ packet switching within ↝ GSM. GPRS will bring Internet Protocol (IP) connectivity to the GSM network, and is sometimes referred to as 2½G, in contrast to ↝ UMTS, which is the third-generation standard for mobile cellular networks.

GPRS supports a data transfer rate of up to 115 kilobits per second (kbps), compared with the 9.6 kbps of standard GSM. Another advantage of GPRS is that is always 'on', rather than requiring that the user dial up to establish a connection in order to transmit or receive data.

In June 2000, ↝ BT Cellnet introduced a limited-coverage GPRS service in the UK for business customers.

graphical user interface *GUI* or *WIMP*, type of ↝ user interface in which programs and files appear as icons (small pictures), user options are selected from pull-down menus, and data are displayed in windows (rectangular areas), which the operator can manipulate in various ways. The operator uses a pointing device, typically a ↝ mouse, to make selections and initiate actions.

The concept of the graphical user interface was developed by the Xerox Corporation in the 1970s, was popularized with the Apple Macintosh computers in the 1980s, and is now available on many types of computer – most notably as Windows, an operating system for IBM PC-compatible microcomputers developed by the software company Microsoft.

graphic file format format in which computer graphics are stored and transmitted. There are two main types: ↝ raster graphics in which the image is stored as a ↝ bit map (arrangement of dots), and ↝ vector graphics, in which the image is stored using geometric formulas. There are many different file formats, some of which are used by specific computers, operating systems, or applications. Some formats use file compression, particularly those that are able to handle more than one colour.

graphics see ↝ computer graphics.

graphics board another name for ↝ graphics card.

graphics card peripheral device that processes and displays graphics.

Graphics Interchange Format picture file format usually abbreviated to ↝ GIF.

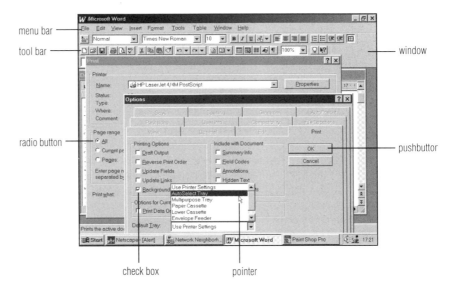

menu bar

tool bar

radio button

window

pushbuttor

check box

pointer

graphical user interface
A typical graphical user interface (GUI), where the user moves around the system by clicking on representative buttons or icons using the mouse.

graphics tablet or *bit pad*, input device in which a stylus or cursor is moved, by hand, over a flat surface. The computer can keep track of the position of the stylus, so enabling the operator to input drawings or diagrams into the computer.

A graphics tablet is often used with a form overlaid for users to mark boxes in positions that relate to specific registers in the computer, although recent developments in handwriting recognition may increase its future versatility.

graphics tablet
A graphics tablet enables images drawn freehand to be translated directly to the computer screen.

graph plotter alternative name for a ↩ plotter.

greeking method used in ↩ desktop publishing and other page make-up systems for showing type below a certain size on screen. Rather than the actual characters being displayed, either a grey bar or graphics symbols are used. Greeking is usually employed when a general impression of the page lay-out is required.

green computing gradual movement by computer companies toward incorporating energy-saving measures in the design of systems and hardware. The increasing use of energy-saving devices, so that a computer partially shuts down during periods of inactivity, but can reactivate at the touch of a key, could play a significant role in energy conservation.

It is estimated that worldwide electricity consumption by computers amounts to 240 billion kilowatt hours per year, equivalent to the entire annual consumption of Brazil. In the USA, carbon dioxide emissions could be reduced by 20 million tonnes per year – equivalent to the carbon dioxide output of 5 million cars – if all computers incorporated the latest 'sleep technology' (which shuts down most of the power-consuming features of a computer if it is unused for any length of time).

Although it was initially predicted that computers would mean 'paperless offices', in practice the amount of paper consumed continues to rise. Other environmentally costly features of computers include their rapid obsolescence, health problems associated with monitors and keyboards, and the unfavourable economics of component recycling.

GreenNet international computer network used by environmental activists to exchange information and news.

grep acronym for *global regular expression print*, Unix command that allows full-text searching within files. On the Net, grep is sometimes used as an all-purpose synonym for 'search'.

grey scales method of representing continuous tone images on a screen or printer. Each dot in the ☞ bit map is represented by a number of bits and can have a different shade of grey. Compare with ☞ dithering where shades are simulated by altering the density and the pattern of black dots on a white background.

groupware software designed to be used collaboratively by a small group of users, each with his/her own computer and a copy of the software. Examples of groupware are Lotus Notes and Novell GroupWise, both of which provide facilities for sending e-mail and sharing documents.

Standard business applications such as word processors are spoken of as 'groupware-enabled' if they provide facilities for a number of users to make revisions and incorporate them all into a final version. See also ☞ computer-supported collaborative work.

Grove, Andy (1936–) Hungarian-born US computer entrepreneur, who founded the microprocessor manufacturing company ☞ Intel, of which he is chairman.

Grove graduated from the City College of New York in 1960 with a degree in Chemical Engineering, and received his PhD from the University of California, Berkeley, in 1963. He then joined the research and development laboratory of Fairchild Semiconductor, becoming assistant director of this department in 1967.

Grove was one of the founders of Intel in July 1968, becoming president in 1979 and chief executive in 1987. Ten years later, he became chairman also, ceasing to be chief executive in May 1998, when he was succeeded by Craig Barrett.

Visitors to Intel's Web site can view a 360° panorama of Grove's office cubicle.

GSM originally an abbreviation for *Group Système Mobile* (French) but now said to stand for *Global System for Mobile* (communications).

GUI abbreviation for ↝ graphical user interface.

GZip compression software, properly called ↝ GNU Zip, commonly used on the Internet. Files compressed using GZip can be recognized by the file extension '.GZ'. The software is published by the ↝ Free Software Foundation and was originally developed for Unix, although a DOS version is readily available.

hacking unauthorized access to a computer, either for fun or for malicious or fraudulent purposes. Hackers generally use microcomputers and telephone lines to obtain access. In computing, the term is used in a wider sense to mean using software for enjoyment or self-education, not necessarily involving unauthorized access. The most destructive form of hacking is the introduction of a computer ↝ virus.

Hacking can be divided into four main areas: ↝ viruses, ↝ phreaking, software piracy (stripping away the protective coding that should prevent the software being copied), and accessing operating systems.

A 1996 US survey co-sponsored by the FBI showed 41% of academic, corporate, and government organizations interviewed had had their computer systems hacked into during 1995. White hat hackers are computer experts hired by companies to hack into their networks to expose weaknesses in security.

In the UK, hacking is illegal under the ↝ Computer Misuse Act 1990.

A survey 1993–96 of 10,000 organizations in the UK showed that only 3% had been troubled by hackers.

Famous hackers include, in the USA, Kevin ↝ Mitnick and, in the UK, Rob Schifreen and Steve Gold, who in 1984 hacked into Prince Philip's mail box on the British Telecom service Prestel.

half duplex ↝ modem setting which controls whether or not characters echo to (appear on) the screen. See ↝ full duplex.

halftone term used in the publishing industry for a black-and-white photograph, indicating the many shades of grey that must be reproduced.

handle term used on ↝ Internet Relay Chat and other live chat services for a nickname.

A given user's handle may or may not be the same as his/her ↝ user-ID; on many systems users are allowed to pick any name they like to use on chat systems as long as it is not already taken by another user.

Handles are also used on CB and ham radio, and hackers use handles, for cultural reasons as much as to disguise their real identities.

handshake exchange of signals between two devices that establishes the communications channels and protocols necessary for the devices to send and receive data.

handwriting recognition ability of a computer to accept handwritten input and turn it into ↝ digital data that can be processed and displayed or stored as ↝ ASCII characters on the computer screen.

In the 1990s, handwriting recognition was widely adopted for use on handheld computers, especially the 'palmtop' models which do not have a physical keyboard. The recognition systems in these machines need to be trained to optimize recognition of the user's writing, and cannot recognize cursive (joined up) handwriting. However, they can be very effective once users become aware of and allow for their limitations.

hard copy computer output printed on paper.

hard disk storage device usually consisting of a rigid metal ⤳ disk coated with a magnetic material. Data are read from and written to the disk by means of a disk drive. The hard disk may be permanently fixed into the drive or in the form of a disk pack that can be removed and exchanged with a different pack. Hard disks vary from large units with capacities of more than 3,000 megabytes, intended for use with mainframe computers, to small units with capacities as low as 20 megabytes, intended for use with microcomputers.

A hard disk drive that is only thumbnail-sized was released by IBM in 1999, holding 340 megabytes. A one-gigabyte version was released in 2000.

hard-sectored disk floppy disk that is sold already formatted, so that ⤳ disk formatting is not necessary. Usually sectors are marked by holes near the hub of the disk. This system is now obsolete.

hardware mechanical, electrical, and electronic components of a computer system, as opposed to the various programs, which constitute ⤳ software.

Hardware associated with a microcomputer might include the power supply and housing of its processor unit, its circuit boards, VDU (screen), disk drive, keyboard, and printer.

hash function ⤳ algorithm that calculates a value from the content of a message which can then be used to detect alterations to the original message.

Similar to a ⤳ checksum but with greater security, hash functions play an important role in secure cryptographic systems (see ⤳ cryptography), where authentication is as important as hiding the data from third parties.

hashing process used to convert a record, usually in a database, into a number that can be used to retrieve the record, or check its validity. The 'hashing algorithm', which may be based on manipulating the ASCII values of letters, will be devised so that different records give a useful range of results. Hashing is faster than storing things alphabetically, for example, where some areas may have lots of very similar records (for example, under c, s, or t) while others are little used (q, x, z).

hash total ⤳ validation check in which an otherwise meaningless control total is calculated by adding together numbers (such as payroll or account numbers) associated with a set of records. The hash total is checked each time data are input, in order to ensure that no entry errors have been made.

HCI abbreviation for ⤳ human–computer interaction.

header line or lines of text that appear at the beginning of each e-mail or Usenet message sent across the Internet. The header includes important routing and identifying information, such as the sender's name, recipient's name (either a person or a newsgroup), date, time, and machine used when the message was composed, and the path by which the message arrived at its destination.

In the case of Usenet postings, it also indicates if the message is intended for more than one group. The exact material is determined by ⮡ RFC (requests for comments) and discussion.

helper application in Web ⮡ browsers, an external application that adds the ability to display certain types of files. Common helper applications include ⮡ RealAudio, which allows browsers to play live sound tracks such as radio broadcasts or recorded lectures; ⮡ Acrobat; and mIRC, which allows access to ⮡ Internet Relay Chat via the World Wide Web.

hertz SI unit (symbol Hz) of frequency (the number of repetitions of a regular occurrence in one second). Radio waves are often measured in megahertz (MHz), millions of hertz, and the ⮡ clock rate of a computer is usually measured in megahertz. The unit is named after German physicist Heinrich Hertz.

heuristics process by which a program attempts to improve its performance by learning from its own experience.

Hewlett, William R (1913–   ) US electrical engineer. With his friend, David Packard, he formed ⮡ Hewlett-Packard in 1939 in Palo Alto, California. They began by producing resistance-capacitance audio oscillators in a garage. He was actively involved in the company until 1987.

Hewlett was born in Ann Arbor, Michigan. He graduated from Massachusetts Institute of Technology in 1936.

Hewlett-Packard often abbreviated to *HP*, major manufacturer of computer and telecommunications hardware, founded 1939 by William ⮡ Hewlett and David Packard and based in Palo Alto, California, USA. In 1996 the company was manufacturing more than 24,000 products, including medical equipment, analytical instruments, calculators, PCs, printers, workstations, and palmtops.

HP's sales grew dramatically from $13.2 billion in 1990 to $38.4 billion in 1996.

hexadecimal number system or *hex*, number system to the base 16, used in computing. In hex the decimal numbers 0–15 are represented by the characters 0, 1, 2, 3, 4, 5, 6, 7, 8, 9, A, B, C, D, E, F.

Hexadecimal numbers are easy to convert to the computer's internal ⮡ binary code and are more compact than binary numbers.

Each place in a number increases in value by a power of 16 going from right to left; for instance, 8F is equal to 15 + (8 × 16) = 143 in decimal. Hexadecimal numbers are often preferred by programmers writing in low-level languages because they are more easily converted to the computer's internal ⮡ binary (base-two) code than are decimal numbers, and because they are more compact than binary numbers and therefore more easily keyed, checked, and memorized. (See also ⮡ ASCII.)

hidden file computer file in an ᐳ MS-DOS system that is not normally displayed when the directory listing command is given. Hidden files include certain system files, principally so that there is less chance of modifying or deleting them by accident, but any file can be made hidden if required.

hierarchical storage management organization of data storage so that information which is used most often is stored using the fastest access technology, and information used less often is stored on slower and less expensive storage devices.

For example, information that is accessed regularly will be kept in the main ᐳ memory (fast, but expensive). Information that is required a little less often will be stored on hard disk (slower than memory, but less expensive), and information that is needed only occasionally is stored on optical devices or magnetic tape (very slow access time, but low in cost).

hierarchy on Usenet, the structure for naming ᐳ newsgroups. All newsgroups on Usenet are assigned to a major group. The ᐳ Big Seven hierarchies were the first to be set up, and setting up a new newsgroup in these involved following more or less formal procedures. The ᐳ alt hierarchy was set up to allow more flexibility. The biz hierarchy was set up 1994, after the first incidence of ᐳ spamming, to give advertising its own place.

A number of other hierarchies are available, set up for specific countries (de is Germany, dk is Denmark, uk is Britain); for Internet Service Providers (Demon, CompuServe, and AOL all have their own local groups); or for individual companies.

These newsgroups may be local and reserved for a specific audience, or they may be propagated throughout the world; it is up to the organizations to decide whether to make them available and up to individual Internet Service Providers to take them if they think enough of their users would be interested in the material.

high-definition television *HDTV*, ᐳ television system offering a significantly greater number of scanning lines, and therefore a clearer picture, than that provided by conventional systems. Typically, HDTV has about twice the horizontal and vertical resolution of current 525-line (such as the American standard, NTSC) or 625-line standands (such as the British standard, PAL); a frame rate of at least 24 Hz; and a picture aspect ratio of 9:16 instead of the current 3:4. HDTV systems have been in development since the mid-1970s.

The Japanese HDTV system, or HiVision as it is trade-named in Japan, uses 1,125 scanning lines and an aspect ratio of 16:9 (widescreen) instead of the squarish 4:3 that conventional television uses. A European HDTV system, called HD-MAC, using 1,250 lines, is under development. HDTV is already being broadcast in the USA, but the high cost of suitable television sets means few people are watching.

high-level language programming language designed to suit the requirements of the programmer; it is independent of the internal machine code of any particular computer. High-level languages are used to solve problems and are often described as problem-oriented languages – for example, ↬ BASIC was designed to be easily learnt by first-time programmers; ↬ COBOL is used to write programs solving business problems; and ↬ FORTRAN is used for programs solving scientific and mathematical problems. In contrast, low-level languages, such as ↬ assembly languages, closely reflect the machine codes of specific computers, and are therefore described as machine-oriented languages.

Unlike low-level languages, high-level languages are relatively easy to learn because the instructions bear a close resemblance to everyday language, and because the programmer does not require a detailed knowledge of the internal workings of the computer. Each instruction in a high-level language is equivalent to several machine-code instructions. High-level programs are therefore more compact than equivalent low-level programs. However, each high-level instruction must be translated into machine code – by either a ↬ compiler or an ↬ interpreter program – before it can be executed by a computer. High-level languages are designed to be portable – programs written in a high-level language can be run on any computer that has a compiler or interpreter for that particular language.

high memory first 64 kilobytes in the ↬ extended memory of an ↬ MS-DOS system. The operating system itself is usually installed in this area to allow more conventional memory (below 640 kilobytes) for applications.

High-Sierra format standard format for writing CD-ROM disks; see ↬ ISO 9660.

hinting method of reducing the effects of ↬ aliasing in the appearance of ↬ outline fonts. Hinting makes use of a series of priorities so that noticeable distortions, such as uneven stem weight, are corrected. ↬ PostScript Type 1 and ↬ TrueType fonts are hinted.

history list of sites visited by a Web ↬ browser during the current session. The history is usually stored as a list of page titles and is accessed via the browser's menu system. The purpose is to make it easy for users to go back to a recently visited site.

hit request sent to a ↬ file server.

Sites on the World Wide Web often measure their popularity in numbers of hits. However, this is misleading, as a single Web page may be made up of many files, each of which counts as a hit when a user downloads the whole page. Counting individual visits is a better indication of a site's success.

Hoff, Ted (1937–) born Marcian Edward Hoff, Jr, inventor of the microprocessor. Working at Intel, Hoff conceived the idea of putting a computer on a single integrated circuit or microchip, to simplify the development of a range of pocket calculators for a Japanese company called Busicom.

Hollerith, Herman (1860–1929) US inventor of a mechanical tabulating machine, the first device for high-volume data processing. Hollerith's tabulator was widely publicized after being successfully used in the 1890 census. The firm he established, the Tabulating Machine Company, was later one of the founding companies of ↝ IBM.

Hollerith was born in Buffalo, New York, and attended the Columbia University School of Mines. From 1884 to 1896 he worked for the US Patent Office.

Working on the 1880 US census, he saw the need for an automated recording process for data, and had the idea of punching holes in cards or rolls of paper. By 1889 he had developed machines for recording, counting, and collating census data. The system was used in 1891 for censuses in several countries, and was soon adapted to the needs of government departments and businesses that handled large quantities of data.

hologram three-dimensional image produced by ↝ holography. Small, inexpensive holograms appear on credit cards and software licences to guarantee their authenticity.

holography method of producing three-dimensional (3-D) images, called ↝ holograms, by means of laser light. Holography uses a photographic technique (involving the splitting of a laser beam into two beams) to produce a picture, or hologram, that contains 3-D information about the object photographed. Some holograms show meaningless patterns in ordinary light and produce a 3-D image only when laser light is projected through them, but reflection holograms produce images when ordinary light is reflected from them (as found on credit cards).

Although the possibility of holography was suggested as early as 1947 (by Hungarian-born British physicist Dennis Gabor), it could not be demonstrated until a pure coherent light source, the laser, became available in 1963. The first laser-recorded holograms were created by Emmett Leith and Juris Upatnieks at the University of Michigan, USA, and Yuri Denisyuk in the Soviet Union.

The technique of holography is also applicable to sound, and bats may navigate by ultrasonic holography. Holographic techniques also have applications in storing dental records, detecting stresses and strains in construction and in retail goods, detecting forged paintings and documents, and producing three-dimensional body scans. The technique of detecting strains is of widespread application. It involves making two different holograms of an object on one plate, the object being stressed between exposures. If the object has distorted during stressing, the hologram will be greatly changed, and the distortion readily apparent.

Using holography, digital data can be recorded page by page in a crystal. 10,000 pages (100 megabytes) of digital data can be stored in an iron-doped lithium niobate crystal measuring 1 cm^3.

home page opening page on a particular site on the World Wide Web. The term is also used for the page which loads automatically when a user opens a Web ↝ browser, and for a user's own personal Web pages.

Many Internet Service Providers provide free space to allow all their users to create and maintain their own home pages.

hop on the Internet, an intermediate stage of the journey taken by a message travelling from one site to another.

Internet messages must travel through many machines to get to their destinations. The exact route is recorded in the ↝ bang path.

Hopper, Grace (1906–1992) born Grace Brewster Murray, US computer pioneer and mathematician who created the first compiler and helped invent the computer language ↝ COBOL. She also coined the term 'debug'.

Hopper was educated at Vassar and Yale. She volunteered for duty in World War II with the Naval Ordinance Computation Project. This was the beginning of a long association with the Navy (she was appointed rear admiral in 1983). After the war, Hopper joined a firm that eventually would become the Univac division of Sperry-Rand, to manufacture a commercial computer.

In 1945 she was ordered to Harvard University to assist Howard ↝ Aiken in building a computer. One day a breakdown of the machine was found to be due to a moth that had flown into the computer. Aiken came into the laboratory as Hopper was dealing with the insect. 'Why aren't you making numbers, Hopper?' he asked. Hopper replied: 'I am debugging the machine!'

Hopper's main contribution was to develop the first English-like data processing compiler, B-0 (Flow-Matic). In 1959, she was invited to join a Pentagon team attempting to create and standardize a single computer language for commercial use. This led to the development of ↝ COBOL (Common Business-Oriented Language), still one of the most widely used languages.

host or *host computer*, large computer that supports a number of smaller computers or terminals that are connected to it via a network. Hosts may be mainframe computers that service large number of terminals or green screens, or, for example, Internet hosts that serve Web pages and files to personal computers attached via the Internet.

hostname alternative name given to a computer when it is connected to the ↝ Internet. The hostname is used instead of the unique Internet address which is in the form for four numbers. The hostname is an alias, or nickname, and is easier to remember than the number.

One of the roles of the Domain Name Service is to maintain tables of Internet addresses and their corresponding hostnames.

hot key key stroke (or sequence of key strokes) that triggers a memory-resident program. Such programs are called ↝ terminate and stay resident. Hot keys should be chosen so that they do not conflict with key sequences in commonly used applications.

TIP

hot key

Ctrl|Alt|Del is a useful hot key sequence to try if your computer is not responding to your input. This hot key sequence will restart your computer.

hotlist stored list of favourite sites which allows users to move quickly to frequently used resources. See also ↝ bookmark; ↝ favourites.

hot-swapping technique that allows a user to exchange components without having to shut down the entire system.

The most common example of hot-swapping is ↝ PCMCIA (*personal computer memory card interface adapter*), or PC Card, components: a user with only one PCMCIA slot can exchange a modem for a network card or hard disk while the machine is running. Special software recognizes the components and allows their immediate use.

HP abbreviation for ↝ Hewlett-Packard.

HPGL abbreviation for *Hewlett-Packard Graphics Language*, file format used in ↝ vector graphics. HPGL is often generated by ↝ CAD systems.

href tag in HTML (hypertext markup language) that indicates that the following text is a link either to another portion of the same document or to an external document on the same or a remote site.

HSCSD abbreviation for *High Speed Circuit Switched Data*, wireless service introduced in 2000 by UK mobile phone operator Orange, allowing users of ↝ laptop computers and ↝ personal digital assistants (PDAs) to transmit data at a speed of 28.8 kilobytes per second (kbps). HSCSD is a rival of ↝ GPRS, which requires the use of a ↝ mobile phone to connect laptops and PDAs.

HTML abbreviation for *Hypertext Markup Language*, standard for structuring and describing a document on the ↝ World Wide Web. The HTML standard provides labels for constituent parts of a document (for example headings and paragraphs) and permits the inclusion of images, sounds, and 'hyperlinks' to other documents. A ↝ browser program is then used to convert this information into a graphical document on-screen. The specifications for HTML version 4, called ↝ Dynamic HTML, were adopted at the end of 1997.

HTML is a specific example of ↝ SGML (the international standard for text encoding). As such it is not a rigid standard but is constantly being improved to incorporate new features and allow greater freedom of design.

HTML extension any proprietary addition to the standard specification of HTML (hypertext markup language).

Both Microsoft and Netscape, publishers of the two leading Web ↝ browsers, have built in such extensions, which are controversial as they clash with the basic ideal that the Net should operate on open standards which allow interoperability. In general, any browser should be able to log on to any site and be able to access most of its information, but the features implemented with proprietary extensions will only display correctly with a browser that supports those extensions.

HTTP abbreviation for *Hypertext Transfer Protocol*, ↜ protocol used for communications between client (the Web ↜ browser) and ↜ server on the World Wide Web.

hub central distribution point in a computer ↜ network.

human–computer interaction exchange of information between a person and a computer, through the medium of a ↜ user interface, studied as a branch of ergonomics.

Hypercard computer application developed for the Apple ↜ Macintosh, in which data are stored as if on cards in a card-index system. A group of cards forms a stack. Additional features include the ability to link cards in different ways and, by the use of software buttons (icons that can be clicked or double clicked with a mouse), to access other data. Hypercard is very similar to ↜ hypertext, although it does not conform to the rigorous definition of hypertext.

hyperlink link from one document to another or, within the same document, from one place to another. It can be activated by clicking on the link with a ↜ mouse. The link is usually highlighted in some way, for example by the inclusion of a small graphic. Documents linked in this way are described as ↜ hypertext. Examples of programs that use hypertext and hyperlinks are ↜ Windows help files, ↜ Acrobat, and ↜ Mosaic.

hypermedia system that uses links to lead users to related graphics, audio, animation, or video files in the same way that ↜ hypertext systems link related pieces of text. The World Wide Web is an example of a hypermedia system, as is ↜ Hypercard.

hypertext system for viewing information (both text and pictures) on a computer screen in such a way that related items of information can easily be reached. For example, the program might display a map of a country; if the user clicks (with a ↜ mouse) on a particular city, the program will display information about that city.

Hytelnet contraction of *hypertext browser for Telnet-accessible sites on the Internet*, program developed in 1990 which indexes Telnet-accessible sites on the Internet so that users can quickly look up the necessary access information.

Versions of Hytelnet exist for PCs, DEC VAXes, and Unix machines. Hytelnet is distributed as ↜ shareware; it is updated via the HYTEL-L electronic mailing list.

IAB abbreviation for ⮑ Internet Architecture Board.

IBM abbreviation for *International Business Machines*, multinational company, the largest manufacturer of computers in the world. The company is a descendant of the Tabulating Machine Company, formed in 1896 by US inventor Herman ⮑ Hollerith to exploit his punched-card machines. It adopted its present name in 1924. By 1991 it had an annual turnover of $64.8 billion and employed about 345,000 people, but in 1992 and 1993 it made considerable losses. The company acquired Lotus Development Corporation in 1995. By 1997 IBM had, under new management, recovered financially, with an annual turnover of $76 billion, which means it is still a dominant industry player.

Its acquisition of the Lotus Development Corporation gave IBM access to its wide range of innovative software, including the 1-2-3 spreadsheet and Notes, a market leader in groupware.

Founded in 1924, by former cash register salesman Tom Watson, IBM grew to monopolize the mechanical data processing business, and in the 1950s, thanks mainly to Tom Watson Jr, quickly took over the new electronic (computer-based) data processing business, too. IBM's sales increased from $734 million in 1956 to $51 billion in 1986, when the company dominated most computer markets: mainframes, minicomputers, personal computers, and networking. However, the rise of powerful microprocessors and the 'open systems' movement destroyed much of IBM's power; in the early 1990s it lost billions of dollars and shed almost half its 420,000 staff.

IBM became an important patron of modern design in the post-1945 years. Tom Watson Jr hired Eliot Noyes as chief design consultant. Previously an employee of Norman Bel Geddes, Noyes ensured that IBM worked with the best architects – among them Ludwig Mies van der Rohe and Marcel Breuer – and designed many of the company's machines, including the 'Selectric' electric typewriter in 1961.

IBM-compatible clone of an IBM PC; synonymous with PC-compatible.

Although there were successful personal computers before the PC, IBM set the most common standard for these machines when it launched the PC in 1981. It created a clone industry by using readily available parts in the IBM PC, instead of developing proprietary parts itself. The success of the PC established Intel processors and Microsoft software as industry standards.

iBook stylish ⮑ Apple notebook computer, with a case in blueberry or tangerine, launched in 1999 as a portable version of the ⮑ iMac desktop computer. The iBook contains a 6 gigabyte disk drive and a 56-kilobits-per-second modem.

ICANN acronym for *Internet Corporation for Assigned Names and Numbers*, not-for-profit organization set up by the US government in 1999 to oversee the issuing of top-level Internet ⮑ domain names. The private company Network Solutions had previously held a monopoly on this. ICANN has licensed many other companies to issue top-level domain names.

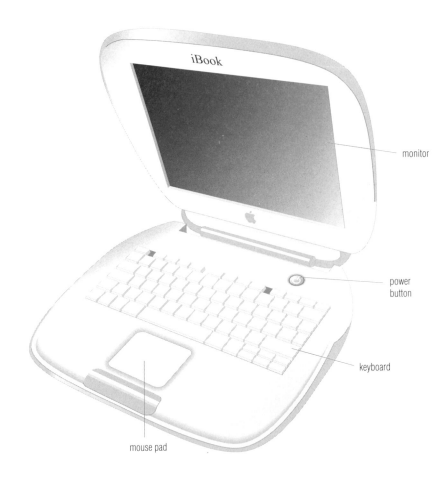

iBook

monitor

power
button

keyboard

mouse pad

iBook
*The iBook is Apple's
industrial-style portable
computer, with protective
casing and integral carrying
handle. Recently released
versions feature a built-in
DVD (digital versatile disk)
player and digital movie
maker.*

ICE acronym for *Information Content Exchange*, protocol developed in 1998 for the transfer of data to partnering Web sites. Applications based on ICE allow companies to construct syndicated publishing networks, Web superstores, and online reseller channels.

Companies that have working examples and implementations of ICE include Vignette, Kinecta, Microsoft, Xenosys, Macromedia, Intershop, Quark, and ArcadiaOne.

icon small picture on the computer screen, or ↝ VDU, representing an object or function that the user may manipulate or otherwise use. It is a feature of ↝ graphical user interface (GUI) systems. Icons make computers easier to use by allowing the user to point to and click with a ↝ mouse on pictures, rather than type commands.

ICQ abbreviation for *I seek you*, software system created by Mirabilis Ltd that enables Internet users to locate one another online so that they can chat or exchange messages. Both users must run the software for the system to work.

IDEA acronym for *International Data Encryption Algorithm*, encryption
➥ algorithm, developed in 1990 in Zürich, Switzerland. For reasons of speed, it is
used in the encryption program ➥ Pretty Good Privacy (PGP) along with ➥ RSA.

id Software software company that publishes popular games such as ➥ *Doom*
and *Quake*, based in Texas, USA. An entire subculture has built up around id's
games because of its habit of releasing ➥ source code to enable fans to write
their own additional game levels using settings of their own choice.

  The company's first major product was the 1992 game *Wolfenstein 3-D*, in
which players move around a series of complicated mazes retrieving treasure
and shooting Nazi troops and guard dogs. *Quake*, released in 1996, uses
complex, carefully styled 3-D graphics, adds vertical movement and underwater
caves, and includes a gruesome collection of fierce aliens. Both *Doom* and
Quake can be played competitively over networks, including the Internet.

IETF abbreviation for ➥ Internet Engineering Task Force.

i.Link Sony Corporation's branded name for the IEEE ➥ 1394 serial port and
bus. Sony has licensed the name and logo to other companies including
Hitachi, Matsushita, Sharp, and Victor of Japan (JVC).

IMA abbreviation for ➥ Interactive Multimedia Association.

iMac stylish ➥ Apple desktop computer, launched in 1998, with monitor cases
in bright colours (including tangerine, strawberry, blueberry, grape, and lime).
Some models contain digital video technology, and all may be connected to the
Internet via wireless technology.

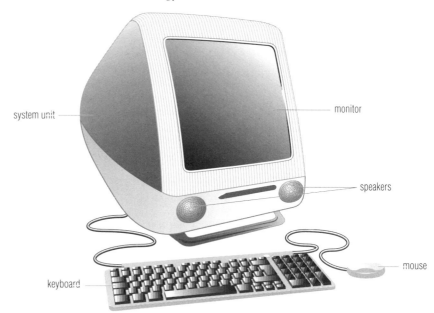

iMac
The iMac is a desktop computer with integral monitor, developed by Apple. It relies on two standardized USB (Universal Serial Bus) ports to link to peripheral devices such as printers and floppy-disk drives.

system unit

monitor

speakers

mouse

keyboard

image compression one of a number of methods used to reduce the amount of information required to represent an image, so that it takes up less computer memory and can be transmitted more rapidly and economically via telecommunications systems. It plays a major role in fax transmission and in videophone and multimedia systems.

image map on the World Wide Web, a large image with multiple hot spots on which users click to navigate around the site.

image processing technique for cleaning up and digitally retouching photographs.

A lot of the fundamental work involved in developing image processing techniques was done at the Jet Propulsion Laboratory in Pasadena, California, USA, which manages unmanned space flight for NASA. Pictures taken in-flight of planets have drop-out areas where data is missing due to static or other interference. These pictures are also often taken using parts of the spectrum which the human eye cannot see. Accordingly, computer ↝ algorithms had to be developed to fill in the missing data and compute the correct colours. The images produced in this way are made available publicly and often appear in the media.

immediate access memory ↝ memory provided in the ↝ central processing unit to store the programs and data in current use.

immersive in ↝ virtual reality, term describing the sense that the user is completely surrounded by and immersed in the virtual world.

impact printer computer printer that creates characters by striking an inked ribbon against the paper beneath. Examples of impact printers are dot-matrix printers, daisywheel printers, and most types of line printer.

Impact printers are noisier and slower than nonimpact printers, such as ink-jet and laser printers, but can be used to produce carbon copies.

import file file that can be read by a program even though it was produced as an ↝ export file by a different program or make of computer.

incremental backup ↝ backup copy of only those files that have been modified or created since the last incremental or full backup.

indexed sequential file type of ↝ file access in which an index is used to obtain the address of the ↝ block containing the required record.

indexing computerized service on the Internet that automatically scans ↝ servers and compiles lists of the information they hold to make it easier for users to find what they are looking for.

Indexing servers for ↝ FTP (File Transfer Protocol) are called Archie servers. On the World Wide Web, the best-known indexing service is ↝ Yahoo!, which organizes sites by categories and subcategories, and also allows free-form searching.

Industrial Light & Magic *ILM*, company that creates special effects for films and which has broken new ground in computer animation techniques (see ➴ animation, computer). ILM was set up in 1975 by US director George Lucas to create special effects for his *Star Wars* films, and is based in San Rafael, California, USA.

The company's best-known computer-generated effects include the sea creature in *The Abyss* (1990), the liquid-metal man in *Terminator 2* (1991), and the dinosaurs in *Jurassic Park* (1993).

information superhighway popular collective name for the ➴ Internet and other related large-scale computer networks. The term was first used in 1993 by US vice-president Al Gore in a speech outlining plans to build a high-speed national data communications network.

information technology *IT*, collective term for the various technologies involved in processing and transmitting information. They include computing, telecommunications, and microelectronics. The term became popular in the UK after the Government's 'Information Technology Year' in 1972.

Word processors, databases, and spreadsheets are just some of the computing ➴ software packages that have revolutionized work in the office environment. Not only can work be done more quickly than before, but IT has given decision-makers the opportunity to consider far more data when making decisions.

infotainment contraction of *information and entertainment*, term applied to software that seeks to inform and entertain simultaneously. Many non-fiction ➴ CD-ROM titles are classified as infotainment, such as multimedia encyclopedias or reference disks. Compare ➴ edutainment.

infrastructure on the Internet, the underlying structure of telephone links, leased lines, and computer programs that makes communication possible.

ink-jet printer computer printer that creates characters and graphics by spraying very fine jets of quick-drying ink onto paper. Ink-jet printers range in size from small machines designed to work with microcomputers to very large machines designed for high-volume commercial printing.

Because they produce very high-quality printing and are virtually silent, small ink-jet printers (along with ➴ laser printers) are replacing impact printers, such as dot-matrix and daisywheel printers, for use with microcomputers.

inline graphics on the ➴ World Wide Web, images included in Web pages which can be downloaded and viewed on the fly. Web ➴ browsers display these graphics automatically without any action required by the user. Those with slow connections, however, may choose to turn these off in the interests of speed and just view the text.

inline video on the ➴ World Wide Web, video files included in Web pages which can be played back on the fly. Web ➴ browsers typically require a ➴ helper application or ➴ plug-in to be installed to play these files.

---

eHow

http://www.ehow.com/

Site providing over 15,000 step-by-step guides to a wide range of topics, both techncial and non-technical. Each guide is linked to related articles and other relevant Web sites, and includes an indication of the skill level involved to complete the task.

WEB LINK

TIP

inline video

Most Web sites which include inline video have links to the necessary software for users who aren't already equipped.

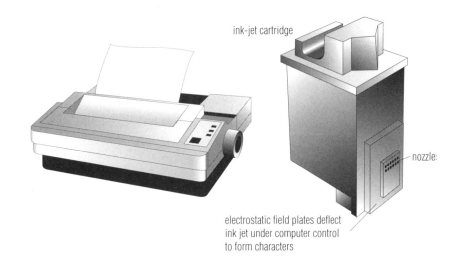

ink-jet cartridge

nozzle:

electrostatic field plates deflect
ink jet under computer control
to form characters

ink-jet printer
High-quality print images
are produced by ink-jet
printers by squirting ink
through a series of nozzles.

input device device for entering information into a computer. Input devices include ⤳ keyboards, ⤳ joysticks, mice, ⤳ light pens, touch-sensitive screens, ⤳ scanners, ⤳ graphics tablets, ⤳ speech-recognition devices, and vision systems. Compare ⤳ output device.

Input devices that are used commercially – for example, by banks, postal services, and supermarkets – must be able to read and capture large volumes of data very rapidly. Such devices include *document readers* for ⤳ magnetic-ink character recognition (MICR), ⤳ optical character recognition (OCR), and ⤳ optical mark recognition (OMR); mark-sense readers; bar-code scanners; magnetic-strip readers; and point-of-sale (POS) terminals. Punched-card and paper-tape readers were used in earlier commercial applications but are now obsolete.

Institute for the Management of Information Systems *IMIS*, UK information technology professional body. The IMIS was formed in 1978 from a merger of the Data Processing Management Association and the Institute of Data Processing, both founded in the 1960s. The present name was introduced in 1998.

instruction register special memory location used to hold the instruction that the computer is currently processing. It is located in the control unit of the ⤳ central processing unit, and receives instructions individually from the immediate-access memory during the fetch phase of the ⤳ fetch-execute cycle.

instruction set complete set of machine-code instructions that a computer's ⤳ central processing unit can obey.

integrated circuit *IC* or *silicon chip*, miniaturized electronic circuit produced on a single crystal, or chip, of a semiconducting material – usually silicon. It may contain many millions of components and yet measure only 5 mm/0.2 in square and 1 mm/0.04 in thick. The IC is encapsulated within a plastic or ceramic case, and linked via gold wires to metal pins with which it is connected to a ⏁ printed circuit board and the other components that make up such electronic devices as computers and calculators.

Integrated Services Digital Network *ISDN*, internationally developed telecommunications system for sending signals in ⏁ digital format. It involves converting the 'local loop' – the link between the user's telephone (or private automatic branch exchange) and the digital telephone exchange – from an ⏁ analogue system into a digital system, thereby greatly increasing the amount of information that can be carried. The first large-scale use of ISDN began in Japan in 1988.

ISDN has advantages in higher voice quality, better quality faxes, and the possibility of data transfer between computers faster than current modems. With ISDN's Basic Rate Access, a multiplexer divides one voice telephone line into three channels: two B bands and a D band. Each B band offers 64 kilobits per second and can carry one voice conversation or 50 simultaneous data calls at 1,200 bits per second. The D band is a data-signalling channel operating at 16 kilobits per second. With Primary Rate Access, ISDN provides 30 B channels.

British Telecom began offering ISDN to businesses in 1991, with some 47,000 ISDN-equipped lines. Its adoption in the UK is expected to stimulate the use of data-communications services such as faxing, teleshopping, and home banking. New services may include computer conferencing, where both voice and computer communications take place simultaneously, and videophones.

Intel manufacturer of the ⏁ microprocessors that form the basis of the IBM PC range and its clones. Intel developed the first microprocessor, the 4004, in 1971, and has largely retained compatibility throughout the x86 range from the 8086 to the 80486 and the ⏁ Pentium or 586 released in 1993. Intel's current strategy is to promote the use of the Pentium II processor, introduced in 1997, while it is developing its next-generation chip, code-named Merced, in conjunction with Hewlett-Packard.

Intel is thought to supply the processors for almost 90% of the world's personal computers.

A boycott of the new version of the company's computer chip, Pentium III, was called for on 25 January 1999 by several groups worried about Internet privacy. The chip is expected to carry a built-in identification number that would allow Web site operators to identify the computer and record the user's surfing habits. Intel believes the identification number would cut down on computer fraud.

intellectual property material such as computer software, magazine articles, songs, novels, or recordings which can be described as the expression of ideas fixed in a tangible form.

ISDN Tutorial

http://www.ralphb.net/ISDN/

Guide to ISDN for both beginners and advanced users. It begins with a definition of ISDN and a description of its benefits, and moves on to the various interfaces and protocols.

WEB LINK

Generally, intellectual property is protected by copyright law, and distribution, sale, and copying of such material is restricted so that the creators can be paid for their work. On the Internet, intellectual property may include the words, graphics, audio files, and other material which make up pages on the World Wide Web, as well as the words written by individuals in e-mail or on Usenet.

intellectual property rights right of control over the copying, distribution, and sale of ↝ intellectual property which is codified in the copyright laws.

The future of intellectual property rights is unclear, as the Internet makes mass distribution and copying quick and easy. In the mid-1990s, many schemes were being considered for using encryption to mark computer files or prevent copying in an effort to safeguard these rights. The ↝ World Intellectual Property Organization runs an online arbitration service for disputes over Internet addresses.

intelligent agent another name for ↝ agent.

intelligent terminal ↝ terminal with its own processor which can take some of the processing load away from the main computer.

interactive describing a computer system that will respond directly to data or commands entered by the user. For example, most popular programs, such as word processors and spreadsheet applications, are interactive. Multimedia programs are usually highly interactive, allowing users to decide what type of information to display (text, graphics, video, or audio) and enabling them (by means of ↝ hypertext) to choose an individual route through the information.

interactive computing system for processing data in which the operator is in direct communication with the computer, receiving immediate responses to input data. In ↝ batch processing, by contrast, the necessary data and instructions are prepared in advance and processed by the computer with little or no intervention from the operator.

interactive media new technology such as ↝ CD-ROM and online systems which allow users to interact with other users or to choose their own path through the material.

The newest attempts to create interactive media are books published on the World Wide Web which allow readers to use ↝ hyperlinks to move around the material at will in the order they choose. Other interactive media include plans for films and other projects which allow viewers to choose how to follow the story, which characters to focus on, or which plot threads to follow.

Interactive Multimedia Association *IMA*, organization founded in 1987 to promote the growth of the multimedia industry. Based in Anapolis, Maryland, USA, the IMA runs special interest groups, summit meetings, conferences, and trade shows for its member companies.

interactive television services provided through a television set that enable interaction by the viewer. Interactive TV services include ∿ electronic commerce (for example, home shopping and banking), ∿ video-on-demand, and the ability to select camera angles and to replay action, usually for sporting events. See ∿ Open.

interactive video *IV*, computer-mediated system that enables the user to interact with and control information (including text, recorded speech, or moving images) stored on video disk. IV is most commonly used for training purposes, using analogue video disks, but has wider applications with digital video systems such as CD-I (Compact Disc Interactive, from Philips and Sony) which are based on the CD-ROM format derived from audio compact discs.

Intercast ∿ Intel device that adds TV reception capability to a PC and uses blank lines to deliver data. A number of leading PC manufacturers expect to bundle Intercast TV tuner boards with new computer systems.

interface point of contact between two programs or pieces of equipment. The term is most often used for the physical connection between the computer and a peripheral device, which is used to compensate for differences in such operating characteristics as speed, data coding, voltage, and power consumption. For example, a printer interface is the cabling and circuitry used to transfer data from a computer to a printer, and to compensate for differences in speed and coding.

Common standard interfaces include the Centronics interface, used to connect parallel devices, and the ∿ RS-232 interface, used to connect serial devices. For example, in many microcomputer systems, an RS-232 interface is used to connect the microcomputer to a modem, and a Centronics device is used to connect it to a printer.

interlacing technique for increasing resolution on computer graphic displays. The electron beam traces alternate lines on each pass, providing twice the number of lines of a noninterlaced screen. However, screen refresh is slower and screen flicker may be increased over that seen on an equivalent noninterlaced screen.

TIP

internal modem

The disadvantages of an internal modem are that it can't easily be swapped from one computer to another, requires greater skill to install (except for PCMCIA), and has no external displays of lights to give users feedback.

intermercial contraction of interstitial commercial, advertising screen interposed between one Web page, where the user mouse-clicks on a link, and the destination page that the user is trying to reach.

internal modem ∿ modem that fits into a slot inside a personal computer. On older PCs, an internal modem may prove a better choice for high-speed data communications than an external modem, as it may have built-in features which make up for features missing in older computers. Internal modems are generally also cheaper, except for the small-sized ∿ PCMCIA types.

The disadvantages are that an internal modem cannot easily be swapped from one computer to another, require greater skill to install (again except for PCMCIA), and have no external displays of lights to give users feedback.

Interactive Television

Interacting with your television set Interactive television is any use of a television set where viewers do not merely passively watch the programme but are able to 'interact' by controlling what they are presented with. Trials of interactive television services have been taking place for the last 30 years. Because the television set is present in over 90% of homes in the developed world (99% in the USA and Japan), it seemed an ideal medium for home shopping and banking, playing games, and receiving information.

During the 1990s, both the power of the personal computer and the speed of data transmissions increased tremendously, leading to the development of the Internet as a global commercial medium. For a time, it seemed that there would no longer be any need for interactive television. The idea has persisted, however, because PC penetration (even in the USA) is nowhere near as high as that of television. Interactive television therefore retains its attraction as a means of reaching all those households that feel Internet access via a PC is either too expensive or too technical for them.

t-Commerce Home shopping, banking, and so on via television are becoming known as television commerce, or t-commerce. Interactive television providers are interested in incorporating smart-card readers into set-top boxes, so that money can be downloaded from a viewer's bank account onto a smart card. This would allow low-value items to be bought without the need for a credit card. Banks and shops have been keen to stress that online shopping will not mean the closure of branches or a reduction in the number of staff employed in them. In the UK, however, many bank branches in rural locations are already being closed as a result of the proliferation of electronic services.

Enhanced television Another form of interactivity consists of allowing viewers to select camera angles for sporting events, and letting them replay parts of a match alongside the live footage. A proposed development is live, online betting, which will need regulatory approval. In addition, viewers can actively participate in quiz shows, where they can compete alongside the studio contestants to win prizes. Educational programmes can also contain interactive sequences, providing a personalized version of the programme, together with local information, addresses, and so on.

Video-on-demand Viewers will be able to watch programmes whenever they like with video-on-demand (VOD). With programmes transmitted over broadband connections such as cable or ADSL (asymmetric digital subscriber line) telephone lines, VOD will allow viewers to stop, pause, rewind, and fast-forward in the same way that a video recorder does. Satellite and cable television companies already provide feature films on a near video-on-demand basis, where the same film is shown on several channels simultaneously, with staggered starting times. Although VOD has usually been associated with feature films, there is no reason why any type of programme should not be shown in this way.

Time-shifted television The US company TiVo produces special digital set-top boxes (manufactured under licence by Philips and Sony) containing a hard disk. The TiVo box acts as a highly sophisticated video recorder, allowing up to 30 hours of television programmes to be stored and replayed. The device is able to scan the television schedules in advance, and automatically select and record programmes the user is likely to enjoy, based on previous viewing preferences. It also allows the viewer to 'pause' live programmes. The TiVo service was launched in the UK in the autumn of 2000.

The Internet on TV A number of companies provide access to the Web and an e-mail service through the television set. To be able to use such a service properly requires the use of a keyboard, usually with an infrared connection to the set-top box. For several years, Microsoft has provided a WebTV service in the USA. In June 2000, both Microsoft and America Online (AOL) announced that they would deliver competing interactive television services, both featuring set-top boxes that allow programmes to be stored on disk. The AOL service will also allow users to 'chat' online with

Interactive Television (continued)

other viewers of the same programme, while Microsoft's UltimateTV will allow users to participate in game shows.

TV/PC convergence The convergence of the television set and the PC has been forecast for many years. A number of commentators have disputed that this will ever happen, however, pointing to the fundamentally different ways in which each device is used. Certainly, although television tuner boards have been available for the PC for several years, demand for them has been small. As broadband Internet access becomes available, however, television programmes and feature films will increasingly come to the PC via the Web. Although full convergence may never come about, nevertheless each device seems to be taking on the role of the other to a certain extent.

Alan Stewart

International Organization for Standardization *ISO*, international organization founded in 1947 to standardize technical terms, specifications, units, and so on. Its headquarters are in Geneva, Switzerland.

International Telecommunications Union *ITU*, international organization, based in Geneva, Switzerland, which manages telecommunications standards such as ⮡ modem speeds and ⮡ protocols. ITU activities include the coordination, development, regulation, and standardization of telecommunications.

The ITU has two permanent standards-making committees, the International Telegraph and Telephone Consultative Committee (CCITT) and the International Radio Consultative Committee (CCIR).

International Traffic in Arms Regulations US laws which prohibit the export of strong encryption by classifying it as a munition. Non-US users of common products such as ⮡ Netscape and ⮡ Lotus Notes are affected by these laws, as outside the USA American software suppliers must weaken the encryption built in to protect sensitive data.

In the mid-1990s several bills were introduced into the US Congress attempting to change these laws.

Internet global computer network connecting governments, companies, universities, and many other networks and users. ⮡ Electronic mail, ⮡ electronic conferencing, ⮡ online shopping, and educational and chat services are all supported across the network, as is the ability to access remote computers and send and retrieve files. In 1998 the Internet generated $301 billion in revenue, according to a report released in June 1999 by researchers at the University of Texas, USA. The Internet also created 1.2 million jobs in 1998. By June 2000, the number of Internet users worldwide was estimated to be 305 million. Of these, 137 million were in the USA and Canada, 83 million in Europe (with 16 million each in the UK and Germany), and 69 million in the Asia/Pacific region. A figure of 720 million users worldwide has been predicted for the end of 2005.

The technical underpinnings of the Internet were developed as a project funded by the US Defense Advanced Research Project Agency (DARPA) to research how to build a network that would withstand bomb damage. The Internet itself began in the mid-1980s with funding from the US National Science Foundation as a means to allow US universities to share the resources of five regional supercomputing centres. The number of users grew quickly, and in the early 1990s access became cheap enough for domestic users to have their own links on home personal computers. As the amount of information available via the Internet grew, indexing and search services such as Gopher, Archie, Veronica, and WAIS were created by Internet users to help both themselves and others. The newer World Wide Web allows seamless browsing across the Internet via ⮑ hypertext.

There has been a rapid growth of venture capital invested in companies involved in Internet operations. In 1999, the Internet grew by 62%, according to a study released in June 2000 by the University of Texas. Internet-related activities accounted for nearly 2.5 million jobs, including 650,000 which were newly created, and almost $524 billion/£328 billion in revenue. The study predicted that the same growth rate could take place again in 2000.

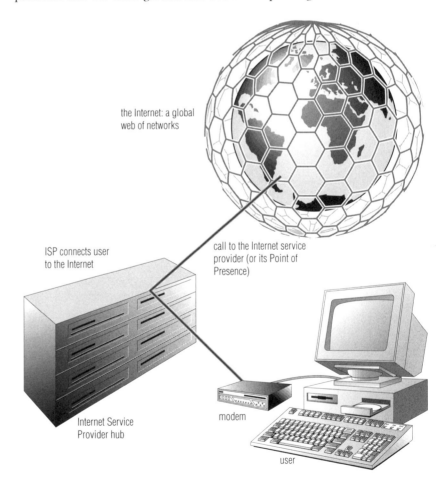

the Internet: a global web of networks

ISP connects user to the Internet

call to the Internet service provider (or its Point of Presence)

Internet Service Provider hub

modem

user

Internet
The Internet is accessed by users via a modem to the service provider's hub, which handles all connection requests. Once connected, the user can access a whole range of information from many different sources, including the World Wide Web.

US vice-president Al Gore announced plans, in April 1998, for Internet2 that will run on a second network Abilene, operated by private contractors, to provide a high-speed data communications backbone to serve the 170 US research universities, enabling them to bypass the congestion on the Internet. The network became operational in 1999.

Internet Architecture Board *IAB*, committee that coordinates the development of Internet ↝ standards. Set up 1983, the IAB is a technical advisory group of the ↝ Internet Society. Its responsibilities include architectural oversight for the ↝ protocols and procedures used by the Internet, standards process oversight and appeal, editorial management and publication of ↝ RFC (request for comments) documents, and advising the Internet Society concerning technical, architectural, procedural, and some policy matters.

Internet-enabled facility that allows desktop applications to exchange information directly across the Internet. The most common Internet facility to build in is e-mail. Also popular is integrated Web access, so that a user can click on a ↝ URL (uniform resource locator) from inside an application such as a word processor or personal information manager and be taken directly to that page on the World Wide Web.

Internet Engineering Task Force *IETF*, international group which supervises the development of ↝ RFC (requests for comments), ↝ protocols, and other engineering design for the Internet, reporting to the ↝ Internet Architecture Board. It was formed in 1986 and is based in Reston, Virginia, USA.

Internet Explorer Web ↝ browser created by Microsoft in 1995 to compete with ↝ Netscape Navigator. Internet Explorer is given away free by Microsoft and bundled with its Windows program. This is one of the bones of contention between ↝ Microsoft and the US Justice Department.

Internet phone technology allowing users of the World Wide Web to talk to each other in more or less real time, via microphones and headsets. Network delays mean such connections are not as good quality as traditional telephone connections, but they are much cheaper for long-distance calls since users pay only for their local telephone connection to the Internet.

The earliest products were limited in that they only allowed users to talk to each other if both were logged on to the Vocaltec Web site at the same time. More recent products make it possible for a person using the Internet to dial any telephone in the world.

In mid-1996, a group of US telephone companies asked the Federal Communications Commission to protect their business interests by regulating Internet telephony. The Voice on the Net (VON) coalition opposes this regulation.

Internet Relay Chat *IRC*, service that allows users connected to the Internet to chat with each other over many channels. There are probably hundreds of IRC channels active at any one time, covering a variety of topics. Many abbreviations are used to cut down on typing.

Internet Service Provider *ISP*, any company that sells dial-up access to the Internet. Several types of company provide Internet access, including online information services such as ↩ CompuServe and ↩ America Online (AOL), electronic conferencing systems such as the ↩ WELL and ↩ Compulink Information eXchange, and local bulletin board systems (BBSs). Most recently founded ISPs, such as ↩ Demon Internet and ↩ PIPEX, offer only direct access to the Internet without the burden of running services of their own just for their members.

Such companies typically work out cheaper for their users, as they charge a low, flat rate for unlimited usage. By contrast, commercial online services typically charge by the hour or minute.

The second largest Internet service provider, after AOL, was formed in the USA by the merger of Mindspring Enterprises, based in Atlanta, Georgia, and Earthlink Network in Pasadena, California, completed in February 2000. Mindspring had a market value of about $1.5 billion and EarthLink was worth about $2 billion. The deal created a company named Earth-Link with more than 3 million subscribers (to AOL's 20 million).

In September 1998, the UK ISP scene was revolutionized by the launch by Dixons, the UK high-street electrical retailer, of ↩ Freeserve, the first ISP with no registration or set-up fees and no monthly subscription charges. Users still have to pay for local-rate telephone connection charges. In 2000, this freedom from charges was taken a step further with the launch of services free of telephone charges, but in some cases with a flat fee, by ↩ BT, ↩ AltaVista, ↩ ntl, and others. BT also introduced a flat-fee broadband service utilising ↩ ADSL.

Internet Society *ISOC*, global volunteer group that works to coordinate and develop the Internet and its underlying technology. It was founded in 1992 and is based in Reston, Virginia, USA; the president (1996) is Vinton Cerf. Members include individuals, companies, nonprofit-making organizations, and government agencies.

Internet Talk Radio or Internet multicasting service, service that broadcasts radio programmes of interest to the technical community, such as *Geek of the Week*. Based in Washington, DC, USA, the service broadcasts via ↩ MBONE.

Internet worm virus; see ↩ worm.

ISP	Web address	Subscription	E-mail addresses	Proprietary Content	Free Web space (MB)	Helpline
AOL	www.aol.co.uk	monthly sub	5	yes	10	free
BT Internet	www.btinternet.com	monthly sub	5	no	10	local rate
Cable & Wireless Lite	www.cwcom.net	free to C&W customers	5	yes	20	national rate
CompuServe	www.compuserve.co.uk	monthly sub	5	yes	10	national rate
ClaraNET	www.clara.net	monthly sub	unlimited	no	25	free
Demon	www.demon.net	monthly sub	unlimited	no	20	national rate
Easynet	www.easynet.co.uk	monthly sub	5	no	unlimited	free
Freeserve	www.freeserve.net	free	unlimited	yes	15	50p per minute
LineOne	www.lineone.net	free	unlimited	yes	10	50p per minute
MSN Freeweb	www.msn.co.uk	free	1	yes	none	national rate
Virgin Net	www.virgin.net	free	5	yes	10	50p per minute
Which? Online	www.which.net	monthly sub	5	yes	5	£1 per minute
WHSmith Online	www.whsmith.co.uk	free	unlimited	yes	12	national rate

Internet Service Providers
Selected ISPs as of March 2000

Internet Talk Radio

http://museum.media.org/radio/

Internet Talk Radio makes audio files of its programmes available for download via file transfer protocol (FTP) and also on the World Wide Web.

WEB LINK

InterNIC service that administers domain names and maintains a number of Internet user directories. Users interested in registering a particular domain name can use the InterNIC's resources to check if the domain name or a similar one is already in use. See ⇔ ICANN.

interpolation mathematical technique for using two values to calculate intermediate values. It is used in ⇔ computer graphics to create smooth shadings.

interpreter computer program that translates and executes a program written in a high-level language. Unlike a ⇔ compiler, which produces a complete machine-code translation of the high-level program in one operation, an interpreter translates the source program, instruction by instruction, each time that program is run.

Because each instruction must be translated each time the source program is run, interpreted programs run far more slowly than do compiled programs. However, unlike compiled programs, they can be executed immediately without waiting for an intermediate compilation stage.

interrupt signal received by the computer's central processing unit that causes a temporary halt in the execution of a program while some other task is performed. Interrupts may be generated by the computer's internal electronic clock (clock interrupt), by an input or output device, or by a software routine. After the computer has completed the task to which it was diverted, control returns to the original program.

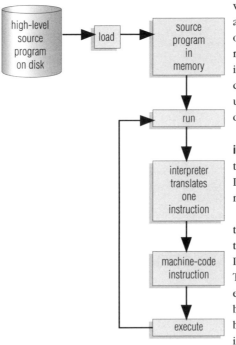

For example, many computers, while printing a long document, allow the user to carry on with other work. When the printer is ready for more data, it sends an interrupt signal that causes the computer to halt work on the user's program and transmit more data to the printer.

intranet use of software and other technology developed for the Internet on internal company ∽ networks.

Many company networks (and those of other organizations) use the same ∽ protocols as the Internet, namely ∽ TCP/IP. Therefore the same technology that enables the World Wide Web can be used on an internal network to build an organization-wide web of internal documents that is familiar, easy to use, and comparatively inexpensive.

interpreter
The sequence of events when running an interpreter on a high-level language program. Instructions are translated one at a time, making the process a slow one; however, interpreted programs do not need to be compiled and may be executed immediately.

inverse multiplexing technique for combining individual low-bandwidth channels into a single high-bandwidth channel. It is used to create high-speed telephone links for applications such as ∽ videoconferencing which require the transmission of huge quantities of data.

inverse video or *reverse video*, display mode in which images on a display screen are presented as a negative of their normal appearance.

For example, if the computer screen normally displays dark images on a light background, inverse video will change all or part of the screen to a light image on a dark background.

Inverse video is commonly used to highlight parts of a display or to mark out text and pictures that the user wishes the computer to change in some way. For example, the user of a word-processing program might use a pointing device such as a ∽ mouse to mark in inverse video a paragraph of text that is to be deleted from the document.

inverted index or *inverted file*, file that reorganizes the structure of an existing data file to enable a rapid search to be made for all records having one field falling within set limits.

For example, a file used by an estate agent might store records on each house for sale, using a reference number as the key field for ↝ sorting. One field in each record would be the asking price of the house. To speed up the process of drawing up lists of houses falling within certain price ranges, an inverted file might be created in which the records are rearranged according to price. Each record would consist of an asking price, followed by the reference numbers of all the houses offered for sale at this approximate price.

I/O abbreviation for *input/output*, see ↝ input devices and ↝ output devices. The term is also used to describe transfer to and from disk – that is, disk I/O.

Iomega leading manufacturer of removable storage and back-up devices, in direct competition with Syquest. Based in Roy, Utah, USA, Iomega's two most popular products are the Zip drive, which uses inexpensive 100Mb disks, and the Jaz drive, which uses 1Gb disks.

IP address abbreviation for *Internet protocol address*, numbered ↝ address assigned to an Internet host. Traditionally, IP addresses are ↝ 32-bit, which means that numbered addresses have four sections separated by dots, each a decimal number between 0 and 255.

IRC abbreviation for ↝ Internet Relay Chat.

IrDA abbreviation for Infrared Data Association, which sets the standard by which infrared signals may be used to beam data between two devices: for example, between two computers, or a computer and a printer. Users of handheld computers frequently exchange electronic business cards or ↝ vCards using built-in IrDA ports.

IRQ abbreviation for *interrupt request*, request for an ↝ interrupt to be generated to allow programs and devices to function even while the computer is performing another task. A PC-compatible computer uses a series of interrupt requests numbered from IRQ0 to IRQ9, which are assigned to devices such as sound cards, mice, and serial communications ports.

ISA bus abbreviation for *industry standard architecture bus*, 16-bit data ↝ bus introduced in 1984 with the IBM PC AT and still in common use in PCs, alongside the superior ↝ PCI bus. PC hardware and software manufacturers would like to get rid of the ISA bus as it is not compatible with ↝ Plug and Play.

ISDN abbreviation for ↝ Integrated Services Digital Network, a telecommunications system.

ISO 9660 standard file format for ↝ CD-ROM disks, synonymous with ↝ High-Sierra format. This format is compatible with most systems, so the same disk can contain both Apple Macintosh and PC versions.

ISOC abbreviation for ↝ Internet Society.

ISP abbreviation for ↝ Internet Service Provider.

iteration method of solving a problem by performing the same steps repeatedly until a certain condition is satisfied. For example, in one method of ↝ sorting, adjacent items are repeatedly exchanged until the data are in the required sequence.

ITU abbreviation for *International Telecommunications Union*, the standards-setting body for the communications industry.

jack small plug allowing users to connect peripherals to CPUs ($\leftharpoondown$ central processing units).

Jacquard, Joseph Marie (1752–1834) French textile manufacturer. He invented a punched-card system for programming designs on a carpetmaking loom (the Jacquard loom). In 1801 he constructed looms that used a series of punched cards to control the pattern of longitudinal warp threads depressed before each sideways passage of the shuttle. On later machines the punched cards were joined to form an endless loop that represented the 'program' for the repeating pattern of a carpet.

Jacquard-style punched cards were used in the early computers of the 1940s–1960s.

Jacquard was born in Lyon and inherited a small weaving business. He invented the Jacquard loom after becoming bankrupt, and worked on improving it at the Paris Conservatoire des Arts et Métiers from 1804. In Lyon and elsewhere, his machines were smashed by weavers who feared unemployment. By 1812 there were 11,000 Jacquard looms working in France, and they were introduced into many other countries.

Jacquard's attachment for pattern weaving, which was later improved by others, allowed patterns to be woven without the intervention of the weaver. Weavers had always had to plan the pattern before they began their task. This planning now became the essential feature of the weaver's job, and once the pattern had been punched onto cards, it could be used over and over again.

Jacquard system use of punched cards to direct the operation of a loom in weaving patterns. It was devised by French engineer Joseph Jacquard, and is similar to a system first used in China in the 3rd century bc, where a loom was controlled by a memory frame with silk threads of varying lengths.

jaggies 'stepped' appearance of curved or diagonal lines in computer graphics caused by $\leftharpoondown$ aliasing.

JANET acronym for *Joint Academic Network*, network linking academic and research institutes in the UK. JANET is composed of many interconnected smaller networks, controlled by a committee called the Joint Network Team. Sites which subscribe to the network can communicate with each other, with other academic networks, and with external services.

Java programming language much like C developed by James Gosling at $\leftharpoondown$ Sun Microsystems in 1995. Java has been adopted as a multipurpose, cross-platform lingua franca for network computing, including the $\leftharpoondown$ World Wide Web. When users connect to a server that uses Java, they download a small program called an $\leftharpoondown$ applet onto their computers. The applet then runs on the computer's own processor via a $\leftharpoondown$ Java Virtual Machine program or JVM. In 2000 Java 2 Micro Edition was released, designed for use in handheld devices, phones, and pagers.

Java 3D set of special 3-dimensional graphics functions built into the latest version of the ⤳ Java programming language. Java 3D allows programmers to develop 3D models and ⤳ virtual worlds. Because Java programs are portable, and can be run using a Web ⤳ browser, Java 3D is becoming a serious alternative to another computing language, ⤳ VRML, for developing Web-based virtual worlds.

Java Beans specification devised by ⤳ Sun Microsystems, according to which ⤳ object-oriented programs can be created in the ⤳ Java language. A Java Bean is similar to an ⤳ ActiveX control in Microsoft's software architecture.

JavaScript ⤳ scripting language commonly used to add interactive elements to Web pages. JavaScript was developed by ⤳ Netscape Communications as LiveScript (it was not derived from Java) and has been standardized by ⤳ ECMA as ECMAScript.

Java Virtual Machine *JVM*, program that sits on top of a computer's usual operating system and runs Java ⤳ applets.

Different computers require different JVMs but they should run the same Java code. This means that servers only need to provide one version of each applet, instead of different 'native code' versions for PCs, Apple Macintoshes, and Unix workstations, as is the case with other plug-ins.

A JVM is commonly supplied as part of a Web browser but may be included as part of the operating system.

Because the JVM interprets Java code – applets are not compiled into processor-specific machine code like normal programs – Java tends to be slow. However, a just-in-time compiler (JIT) can be used to compile code on the fly for faster results. Another problem is that not all JVMs are the same, and incompatibilities mean applets may not in fact run correctly on every machine, as intended.

Jobs, Steven Paul (1955–   ) US computer entrepreneur. He cofounded ⤳ Apple Computer Inc with Stephen ⤳ Wozniak in 1976, and founded ⤳ NeXT Technology Inc in 1985. In 1986 he bought Pixar Animation Studios, the computer animation studio spun off from George Lucas's LucasFilm.

Jobs has been involved with the creation of three different types of computer: the Apple II personal computer in 1977, the Apple ⤳ Macintosh in 1984 – marketed as 'the computer for the rest of us' – and the NeXT workstation in 1988. The NeXT was technically the most sophisticated and powerful design, but it became a commercial disaster, and in 1993 NeXT abandoned hardware manufacturing to concentrate on its highly-regarded Unix-based ⤳ object-oriented operating system, NeXTStep. Apple Computer bought NeXT at the end of 1996 to obtain NextStep, and Jobs returned to Apple in an advisory capacity. However, he soon took over as acting chief executive officer of the struggling firm in 1997, his position becoming permanent in 2000.

Born in Silicon Valley, California, Jobs began working for Atari designing computer games in 1972 after dropping out of college. He started working with Steve Wozniak making home computers in a garage.

joystick input device that signals to a computer the direction and extent of displacement of a hand-held lever. It is similar to the joystick used to control the flight of an aircraft.

Joysticks are sometimes used to control the movement of a cursor (marker) across a display screen, but are much more frequently used to provide fast and direct input for moving the characters and symbols that feature in computer games. Unlike a ↝ mouse, which can move a pointer in any direction, simple games joysticks are often capable only of moving an object in one of eight different directions. Today, many joysticks and control pads feature some form of ↝ force feedback.

JPEG abbreviation for *Joint Photographic Experts Group*, used to describe a compression standard set up by that group and now widely accepted for the storage and transmission of colour images. The JPEG compression standard reduces the size of image files considerably.

jump programming instruction that causes the computer to branch to a different part of a program, rather than execute the next instruction in the program sequence. Unconditional jumps are always executed; conditional jumps are only executed if a particular condition is satisfied.

jumper rectangular plug used to make connections on a circuit board. By pushing a jumper onto a particular set of pins on the board, or removing another, users can adjust the configuration of their computer's circuitry. Most home users, however, prefer to leave the insides of their machines with all the factory settings intact.

justification in printing and word processing, the arrangement of text so that it is aligned with either the left or right margin, or both.

Left-justified text has lines of different length that are perfectly aligned with the left margin but not with the right margin. The left margin is straight but the right margin is uneven, or ragged. Right-justified text, normally only used for columns of numbers, has lines of different length that are perfectly aligned with the right margin but not with the left margin. The right margin is straight but the left margin is ragged. Fully justified text has lines of the same length that are perfectly aligned with both the left and the right margins. Both margins are even. Many word processors can automatically produce fully justified text by inserting extra spaces between the words in each line, or by adjusting the spacing between the letters (microspacing).

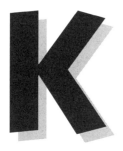

KA9Q ↝ TCP/IP protocol named after the call sign of Philip Karn, the radio ham who wrote it for ↝ packet radio. The system proved also to be useable on telephone connections, and so was adapted to several other computer platforms. It formed the basis of connections to ↝ Demon Internet for many years.

Kapor, Mitchell (1951–) US entrepreneur and software designer who founded Lotus Development Corporation, a leading business software company, in 1982. Eight years later, he co-founded the Electronic Frontier Foundation, a non-profit-making organization concerned with protecting civil liberties, in particular freedom of speech on the Internet. Kapor is also a professor of media arts and sciences at the Massachussetts Institute of Technology.

Kay, Alan (1940–) US computing expert who became a key figure in the development of ↝ graphical user interfaces (later popularized by the Apple Macintosh) and object-oriented languages (Smalltalk) while working at Xerox's Palo Alto Research Centre (PARC) throughout the 1970s. Kay also came up with the inspirational idea of the DynaBook, a sort of computer-based personal digital assistant. Kay spent 1984–96 as an Apple Fellow, working mainly on future-oriented projects with children. In 1996 he joined Walt Disney Imagineering as a Disney Fellow.

Kerberos system of symmetric ↝ key cryptography developed at the Massachussetts Institute of Technology.

kermit ↝ file-transfer protocol, originally developed at Columbia University and made available without charge. Kermit is available as part of most communications packages and available on most operating systems, but it is now rarely used on the Internet. Kermit is named after the frog in *Sesame Street* and *The Muppets*.

key in cryptography, the password needed to both encode and decipher a file. The key performs a sequence of operations on the original data. The recipient of the encoded file will need to apply another key in order to reverse all the operations in the correct order. Current encryption techniques such as ↝ Pretty Good Privacy (PGP) make use of a ↝ public key and a secret one.

keyboard input device resembling a typewriter keyboard, used to enter instructions and data. There are many variations on the layout and labelling of keys. Extra numeric keys may be added, as may special-purpose function keys, whose effects can be defined by programs in the computer.

key escrow in ↝ public key cryptography, requirement that users store copies of their private keys with the government or other authorities for release to law enforcement officials upon production of the necessary legal documents.

Key escrow was first proposed in the USA, where it was built into the controversial ↝ Clipper chip. In 1996, both the USA and the European Union were considering legislation requiring users of strong encryption to escrow their keys to protect law enforcement interests.

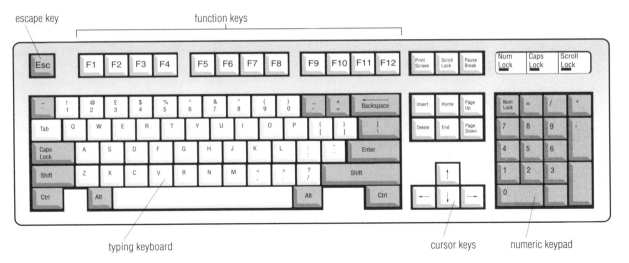

escape key   function keys

typing keyboard   cursor keys   numeric keypad

keyboard
A standard 102-key keyboard. As well as providing a QWERTY typing keyboard, the function keys (labelled F1–F12) may be assigned tasks specific to a particular system.

key field selected field, or portion, of a record that is used to identify that record uniquely; in a file of records it is the field used as the basis for ↪ sorting the file. For example, in a file containing details of a bank's customers, the customer account number would probably be used as the key field.

key frame in animation, a frame which was drawn by the user rather than generated by the computer. Animators feed a sequence of key frames into the computer, allowing the program to draw the intervening stages in a process known as tweening.

key-to-disk system or *key-to-tape system*, system that enables large amounts of data to be entered at a keyboard and transferred directly onto computer-readable disks or tapes.

Such systems are used in ↪ batch processing, in which batches of data, prepared in advance, are processed by computer with little or no intervention from the user. The preparation of the data may be controlled by a minicomputer, freeing a larger, mainframe computer for the task of processing.

Kilby, Jack St Clair (1923–) US electrical engineer, co-inventor of the ↪ integrated circuit, popularly known as the microchip, for which he was awarded the 2000 Nobel Prize for Physics (shared with Zhores Alferov and Herbert Kroemer). The integrated circuit was developed independently by Kilby at Texas Instruments, Dallas, Texas, in 1958 and by Robert ↪ Noyce at Fairchild Semiconductor in California in 1959.

Kilby was the first to produce a working chip, but when Noyce's patent application was challenged by Texas Instruments, the courts found in Noyce's favour. While Noyce went into chip manufacturing at Intel, Kilby developed applications such as calculators – which helped to establish Texas Instruments as a leader in this field – and promoted the widespread use of microchips. Integrated circuits have allowed microelectronics to dominate all modern technology and can be regarded as one of the most influential inventions of the 20th century. They are used in all modern electronics equipment, ranging from washing machines to satellites and have allowed the rapid development of increasingly faster and more compact computers.

Kilby was born in Jefferson City, Missouri. He works for Texas Instruments as a consultant and was distinguished professor of electrical engineering at Texas A&M University, College Station, Texas from 1978 until 1984.

killer application program so good or so compelling to certain potential users that they buy the computer that the program runs on for no other reason than to be able to use that program.

Killer applications are very rare. The most successful was VisiCalc, the first spreadsheet to run on a personal computer (the original Apple II microcomputer). VisiCalc succeeded as a killer application because it provided a unique tool for accountants to manipulate numbers easily without the need for programming skills. Another clear example is PageMaker, the first desktop publishing program, which was responsible for selling the Apple ⟿ Macintosh to the design and publishing community.

The ⟿ World Wide Web is the killer application for the Internet: by bringing visual excitement and ease of use to the Internet, it inspired people to buy new computers capable of supporting Web ⟿ browsers.

killfile file specifying material that you do not wish to see when accessing a ⟿ newsgroup. By entering names, subjects, or phrases into a killfile, users can make ⟿ Usenet a more pleasant experience, filtering out tedious threads, offensive subject headings, ⟿ spamming, or contributions from other irritating subscribers.

kilobyte *K* or *KB*, unit of memory equal to 1,024 ⟿ bytes. It is sometimes used, less precisely, to mean 1,000 bytes.

In the metric system, the prefix 'kilo-' denotes multiplication by 1,000 (as in kilometre, a unit equal to 1,000 metres). However, computer memory size is based on the ⟿ binary number system, and the most convenient binary equivalent of 1,000 is 2^{10}, or 1,024.

kiosk any computer that has been set up to act as an information centre in a public place. Users navigate the display using keyboards or ⟿ touch screens, but are never allowed to access the computer's operating system. A kiosk in a museum might show an interactive multimedia display, or one in a library might give readers access to catalogues.

knowbot program that will search a system or a network, such as the Internet, seeking and retrieving information on behalf of a user and reporting back when it has found it. An example is the Knowbot Information Service, which can process users' queries by e-mail.

knowledge-based system *KBS*, computer program that uses an encoding of human knowledge to help solve problems. It was discovered during research into ⏎ artificial intelligence that adding heuristics (rules of thumb) enabled programs to tackle problems that were otherwise difficult to solve by the usual techniques of computer science.

Chess-playing programs have been strengthened by including knowledge of what makes a good position, or of overall strategies, rather than relying solely on the computer's ability to calculate variations.

knowledge management process by which an organization gathers, organizes, shares, and analyses its knowledge. Data entered via a ⏎ keyboard, a ⏎ scanner, or ⏎ voice input can be catalogued, indexed, filtered, and linked. The information can then be refined, for example through ⏎ data mining, in preparation for dissemination.

Kurzweil, Raymond C (1948–) US computer scientist and entrepreneur. He developed a print-to-speech reading machine for the blind in 1976 and a computer music keyboard in 1984. A pioneer in automated speech-recognition, he founded Kurzweil Applied Intelligence in 1982, which introduced the Kurzweil Voicesystem in 1985; technology to transfer speech directly to a computer. His VoiceMED technology for voice-controlled patient reporting, introduced in 1986, has been widely used by physicians and hospitals. Kurzweil was born in New York City.

LAN abbreviation for ⇌ local area network.

Lanier, Jaron (1960–) US computing innovator who coined the term ⇌ virtual reality (VR), and set up a small company, VPL Research Inc, to produce the first VR headsets and data gloves. The headsets enabled wearers to experience graphical worlds created by high-powered computers and to 'meet' in virtual spaces. In 1996 he was chief scientist at New Leaf Systems Inc, and visiting scholar at Columbia University's Department of Computer Science and New York University's Tisch School of the Arts. Lanier is also a musician, a composer, and a painter.

Laplink software that allows intelligent transfer of files between computers. Laplink is a key tool for those managing files across more than one computer, such as a mobile executive who has both a desktop computer at his office and a laptop for travelling. It is published by US company Traveling Software.

laptop computer portable microcomputer, small enough to be used on the operator's lap. It consists of a single unit, incorporating a keyboard, ⇌ floppy disk and ⇌ hard disk drives, and a screen. The screen often forms a lid that folds back in use. It uses a liquid-crystal or gas-plasma display, rather than the bulkier and heavier cathode-ray tubes found in most display terminals. A typical laptop computer measures about 210 x 297 mm/8.3 x 11.7 in (A4), is 5 cm/2 in in depth, and weighs less than 3 kg/6 lb 9 oz. In the 1980s there were several types of laptop computer, but in the 1990s designs converged on systems known as ⇌ notebook computers.

laser printer computer printer in which the image to be printed is formed by the action of a laser on a light-sensitive drum, then transferred to paper by means of an electrostatic charge. Laser printers are page printers, printing a complete page at a time. The printed image, which can take the form of text or pictures, is made up of tiny dots, or ink particles. The quality of the image generated depends on the fineness of these dots – most laser printers can print up to 120 dots per cm/300 dots per in across the page.

laser printer
A laser printer works by transferring tiny ink particles contained in a toner cartridge to paper via a rubber belt. The image is produced by laser on a light-sensitive drum within the printer.

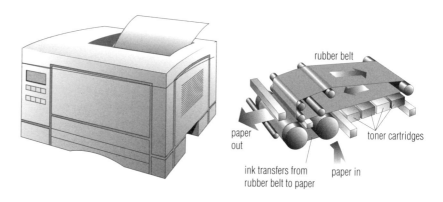

A typical desktop laser printer can print about 4–20 pages per minute. The first low-cost laser printer suitable for office use appeared in 1984.

Laser printers range in size from small black-and-white machines designed to work with microcomputers to very large colour machines designed for high-volume commercial printing. Because they produce very high-quality print and are virtually silent, small laser printers (along with ⇌ ink-jet printers) have replaced dot-matrix and daisywheel printers as the most popular type of microcomputer printer.

latency time needed for an electronic message to travel across a communications system and for the remote system to respond. Latency is inherent in all computer systems because nothing happens instantly, but usually things happen so quickly that the delay does not matter. However, latency is a critical factor in real-time systems where something is being controlled: a robot arm, for example, or an aircraft wing. It particularly concerns users when they want things to happen quickly – as when playing fast action games over a network – or when distance means the latency (delay) is very large. For example, a control message could take hours or days to reach a spacecraft.

lathe shape in graphics software, a cross-sectional representation of a symmetrical three-dimensional object. The object's shape can be changed by using a mouse-operated tool, much as a piece of wood can be carved on a lathe.

launch to start up a program. Many applications contain embedded programs (such as help screens or formatting options), with the result that users may launch programs without being aware they are doing so.

LCD abbreviation for ⇌ liquid-crystal display.

LDAP abbreviation for *Lightweight Directory Access Protocol,* Internet standard that enables a client PC or workstation to look up an e-mail address on an LDAP server over a ⇌ TCP/IP network. LDAP is a simplified version of the 'heavyweight' X.500 directory access protocol in the ⇌ OSI (Open Systems Interconnection) standards suite.

leased line permanent dedicated digital telephone link used for round-the-clock connection within a network or between offices. For example, a bank may use leased lines to carry financial data between branches and head office. The infrastructure of the Internet is a network of leased lines that deliver guaranteed ⇌ bandwidth at a fixed cost, regardless of how much traffic they carry. The enormous economies produced by the heavy use of such lines makes the Net a very cheap method of communication.

LED abbreviation for ⇌ light-emitting diode.

legacy application inherited application, usually an old one that runs on a large minicomputer or mainframe, and that may be too important to scrap or too expensive to change. 'Legacy' implies that such applications are valuable and should be looked after. Those who want to be rid of legacy applications use different metaphors, such as 'slum clearance'.

legacy system old system with which new technology must be compatible.

Leibniz, Gottfried (1646–1716) German inventor of the first calculating machine able to perform all four basic arithmetical operations. Leibniz knew of a calculator developed by Blaise ⤳ Pascal, which could add and subtract. He extended the idea to handle multiplication and division.

library program one of a collection, or library, of regularly used software routines, held in a computer backing store. For example, a programmer might store a routine for sorting a file into ⤳ key field order, and so could incorporate it easily into any new program being developed instead of having to rewrite it.

light-emitting diode *LED*, electronic component that converts electrical energy into light or infrared radiation in the range of 550 nm (green light) to 1300 nm (infrared). They are used for displaying symbols in electronic instruments and devices. An LED is a diode made of semiconductor material, such as gallium arsenide phosphide, that glows when electricity is passed through it. The first digital watches and calculators had LED displays, but many later models use ⤳ liquid-crystal displays.

In 1993 chemists at the University of Cambridge, England, developed LEDs from the polymer poly(p-phenylenevinyl) (PPV) that emit as much light as conventional LEDs and in a variety of colours.

A new generation of LEDs that can produce light in the mid-infrared range (300–1000 nm) safely and cheaply were developed by British researchers in 1995, using thin alternating layers of indium arsenide and indium arsenide antimonide.

light pen device resembling an ordinary pen, used to indicate locations on a computer screen. With certain computer-aided design (⤳ CAD) programs, the light pen can be used to instruct the computer to change the shape, size, position, and colours of sections of a screen image.

The pen has a photoreceptor at its tip that emits signals when light from the screen passes beneath it. From the timing of this signal and a gridlike representation of the screen in the computer memory, a computer program can calculate the position of the light pen.

line input in audio systems, direct input to a tape recorder from a device such as another recorder, rather than a microphone.

line printer computer ⤳ printer that prints a complete line of characters at a time. Line printers can achieve very high printing speeds of up to 2,500 lines a minute, but can print in only one typeface, cannot print graphics, and are very noisy. Today, most users prefer ⤳ laser printers.

link image or item of text in a ⤳ World Wide Web document that acts as a route to another Web page or file on the Internet. Links are created by using ⤳ HTML to combine an on-screen 'anchor' with a hidden Hypertext Reference (HRF), usually the ⤳ URL (Web address) of the item in question.

Linux contraction of *Linus Unix*, operating system based on an original core program written by Linus Torvalds, a 22-year-old student at the University of Helsinki, Finland, in 1991–92. Linux is a nonproprietary system, made up of freely-available ('open source') code created over several years by ⤳ Unix enthusiasts all over the world. Each programmer retains the copyright to his or her creation, but makes it freely available on the Internet. Linux retains the flexibility and many of the advanced programming features that make Unix popular for technically minded users, but can run on an ordinary PC instead of an expensive Unix workstation.

LINX, the contraction of *London Internet Exchange*, Docklands-based hub for all Internet traffic within the UK, run by the main British Internet Service Providers as a joint enterprise. By making sure that all traffic between British Internet users stays in the UK, the LINX improves the speed and reliability of network connections.

liquid-crystal display *LCD*, display of numbers (for example, in a calculator) or pictures (such as on a pocket television screen) produced by molecules of a substance in a semiliquid state with some crystalline properties, so that clusters of molecules align in parallel formations. The display is a blank until the application of an electric field, which 'twists' the molecules so that they reflect or transmit light falling on them. The two main types of LCD are passive matrix and active matrix.

LISP contraction of *list processing*, high-level computer-programming language designed for manipulating lists of data items. It is used primarily in research into ⤳ artificial intelligence (AI).

Developed in the late 1950s, and until recently common only in university laboratories, LISP is used more in the USA than in Europe, where the language ⤳ PROLOG is often preferred for AI work.

LISTSERV program that receives incoming messages for a mailing list and redistributes them to subscribers. Listserv was originally written for IBM mainframes but there are now many alternatives for Unix machines and PCs, such as ⤳ Majordomo.

local area network *LAN*, ⤳ network restricted to a single room or building. Local area networks enable around 500 devices, usually microcomputers acting as workstations, as well as peripheral devices, such as printers, to be connected together.

Central to the LAN is the file server, which controls user access to the network. The print server processes and controls all print jobs being sent via the network to a connected printer.

local bus extension of the central processing unit (CPU) ∽ bus (electrical pathway), designed to speed up data transfer between the CPU, disks, graphics boards, and other devices. The ∽ PCI bus has become the standard on PCs and more recently has been adopted for the Apple Macintosh.

local variable ∽ variable that can be accessed only by the instructions within a particular ∽ subroutine.

log file file that keeps a record of computer transactions. A log file might track the length and type of connection made to a network, or compile details of faxes sent by computer.

logic gate or *logic circuit*, in electronics, one of the basic components used in building ∽ integrated circuits. The five basic types of gate make logical decisions based on the functions NOT, AND, OR, NAND (NOT AND), and NOR (NOT OR). With the exception of the NOT gate, each has two or more inputs.

Information is fed to a gate in the form of binary-coded input signals (logic value 0 stands for 'off' or 'low-voltage pulse', logic 1 for 'on' or 'high-voltage'), and each combination of input signals yields a specific output (logic 0 or 1). An OR gate will give a logic 1 output if one or more of its inputs receives a logic 1 signal; however, an AND gate will yield a logic 1 output only if it receives a logic 1 signal through both its inputs. The output of a NOT or inverter gate is the opposite of the signal received through its single input, and a NOR or NAND gate produces an output signal that is the opposite of the signal that would have been produced by an OR or AND gate, respectively. The properties of a logic gate, or of a combination of gates, may be defined and presented in the form of a diagram called a truth table, which lists the output that will be triggered by each of the possible combinations of input signals. The process has close parallels in computer programming, where it forms the basis of binary logic.

circuit symbols

input
input ——— output   OR gate   AND gate   NOT or inverter gate   NOR gate   NAND gate

truth tables

logic gate
The circuit symbols for the five basic types of logic gate: OR, AND, NOT, NOR, and NAND. The truth table displays the output results of each possible combination of input signal.

inputs		output	inputs		output	inputs	output	inputs		output	inputs		output
0	0	0	0	0	0	0	1	0	0	1	0	0	1
0	1	1	0	1	0	1	0	0	1	0	0	1	1
1	0	1	1	0	0			1	0	0	1	0	1
1	1	1	1	1	1			1	1	0	1	1	0

OR gate   AND gate   NOT gate   NOR gate   NAND gate

US computer scientists announced the construction of logic gates from DNA in 1997. Rather than responding to an electronic signal their DNA gates respond to nucleotide sequences.

LOGO (Greek *logos* 'word') high-level computer programming language designed to teach mathematical concepts. Developed in about 1970 at the Massachusetts Institute of Technology, it became popular in schools and with home computer users because of its 'turtle graphics' feature. This allows the user to write programs that create line drawings on a computer screen, or drive a small mobile robot (a 'turtle' or 'buggy') around the floor.

LOGO encourages the use of languages in a logical and structured way, leading to 'microworlds', in which problems can be solved by using a few standard solutions.

log off or *log out*, process by which a user identifies himself or herself to a multiuser computer and leaves the system.

log on or *log in*, process by which a user identifies himself or herself to a multiuser computer and enters the system. Logging on usually requires the user to enter a password before access is allowed.

look-and-feel general appearance of a user interface (usually a ⮑ graphical user interface). The concept of look-and-feel was the subject of several court cases in the USA. ⮑ Apple sued ⮑ Microsoft on the basis that the look-and-feel of Microsoft ⮑ Windows infringed its copyright. The case was decided principally in Microsoft's favour.

loop short for ⮑ program loop.

loopback any connection that sends an output signal to the same system's input. Loopback adaptors are used in electrical testing.

lossless compression ⮑ data compression technique that reduces the number of ⮑ bits used to represent data in a file, thereby reducing its size while retaining all the original information. This makes it suitable for computer code and text files. Lossless compression typically achieves space savings of 30%.

lossy compression ⮑ data compression technique that dramatically reduces the size of a file by eliminating superfluous data. The lost information is either unnoticeable to the user, or can be recovered during decompression by extrapolation of the existing data. ⮑ JPEG and MPEG are lossy methods that can reduce the size of graphics, audio, and video files by over 90%.

Lotus 1-2-3 ⮑ spreadsheet computer program, produced by Lotus Development Corporation. It first appeared in 1982 and its combination of spreadsheet, graphics display, and data management contributed to the rapid acceptance of the IBM Personal Computer in businesses.

TIP

loopback

On the Internet, certain addresses are loopback addresses; that is, attempting to access that address takes the user back to his or her own system.

Lotus Notes business software combining database and message facilities to help people in an organization to share information and work together. Notes is a very versatile ↝ groupware program that can be customized to suit the needs of the organization.

Although commentators had believed Notes to be under threat from cheaper Internet-based solutions, in fact its popularity increased in the late 1990s, when Lotus lowered the price of Notes and released its Domino software which acts as both a Notes server and a Web server.

low-level language programming language designed for a particular computer and reflecting its internal ↝ machine code; low-level languages are therefore often described as machine-oriented languages. They cannot easily be converted to run on a computer with a different central processing unit, and they are relatively difficult to learn because a detailed knowledge of the internal working of the computer is required. Since they must be translated into machine code by an ↝ assembler program, low-level languages are also called ↝ assembly languages.

In contrast, ↝ high-level languages are designed to solve particular problems and are therefore described as problem-oriented languages.

LSI abbreviation for *large-scale integration*, technology that enables whole electrical circuits to be etched into a piece of semiconducting material just a few millimetres square.

By the late 1960s a complete computer processor could be integrated on a single chip, or ↝ integrated circuit, and in 1971 the US electronics company Intel produced the first commercially available ↝ microprocessor. Very large-scale integration (↝ VLSI) results in even smaller chips.

lurk to read a ↝ Usenet newsgroup without making a contribution. Before introducing themselves to the group, it is advisable for newcomers to lurk for a week or two in order to assess its members and their methods. That way, they can avoid posting an inappropriate message and attracting ↝ flames.

Lycos ↝ search engine for the ↝ World Wide Web. Lycos is a database compiled by Web ↝ crawlers that comb the Internet for Web, ↝ FTP and ↝ Gopher sites, indexing them by title, headings, keywords, and text.

Lycos, named after a particularly voracious hunting spider, started as a research project at Carnegie Mellon University in Pittsburgh, USA, but became a commercial venture in 1995. By August 1996 Lycos had indexed over 60 million ↝ URLs. In 2000, a \$12.5 billion offer was made for Lycos by Terra Networks, an ↝ Internet Service Provider, whose majority shareholder is Telefonica, the privatized Spanish national telecommunications operator.

Lynx text-only Web browser for ↝ Unix computers.

Lycos

http://www.lycos.com

Lycos can be reached at their Web site.

WEB LINK

LZW compression abbreviation for *Lempel-Zif-Welsh compression*, data compression system used to reduce the size of data files and thus shorten the time needed to transmit them. LZW compression is the basis of the ↩ GIF graphics interchange format. When US computer company Unisys announced in 1995 that it wanted licence fees for the use of LZW compression for commercial applications, users began to develop alternatives such as ↩ Portable Network Graphics (PNG).

machine code set of instructions that a computer's central processing unit (CPU) can understand and obey directly, without any translation. Each type of CPU has its own machine code. Because machine-code programs consist entirely of binary digits (bits), most programmers write their programs in an easy-to-use ⇨ high-level language. A high-level program must be translated into machine code – by means of a ⇨ compiler or ⇨ interpreter program – before it can be executed by a computer.

Where no suitable high-level language exists or where very efficient machine code is required, programmers may choose to write programs in a low-level, or assembly, language, which is eventually translated into machine code by means of an ⇨ assembler program.

Microprocessors (CPUs based on a single integrated circuit) may be classified according to the number of machine-code instructions that they are capable of obeying: ⇨ CISC (complex instruction set computer) microprocessors support up to 200 instructions, whereas ⇨ RISC (reduced instruction set computer) microprocessors support far fewer instructions but execute programs more rapidly.

machine-readable of data, readable directly by a computer without the need for retyping. The term is usually applied to files on disk or tape, but can also be applied to typed or printed text that can be scanned for ⇨ optical character recognition or ⇨ bar codes.

Macintosh range of microcomputers originally produced by ⇨ Apple Computer. The Apple Macintosh, introduced in 1984, was the first popular microcomputer with a ⇨ graphical user interface. The success of the Macintosh prompted other manufacturers and software companies to create their own graphical user interfaces. Most notable of these are Microsoft Windows, which runs on IBM PC-compatible microcomputers, and OSF/Motif, from the Open Software Foundation, which is used with many Unix systems.

Apple introduced its stylish ⇨ iMac computer in 1998, followed by a laptop version, the ⇨ iBook, in 1999.

macro in computer programming, a new command created by combining a number of existing ones. For example, a word processing macro might create a letterhead or fax cover sheet, inserting words, fonts, and logos with a single keystroke or mouse click. Macros are also useful to automate computer communications – for example, users can write a macro to ask their computer to dial an ⇨ Internet Service Provider (ISP), retrieve e-mail and ⇨ Usenet articles, and then disconnect. A macro key on the keyboard combines the effects of pressing several individual keys.

macro virus computer virus that hides in Microsoft Word documents or, less commonly, Excel files.

magnetic-ink character recognition *MICR*, technique that enables special characters printed in magnetic ink to be read and input rapidly to a computer. MICR is used extensively in banking because magnetic-ink characters are difficult to forge and are therefore ideal for marking and identifying cheques.

Macintosh Tips and Tutorials

http://home.earthlink.net/
~ohora/index.html

Dedicated to 'less experienced computer users', this site offers a large number of tips for Macintosh or iMac computers. The tips are clearly laid out and come complete with illustrations to ease the learning process. Also featured are several tutorials that guide the user through word processing, graphics, databases, and many other subjects.

WEB LINK

Data Powers of Ten

http://www.ccsf.caltech.
edu/~roy/dataquan/

Collection of estimates of the quantities of data contained by various magnetic media. Includes interesting facts about the number of books needed to store the same amount of information as on magnetic media.

WEB LINK

magnetic strip or *magnetic stripe*, thin strip of magnetic material attached to a plastic card and used for recording data. Magnetic strips are used on credit cards, bank cards (as used at cash dispensing machines), telephone cards, and railway tickets.

magnetic tape narrow plastic ribbon coated with an easily magnetizable material on which data can be recorded. It is used in sound recording, audiovisual systems (videotape), and computing. For mass storage on commercial mainframe computers, large reel-to-reel tapes are still used, but cartridges are becoming popular. Various types of cartridge are now standard on minis and PCs, while audio cassettes are sometimes used with home computers.

Magnetic tape was first used in sound recording in 1947, and made overdubbing possible, unlike the direct-to-disc system it replaced. Two-track tape was introduced in the 1950s and four-track in the early 1960s; today, studios use 16-, 24-, or 32-track tape, from which the tracks are mixed down to a stereo master tape.

In computing, magnetic tape was first used to record data and programs in 1951 as part of the UNIVAC 1 system. It was very popular as a storage medium for external memory in the 1950s and 1960s. Since then it has been largely replaced by magnetic ⇌ disks as a working medium, although tape is still used to make backup copies of important data. Information is recorded on the tape in binary form, with two different strengths of signal representing 1 and 0.

mailbox folder in which electronic mail is stored, typically divided into 'in' and 'out' trays. Users usually have two mailboxes: one on their PC, and another at their mail ⇌ server at the ⇌ Internet Service Provider (ISP), where incoming messages await collection.

mailbox name in an e-mail address, the name to the left of the @ sign, signifying the individual's mailbox for handling mail. All e-mail addresses appear in the form mailbox name@domain name.

mail-enabled piece of software that can generate ⇌ e-mail without launching a separate electronic mail program.

mailing list list of people who receive a given piece of ⇌ e-mail. Mailing lists are an easy way for people to share professional and technical information: hackers (see ⇌ hacking) often set up ad hoc mailing lists so that they can collaborate on a single piece of programming. It is also possible to join mailing lists devoted to special topics and social and leisure interests.

mail merge feature offered by some word-processing packages that enables a list of personal details, such as names and addresses, to be combined with a general document outline to produce individualized documents.

For example, a club secretary might create a file containing a mailing list of the names and addresses of the club members. Whenever a letter is to be sent to all club members, a general letter outline is prepared with indications as to where individual names and addresses need to be added. The mail-merge feature then combines the file of names and addresses with the letter outline to produce and print individual letters addressed to each club member.

mail reflector ↝ e-mail address that acts as an ↝ alias, redistributing all mail received to another address or to a ↝ mailing list. Individuals use mail reflectors to hide their true identities or to forward messages following a change of e-mail address.

The same method can be used to address a particular group of people – for example, Bloggs College might create mail reflectors for all staff (staff@bloggs.ac.uk), for students (students@bloggs.ac.uk), former students (alumni@bloggs.ac.uk), and so on.

mail server software in client/server computing (see ↝ client–server architecture), software that stores e-mail and distributes it only to the authorized recipient.

mainboard new (and more politically correct) name for a ↝ motherboard.

mainframe large computer used for commercial data processing and other large-scale operations. Because of the general increase in computing power, the differences between the mainframe, ↝ supercomputer, ↝ minicomputer, and ↝ microcomputer (personal computer) are becoming less marked.

Mainframe manufacturers include IBM, Amdahl, Fujitsu, and Hitachi. Typical mainframes have from 128 MB to 4 GB of memory and hundreds of gigabytes of disk storage.

Majordomo ↝ freeware mailing list processor for ↝ Unix systems.

mark sensing technique that enables pencil marks made in predetermined positions on specially prepared forms to be rapidly read and input to a computer. The technique makes use of the fact that pencil marks contain graphite and therefore conduct electricity. A mark sense reader scans the form by passing small metal brushes over the paper surface. Whenever a brush touches a pencil mark a circuit is completed and the mark is detected.

mask restriction placed on the type of character that can be entered in a given field of a database or spreadsheet. For example, a 'dd-mm-yy' mask will only allow operators to enter a date in the field, and a field operating under a text mask will accept only letters, not numbers. See also ↝ validation.

Mauchly, John William (1907–1980) US physicist and engineer who, in 1946, constructed the first general-purpose computer, the ENIAC, in collaboration with John ↝ Eckert. Their company was bought by Remington Rand in 1950, and they built the UNIVAC 1 computer in 1951 for the US census.

The work on ENIAC was carried out by the two during World War II, and was commissioned to automate the calculation of artillery firing tables for the US Army. In 1949 Mauchly and Eckert designed a small-scale binary computer,

BINAC, which was faster and cheaper to use. Punched cards were replaced with magnetic tape, and the computer stored programs internally.

Mauchly was born in Cincinnati, Ohio, and studied at Johns Hopkins University, becoming professor of physics at Ursinus College in Collegeville, Pennsylvania. In 1941 he moved to the Moore School of Electrical Engineering of the University of Pennsylvania, and became principal consultant on the ENIAC project. A dispute over patent policy with the Moore School caused Mauchly and Eckert to leave and set up a partnership in 1948. Mauchly was a consultant to Remington Rand (later Sperry Rand) 1950–59 and again from 1973, after setting up his own consulting company in 1959.

MBONE contraction of *multicast backbone*, layer of the Internet designed to deliver ☞ packets of multimedia data, enabling video and audio communication. It can be used for telephony and video-conferencing – however, it can deliver a maximum of only five video frames per second, as opposed to television's 30. Large rock concerts are occasionally broadcast on the MBONE.

MCI US-based long distance telecommunications company, active in Net communications since the 1980s, when it ran the backbone for the National Science Foundation's ☞ NSFnet.

In 1997 MCI was acquired by rival telecommunications company WorldCom, the new company being known as MCI WorldCom. In October 1999 MCI WorldCom acquired ☞ Sprint, the third-largest carrier of long distance calls in the USA. The new company is named WorldCom and is expected to have annual revenues of more than $50 billion, 142,000 employees, and more than 40 million private and business customers, giving it about 30% of the long distance market in the USA and making it a rival to AT&T.

m-commerce contraction of ☞ mobile commerce.

media singular *medium*, collective name for materials on which data can be recorded. For example, paper is a medium that can be used to record printed data; a floppy disk is a medium for recording magnetic data.

megabyte *MB*, unit of memory equal to 1,024 ☞ kilobytes. It is sometimes used, less precisely, to mean 1 million bytes.

memory part of a system used to store data and programs either permanently or temporarily. There are two main types: immediate access memory and backing storage. Memory capacity is measured in ☞ bytes or, more conveniently, in kilobytes (units of 1,024 bytes) or megabytes (units of 1,024 kilobytes).

Immediate access memory, or internal memory, describes the memory locations that can be addressed directly and individually by the central processing unit. It is either read-only (stored in ROM, PROM, and EPROM chips) or read/write (stored in RAM chips). Read-only memory stores information that must be constantly available and is unlikely to be changed. It is nonvolatile – that is, it is not lost when the computer is switched off.

Read/write memory is volatile – it stores programs and data only while the computer is switched on.

Backing storage, or external memory, is nonvolatile memory, located outside the central processing unit, used to store programs and data that are not in current use. Backing storage is provided by such devices as magnetic ⮑ disks (floppy and hard disks), ⮑ magnetic tape (tape streamers and cassettes), optical disks (such as ⮑ CD-ROM), and ⮑ bubble memory. By rapidly switching blocks of information between the backing storage and the immediate-access memory, the limited size of the immediate-access memory may be increased artificially. When this technique is used to give the appearance of a larger internal memory than physically exists, the additional capacity is referred to as ⮑ virtual memory.

memory address number specifying the location of a particular item in a computer's ⮑ RAM.

memory resident present in the main (⮑ RAM) memory of the computer. For an application to be run, it has to be memory resident. Some applications are kept in memory (see ⮑ terminate and stay resident), while most are deleted from the memory when their task is complete. However, the memory is usually not large enough to hold all applications and ⮑ swapping in and out of memory is necessary. This slows down the application.

menu list of options, displayed on screen, from which the user may make a choice – for example, the choice of services offered to the customer by a bank cash dispenser: withdrawal, deposit, balance, or statement. Menus are used extensively in ⮑ graphical user interface (GUI) systems, where the menu options are often selected using a pointing device called a ⮑ mouse.

message-ID special number given to every item of ⮑ e-mail as it travels across the Internet. Message-IDs are especially important for controlling traffic in ⮑ Usenet. Articles are initially offered across the network by their message-IDs, enabling ⮑ news servers to check whether they have already received them and either take the rest of the message or move on to the next message-ID.

metadata data about data. Originally a term used by the information science community, it is becoming much more common with the growth of the ⮑ Internet. On the Web, metadata describes the content of a Web page. It might record the name of the author and the date the page was created, and may contain keywords to describe the Web page to ⮑ search engines. The metadata is not displayed on the Web page itself, but makes the page more understandable to Web ⮑ crawlers and Web ⮑ robots.

Much of the current work of the World Wide Web (WWW) Consortium is directed at designing metadata standards for Web documents.

meta-search engine search utility, usually accessed via a Web site, that sends search strings to a number of individual search engines. This makes it possible to query up to five or more search engines – for example AltaVista, HotBot, or Lycos – at the same time. Popular meta-search engines include Dogpile and Mama.

meta-tags in Web pages, ⮑ tags used to document the page and/or provide information that can be used by search engines to classify or index the page, not to control the display of information. Some Web programmers use meta-tags to try to cheat search engines – for example by repeating words frequently, or by using popular search words that have no relevance to the page – while search engine programmers make considerable efforts to negate this misuse. The battle is unseen by most Web users, who rarely use the browser's view source menu item to read meta-tags.

Metropolitan Area Exchange *MAE*; or *Ethernet*, at an MAE, a number of ⮑ Internet Service Providers, or ISPs, link up to exchange data – usually via an ⮑ Ethernet network – without that data having to pass across an Internet backbone. Before UK ISPs linked their systems at the ⮑ LINX in London, e-mail from one to another might be routed via the USA. America's first two MAEs were set up on opposite coasts and known as MAE East and MAE West.

metropolitan area network *MAN*, high-speed communications network within the environs of a city or metropolitan area. In the UK, MANs are starting to become more common as more schools, colleges, and public services become linked to the ⮑ Internet. MANs provide a high-speed network ⮑ backbone for all of these services, and the high cost of building the MAN can be recovered by charging commercial organisations to use it to gain faster access to the Internet.

MICR abbreviation for ⮑ magnetic-ink character recognition.

microbilling technique of charging for software by usage. Instead of being sold to users in a box over the counter, programs are divided into small segments which can be quickly downloaded over a network on demand. Each time the program is used, the customer's account is debited by a small amount.

microchip popular name for the silicon chip, or ⮑ integrated circuit.

microcomputer or *micro or personal computer*, small desktop or portable ⮑ computer, typically designed to be used by one person at a time, although individual computers can be linked in a network so that users can share data and programs.

Its central processing unit is a ⮑ microprocessor, contained on a single integrated circuit.

Microcomputers are the smallest of the four classes of computer (the others are ⮑ supercomputer, ⮑ mainframe, and ⮑ minicomputer). Since the appearance in 1975 of the first commercially available microcomputer, the Altair 8800, micros have become ubiquitous in commerce, industry, and education.

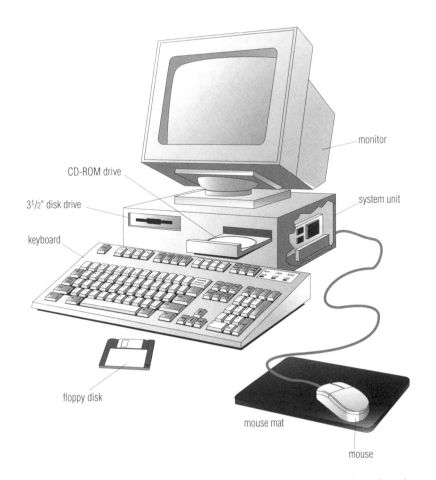

microcomputer
The component parts of the microcomputer: the system unit contains the hub of the system, including the central processing unit (CPU), information on all of the computer's peripheral devices, and often a fixed disk drive. The monitor (or visual display unit) displays text and graphics, the keyboard and mouse are used to input data, and the floppy disk and CD-ROM drives read data stored on disks.

microfiche sheet of film on which printed text is photographically reduced. See ↪ microform.

microform generic name for media on which text or images are photographically reduced. The main examples are microfilm (similar to the film in an ordinary camera) and microfiche (flat sheets of film, generally 105 mm/4 in x 148 mm/6 in, holding the equivalent of 420 standard pages). Microform has the advantage of low reproduction and storage costs, but it requires special devices for reading the text. It is widely used for archiving and for storing large volumes of text, such as library catalogues.

Computer data may be output directly and quickly in microform by means of COM (computer output on microfilm/microfiche) techniques.

micropayments payments of very small amounts of money electronically (usually over the Internet), for which credit card payment is inefficient. ↪ E-cash providers, such as ↪ Mondex and ↪ CyberCash, use an electronic 'purse' or 'wallet', in which a monetary value can be stored.

microprocessor complete computer ⇨ central processing unit contained on a single ⇨ integrated circuit, or chip. The appearance of the first microprocessor in 1971 designed by Intel for a pocket calculator manufacturer heralded the introduction of the microcomputer. The microprocessor has led to a dramatic fall in the size and cost of computers, and ⇨ dedicated computers can now be found in washing machines, cars, and so on. Examples of microprocessors are the Intel Pentium family and the IBM/Motorola PowerPC, used by Apple Computer.

Texas Instruments introduced in January 1997 a digital-signal microprocessor chip that can process 1.6 billion instructions a second. This is about 40 times more powerful than a chip now found in today's computer modem. The new chip can reduce the time needed to download a file from the Internet from ten minutes to less than five seconds.

Microsoft US corporation, now the world's largest software supplier. Microsoft's first major product was a version of BASIC, written for the MITS Altair in 1975, and adopted by most of the desktop computer industry. Through ⇨ MS-DOS, written for IBM, ⇨ Windows, and related applications it has steadily increased its hold on the personal computer market.

Microsoft was founded by Bill ⇨ Gates and Paul ⇨ Allen in 1975. Bill Gates was the company's chief executive until January 2000, when he stepped down in order to spend more time on developing new technologies, becoming 'chief software architect'. The title of chief executive was handed to Steve Ballmer, the company's president since 1998.

In 1996, Microsoft launched another new operating system, Windows CE (Consumer Electronics), for handheld computers, pen-operated personal digital assistants, in-car systems, and similar applications. Suppliers of CE-based HPCs (handheld personal computers) include Casio, Compaq, Hewlett-Packard, Philips, and Sharp. Windows CE version 2 is also used in an improved version of WebTV: a set-top box that enables users to surf the Internet on their television sets. Microsoft purchased WebTV Networks for $425 million in 1997. The first companies to supply WebTV systems were Philips, Sony, and Mitsubishi.

A US federal probe into charges that Microsoft was engaging in anticompetitive behaviour was carried out in 1990–93, from which date the US Justice Department launched its own investigations. Under a settlement reached in 1994, Microsoft agreed to end the uncompetitive practice 'per processor' pricing, whereby PC manufacturers paid a fee for each machine produced irrespective of the software to be installed. The Justice Department started another case in 1997, accusing Microsoft of breaking this settlement by tying the installation of Windows 95 to the installation of Microsoft's free Web browser, Internet Explorer. In December the company was ordered to change its marketing policy.

America's Justice Department and 20 states charged Microsoft in May 1998 with breaking antitrust laws. Microsoft was accused of abusing its monopoly power against Netscape, its main competitor in Internet browsers. However, the US government suffered a major legal defeat in its campaign against Microsoft in late June 1998. An appeal court ruled that Microsoft was quite within its rights to combine its Internet browser with its operating system. After this judgement was overturned in April 2000, and the US government issued proposals to smash the company's virtual monopoly, Microsoft proposed instead to remove restrictive clauses on its contracts with PC manufacturers and to allow other software suppliers easier access to consumers who use some, but not all, of the Microsoft package. However, in June 2000, a federal judge ruled that the company should be split into two companies. Microsoft launched another appeal, which went in its favour in September 2000 when the US Supreme Court ruled that the appeal against the ruling that their software businesses should be split up should first be heard by a lower appeal court. This could delay by up to two years the resolution of the case, allowing Microsoft to continue its business practices unhindered.

Microsoft's first program was a version of the ➴ BASIC computer language written for the MITS Altair, the first personal computer. In 1980, when it had a staff of 40, Microsoft was contracted to produce a BASIC and DOS (Disk Operating System) for IBM's first mass market microcomputer, the IBM PC. With the success of the IBM PC, Microsoft grew rapidly to 6,000 staff and a turnover of $1 billion in 1990, when it launched Windows 3, a hugely successful graphical user interface for DOS. With the launch of Windows 95 and Windows 98, and ancilliary sales of Windows applications (Word, Excel, Microsoft Office) and CD-ROM programs (for example *Encarta* and *Cinemania*), Microsoft then grew to more than 20,000 staff and a turnover of $14.5 billion in 1998. The accompanying growth in the value of the company's shares created three billionaires (Gates, Allen, and Steve Ballmer) while hundreds, perhaps thousands, of Microsoft's programmers have become millionaires.

Microsoft closed a deal with Tandy's RadioShack, in November 1999, to create 'stores within stores', to sell dial-up, high-speed Internet access in the 7,000 new outlets.

Microsoft Network *MSN*, online service operated by ➴ Microsoft.

Microsoft Word word-processing program for PCs and Apple ➴ Macintoshes. See ➴ Word.

MIDI acronym for *musical instrument digital interface*, manufacturer's standard allowing different pieces of digital music equipment used in composing and recording to be freely connected.

The information-sending device (any electronic instrument) is called a controller, and the reading device (such as a computer) the sequencer. Pitch, dynamics, decay rate, and stereo position can all be transmitted via the interface. A computer with a MIDI interface can input and store the sounds produced by the connected instruments, and can then manipulate these sounds in many different ways. For example, a single keystroke may change the key of an entire composition. Even a full written score for the composition may be automatically produced.

mil abbreviation for *military*, in the Internet's ↝ domain name system (DNS), one of the top-level domains along with net, gov, org, com, and net. US military organizations typically have Internet addresses of the form name.mil.

MIME acronym for *Multipurpose Internet Mail Extensions*, standard for transferring multimedia ↝ e-mail messages and ↝ World Wide Web ↝ hypertext documents over the Internet. Under MIME, binary files (any file not in plain text, such as graphics and audio) are translated into a form of ↝ ASCII before transmission, and then turned back into binary form by the recipient.

minicomputer multiuser computer with a size and processing power between those of a ↝ mainframe and a ↝ microcomputer. Nowadays almost all minicomputers are based on ↝ microprocessors.

Minicomputers are often used in medium-sized businesses and in university departments handling ↝ database or other commercial programs and running scientific or graphical applications.

Minitel dedicated terminal attached to France's teletext system, Teletel, which was launched in 1981 and has millions of users. Many Minitels – most of which have small black and white screens – were installed on free loan by France Telecom to subscribers who opted not to have telephone directories, and the online directory is still the most widely used Minitel service. Erotic 'chat lines' have also proved very popular. Today in France, many PC users access Teletel using software that emulates a Minitel terminal.

mips acronym for *million instructions per second*, measure of the speed of a processor. It does not equal the computer power in all cases.

mirror site archive site which keeps a copy of another site's files for downloading by ↝ FTP. Software archives such as those of the University of Michigan, and the many companies that distribute software by FTP, have several mirror sites around the world, so that users can choose the nearest site.

MIT media lab one of several important computer research centres at the Massachussetts Institute of Technology in Cambridge, Massachussetts, USA. The MIT media lab is at the forefront of multimedia technology.

Mitnick, Kevin (1963–   ) US computer criminal known as 'the world's most wanted hacker' (see ↝ hacking) during the three years he spent on the run before being caught in 1994. Mitnick was a compulsive hacker who specialized in penetrating communications systems including ↝ MCI, Pacific Bell, the Manhattan telephone system, and a Pentagon defence computer.

In January 2000, Mitnick was released from prison, after serving five years. Mitnick claims that the harm he caused was grossly exaggerated.

mixer in sound recording, equipment that allows an engineer to set a different volume level for each individual sound track so that solos can be highlighted

MIME

http://www.oac.uci.edu/
indiv/ehood/MIME/

MIME can be reached at their Web site.

WEB LINK

and loud instruments can be kept from dominating softer ones. Multimedia systems that allow recording generally include similar, though not as sophisticated, functions through software. This is useful in applications such as adding background music to a scene where two people are talking and it is important to hear the voices clearly over the music.

MMX umbrella name for improvements to the Intel Pentium line of processors in 1996, including 57 new instructions to handle multimedia and communications data. From 1997, all new Pentium chips included MMX as standard, such as the Pentium II range. MMX may be an abbreviation for MultiMedia eXtensions.

mnemonic short sequence of letters used in low-level programming languages (see ↝ low-level language) to represent a ↝ machine code instruction.

mobile commerce or *m-commerce*, ↝ electronic commerce accessed using a mobile device, such as a ↝ mobile phone or a ↝ personal digital assistant, instead of a ↝ personal computer connected to a fixed telephone line. See also ↝ GPRS, ↝ UMTS, and ↝ WAP.

mobile phone cordless telephone linked to a digital cellular radio network. Mobile phones can connect to the Internet via a datacard, which converts computer data into a form that can be passed over the network and vice versa. Users can connect them to a ↝ laptop computer and others incorporate a full pocket organizer. A trend for greater integration of phone and computer emerged in 1996, leading to the arrival of ↝ WAP phones in 1999.

In 1999 both Ericsson, a Swedish mobile phone producing company, and ↝ BT announced agreements with ↝ Microsoft to develop cellular phones that connect to the Internet using Microsoft's Mobile Explorer, allowing people to read their e-mail and browse the Web via wireless devices; see ↝ WAP (wireless application protocol).

The British public health minister Tessa Jowell announced in April 1999 the setting up of an expert panel to review the radiation risks of mobile phones under the guidance of the National Radiological Protection Board. The panel's report in 2000 was inconclusive.

Some scientific research has found a link between mobile phone use and brain tumour incidence but the proof is far from conclusive. To determine whether there is a risk, the World Health Organization (WHO) announced in 1999 that it is organizing a large study to compare the mobile phone use of 3,000 mobile phone users with brain tumours, with the usage by a cancer-free control group. The $6 million study will be partly financed by mobile phone companies.

model set of assumptions and criteria based on actual phenomena, used to conduct a ↝ computer simulation. Models are used to predict the behaviour of a system such as the movement of a hurricane or the flow of goods from a store. In industry, they are an important tool for testing new products:

Mobile Internet

Data on the mobile phone In the last few years, the take-up of mobile phone services has been quite phenomenal, particularly in northern Europe and Japan. This is one area of high technology where the USA is not in the lead. Reasons for this include the lack of a single transmission standard like GSM (Global System for Mobile), continuing large-scale use of analogue rather than digital phones, and the sharing of the high cost of a mobile call between the caller and the receiver of the call.

Among young people especially, the use of the Short Messaging System (SMS) is more popular than making voice calls, because it is quicker (and therefore cheaper) to send a message than to speak to someone. Mobile phones can now be connected to the Internet, using Wireless Application Protocol (WAP) in Europe and i-Mode in Japan. WAP phones allow their users to go beyond the 160 characters of an SMS message, allowing them to send and receive Internet e-mail by phone and to access WAP-enabled Web sites. i-Mode also provides e-mail facilities and access to the Web.

The 'next big thing'? According to the hype, the mobile Internet will be a huge success. Its supporters point to the success of SMS, and to the ever-increasing number of mobile phone users (forecast to be about 1.2 billion worldwide by 2005, compared to around 720 million desktop Internet users). Therefore, runs the argument, those millions of mobile phone users will want to access the Internet from their phones and take part in mobile commerce. Finland (with almost 70% mobile phone penetration in 2000) is often held up as an indication of what the future has in store for the rest of the world. Even in Finland, however, there are many pilot projects and a great deal of wishful thinking, but not very much hard evidence of the success of the mobile Internet.

Tomorrow's world In a few years' time, the mobile Internet will have the features that we take for granted in the fixed-line Internet today. Mobile devices will be a cross between today's mobile phones and handheld/laptop computers, with fairly large, colour screens that can display Web pages in all their video and audio glory. Tomorrow's mobiles will also have small keyboards, so that e-mail messages can be keyed in with ease, and the devices will connect to the Internet at high data transfer speeds.

WAP: the reality today Anyone expecting today's mobile to bear any resemblance to the picture painted above is going to be sorely disappointed. The WAP phones available now have tiny, monochrome screens, which can display text and very basic graphics. Web pages have to be re-coded using Wireless Markup Language (WML) in order for it to be possible to view them on a WAP phone. Very few mobile phones have an attachable keyboard, so e-mail messages have to be keyed in laboriously using the letters of the alphabet associated with the phone's numeric keypad. WAP uses GSM, so WAP messages are limited by the speed of GSM, which is only 9.6 Kbps.

Mobile applications The applications foreseen for mobile phones include existing fixed-line services, such as banking, shopping, share-dealing, traffic information, and news services. In addition, however, a number of new services specific to the mobile world are emerging, which utilize the ability of mobile operators to pinpoint the location of the user down to within a few metres. These new 'location-based' services include information on the weather, restaurants, clubs, cinemas, bricks-and-mortar shops, and local taxi services.

Mobile applications that are being introduced by businesses include the integration of mobile phones into supply chain applications, such as enterprise resource planning and electronic marketplaces, as well as sales force automation and customer relationship management systems. In addition, warnings can be sent to the mobile phones of maintenance staff about the performance of machinery and vehicles, and jobs can be assigned to mobile workers in areas such as transport, utilities, field service, health care, and security. Fleet management is also expected to be a big growth area for mobiles.

Third generation Universal Mobile Telecommunications System (UMTS) is the third generation (3G) of mobile

Mobile Internet (continued)

phone standards, which is expected to come into use in Japan and the Isle of Man in 2001, in the European Union in 2002, and in the USA by around 2004. The higher data transfer rates (initially 38.4 Kbps, rising to 2 Mbps) will allow UMTS to usher in the kind of scenario envisaged above. Several European governments, including those of Germany and the UK, have auctioned 3G licences, raising tens of billions for their coffers.

Before the arrival of UMTS, however, General Packet Radio System (GPRS), sometimes referred to as 2½G, will have brought a considerable improvement on GSM's slow access speeds. GPRS, which allows data transfer at 11.5 Kbps, was already being implemented for business users in the UK by mid-2000.

Alan Stewart

engineers subject ⮑ virtual prototypes of aircraft or bridges to various scenarios to find out what adjustments are necessary to the design. However, a model is only as good as the assumptions that underlie it.

Models may run at the same speed of the real situation (real-time models) or run at faster or slower speeds.

Models are also the basis for ⮑ expert systems, which simulate the knowledge of a human expert.

modem contraction of *modulator/demodulator*, device for transmitting computer data over telephone lines. Such a device is necessary because the ⮑ digital signals produced by computers cannot, at present, be transmitted directly over the telephone network, which uses analogue signals. The modem converts the digital signals to analogue, and back again.

Modems are used for linking remote terminals to central computers and enable computers to communicate with each other anywhere in the world. In 1997, the fastest standard modems transmitted data at a nominal rate of about 33,600 bps (bits per second), often abbreviated to 33.6K.

56K modems launched in 1997 achieve higher speeds by using a digital connection to the user's computer, while using a conventional analogue connection in the other direction. In theory the downstream link can transfer data at 56 Kbps but in practice, speeds are usually 45–50K or less, depending on the quality of the phone line and other factors.

Initially there were two competing 56K systems – K56Flex from Rockwell and Lucent Technologies, and X2 from 3Com/US Robotics – though many users waited for the ITU to agree a standard system called a V.90 (see ⮑ V numbers).

moderator person or group of people that screens submissions to certain ⮑ newsgroups and ⮑ mailing lists before passing them on for wider circulation. The aim of moderation is not to censor, but to ensure that the quality of debate is maintained by filtering out ⮑ spamming, irrelevant ('off-topic'), or gratuitously offensive postings.

TIP

moderator

If you try to post a message to a moderated newsgroup, it will actually be e-mailed directly to the moderator. You may have to wait a few days before it is read and passed on to the newsgroup.

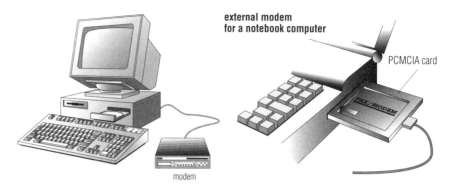

external modem
for a notebook computer

PCMCIA card

FAX/MODEM

modem

internal modem

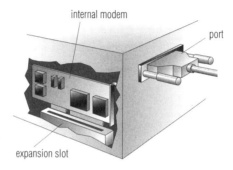

internal modem

port

expansion slot

modem
Modems are available
in various forms:
microcomputers may use
a plug-in device
connected through a
communications port, or an
internal device, which takes
the form of an expansion
board inside the computer.
Notebook computers use
an external modem
connected via a special
interface card.

Mondex ⤳ e-cash system operating on a ⤳ smart card. The card's microchip contains a 'purse' divided into five separate pockets that allow up to five different currencies to be held on the card electronically at any one time. The microchip also contains security programs that protect transactions between one Mondex card and another.

monitor or *screen*, output device on which a computer displays information for the benefit of the operator user – usually in the form of a ⤳ graphical user interface such as ⤳ Windows. The commonest type is the cathode-ray tube (CRT), which is similar to a television screen. Portable computers often use ⤳ liquid crystal display (LCD) screens. These are harder to read than CRTs, but require less power, making them suitable for battery operation.

MOO abbreviation for *MUD, object-oriented,* ⤳ MUD (multi-user dungeon) that uses ⤳ object-oriented programming, enabling participants to create their own personalized characters – which may well be specially equipped to attack the characters created by other players.

Moog, Robert (1934–) US engineer who developed the first synthesizers widely used in popular music. Moog is also known for building theremins, an electronic instrument which musicians play by moving their hands between two antennas. In 1996 his company, Big Briar, based in Asheville, North Carolina, announced a ⇝ MIDI interface for theremins.

Moore, Gordon (1928–) US cofounder, with Robert ⇝ Noyce, of microchip manufacturer ⇝ Intel in 1968.

In 1965, when writing an article for the 35th anniversary edition of *Electronics* magazine, Moore formulated what has since been named Moore's Law: the number of components that could be squeezed onto a silicon chip would double every year. Moore updated this prediction in 1975 from doubling every year to doubling every two years. These observations proved remarkably accurate – the processing technology of 1996, for example, was some 8 million times more powerful than that of 1966 – partly because chip manufacturers tried to keep up with Moore's Law so as to avoid falling behind their rivals.

morphing metamorphosis of one shape or object into another by computer-generated animation. First used in film-making in 1990, it has transformed cinema special effects. Conventional animation is limited to two dimensions; morphing enables the creation of three-dimensional transformations.

To create such effects, the start and end of the transformation must be specified on screen using a wire-frame model that mathematically defines the object. To make the object three-dimensional, the wire can be extruded from a cross-section or turned as on a lathe to produce an evenly turned surface. This is then rendered, or filled in, and shaded. Once the beginning and end objects have been created, the computer can calculate the morphing process.

Mosaic ⇝ browser program used for searching the ⇝ World Wide Web. It was distributed free of charge on the Internet as NCSA Mosaic, and made a significant contribution to the huge growth in the Internet's popularity.

Mosaic was developed at the National Center for Supercomputing Applications at the University of Illinois in 1993, and the team behind it went on to create ⇝ Netscape Navigator, which quickly became a ⇝ killer application for browsing the Web. The Spyglass version of Mosaic was used as the basis for Microsoft's ⇝ Internet Explorer browser.

motherboard ⇝ printed circuit board that contains the main components of a microcomputer. The power, memory capacity, and capability of the microcomputer may be enhanced by adding expansion boards to the motherboard, now more commonly called a mainboard.

Motorola US semiconductor and electronics company. In computing, Motorola is best known for the 680x0 series of microprocessors used for many years by the Apple ⇝ Macintosh range and other computers. Its main microprocessor is the ⇝ PowerPC chip.

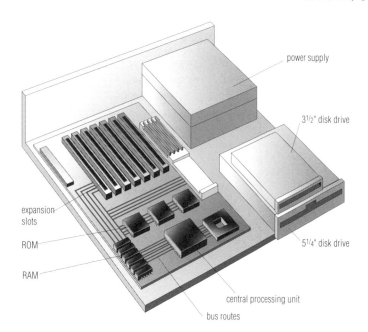

power supply

3½" disk drive

expansion slots

ROM

RAM

5¼" disk drive

central processing unit

bus routes

motherboard
The position of a motherboard within a computer's system unit. The motherboard contains the central processing unit, Random Access Memory (RAM) chips, Read-Only Memory (ROM), and a number of expansion slots.

mouse input device used to control a pointer on a computer screen. It is a feature of ⇝ graphical user interface (GUI) systems. The mouse is about the size of a pack of playing cards, is connected to the computer by a wire, and incorporates one or more buttons that can be pressed. Moving the mouse across a flat surface causes a corresponding movement of the pointer. In this way, the operator can manipulate objects on the screen and make menu selections.

The mouse was invented 1963 at the Stanford Research Institute, USA, by Douglas ⇝ Engelbart, and developed by the Xerox Corporation in the 1970s. The first was made of wood; the Microsoft mouse was introduced in 1983, and the Apple Macintosh mouse in 1984. Mice work either mechanically (with electrical contacts to sense the movement in two planes of a ball on a level surface), or optically (photocells detecting movement by recording light reflected from a grid on which the mouse is moved).

mouse, 3D input device used to control a pointer on a computer screen. A conventional ⇝ mouse works for 2-dimensional applications, but for 3-dimensional (3D) applications this pointing device with 6 degrees of freedom is becoming increasingly common. Most 3D mice are constructed with some graspable object, usually a ball, attached to a stationary base. Small movements are applied to the ball in various directions: up/down, side-to-side, twisting, and pitching. These movements are fed back to the computer, where they are translated to move an object around a 3D space on the screen.

Some of the more advanced ➥ virtual reality games for computers are able to be operated by 3D mice.

MP3 contraction of MPEG-1 Audio Layer 3, specification for a way of compressing digital sound files with very little loss of quality. This method allows music files, for instance of pop records, to be distributed via the Internet at low cost. MP3 is Layer 3 of the MPEG-2 video compression system developed by the Moving Pictures Expert Group (MPEG).

MPC abbreviation for *Multimedia PC*, standard defining the minimum specification for developing and running CD-ROM software. It has been rendered largely obsolete by the fact that most of today's PCs include multimedia features as a matter of course. The current MPC specification, MPC III, requires at least 8 MB of RAM, a 75MHz Pentium processor, a VGA monitor, and a quad-speed CD-ROM disk drive.

MPR-II abbreviation for *Mat och ProvRad*, Swedish standard that limits the amount of possibly harmful electromagnetic radiation that may be produced by visual display units (VDUs). A monitor tested for MPR-II compliance should have low emission rates.

MSCDEX.EXE abbreviation for *Microsoft Compact Disc Extensions*, device driver used by Microsoft MS-DOS and Windows 3 to provide access to files on CD-ROM drives as though they were on a hard drive or floppy disk.

MS-DOS abbreviation for *Microsoft Disk Operating System*, computer ➥ operating system produced by Microsoft Corporation, widely used on ➥ microcomputers with Intel x86 and Pentium-family microprocessors. A version called PC-DOS is sold by IBM specifically for its personal computers. MS-DOS and PC-DOS are usually referred to as DOS. MS-DOS first appeared in 1981, and was similar to an earlier system from Digital Research called CP/M.

MTBF abbreviation for *mean time between failures*, the statistically average time a component can be used before it goes wrong. The MTBF of a computer hard disk, for example, is around 150,000 hours.

MUD acronym for *multi-user dungeon* or *multi-user domain*, interactive multi-player game, played via the Internet or modem connection to one of the participating computers. MUD players typically have to solve puzzles, avoid traps, fight other participants, and carry out various tasks to achieve their goals.

The first MUD was called *MUD*, and was written by British programmers Roy Trubshaw and Richard Bartle to run on a DEC System 10 mainframe at the University of Essex, England, in 1979.

Making MP3s

http://www.mp3-faq.
org/faq3.html

Series of well-organized FAQs on how to make MP3 music files, and how to deal with problems. Written and updated by members of newsgroups interested in MP3s, this is an excellent site for answers to specific technical questions.

WEB LINK

MUD Resource Collection

http://www.godlike.com/
muds/

Useful and illuminating information on MUSHes (*multi-user shared hallucinations*) and MUDes (*multi-user dungeons*). The site includes a list of FAQs on these online, interactive environments, research accounts, links to useful resources on MUD information, and MUSH listings.

WEB LINK

Music Distribution

Introduction Thanks to compression technology, downloading music from a Web site is now a relatively painless operation. This should be great news for record companies and consumers alike. By selling music tracks to the public via the Web, record companies ought to be able to reduce packaging and distribution costs to something close to zero. This should in turn mean lower prices for the rest of us. That's the theory. In practice, the music industry has approached the Internet with a singular lack of enthusiasm.

The rise of MP3 Record companies are faced with a conundrum. On the one hand, there is growing demand for downloadable music. At the same time, the industry fears that the new technology will undermine its existing business model.

The demand has largely been driven by a compression technology known as MP3. Short for Moving Picture Experts Group, Audio Layer-3, MP3 was developed in Germany by the Fraunhofer Institut in the late 1980s. A piece of music encoded in this format can be compressed at various ratios, allowing faster downloading via the Internet. For example, a four-minute track compressed at a ratio of 10:1 should take around 10 to 15 minutes to download via a 56-kilobyte modem.

The MP3 revolution really began to gain momentum with the appearance of WinAMP, a PC-based software application designed to allow computer users to archive and play files encoded in the new format. WinAMP was quickly followed onto the market by a series of rival players, notably MusicMatch and Sonique. So far, it was largely a format for geeks. However, when US electronics firm Diamond launched a Walkman-style device known as Rio, MP3 began to reach out to the mass consumer market.

This presented a problem for the record industry. MP3 files can be copied and recopied with impunity. Once a track has been downloaded, it can be placed on a Web site or simply e-mailed to others. Thus, an MP3 track sold to an individual consumer can end up on the hard drives of thousands of others. In other words, music companies cannot protect their intellectual property.

Without backing from major labels, legal MP3 sites have been largely confined to offering music from new artists or small independent labels. For instance, Peoplesound.com provides a forum for unsigned acts, while iCrunch specializes in online distribution for small dance labels.

Nevertheless, tracks by artists signed to big-name labels are easy to come by on the Web. A few are available through legitimate operations such as MP3.com, but there are countless, often short-lived, sites providing access to pirated material.

More radically, peer-to-peer networks have emerged. The first of these was Napster, a system based around registered users equipped with special software. By logging on to the Napster site, any registered individual can search the hard disks of other members for specific MP3 files. This type of system, facilitating the swapping of files on an industrial basis, is the music industry's worst nightmare. At the time of writing, legal action by the US Record Industry Association was putting the future of Napster in doubt.

Closing Napster and other peer-to-peer systems would not necessarily solve the industry's problem, however. The genie is out of the bottle. Music-file swapping is a fact of life.

The record company response In terms of compression technology, MP3 is by no means the only game in town. Liquid Audio functions in a similar way in terms of compression, but it includes security features to prevent recopying. The major record companies have also banded together to produce their own system, known as SDMI (Secure Digital Music Initiative). However, MP3 has a head start, simply because there are a wide range of players and devices on the market. The record industry has a game of catch-up to play.

Nevertheless, the record companies have pushed ahead with their own plans. In April 2000, Sony Music's US operation offered selected singles for download at $2.50 a time. EMI followed later in the year with selected singles and album tracks. Others are expected to follow suit.

Rather than simply offering music from their own sites, both companies

Music Distribution (continued)

worked through the online properties of existing record industry retailers. This was an important point. For the foreseeable future, the vast majority of music sales will continue to involve CDs and cassettes sold through record stores. It is therefore vital that the big labels remain on good terms with distributors and retailers. In offering music online, the big record labels have been at pains to keep retailers in the loop. The middleman is still very much in place, as is the pricing structure.

As the value of sales via download grows, the record companies are likely to intensify their efforts to keep control of intellectual property. Research is currently underway into systems that will track user activity to allow record companies to find perpetrators of copyright infringement.

All this is a long way from the freewheeling culture of the Internet, where content often acts as a loss leader, financed by advertising and e-commerce. Record companies do not want to change their business plans, but they may have to.

Trevor Clawson

multicasting sending a simultaneous message across a ↝ network to two or more workstations.

multimedia computerized method of presenting information by combining audio and video components using text, sound, and graphics (still, animated, and video sequences). For example, a multimedia database of musical instruments may allow a user not only to search and retrieve text about a particular instrument but also to see pictures of it and hear it play a piece of music. Multimedia applications emphasize interactivity between the computer and the user.

As graphics, video, and audio are extremely demanding of storage space, multimedia PCs are usually fitted with ↝ CD-ROM drives because of the high storage capacity of CD-ROM disks.

In the mid-1990s, developments in compression techniques and software made it possible to incorporate multimedia elements into Internet Web sites.

multiplexer in telecommunications, a device that allows a transmission medium to carry a number of separate signals at the same time – enabling, for example, several telephone conversations to be carried by one telephone line, and radio signals to be transmitted in stereo.

In frequency-division multiplexing, signals of different frequency, each carrying a different message, are transmitted. Electrical frequency filters separate the message at the receiving station. In time-division multiplexing, the messages are broken into sections and the sections of several messages interleaved during transmission. Pulse-code modulation allows hundreds of messages to be sent simultaneously over a single link.

multisession ability of a compact disc or other ↝ WORM ('write once, read many times') medium, to record information at different times. Multisession technology allows archives to be built up gradually, as in the ↝ PhotoCD system, where users can progressively fill up a CD as they take pictures.

Multimedia Glossary

http://www.uncg.edu/irc/mm/terms/terms.htm

Extensive glossary of multimedia terms that features illustrations and links to related articles and Web sites. For the uninitiated, there is also a brief explanation of multimedia itself.

WEB LINK

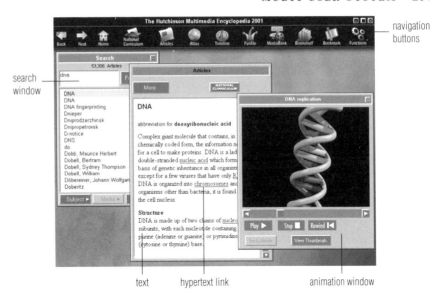

navigation
buttons

search
window

text hypertext link animation window

multimedia
An example of how various elements can be combined to create a multimedia presentation. Text is combined with still images, and icons signify related video, audio, and hypertext links.

multitasking or *multiprogramming*, system in which one processor appears to run several different programs (or different parts of the same program) at the same time. All the programs are held in memory together and each is allowed to run for a certain period.

For example, one program may run while other programs are waiting for a peripheral device to work or for input from an operator.

The ability to multitask depends on the ∽ operating system rather than the type of computer. Unix is one of the commonest.

multi-threading executing two or more ∽ threads, or sections, of a program at a time. Multi-threading is much faster than ∽ multitasking because it switches very quickly between instructions.

multi-user dungeon interactive game usually abbreviated to ∽ MUD.

multi-user shared hallucination interactive game usually abbreviated to ∽ MUSH.

multi-user system or *multiaccess system*, operating system that enables several users to access centrally stored data and programs simultaneously over a network. Each user has a terminal, which may be local (connected directly to the computer) or remote (connected to the computer via a modem and a telephone line).

Multiaccess is usually achieved by time-sharing: the computer switches very rapidly between terminals and programs so that each user has sole use of the computer for only a fraction of a second but can work as if she or he had continuous access.

Multi-user systems are becoming increasingly common in the workplace, and have many advantages – such as enabling employees to refer to and update a shared corporate database. The travel industry uses a multi-user system to manage bookings of airline tickets; travel agents around the world using the system can access information on available seats as readily as an airline's own office.

MUSE acronym for *multi-user shared environment*, type of ↷ MUD.

MUSH acronym for *multi-user shared hallucination*, ↷ MUD (multi-user dungeon) that can be altered by the players. Participants in a MUSH construct new environments or 'rooms' and devise new obstacles to challenge other players.

name server abbreviated from *domain name server*, on the Internet, a type of ➷ server which matches an Internet Protocol address to a ➷ domain name and vice versa.

Humans remember names, but computers work with numbers. Domain name servers translate between the two, so that a human can type an e-mail address such as janedoe@anywhere.com and the computer can route the message correctly.

NAND gate type of ➷ logic gate.

Napier, John (1550–1617) 8th Laird of Merchiston, Scottish mathematician who invented logarithms in 1614 and 'Napier's bones', an early mechanical calculating device for multiplication and division.

It was Napier who first used and then popularized the decimal point to separate the whole number part from the fractional part of a number.

Napier was born in Merchiston Castle, near Edinburgh, and studied at St Andrews. He never occupied any professional post.

English mathematician Henry Briggs went to Edinburgh in 1616 to discuss the logarithmic tables with Napier. Together they worked out improvements, such as the idea of using the base ten.

National Computing Centre *NCC*, UK centre set up in 1966 to offer advice and technical assistance to businesses on every aspect of information technology. The NCC is also the world's largest provider of escrow services for source code, a service necessary for businesses using custom-built software from a single supplier. It is based in Manchester.

The NCC produces various reports, including guidelines for IT managers, an annual salary survey, and an annual business information security survey.

National Education and Research Network communications backbone usually abbreviated to ➷ NERN.

National Grid for Learning *NGfL*, UK government initiative to provide both school teachers and their pupils with up-to-date educational materials via the Internet. The initial framework was launched by Prime Minister Tony Blair in November 1998.

Since it was launched, the NGfL has grown to well over 5,000 Web pages of hosted content and 250,000 pages of indexed content. The Learning Resource Index, accessible from the NGfL's home page, is a searchable index of all sites within the NGfL.

National Information Infrastructure *NII*, US network, often referred to as the information superhighway, that embraces every component of the Internet – from the satellites that carry the data to the PCs and telephone links that Americans use to access the Net. The NII was a 1995 US government initiative, the implementation of which was left to the private sector. The project aims to give all Americans access to the country's information and computing resources.

National Information Infrastructure

http://nii.nist.gov/nii/niiinfo.html

NII can be reached at their Web site.

WEB LINK

National Institute of Standards and Technology *NIST*, US body that plays an important role in setting computing and communications standards. NIST's Advanced Technology Program, which gives financial assistance to companies developing technologically advanced products during the research and development period, has played a considerable role in nurturing the US computer industry.

navigate to find your way around hyperspace or a ↝ hypertext document, especially when using a ↝ browser.

navigation map specialized tool to help users find their way around a Web site. Colourful graphics overlay a hidden grid, like that on a conventional map, containing ↝ hypertext links. Users navigate by placing their cursor on an image and clicking the mouse, sending a 'map reference' back to the Web site which activates a link. Navigation maps give the designer more control over how the page will appear on the screen, and are more attractive than conventional links.

NDA abbreviation for ↝ nondisclosure agreement.

Negroponte, Nicholas US founder and the director of the ↝ MIT Media Lab and columnist for ↝ *Wired* magazine.

In 1996 he published *Being Digital*, in which he makes an analogy between bits of data ('the DNA of information') and atoms of matter. Negroponte also predicted that mass media such as newspapers and television will give way to consumer-led electronic media in which people will take only the information they need.

Nelson, Ted (Theodore) (1937–) US computer scientist who coined the term ↝ hypertext in 1965 to propose a type of literature that used links embedded in text to connect readers to sources of further information. He went on to develop a global electronic publishing project called Xanadu, and was appointed professor of environmental information at Keio University, Japan, in 1996.

nerd slang term for someone who seems to spend more time interacting with computers than with human beings. The term was originally an abusive one, applied to weedy, diffident but studious US high school students by their more sporty and outgoing colleagues.

NERN abbreviation for *National Education and Research Network*, communications ↝ backbone capable of transferring data at the rate of one gigabit per second. It was designed for computer research, and is not accessible to the public.

net abbreviation for *network*, in the Internet's ↝ domain name system (DNS), one of the top-level domains, along with org, edu, com, gov, and mil. However, the use of the name has not been controlled and a name.net address does not necessarily identify the user as someone who works for a company involved in Internet networking.

Net abuse action that upsets participants in ⮑ Usenet. Common forms include ⮑ spamming (advertising), crossposting (sending the same message to several groups), scams (financial frauds), and attempts to rig or prevent discussions. In theory, ⮑ Internet Service Providers (ISPs) can punish Net abuse by blocking access to the Net, but in practice this sanction is very rarely invoked as the offender merely finds a new ISP.

Netfind ⮑ search engine designed to locate personal ⮑ e-mail addresses. Users supply an individual's name and a possible domain name, and Netfind searches a database of domain names, offering users a series of choices to help narrow down the range of options.

netiquette derived from *'Internet etiquette'*, behaviour guidelines evolved by users of the ⮑ Internet. The rules of netiquette include: no messages typed in upper case (considered to be the equivalent of shouting); new users, or new members of a ⮑ newsgroup, should read the frequently asked questions (FAQ) file before asking a question; no advertising via ⮑ Usenet newsgroups.

Users who contravene netiquette can expect to receive electronic mail ⮑ flames (angry messages) pointing out the error of their ways. The Internet community is fiercely protective of netiquette.

net police or *net cops*, ⮑ Usenet readers who monitor and 'punish' postings which they find offensive or believe to be in breach of ⮑ netiquette. Many unmoderated (see ⮑ moderator) newsgroups are policed by these self-appointed guardians, whose attempts to enforce their vision of the group sometimes make them a target for 'punishment' themselves.

Netscape US software company that supplies Navigator, a World Wide Web ⮑ browser, which is usually referred to as Netscape. Netscape Communications was founded in 1994 as Mosaic Communications, and called its browser Netscape. The names were changed in deference to the University of Illinois, where the Mosaic browser was written. The company was taken over by ⮑ America Online in 1999.

Netscape became very popular by giving away its browser for noncommercial use, and its sales increased rapidly as corporations licensed the browser and Netscape's growing suite of server-based programs. In 1997, Netscape's browser held 60% of the market. However, it suffered when Microsoft gave away copies of its Internet Explorer browser, and distributed it as part of Windows. Netscape has also had to compete with ⮑ Apache, a very popular free Web server program. The company now concentrates on selling its highly regarded server software to large corporations, and on developing its profitable ⮑ portal Web site, Netcenter. In 2000, a beta version was released of the completely revamped Netscape Navigator 6.

Net, the abbreviation for the ⮑ Internet. The term is often used to denote the entire community of people with computer access to the Internet.

NetWare leading ⮑ local area network operating system, supplied by ⮑ Novell.

network method of connecting computers so that they can share data and peripheral devices, such as printers. The main types are classified by the pattern of the connections – star or ring network, for example – or by the degree of geographical spread allowed; for example, ⮑ local area networks (LANs) for communication within a room or building, and ⮑ wide area networks (WANs) for more remote systems. Internet is the computer network that connects major English-speaking institutions throughout the world, with millions of users. JANET (joint academic network), a variant of Internet, is used in Britain. SuperJANET, launched in 1992, is an extension of this that can carry 1,000 million bits of information per second.

One of the most common networking systems is Ethernet, developed in 1973 (released 1980) at Xerox's Palo Alto Research Center, California, by R M Metcalfe and D R Boggs.

network computer *NC*, simple computer consisting essentially of a microprocessor, a ⮑ RAM chip, and a monitor. NCs are designed to function as part of a network, connected to a central ⮑ server via the Internet or an ⮑ intranet, downloading software (especially ⮑ object oriented programs) as required.

The absence of internal storage makes them much cheaper to maintain than PCs, and they are easier to manage and upgrade, as all the software is stored in one place. Some commentators had believed that the NC would eventually replace the networked PC as the standard computer set-up for business, especially for tasks previously performed using dumb terminals. In fact, the NC has rather been eclipsed by the ⮑ Windows-Based Terminal.

network interface card *NIC*, item of computer hardware that allows computers to be connected to a computer network.

network operating system *NOS*, software designed to enable a ⮑ LAN or other network to operate. The main task of every NOS is to tell both the central ⮑ file server and the ⮑ workstations connected to it how to communicate with each other. Network operating systems may also include security and backup features, remote access facilities, and a centralized database.

Network Time Protocol *NTP*, ⮑ Internet standards by which computers can tell each other the time. It is important for computer systems to have the correct date and time, and especially important for online transaction processing systems such as banks. NTP ⮑ servers base their own clocks on the times transmitted from super-accurate atomic clocks. Other computers, which represent clients, periodically check their own time with that of the NTP server, to remain in accordance.

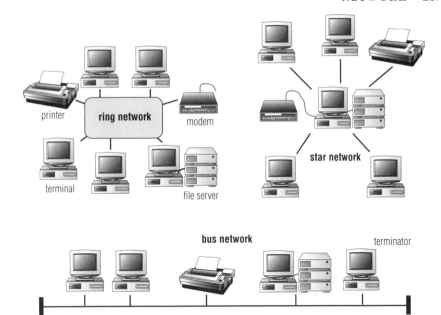

network
Local area networks can be connected together in a ring circuit or in a star arrangement. In the ring arrangement, signals from a terminal or peripheral circulate around the ring to reach the terminal or peripheral addressed. In the star arrangement, signals travel via a central controller. In a bus nework all elements are connected off a single cable that is terminated at each end.

neural network artificial network of processors that attempts to mimic the structure of nerve cells (neurons) in the human brain. Neural networks may be electronic, optical, or simulated by computer software.

A basic network has three layers of processors: an input layer, an output layer, and a 'hidden' layer in between. Each processor is connected to every

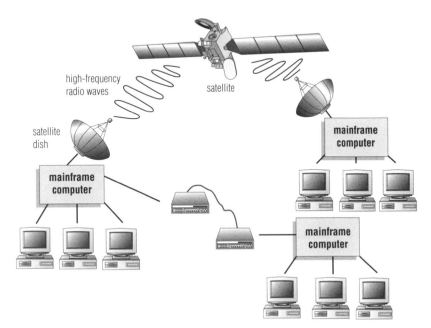

network
A wide area network is used to connect remote computers via telephone lines or satellite links. The ISDN (Integrated Services Digital Network) telecommunications network allows high-speed transfer of digital data.

other in the network by a system of 'synapses'; every processor in the top layer connects to every one in the hidden layer, and each of these connects to every processor in the output layer. This means that each nerve cell in the middle and bottom layers receives input from several different sources; only when the amount of input exceeds a critical level does the cell fire an output signal. The chief characteristic of neural networks is their ability to sum up large amounts of imprecise data and decide whether they match a pattern or not. Networks of this type may be used in developing robot vision, matching fingerprints, and analysing fluctuations in stock-market prices. However, it is thought unlikely by scientists that such networks will ever be able accurately to imitate the human brain, which is very much more complicated; it contains around 10 billion nerve cells, whereas current artificial networks contain only a few hundred processors.

TIP

newbie

Newbies are recommended to lurk for a week or two before adding their voices to the USENET hubbub.

newbie insulting term for a new user of a ↝ Usenet newsgroup, whose naive or off-topic comments irritate established members of the group. A classic newbie *faux pas* is to post a question that is answered in the group's ↝ FAQ (file of frequently asked questions).

new media general term for ↝ CD-ROM, the ↝ World Wide Web, and other electronic media, including ↝ multimedia.

Most publishing companies now have a 'new media' division which manages a ↝ Web site and studies how best to compete and exploit the company's assets in the electronic future.

newsgroup discussion group on the ↝ Internet's ↝ Usenet. Newsgroups are organized in seven broad categories: comp. – computers and programming; news. – newsgroups themselves; rec. – sports and hobbies; sci. – scientific research and ideas; talk. – discussion groups; and misc. – everything else. In addition, there are alternative hierarchies such as the wide-ranging and anarchic alt. (alternative). Within these categories there is a hierarchy of subdivisions.

Newsgroups exist for almost any subject one might care to think of, whether serious or frivolous. Because Usenet cannot be censored at source, some of the newsgroups are inevitably tasteless and offensive to many users. Some newsgroups are moderated, however, so that all postings are assessed in order to maintain the standards of debate.

newsreader program that gives access to ↝ Usenet newsgroups, interpreting the standard commands understood by ↝ news servers in a simple, user-friendly interface. Popular newsreaders include rn for ↝ Unix, Turnpike and Agent for PCs, and NewsReader for Macintosh. It is also possible to access Usenet with a ↝ browser such as ↝ Netscape Navigator.

news server computer that stores ↝ Usenet messages for access by users. Most ↝ Internet Service Providers (ISPs) offer a news server as part of the service.

Newton small portable computer, also called a ⤳ personal digital assistant (PDA), produced by ⤳ Apple in 1993 and discontinued in 1998. The Newton combined many functions, including address book, diary, word processor, fax terminal, and e-mailing and Internet browsing facilities, in a pocket-sized unit. Its keyboardless interface and handwriting recognition software allowed users to enter data using a stylus and a touch screen.

NeXTStep ⤳ operating system and development environment, originally created for the ⤳ NeXT workstation, but later made available for other computers, including the IBM PC. NeXTStep is based on ⤳ Unix but contains a high level of ⤳ object orientation. Apple used NeXTStep (more accurately, OpenStep) as the basis for its next-generation Macintosh operating system in 1997.

NeXT Technology Inc US computer manufacturer founded by Steve Jobs in 1985. NeXT's first product was an advanced workstation, the NeXT Cube, aimed at the higher education market. It sold poorly and NeXT abandoned hardware manufacturing to become a software company, Next Software Inc. This was taken over by Apple Computer for $400 million at the end of 1996.

NGfL abbreviation for ⤳ National Grid for Learning.

nickname alternative ⤳ user-id, as used by participants in ⤳ MUDs, ⤳ Internet Relay Chat, and other interactive setups.

NII abbreviation for ⤳ National Information Infrastructure.

Nintendo Japanese ⤳ games console and software manufacturer. In 1996, the company introduced the N64 – the first 64-bit games console – using technology from workstation manufacturer Silicon Graphics Inc. Nintendo's best-known games characters are the 'Super Mario Brothers'.

Nintendo planned to release the Dolphin, its next-generation console, in time for the Christmas 2000 shopping season.

NIST abbreviation for ⤳ National Institute of Standards and Technology.

NNTP abbreviation for *Network News Transfer Protocol*, set of standard procedures by which ⤳ Usenet news is distributed across the Internet. NNTP governs both the way e-mailed messages travel between news servers and the way ⤳ newsreaders retrieve news from servers.

NO CARRIER error message returned by a modem when the telephone line drops unexpectedly because of line noise or other interruptions.

node any device connected to a network, such as a ⤳ router, a ⤳ bridge, a ⤳ hub, or a ⤳ server.

nondisclosure agreement *NDA*, agreement signed with suppliers by manufacturers, programmers, journalists, and others, in exchange for detailed information or copies of new products in advance of their public launch. For example, a manufacturer might sign an NDA to get a copy of a new operating

TIP

No Carrier

Users generally shouldn't have to worry about port addresses, as applications like Telnet and the World Wide Web mostly use standard addresses (for Telnet, port 23) and the client software will fill these in automatically.

Occasionally, a non-standard address will specify a different port, and in these cases the user must add the non-standard port number to the end of the address.

system in order to have compatible hardware ready for the program's launch. NDAs are often required in order to participate in beta (pre-launch) tests of important pieces of software.

nonlinear video editing video editing method that processes compressed video data stored on a hard disk. This makes it much easier for editors to find their way around the material, and enables them to commence editing at any point in the tape – hence the name.

Editors use a computer to rearrange the material and produce an Edit Decision List (EDL) bearing all information on cuts, fades, and other effects. The EDL can then be used to create an automated final edit using the original tapes. The main video editing programs are Avid VideoShop for the Apple Macintosh and Tektronix Lightworks for PCs.

nonvolatile memory ↝ memory that does not lose its contents when the power supply to the computer is disconnected.

NOR gate in electronics, a type of ↝ logic gate.

Northbridge type of ↝ chip inside modern computers. It is the role of the Northbridge chip to act as a buffer between the ↝ central processing unit (CPU), the main ↝ memory, and the expansion ↝ bus. The advantage of the design is that the same set of 'wires' are used by the CPU to talk to the main memory and the ↝ input/output devices.

NOS acronym for ↝ network operating system.

notebook computer small battery-powered portable about A4 in size and about 50 mm/2 in thick. The first notebook computers, such as the Epson HX-20 and Tandy 100, became available in the early 1980s, with the first

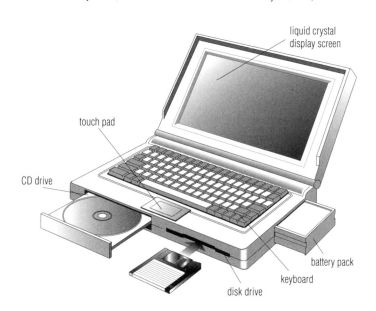

notebook computer
The component parts of a notebook computer. Although as powerful as a microcomputer, the battery pack enables the notebook to be used while travelling.

PC-compatible notebook, the Toshiba T1100, following in 1985. In the 1990s, the notebook format became the standard for portable PCs and Apple PowerBooks.

Many PC manufacturers offer two extra types of notebook computer: an 'ultraportable' and a 'power portable' (nomenclature varies). Ultraportables are typically 20–30 mm/0.8–1.2 in thick and are often supplied with external floppy and CD-ROM drives. They are aimed at mobile users who are willing to make sacrifices for reduced size and weight. Power portables make no such compromises and are aimed at users who want the notebook computer equivalent of a desktop computer. Some manufacturers also offer smaller portable PCs called subnotebooks, which are too small to include a full-size keyboard and screen. See also ↝ laptop computer.

NOT gate or *inverter gate*, in electronics, a type of ↝ logic gate.

Novell US ↝ network operating system specialist. Novell's ↝ NetWare operating system for IBM-compatible PCs dominates the market for ↝ local area networks and is used as an industry standard.

Noyce, Robert Norton (1927–1990) US scientist and inventor, with Jack ↝ Kilby, of the ↝ integrated circuit (microchip), which revolutionized the computer and electronics industries in the 1970s and 1980s. In 1968 he and six colleagues founded the ↝ Intel Corporation, which became one of the USA's leading semiconductor manufacturers.

The integrated circuit was developed independently by Noyce at Fairchild Semiconductor in 1959, and by Jack Kilby at Texas Instruments in 1958. Noyce applied for a patent for the integrated circuit in 1959 and, although this was challenged by Texas Instruments, in 1969 the appeal courts eventually found in his favour. In 1961 he founded his first company, Fairchild Camera and Instruments Corporation, around which Silicon Valley was to grow. The company was the first in the world to understand and exploit the commercial potential of the integrated circuit. It quickly became the basis for such products as the personal computer, the pocket calculator, and the programmable microwave oven. At the time of his death, he was president of Sematech Incorporated, a government–industry research consortium created to help US firms regain a lead in semiconductor technology that they had lost to Japanese manufacturers.

NSFnet abbreviation for *National Science Foundation Network*, network funded by the US National Science Foundation, and an important part of the Internet backbone. In 1993 the National Science Foundation started building a very high speed Backbone Network Service (vBNS) to connect five government supercomputing centres at speeds of up to 2.5 gigabits per second - fast enough to transmit the entire contents of several public libraries every second.

ntl cable television and telecommunications company. In July 1999 ntl announced that it was acquiring the consumer operations of Cable and

Wireless Communications, which would make it the largest cable operator in the UK and Ireland, with a total of 2.8 million customers.

ntl launched the UK's first ↝ interactive television service in 1999, providing news, sport, entertainment, travel, home shopping, and local information services. In 1999 ntl signed an agreement to provide ↝ video-on-demand in partnership with Diva, beginning in the summer of 2000.

NTSC abbreviation for *National Television Standards Committee*, US ↝ television standard signal format. Sometimes believed to stand for 'Never Twice the Same Colour'.

null character character with the ↝ ASCII value 0. A null character is used by some programming languages, most notably C, to mark the end of a character string.

null-modem special cable that is used to connect the ↝ serial interfaces of two computers, so as to allow them to exchange data.

null string string, usually denoted by '–', containing nothing or a ↝ null character. A null string is used in some programming languages to denote the last of a series of values.

object linking and embedding *OLE*, enhancement to ↝ dynamic data exchange, which makes it possible not only to include live data from one application in another application, but also to edit the data in the original application without leaving the application in which the data has been included. (See also ↝ ActiveX.)

object-oriented programming *OOP*, computer programming based on 'objects', in which data items are closely linked to the procedures that operate on them. For example, a circle on the screen might be an object: it has data, such as a centre point and a radius, as well as procedures for moving it, erasing it, changing its size, and so on.

The technique originated with the Simula and Smalltalk languages in the 1960s and early 1970s, but it has now been incorporated into many general-purpose programming languages, including Java, C++, and Eiffel.

object program ↝ machine code translation of a program written in a ↝ source language.

OCR abbreviation for ↝ optical character recognition.

octal number system number system to the base eight, used in computing. The highest digit that can appear in the octal system is seven. Whereas normal decimal, or base-ten, numbers may be considered to be written under column headings based on the number ten, octal, or base-eight, numbers can be thought of as written under column headings based on the number eight. The octal number 567 is therefore equivalent to the decimal number 375, since $(5 \times 64) + (6 \times 8) + (7 \times 1) = 375$.

The octal number system is sometimes used by computer programmers as an alternative to the ↝ hexadecimal number system.

OEM abbreviation for ↝ original equipment manufacturer.

office automation introduction of computers and other electronic equipment, such as fax machines, to support an office routine. Increasingly, computers are used to support administrative tasks such as document processing, filing, mail, and schedule management; project planning and management accounting have also been computerized.

office suite set of bundled programs designed especially for business use. An office suite will typically contain a ↝ spreadsheet, scheduling and presentation software, ↝ word-processing software, a ↝ database, and ↝ e-mail facilities. The programs are set up to work individually and together, so that the user can (for example) create a report with charts created from a spreadsheet, and then e-mail the document to a list of clients selected from the database. Popular office suites include Lotus SmartSuite and Microsoft Office.

offline not connected, so that data cannot be transferred, for example, to a printer. The opposite of ↝ online.

Package	Manufacturer	Content (word processing; spreadsheet; presentation and other software)
CorelOffice	Corel	with WordPerfect, Quattro Pro, Presentations, and a personal information manager and document packaging tool
Microsoft Office	Microsoft	with Word, Excel, PowerPoint, Mail, Office Assistant, and (Professional version) Access database; allows Web-site hyperlinks
SmartSuite	Lotus	with Word Pro, 1-2-3, Freelance, Approach (database), time management system, and screen action recorder

office suite
Contents and functions
of major office suites

offline browsing downloading and copying Web pages onto a computer so that they can be viewed without being connected to the Internet. By taking advantage of off-peak hours, when telephone charges are low and the network responds faster, offline browsing is a thrifty way of using the ↩ World Wide Web.

Although useful in saving time and money for the person who copies the Web pages, offline browsing is considered antisocial by some who argue that by automatically demanding large numbers of pages from a server in quick succession places a large strain on the server, to the detriment of other browsers. Some web servers are set up to deny access to offline browser programs.

offline editing in video and film, process of editing a scratch copy of the footage rather than the expensively created footage itself. Once the edit has been finalized, the real footage is edited by a machine.

offline reader program that downloads information from ↩ newsgroups, ↩ FTP servers or other Internet resources, storing it locally on a hard disk so that it can be read without running up a large telephone bill.

OLE abbreviation for ↩ object linking and embedding

Olsen, Kenneth (Harry) (1926–) US electrical engineer. He helped build WHIRLWIND and SAGE, two early computers, at the Massachusetts Institute of Technology's Lincoln Laboratory (1950–57). He also supervised the building of the transistorized digital computers TX-O and TX-2. In 1957 he founded and became president of the Digital Equipment Corporation, producing the PDP series of computers. In 1977 he introduced VAX (Virtual Address Extension) machines, and in the 1980s, a series of VAX minicomputers. Digital became one of the largest computer manufacturers in the world, but after the recession of the 1980s struck, he resigned as president and CEO of Digital in 1992. Olsen was born in Bridgeport, Connecticut.

OMR abbreviation for ↩ optical mark recognition.

online connected, so that data can be transferred, for example, to a printer or from a network. The opposite of ☞ offline.

online auction sale of goods, of any type, by auction from a Web site. The items available include surplus goods being auctioned by companies, as well as items offered by individuals. The main online auction houses are the US company ☞ eBay, the UK's QXL, and the French firm Aucland. The main German online auction houses, Alando and Ricardo, were taken over by eBay (in 1999) and QXL (in 2000), respectively.

online help guidance and assistance in using a program which is given by the software itself, instead of a manual or a customer services representative over the telephone.

online service commercial service like ☞ America Online (AOL), ☞ Compulink Information eXchange (CIX), or ☞ CompuServe, which offers proprietary conferencing and other services to subscribers on top of access to the Internet.

Shop Genie

http://www.shopgenie.co.uk/

Shop Genie is a utility that allows you to compare the prices of UK online shops to ensure you get the best deal. Currently it covers the books, music, films, and games market, to help you get the best price you can.

WEB LINK

online shopping selecting and buying merchandise via the ☞ Internet. Towards the end of the 1990s, an increasing range of products and services could be purchased online, for example books (companies such as WHSmith are online), groceries (many major supermarkets offer home shopping via the Internet), travel (including rail and air travel), and holidays. In business, trade over the World Wide Web is known as e-commerce, which can be business-to-consumer (B2C), business-to-business (B2B), or consumer-to-consumer (C2C), such as ☞ online auctions. Retailers online are often referred to as e-tailers.

US consumers spent $7 billion/£4.4 billion shopping online during the 1999 Christmas period, it was announced by an Internet research company. The research also found that 90% of the Internet shoppers they surveyed said that they were satisfied with this type of shopping, compared with 74% recorded for the same period in 1998.

online system originally a system that allowed the computer to work interactively with its users, responding to each instruction as it is given and prompting users for information when necessary. Since almost all the computers used now work this way, 'online system' is now used to refer to large database, electronic mail, and conferencing systems accessed via a dial-up modem. These often have tens or hundreds of users from different places – sometimes from different countries – 'on line' at the same time.

on-site warranty after-sales service offered free by many hardware manufacturers for a limited period after purchase – usually one year. An on-site warranty entitles purchasers to a visit from an peripatetic engineer in case of problems.

Open ☞ interactive television service launched in the UK in 1999, and available free of charge to viewers of BSkyB's digital television service. Open covers home shopping and banking, entertainment (including computer games), information (weather reports, holiday ideas, and sports results), and Internet ⬿ electronic mail (for which special keypads are available).

In July 2000 BSkyB bought out minority shareholders Matsushita and HSBC to take control of Open. BSkyB now owns 80.1% of the company, with the remaining shares being held by ⬿ BT. BSkyB had previously been prevented from offering interactive services such as online gambling, because of stringent agreements the company had signed when Open had been set up.

Open eBook standard for ⬿ electronic books being developed since 1998 by a group of companies, including ⬿ Microsoft, five electronic-book-reader manufacturers, five major publishers, Franklin Electronic (publisher of electronic reference books), and US online bookseller barnesandnoble.com.

OpenGL abbreviation for *Open Graphics Library*, 3-D graphics language developed by US-based workstation manufacturer, Silicon Graphics Inc (SGI), and widely used on Unix workstations. Microsoft has developed its own system called Direct3D, which is part of ⬿ DirectX. However, Microsoft's Windows NT operating system supports OpenGL and Microsoft and SGI are working together to add some OpenGL support to DirectX.

Open Group multivendor industry body formed in February 1996 through the merger of X/Open and the ⬿ Open Software Foundation. One of its functions is to test and brand with an X mark products that conform to open systems standards.

Open Software Foundation *OSF*, software house created in 1988 by several major industry players (including Bull, DEC, Hewlett-Packard, IBM, and Philips) to engineer a standard operating system and user interface for the ⬿ Unix platform. The OSF joined with ⬿ X/Open to form The Open Group in 1996.

open systems systems that conform to ⬿ Open Systems Interconnection or ⬿ POSIX standards. ⬿ Unix was the original basis of open systems and most nonproprietary open systems still use this ⬿ operating system.

The term is also used more loosely to describe any system that can communicate with other systems and to describe other standards, such as ⬿ MS-DOS and ⬿ Windows. Open systems were developed partly to make better communication possible, but also to reduce users' dependence on (and lock-in to) suppliers of proprietary systems.

Open Systems Interconnection *OSI*, ⬿ International Standards Organization standard, defining seven layers of communication protocols. Although OSI is an international standard, existing protocols, such as ⬿ TCP/IP and IBM's Systems Network Architecture are more commonly used in commercial systems.

operating system *OS*, program that controls the basic operation of a computer. A typical OS controls the peripheral devices such as printers, organizes the filing system, provides a means of communicating with the operator, and runs other programs.

Operating system	Developer	Interface	Platform
DOS	Microsoft and IBM 1981	command line	PC
OS/2	IBM and Microsoft 1987	command line GUI	PC
Mac OS	Apple 1984	pioneered GUI	Macintosh
Unix/Linux	AT&T, Red Hat, and others late 1960s–2000	command line GUI	from mainframes to PCs
Windows NT/2000	Microsoft 1993–2000	GUI	PC or RISC-based system
Windows 95/98/00	Microsoft 1995–2000	GUI	PC

operating system
Key features of some major operating systems

Many operating systems were written to run on specific computers, but some are available from third-party software houses and will run on machines from a variety of manufacturers. Examples include Apple's OS 9, Microsoft's ↝ Windows, and Unix.

Unix (developed at AT&T's Bell Laboratories) is the standard on workstations, minicomputers, and supercomputers; it is also used on desktop PCs and mainframes. Windows is the standard on desktop PCs.

optical character recognition *OCR*, technique for inputting text to a computer by means of a document reader. First, a ↝ scanner produces a digital image of the text; then character-recognition software makes use of stored knowledge about the shapes of individual characters to convert the digital image to a set of internal codes that can be stored and processed by computer.

OCR originally required specially designed characters but current devices can recognize most standard typefaces and even handwriting. OCR is used, for example, by gas and electricity companies to input data collected on meter-reading cards, and by ↝ personal digital assistants to recognize users' handwriting.

optical computer computer in which both light and electrical signals are used in the ↝ central processing unit. The technology is still not fully developed, but such a computer promises to be faster and less vulnerable to outside electrical interference than one that relies solely on electricity.

optical disk storage medium in which laser technology is used to record and read large volumes of digital data. Types include ↝ CD-ROM, ↝ WORM, and erasable optical disk.

optical fibre very fine, optically pure glass fibre through which light can be reflected to transmit images or data from one end to the other. Although expensive to produce and install, optical fibres can carry more data than traditional cables, and are less susceptible to interference. Standard optical fibre transmitters can send up to 10 billion bits of information per second by switching a laser beam on and off.

Optical fibres are increasingly being used to replace metal communications cables, the messages being encoded as digital pulses of light rather than as fluctuating electric current. Current research is investigating how optical fibres could replace wiring inside computers.

Bundles of optical fibres are also used in endoscopes to inspect otherwise inaccessible parts of machines or of the living body.

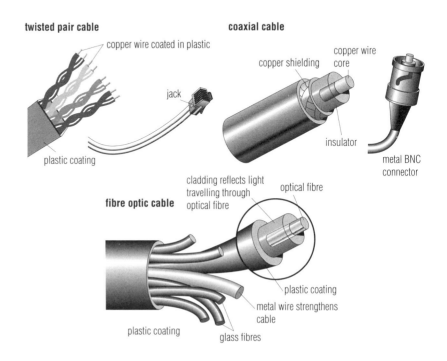

optical fibre
The major differences in construction between twisted pair (telephone), coaxial, and fibre optic cable.

optical mark recognition *OMR*, technique that enables marks made in predetermined positions on computer-input forms to be detected optically and input to a computer. An optical mark reader shines a light beam onto the input document and is able to detect the marks because less light is reflected back from them than from the paler, unmarked paper.

Oracle software development company, founded by Larry ⮑ Ellison in 1977, and originally specializing in ⮑ database management systems. Oracle was initially known as Software Development Laboratories, and then as Relational Technologies. In the high-tech field, its shares are second in value only to those of ⮑ Microsoft.

org abbreviation for *organization*, in the Internet's ⮑ domain name system (DNS), one of the top-level domains, along with com, gov, mil, int edu, and net. Noncommercial organizations, such as charities, typically have Internet addresses of the form name.org.

OR gate in electronics, a type of ⌐ logic gate.

original equipment manufacturer *OEM*, company that manufactures equipment or, illogically, has equipment manufacturered for it by another company. The abbreviation is often used as a verb, as in: 'IBM OEMs PCs from Acer' (in other words, Acer makes PCs with IBM badges for IBM to sell).

OS/2 single-user computer ⌐ operating system produced jointly by Microsoft Corporation and IBM for use on personal computers, particularly when attached to large IBM computers. Its main features were reliability – useful for running file servers – and a powerful object-oriented graphical user interface, Workplace Shell.

OS/2 was announced in 1987 but sales were dismal. Microsoft abandoned it in 1992 to concentrate on Windows. IBM abandoned attempts to sell it on the mass market in 1997, but supports its use as a corporate and network computer operating system.

OSI abbreviation for ⌐ Open Systems Interconnection.

outline font ⌐ font in which the outline of each character is defined by a mathematical formula, making the font scalable to any size. Outline fonts can be output using the resolution of the output device, unlike ⌐ bit map fonts, which can be output at only one size and one resolution. The most common forms of outline fonts are ⌐ PostScript and ⌐ TrueType.

output device any device for displaying, in a form intelligible to the user, the results of processing carried out by a computer.

The most common output devices are the ⌐ VDU (visual display unit, or screen) and the ⌐ printer. Other output devices include graph plotters, speech synthesizers, and COM (computer output on microfilm/microfiche).

over-clocking practice of trying to make a ⌐ central processing unit (CPU) run at a faster ⌐ clock rate than was originally intended by the manufacturer, and so improve performance with minimal costs.

OverDrive chip plug-in replacement for an Intel microprocessor, designed to speed up the PC in which it is used. Intel OverDrive chips are expensive but are cheaper than buying a new PC and offer a simpler upgrade path than replacing the computer's ⌐ motherboard.

overflow error ⌐ error that occurs if a number is outside the computer's range and is too large to deal with.

overlay set of specialized data for use with a larger database. A database of a particular country's geography, for example, that includes roads, towns, and natural features such as rivers and lakes might come with overlays that can be displayed or turned off at the user's command, such as the distribution of speed cameras.

packet unit of data sent across a network. As well as the actual substance of the message, every packet carries error-control information and details of its origin and its final target, enabling a ➝ router to send it on to the intended recipient. This means that packets belonging to the same file can travel via different routes over the network, to be automatically reassembled in the correct sequence when they arrive at their destination. All traffic on the Internet consists of packets. See also ➝ TCP/IP and ➝ X.25.

packet radio use of amateur (ham) radio, instead of telephones, to communicate between computers. A terminal node controller (TNC) replaces the modem, a radio transceiver takes the place of the telephone, and the phone system is replaced by radio waves. Packet radio, which works on several different frequencies, has a complete network of its own, complete with satellite links and terrestrial relays. It cannot be used to access the Internet, but it can be connected through the Internet.

packet switching method of transmitting data between computers connected in a ➝ network. Packet-switched networks do not provide a dedicated connection between two locations, as with a circuit-switched network. Packet-switched networks make more effective use of ➝ bandwidth than circuit-switched networks, and are more resilient to breaks in network links because there are always multiple routes from source to destination.

It is possible for a large message to be broken down into many small packets, each equipped with a sequence number to ensure it can be reassembled properly if some packets take a different route through the network of switches and arrive out of order.

The resilience of packet-switched networks was important to the US Department of Defense, who funded early packet-switching research. It was particularly concerned that the network would continue to work if parts of it were destroyed during a nuclear attack. These were the beginnings of the formation of the Internet.

page-description language control language used to describe the contents and layout of a complete printed page. Page-description languages are frequently used to control the operation of ➝ laser printers. The most popular page-description languages are Adobe Postscript and Hewlett-Packard Printer Control Language.

page printer computer ➝ printer that prints a complete page of text and graphics at a time. Page printers use electrostatic techniques, very similar to those used by photocopiers, to form images of pages, and range in size from small ➝ laser printers designed to work with microcomputers to very large machines designed for high-volume commercial printing.

paging method of increasing a computer's apparent memory capacity. See ➝ virtual memory.

paint program program that enables users to 'paint' a picture on their computer screens, using a variety of brushes, spray-guns, and colours.

Paintshop Pro popular graphics or 'paint' program for Microsoft Windows created by US software house JASC Inc. It is distributed as ❧ shareware.

PAL abbreviation for *Phase Alternation by Line*, video standard used in the UK, other parts of Europe, and China. It has a higher definition and different screen format from the US NTSC standard. Running a television program written for PAL on an ❧ NTSC system can result in the bottom of the screen image being cut off.

palmtop computer or *palm-sized PC*, palm-sized computer that usually does not have a keyboard but is operated by using a stylus on a touch-sensitive screen. Although several companies launched palmtops and ❧ personal digital assistants, the first successful model was Palm Computing's Palm Pilot. (Palm was taken over by modem manufacturer US Robotics, which in turn was taken over by networking company 3Com). In 1998, Casio, Philips, and other companies launched Palm-like palmtops running Microsoft's Windows CE operating system (renamed PocketPC in 2000).

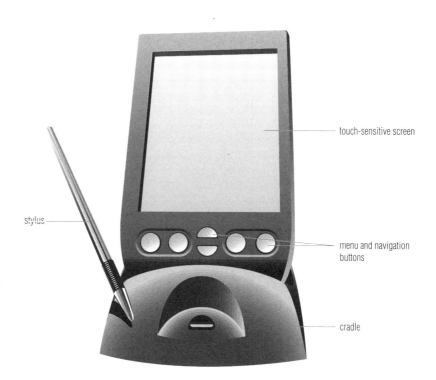

palmtop computer
A palmtop computer, operated by using a pen-like stylus on a touch-sensitive screen, in place of a keyboard. The cradle allows it to connect to and exchange information with a computer terminal.

touch-sensitive screen

stylus

menu and navigation buttons

cradle

Handheld Computers

Background Handheld computers cannot do what most people want them to. This may seem surprising, given that millions of models using operating systems from Palm, Psion, and Microsoft have been sold since 1984, when Psion introduced its first handheld model. But all are severely limited compared to the expectations placed upon them, which can be traced back to two sources: the 1960s TV series *Star Trek* and the 1970s radio series *The Hitchhiker's Guide to the Galaxy*, written by Douglas Adams. Only now does it look as though people will soon be able to buy products with the facilities they have been hankering after for decades.

The sight in the 1960s of William Shatner as Captain Kirk, landing on ancient planets and flipping out a palm-sized machine that could act as a radio, intelligent locator, and general categorizer of knowledge, had a subtle effect on the baby boomers' belief about what computers of the future could and should do. It was voice-activated, and context- and location-sensitive. Similarly, in the radio series, *The Hitchhiker's Guide to the Galaxy* was actually the name of a computerized guidebook. It contained as much information as the hitchhiker could read. While its indexing method was hopeless by any modern standards – the traveller had to look up a number in the index and enter that in order to get to the corresponding entry ('so bad it could have been designed by Microsoft,' Adams later quipped) – it did create the belief that someday one could build a handheld machine able to hold all the knowledge not just in the world, but in the galaxy. And if aliens had them, why shouldn't we?

Psion and Apple The reality of the first retail products was rather different. The Psion 1, the brainchild of David Potter, was launched in 1984. It had a mighty 10 kilobytes of non-volatile memory, an alphabetic keypad, and a one-line, 16-character liquid crystal display (LCD) screen. Entering data was tedious. It would not have passed muster with Captain Kirk. However, its descendants are now widely used by people in jobs requiring simple data collection, including traffic wardens.

In August 1993, Apple Computer launched its $700 Newton, which seemed at the time to promise at least some Star Trek functionality. It had handwriting recognition software, able to 'learn' a person's specific cursive style, and there were promises of wireless communications and word processing. It turned out to be an example of the computer industry's occasional hubris. The software did learn a writing style, but often failed to interpret the letters correctly. The Newton was a flop (officially abandoned in 1998, but dead some years earlier) which poisoned the well for entrepreneurs in the US handheld market for some years. Bill Gates of Microsoft reckoned it put the market for such products back by two years (probably an underestimate).

Palm Computing, founded by Jeff Hawkins and Donna Dubinsky in 1992, managed to survive only by selling itself to US Robotics early in 1996. However, in the UK and Europe, Psion was thriving, and had developed its Psion Organiser 3 series, which had a miniature keyboard and inbuilt software including limited word processing, a calendar, a contacts book, and a spreadsheet program. It looked like a miniaturized version of a laptop computer, and proved very successful in its local market.

Palm Computing But on the west coast of the USA, Hawkins and Dubinsky were developing a palm-sized machine which would have some, at least, of the ease of use of both Captain Kirk's communicator and *The Hitchhiker's Guide to the Galaxy*. Hawkins envisaged a machine (which later became the Palm series) that would not stand alone, but would synchronize and back up its files with a standard PC. Thus it would not have to do everything, only have enough functionality to be useful while out of touch with the PC. For data entry, Hawkins developed a shorthand cursive system called 'Graffiti' which all Palm users have to learn. He tested the ergonomics of the product by carving a block of wood into a size and shape that he could carry around comfortably in his pocket. Function and form thus developed in parallel.

The Palm operating system was hugely popular, even though the basic machine offered only a calendar, an address book, a task and notes list, and

Handheld Computers (continued)

a calculator, plus a search system. Its success stemmed from its ability to coordinate with a PC, the openness of the operating system, and the coincidental rise of the Internet. The first point meant users could access their databases more easily than with tiny keyboards, the second that software developers could write programs to enhance the machine, and the third that those programs could be widely and quickly distributed. Psion, with its EPOC operating system, had attracted some software developers but was held back by its European location (where Internet development lagged by a couple of years compared to the USA) and by lack of connectivity to PCs.

Launched early in 1996, the first Palm computer sold one million units in 18 months. Hawkins and Dubinsky were dismayed by the slow working of the monolithic 3Com, which had bought US Robotics, and left in 1996, with Palm's marketing head Ed Collingen, to set up their own company Handspring. This company licensed the Palm OS, which then had 80% of the world market, served by 100,000 developers, while Psion and Microsoft competed for the remainder.

Microsoft's failure in this market is unusual, but seems to stem from its Windows CE operating system (renamed and rebuilt as PocketPC in spring 2000) being too complex for the limited power of the machines. Windows CE is used in petrol pumps and in set-top boxes for decoding digital television signals.

Handhelds versus mobile phones The future promises rapid change. Until 2000, handheld computers sat apart from mobile phones: an address list on one could not be transferred to another. As usability expert Jakob Nielsen noted, this is absurdly inconvenient. Mobile phones are no good for noting data (such as phone numbers) while you are in a call, but handhelds have been little use for making phone calls.

But Handspring especially has been forcing the pace, as its Visor machines, which use the Palm OS, include a slot called the 'Springboard' where the user can plug in items such as a camera, a memory module, or (from autumn 2000) a GSM modem. Palm rapidly announced that, by the end of 2000, all of its products would have wireless capability. Separately, IBM demonstrated a version of a Palm machine with an add-on board that gave it voice recognition capability, using the ViaVoice technology. Suddenly, the humble handheld was beginning to look like the machine that would be able to do everything.

But mobile-phone makers and Psion have not finished. The so-called 'third generation' of mobile phones, which will have high-speed data connections, were being designed in 2000, and the Symbian consortium (which uses the EPOC operating system) won a contract to provide the operating system for a number of phone companies. What was still unclear at the end of 2000 was whether handheld computers would swallow mobile phones, or vice versa. The handhelds had the functionality, the mobile phones the usability. However, the mobiles rapidly lost that edge as new WAP (Wireless Applications Protocol) phones attempted to squeeze Internet interactivity into a few lines of a monochrome LCD screen. In some respects, it was a step back to 1984. The market's explosive growth may mean that there is room for everyone to survive. In the long term, though, functionality is sure to win out over form.

Charles Arthur

Pantone Matching System trade name for a standard set of colours used in graphics and printing, precisely graded and numbered using a universal system. Colours shown on monitors and computer printers are not reliable enough for most designers, so print graphics programs usually include the facility to specify the desired Pantone colours.

parallax in ⤳ virtual reality, the distance between the viewer's left and right eyes in the virtual world.

This difference is what creates the impression of depth. Right and left images of distant objects look the same; but left and right images of nearby objects look markedly different owing to the difference of perspective. Manipulating this variable in a virtual world helps make objects look large or small.

parallel device device that communicates binary data by sending the bits that represent each character simultaneously along a set of separate data lines, unlike a ↝ serial device.

parallel processing emerging computer technology that allows more than one computation at the same time. Although in the 1990s this technology enabled only a small number of computer processor units to work in parallel, in theory thousands or millions of processors could be used at the same time.

Parallel processing, which involves breaking down computations into small parts and performing thousands of them simultaneously, rather than in a linear sequence, offers the prospect of a vast improvement in working speed for certain repetitive applications.

parallel running method of implementing a new computer system in which the new system and the old system are run together for a short while. The old system is therefore available to take over from its replacement should any faults arise. An alternative method is ↝ pilot running.

parameter variable factor or characteristic. For example, length is one parameter of a rectangle; its height is another. In computing, it is frequently useful to describe a program or object with a set of variable parameters rather than fixed values.

For example, if a programmer writes a routine for drawing a rectangle using general parameters for the length, height, line thickness, and so on, any rectangle can be drawn by this routine by giving different values to the parameters.

Similarly, in a word-processing application that stores parameters for font, page layout, type of ↝ justification, and so on, these can be changed by the user.

parity of a number, the state of being either even or odd. In computing, the term refers to the number of 1s in the binary codes used to represent data. A binary representation has even parity if it contains an even number of 1s and odd parity if it contains an odd number of 1s.

For example, the binary code 1000001, commonly used to represent the character 'A', has even parity because it contains two 1s, and the binary code 1000011, commonly used to represent the character 'C', has odd parity because it contains three 1s. A parity bit (0 or 1) is sometimes added to each binary representation to give all the same parity so that a ↝ validation check can be carried out each time data are transferred from one part of the computer to another. So, for example, the codes 1000001 and 1000011 could have parity bits added and become 01000001 and 11000011, both with even parity. If any bit in these codes should be altered in the course of processing the parity would change and the error would be quickly detected.

Character	Binary code	Parity	Base-ten representation
A	1000001	even	65
B	1000010	even	66
C	1000011	odd	67
D	1000100	even	68

parity
Examples of parity for different letters of the alphabet (represented by binary code)

parity check form of ⤳ validation of data.

parse software facility for breaking down a data stream into individual pieces of information that can be acted upon. On the World Wide Web, for example, data entered by a user can be sent to a database program for storage and later analysis; the ability to do this depends on being able to feed the right bit of data into the right record field.

Pascal French acronym for *program appliqué à la selection et la compilation automatique de la littérature*, high-level computer-programming language. Designed by Niklaus ⤳ Wirth in the 1960s as an aid to teaching programming, it is still widely used as such in universities, and as a good general-purpose programming language. Most professional programmers, however, now use ⤳ C or ⤳ C++. Pascal was named after 17th-century French mathematician Blaise Pascal.

Pascal, Blaise (1623–1666) French mathematician and philosopher, inventor of the first mechanical calculator able to carry 'tens' automatically when adding and subtracting. Pascal's most original work was done in mathematics, but he is now perhaps best known for the programming language that Niklaus ⤳ Wirth named after him.

passive matrix display or *passive matrix LCD*, ⤳ liquid crystal display (LCD) produced by passing a current between an array of electrodes set between glass plates. Passive matrix screens lack the transistors that enhance the performance of ⤳ active matrix LCDs, which makes them relatively inexpensive, but lacking in contrast and slow to react.

password secret combination of characters used in computing to control access and thus to ensure ⤳ data security.

patch modification or update made to a program, consisting of a short segment of additional code. Developers often correct bugs or fine-tune software by releasing a patch which rewrites existing codes and adds new material.

payment service provider *PSP*, company which allows an ⤳ electronic commerce Web site to accept payments online from credit and debit cards, without the need for the site to hold payment details itself. The card transactions are cleared and cardholders' accounts debited immediately. PSPs include Datacash, Netbanx, Secpay, and Worldpay.

PC Card standard for 'credit card' memory and device cards used in ⤳ portable computers. As well as providing ⤳ flash memory, PC Cards can provide either additional disk storage, or modem or fax functionality. PC Card was adopted as being a simpler and more accurate name than ⤳ PCMCIA.

PCI abbreviation for *peripheral component interconnect*, form of ⤳ local bus connection between external devices and the main ⤳ central processing unit. Developed (but not owned) by ⤳ Intel, it was available as 32-bit in 1993, but is now available as 64-bit.

PCL ⤳ page description language, developed by Hewlett Packard for use on Laserjet laser printers. Versions PCL 1 to PCL 4 used ⤳ raster graphics fonts; PCL 5 uses ⤳ outline fonts.

PCMCIA abbreviation for *Personal Computer Memory Card International Association*, another name for a ⤳ PC card.

PCX bitmapped ⤳ graphics file format, originally developed by Z-Soft for use with PC-Paintbrush, but now used and generated by many applications and hardware such as scanners.

PDF abbreviation for *portable document format*, file format created by Adobe's ⤳ Acrobat system that retains the entire content of an electronic document (including layouts, graphics, styled text, and navigation features) regardless of the computer system on which it is viewed. Because they are platform-independent, PDF files are a good way to send documents over the Internet.

PeaceNet computer network dedicated to the cause of world peace and social justice. PeaceNet carries specialist news and information services which are used by many human rights and disarmament organizations. Compare ⤳ GreenNet.

peer-to-peer networking method of file sharing in which computers are linked to each other as opposed to being linked to a central file server.

pen-based computer computer (usually portable), for which input is by means of a pen or stylus, rather than a keyboard. It incorporates handwriting recognition software, although prior to the release of the Apple ⤳ Newton and similar models, this had effectively meant using separate characters rather than 'joined-up' writing.

Pentium microprocessor produced by ⤳ Intel in 1993. The Pentium followed on from the 486 processor and would have been called the 586, but Intel wanted to distinguish its processor from those of rival chip manufacturers, and was unable to register numbers as a trademark. The Pentium family was extended by the Pentium Pro in 1995 and the Pentium II in 1997, and also by the addition of ∾ MMX instructions in 1996. All members of the family are 32-bit chips with 64-bit data buses for faster access to memory and the ∾ PCI expansion bus.

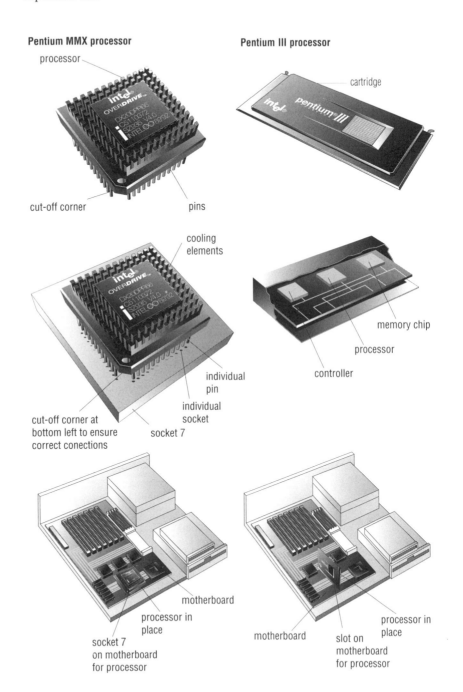

Pentium MMX processor

processor

cut-off corner

pins

cooling elements

cut-off corner at bottom left to ensure correct conections

individual pin

individual socket

socket 7

Pentium III processor

cartridge

memory chip

processor

controller

socket 7 on motherboard for processor

processor in place

motherboard

motherboard

slot on motherboard for processor

processor in place

Pentium
The illustration shows the difference between the Pentium MMX and Pentium III processors, and how they fit into a computer.

The original Pentium had about 3.1 million transistors, the Pentium Pro about 5.5 million, and the Pentium II about 7.5 million. The slowest Pentium ran at 60 MHz, but in 1997 speeds reached 300 MHz in PCs and 450 MHz under laboratory conditions. Intel's most modern processor, the Pentium III, available in 2000, now runs at 1.0 GHz.

peripheral device any item connected to a computer's ⮑ central processing unit (CPU). Typical peripherals include keyboard, mouse, monitor, and printer. Users who enjoy playing games might add a ⮑ joystick or a ⮑ trackball; others might connect a ⮑ modem, ⮑ scanner, or ⮑ integrated services digital network (ISDN) terminal to their machines.

Perl acronym for *Practical Extraction and Report Language*. Perl is a programming language developed by Larry Wall for processing text. However, it has proved extremely popular as a way of writing ⮑ CGI scripts for Web pages.

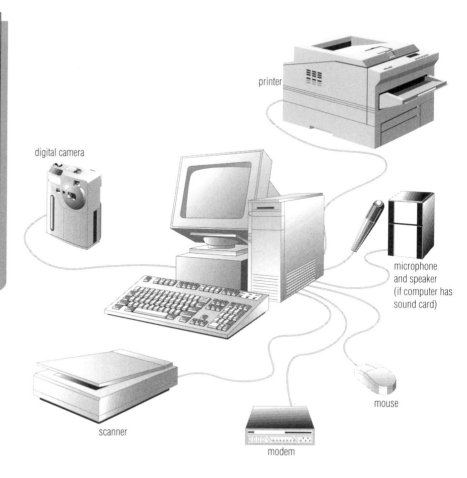

peripheral device
Some of the types of peripheral device that may be connected to a computer include printers, scanners, and modems.

printer

digital camera

microphone and speaker (if computer has sound card)

mouse

scanner

modem

personal computer *PC*, another name for ↝ microcomputer. The term is also used, more specifically, to mean the IBM Personal Computer and computers compatible with it.

The first IBM PC was introduced in the USA in 1981; it had 64 kilobytes of random access memory (RAM) and one floppy-disk drive. It was followed in 1983 by the XT (with a hard-disk drive) and in 1984 by the AT (based on a more powerful ↝ microprocessor). Many manufacturers have copied the basic design, which is now regarded as a standard for business microcomputers. Computers designed to function like an IBM PC were originally known as IBM-compatible computers, but are now more usually called Windows PCs.

personal digital assistant *PDA*, handheld computer designed to store names, addresses, and diary information, and to send and receive faxes and e-mail. They aim to provide a more flexible and powerful alternative to the Filofax or diary.

The market for PDAs with keyboards is being fought between the Psion Series 3 and 5 (strongest in Europe), the Sharp Zaurus range (strongest in Asia), and HPCs (Handheld PCs) and PPCs (Palm-sized PCs) running Microsoft's PocketPC operating system. However, by far the best-selling PDA in 1999 was the Palm Pilot, a very small stylus-operated machine made by US Robotics, a division of 3Com, which held almost 80% of the world market.

personal identification device *PID*, device, such as a magnetic card, carrying machine readable identification, which provides authorization for access to a computer system. PIDs are often used in conjunction with a ↝ PIN.

personal productivity software work-oriented software such as ↝ word processing, ↝ spreadsheets, or ↝ databases.

petaflops jargon for 1,000 trillion computations per second. This is still many years from being realized.

PGML abbreviation for *Precision Graphics Markup Language*, hybrid of ↝ PDF and ↝ HTML under development by ↝ Adobe. PGML is particularly suitable for use on ↝ electronic book readers and ↝ personal digital assistants. See also ↝ ClearType.

PGP abbreviation for the encryption program ↝ Pretty Good Privacy.

Phong shading type of shading used in animation and 3-D graphics, based on a computerized model of how light is reflected from surfaces.

PhotoCD picture storage and viewing system developed by Kodak and Philips. The aim of Kodak's PhotoCD is to allow the user to put up to 100 photos onto compact disc: images are transferred from film to a PhotoCD disk and can then be viewed by means of Kodak's own PhotoCD player, which plugs into a television set, or by using suitable software on a multimedia PC.

PhotoCD is based on multisession ↝ WORM (write-once read many times) technology. The images can be written to the disk in multiple recording sessions.

phreaking using computer technology to make free long-distance phone calls, charge them to another account, or otherwise illegally access the telephone network. In the 1980s, phreaking was semi-respectable among hackers (see ↝ hacking), but it is now less reputable – and thanks to improved security in the phone network, much more difficult. The case of Kevin ↝ Mitnick did much to bring phreaking to public attention.

PICS abbreviation for *Platform for Internet Content Selection*, method of classifying data according to its content. Under PICS, the creator and the reader of a file can add descriptive electronic labels to it, making it possible for users to sort documents according to keywords on the label. The system, introduced in 1996, aims to help parents to control what their children can see on the Internet, for example by blocking access to pornographic or violent material; it also enables people to highlight subjects in which they are especially interested.

PICT object-oriented file format used on the Apple ↝ Macintosh computer. The format uses ↝ QuickDraw and is supported by almost all graphics applications on the Macintosh.

pilot running method of implementing a new computer system in which the work is gradually transferred from the old system to the new system over a period of time. This ensures that any faults in the new system are resolved before the old system is withdrawn. An alternative method is ↝ parallel running.

PIN acronym for *personal identification number*, in banking, a unique number used as a password to establish the identity of a customer using an automatic cash dispenser. The PIN is normally encoded into the magnetic strip of the customer's bank card and is known only to the customer and to the bank's computer. Before a cash dispenser will issue money or information, the customer must insert the card into a slot in the machine (so that the PIN can be read from the magnetic strip) and enter the PIN correctly at a keyboard. This helps to prevent stolen cards from being used to obtain money from cash dispensers.

PING acronym for *Packet Internet Groper*, short message sent over a network by one computer to check whether another is correctly connected to it. By extension, one can 'ping' other people – for example, checking addresses on a ↝ mailing list by sending an ↝ e-mail to all members requesting an acknowledgement.

PIPEX acronym for *public Internet protocol exchange*, UK-based Internet Service Provider which started operations in 1992, specializing in serving the commercial sector. The company became one of the UK's major ➴ backbone providers, was acquired by ➴ UUNET 1996, and was spun off again at the end of 1998.

Pixar Hollywood animation company bought by Steve ➴ Jobs in 1986. In 1995 Pixar, together with Disney, released *Toy Story*, the first ever feature-length computer-animated cartoon film.

pixel derived from *picture element*, single dot on a computer screen. All screen images are made up of a collection of pixels, with each pixel being either off (dark) or on (illuminated, possibly in colour). The number of pixels available determines the screen's resolution. Typical resolutions of microcomputer screens vary from 320 x 200 pixels to 800 x 600 pixels, but screens with 1,024 x 768 pixels or more are now common for high-quality graphic (pictorial) displays.

The number of bits (binary digits) used to represent each pixel determines how many colours it can display: a two-bit pixel can have four colours; an eight-bit (one-byte) pixel can have 256 colours. The higher the resolution of a screen and the more colours it is capable of displaying, the more memory will be needed in order to store that screen's contents.

PKI abbreviation for ➴ public key infrastructure.

PKZIP widely-used shareware file compression utility. Files created with PKZIP (often posted to ➴ newsgroups and ➴ bulletin boards) bear the suffix .zip and are said to be 'zipped'.

plaintext another name for ➴ cleartext.

plan file file publicly accessible on Unix systems that holds whatever information users wish to make public about themselves.

On other services such records may be called a resumé, bio, or directory entry. The purpose is generally the same: to allow users of the same system to find out a little more about the real-world identity of the people with whom they are interacting.

plasma display type of flat display, which uses an ionized gas between two panels containing grids of wires. When current flows through the wires a ➴ pixel is charged causing it to light up.

platform ➴ operating system, together with the ➴ hardware on which it runs.

Platform for Internet Content Selection method of classifying data, usually abbreviated to ➴ PICS.

PlayStation market-leading ➴ games console made by ➴ Sony. The PlayStation holds 75% of the UK video games market, and accounts for nearly half of Sony's profits.

direction buttons

fire buttons

joysticks

PlayStation2
This games console from Sony plays games from either DVDs (digital versatile disks) or original PlayStation CDs (compact discs). It is backwards compatible to enable it to play games from earlier Sony systems. It can also connect to the Internet via its built-in modem, allowing gamers in different countries to play against each other.

Sony launched the PlayStation2 in 2000, in a market that is increasingly lucrative, and competitive. Sega launched its rival console, Dreamcast, in late 1999, and Nintendo was aiming to release its new Dolphin in time for the Christmas 2000 market. The new generation of games consoles promise Internet connectivity and cutting-edge graphics technology. PlayStation2 will be the first backwards-compatible console, allowing existing PlayStation games to be played on the PlayStation2.

plotter or *graph plotter*, device that draws pictures or diagrams under computer control.

Plotters are often used for producing business charts, architectural plans, and engineering drawings. Flatbed plotters move a pen up and down across a flat drawing surface, whereas roller plotters roll the drawing paper past the pen as it moves from side to side.

Plug & Display standard intended to allow digital computers to control digital flat panel displays. Almost all personal computers have an analogue output port to connect to a CRT or monitor. Almost all flat panel (LCD) display screens are therefore provided with the corresponding analogue input port, plus circuitry to convert the analogue signal back to digital. The double-conversion is pointless and degrades quality. However, there are several options for making digital-to-digital connections and, in the short term, Plug & Display looks unlikely to succeed.

plug and play item of hardware or software that configures itself and the user's system automatically when first installed. Having been thus 'plugged' in, it can be used ('played' with) immediately. In the PC industry, suppliers have adopted a form of Plug and Play (PnP) developed by Microsoft and Intel in 1993.

plug-in small add-on file which enhances the operation of an application program, often by enabling it to launch, display, or interpret a file created using another one. The first plug-ins were made for graphics programs in the 1980s, but the practice became very popular in the mid-1990s, when a range of plug-ins became available to enhance the multimedia capabilites of ⌐ Netscape's Navigator ⌐ browser. Plug-ins are often created and distributed by independent developers rather than the manufacturer of the program they extend.

PNG abbreviation for ⌐ Portable Network Graphics.

point and click basic method of navigating a ⌐ Web page or a multimedia CD-ROM. The user points at an object using a cursor and a mouse, and clicks to activate it.

point-of-sale terminal or *POS terminal*, computer terminal used in shops to input and output data at the point where a sale is transacted; for example, at a supermarket checkout. The POS terminal inputs information about the identity of each item sold, retrieves the price and other details from a central computer, and prints out a fully itemized receipt for the customer. It may also input sales data for the shop's computerized stock-control system.

A POS terminal typically has all the facilities of a normal till, including a cash drawer and a sales register, plus facilities for the direct capture of sales information – commonly, a laser scanner for reading bar codes. It may also be equipped with a device to read customers' bank cards, so that payment can be transferred electronically from the customers' bank accounts to the shop's (see ⌐ EFTPOS).

Point-to-Point Protocol method of connecting a computer to the Internet; usually abbreviated to PPP.

polling technique for transferring data from a terminal to the central computer of a ⌐ multiuser system. The computer automatically makes a connection with each terminal in turn, interrogates it to check whether it is holding data for transmission, and, if it is, collects the data.

PoP acronym for *point of presence*, place where users can access a network via a telephone connection. A PoP is a collection of modems and other equipment which are permanently connected to the network. Compare ⌐ vPoP.

POP3 abbreviation for *Post Office Protocol*, on the Internet, one of the two most common mail ⌐ protocols.

Internet Service Providers (ISPs) offer ⌐ SMTP, POP3, or both. The primary difference to most users is the choice of software available. SMTP is older and more flexible, but POP3 is generally simpler for those accessing the Internet via a dial-up account.

pop-up menu menu that appears in a (new) window when an option is selected with a mouse or key-stroke sequence in a ⌐ graphical user interface (GUI), such as Microsoft Windows. Compare with ⌐ pull-down menu.

A seamless network On the Internet, you are your words. (Or your images, animations, full-motion videos, or sounds.) When someone objects to what you say, they object to who you are. When they try to make laws banning what you say, you feel as if they're putting you in prison without a trial. This is the psychology behind the reality that censorship has been one of the hottest topics on the Net since the day the first two ARPA scientists exchanged their first e-mail message.

This doesn't stop governments and other organizations from wanting to try. The attempts take different forms: legislation in the USA, voluntary hotlines in the UK and the Netherlands, technical means to block access to non-approved content in Singapore. None of these methods is perfect, and the Net finds means to bypass all of them. On the non-governmental level, corporations have sought to have material critical to them removed, the Net's central registry of domain names has persistently refused to allow the domain 'f***.com', and intellectual property owners have acted to shut down activities they perceived as infringements of their copyrights.

Each of these phenomena has had its own major battle. US legislation such as the 1997 Communications Decency Act (CDA) was challenged in court and eventually struck down as violating the First Amendment to the US Constitution. The voluntary hotlines work in a limited way, in that they can only request the removal of illegal material from servers in their own countries: Britain's Internet Watch Foundation can't do much about child pornography on a server in the Philippines. The Net's domain name authority, the Internet Corporation for Assigned Names and Numbers, which came into being in 1998, was still considering mid-2000 which names should be allowed. Corporations and intellecutal property holders have the toughest time, as shutting one server down on the Net works like severing the heads of the Hydra of Greek mythology: cut one off and several more spring up elsewhere. In 2000, the major example of this was the ongoing legal action of the Recording Industry Association of America against music services such as MP3.com and Napster. While the legal battles continued, copies of the music files at issue proliferated everywhere.

The problem with successfully blocking information that a group of people perceives as undesirable lies largely in the original design of the Internet as a seamless network that would allow researchers all over the world to share information as easily as if they were alternating seats in front of the same computer. Unlike a phone call, which originates in one identifiable place and ends up in another, data travels the Internet unpredictably. Restricting that flow of data therefore not only impedes the normal workings of the Net, but is also a difficult matter, since material that is banned in one place may well pop up in another (or, in the Net's traditionally defiant style, many others). 'The Net perceives censorship as damage,' Electronic Frontier Foundation co-founder John Gilmore has famously said, 'and routes around it.'

The other significant difficulty in censoring the Net is that each country has its own set of cultural values. The USA is, by European standards, rather straitlaced about nudity, sex, and drugs, but tolerant of hate speech, which is protected under the First Amendment, and of violence. In mid-2000, for example, the French government was trying to block Yahoo!'s US operation from selling Nazi memorabilia to French citizens. Sweden, by contrast, is permissive about sexual material but heavily regulates violence, while the Netherlands is tolerant of both drug-related and sexual content. Even in the area of child pornography, countries differ on the age of consent.

Blocking software and ratings systems For the above reasons, by the end of 1997 many countries were encouraging the development of ratings systems and blocking software. Blocking software typically contains an encrypted database of sites containing material the software publisher considers undesirable, and loads as a separate program onto a PC. When the user tries to access one of the blocked sites, he or she receives either an error message or a warning message from the software. During the late 1990s, blocking software was installed in many libraries and schools in the USA, in spite of the

Censorship on the Internet (continued)

protests of civil liberties groups. Ratings systems, on the other hand, can be used to mark Web sites and Usenet newsgroups. The leading contender, called Platform-Independent Content Selection (PICS), was developed by the World Wide Web Consortium, the group that guides the Web's development. A live strip show Web site, for example, might rate itself 10 in the sexual content category, but 0 for violence. Within the browser, a profile specifies which levels in these and other categories are acceptable. While this sounds complicated for an average user to configure, the idea is that third-party organizations with known agendas (or, potentially, governments) should be able to make available customized profiles for users to download. Such a system solves one of the key problems with blocking software: the uncertainty over what is being blocked. Closer examination of blocking software has revealed that these products typically go far beyond the pornography and violence they claim to filter, and block sites covering issues such as feminism, censorship, and safe sex. However, many 'Netizens' are wary of ratings systems for the same reason they were wary of blocking software: they believe the potential exists for ratings systems to be used to censor the Net, rather than for the stated purpose of empowering users to make their own choices.

Ratings software also faces the problem of deployment: how do you get 100 million Internet users to rate their sites voluntarily? For these reasons, by mid-2000, although organizations continued to talk about the development of PICS and other ratings systems, many technical insiders considered the idea effectively dead.

In the future The chances are that the future will see many more efforts to censor the Net, not just by governments but increasingly by large companies, who by mid-2000 were beginning to dominate Net access. By the end of 1997, moves were afoot to introduce new CDA-style legislation in the USA, and the European Commission proposed an action plan blending the approaches already being tried in Europe: hotlines, self-regulation by ISPs, the deployment of ratings and filtering software, and, especially, international cooperation so that data banned in one place could not find a haven in another. Few on the Net believe, however, that it will ever be possible to regulate the Net completely, because of its size and diversity. What is certain is that governments and other groups will continue to try. The battle continues.

Wendy M Grossman

pornography, Internet material of an explicitly sexual nature, whether it be text, photographs, graphics, audio, or video available on the Internet.

The amount of pornography and the ease of finding it has been exaggerated by both politicians and mass media. Nonetheless, there is material available on the Internet to offend almost everyone, and most governments are either attempting or considering some means of ➷ censorship.

port socket that enables a computer processor to communicate with an external device. It may be an input port (such as a joystick port), or an output port (such as a printer port), or both (an i/o port).

Microcomputers may provide ports for cartridges, televisions and/or monitors, printers, and modems, and sometimes for hard disks and musical instruments (MIDI, the musical-instrument digital interface). Ports may be serial or parallel.

portability characteristic of certain programs that enables them to run on different types of computer with minimum modification. Programs written in a

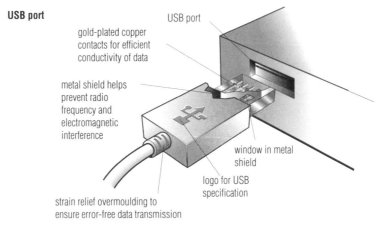

USB port

gold-plated copper contacts for efficient conductivity of data

USB port

metal shield helps prevent radio frequency and electromagnetic interference

window in metal shield

logo for USB specification

strain relief overmoulding to ensure error-free data transmission

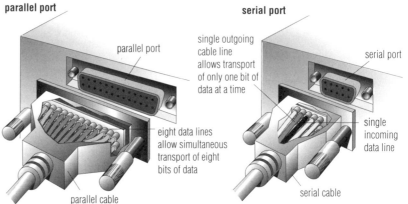

parallel port

parallel port

single outgoing cable line allows transport of only one bit of data at a time

serial port

serial port

eight data lines allow simultaneous transport of eight bits of data

single incoming data line

parallel cable

serial cable

port
The three types of communications port in a microcomputer. The USB port transmits data at a faster rate than a serial or parallel port.

⇨ high-level language can usually be run on any computer that has a compiler or interpreter for that particular language.

portable computer computer that can be carried from place to place. The term embraces a number of very different computers – from those that would be carried only with some reluctance to those, such as ⇨ laptop computers and ⇨ notebook computers, that can be comfortably carried and used in transit.

Portable Network Graphics *PNG*, file format for images created under the auspices of the ⇨ W3C. PNG offers an alternative to the ⇨ GIF format, which ran into problems over its use of ⇨ LZW compression. See also ⇨ graphic file format.

port address on the Internet, a way for a host system to specify which ⇨ server a particular application will use.

portal ⇨ Web site designed to be used as a start-up site for browsing sessions and to provide a gateway to the rest of the Web. To increase their

portal
An example of a portal site on the Web, which presents a variety of ways to make use of the Internet.

attractiveness, portals expanded rapidly in the late 1990s to offer a wide variety of services such as personalized start-up pages, free e-mail, directories, customized news and weather reports, online calendars, games, and free Web space. The first portals were online services such as America Online, which added gateways to the Internet. Others have come from different areas: Yahoo! started as a hierarchical guide to Web sites, Excite as a search engine, and Netscape's Netcenter as the default home page for users of Netscape's Web browser. CNet's Snap! was the first Web site designed to act as a portal.

POSIX acronym for *portable operating system interface for Unix*, ↪ ANSI standard, developed to describe how the programming interfaces and other features of ↪ Unix worked, in order to remove control from the developers, AT&T Bell Laboratories. Subsequently many other (proprietary) ↪ operating systems were modified in order to become POSIX-compliant, that is, they provide an ↪ open systems interface, so that they can communicate with other POSIX-compliant systems, even though the operating systems themselves are internally quite different. See also ↪ open systems interconnection.

post to send a message to a ↪ newsgroup or ↪ bulletin board for others to read.

POS terminal acronym for ⇌ point of sale terminal, a cash register linked to a computer.

posting another word for article.

postmaster ⇌ systems administrator in charge of a mail server. The term is especially used for people who manage the electronic mail system in a ⇌ local area network (LAN) or other local network.

PostScript page-description language developed by Adobe that has become a standard. PostScript is primarily a language for printing documents on laser printers, but it can be adapted to produce images on other types of devices.

PostScript is an object-oriented language, meaning that it treats images, including fonts, as collections of geometrical objects rather than as ⇌ bit maps. PostScript fonts are ⇌ outline fonts stored in the computer memory as a set of instructions for drawing the circles, straight lines, and curves that make up the outline of each character. This means they are also scalable. Given a single typeface definition, a PostScript printer can thus produce a multitude of fonts.

The principal advantage of ⇌ vector graphics over bit-mapped graphics is that object-oriented images take advantage of high-resolution output devices whereas bit-mapped images do not. A PostScript drawing looks much better when printed on a 600 ⇌ dpi printer than on a 300 dpi printer. Object-oriented images also generally require less memory than bit-mapped images.

PowerPC ⇌ microprocessor produced by IBM and ⇌ Motorola, originally as a challenger to Intel, though now being directed towards industrial uses.

The PowerPC was based on IBM's multichip POWER (Performance Optimization With Enhanced RISC) architecture introduced with the RS/6000 line of Unix workstations and servers in 1990. When Apple decided to switch to the PowerPC processor, its previous chip supplier, Motorola, switched from its own 88000 ⇌ RISC processor to join a triumvirate backing the PowerPC. However, the group failed to make any impact on Intel and Apple's sales declined in 1995–97.

PowerPoint ⇌ presentation graphics program made by ⇌ Microsoft and sold mainly as part of Microsoft Office.

PPP abbreviation for *Point-to-Point Protocol*, newer of the two standard methods for connecting a computer to the Internet via a modem and the public switched telephone network (⇌ PSTN). Unlike the earlier ⇌ SLIP, PPP can handle both ⇌ synchronous and ⇌ asynchronous communication and provides ⇌ error detection.

presentation graphics program that helps users to create presentations such as visual aids, handouts, and overhead slides. Presentation graphics programs process artwork, graphics, and text to produce a series of 'slides' – images which help speakers to get their message across. Leading programs include

10 Minute Guide to PowerPoint

http://sunsite.net.edu.cn/tutorials/tmg-power/

Useful guide to Microsoft's presentation graphics software PowerPoint, explaining everything you need to know in an easy to understand language.

WEB LINK

Software	Manufacturer	Description
Adobe Persuasion	Adobe	with outlines, speaker's notes
ASAP WordPower	SPC	few features but extremely simple to use
Astound	Gold Disk	easy-to-use business presentation package with multimedia features
Freelance	Lotus	full of features; very effective outline view
PowerPoint	Microsoft	allows incorporating spreadsheet and word processing elements into presentations
Presentation	Corel	formerly WordPerfect Presentation

presentation graphics
A selection of presentation graphics programs

Microsoft ↝ PowerPoint and (for ↝ multimedia presentations, incorporating moving pictures, and sounds) Macromedia Director.

Prestel ↝ viewdata service that provides information on the television screen via the telephone network. The service was first offered to the public by British Telecom – then a division of the General Post Office – in 1979. It never lived up to expectations and British Telecom sold off what remained in 1995.

Prestel On-Line is now a subsidiary of Thus (formerly Scottish Telecom) specializing in Internet access and content provision.

Pretty Good Privacy *PGP*, strong encryption program that runs on personal computers and is distributed on the Net free of charge. It was written by Phil ↝ Zimmermann and released to the Net in 1991 amid growing fears that the USA would pass a law requiring all secure communications systems to incorporate a 'back door' to make it easy for law enforcement officials to read encrypted messages.

PGP is based on the ↝ RSA ↝ algorithm and uses ↝ public-key cryptography; its source code has been released to the cryptographic community for study and testing. Since version 1.0, its development has proceeded in multiple locations around the world to avoid conflicts with the US laws banning the export of strong encryption. A companion product, PGPfone, released in 1996, runs across the Internet to give users the equivalent of a military grade secure telephone.

In 1996, Zimmermann founded PGP Inc, which was acquired by computer security software developer Network Associates in 1997.

print to transfer data to a ↝ printer, to a screen or to another file.

printed circuit board *PCB*, electrical circuit created by laying (printing) 'tracks' of a conductor such as copper on one or both sides of an insulating board. The PCB was invented in 1936 by Austrian scientist Paul Eisler, and was first used on a large scale in 1948.

PGP for Beginners

http://axion.physics.ubc.ca/pgp-begin.html

This tutorial introduces users to PGP, showing them how to download and install PGP, as well as how to encrypt and decrypt files and how to send anonymous mail.

WEB LINK

Components such as integrated circuits (chips), resistors, and capacitors can be soldered to the surface of the board (surface-mounted) or, more commonly, attached by inserting their connecting pins or wires into holes drilled in the board. PCBs include ↝ motherboards, ↝ expansion boards, and adaptors.

printer output device for producing printed copies of text or graphics. Types include the daisywheel printer, which produces good-quality text but no graphics; the dot matrix printer, which produces text and graphics by printing a pattern of small dots; the ↝ ink-jet printer, which creates text and graphics by spraying a fine jet of quick-drying ink onto the paper; and the ↝ laser printer, which uses electrostatic technology very similar to that used by a photocopier to produce high-quality text and graphics.

Printers may be classified as impact printers (such as daisywheel and dot-matrix printers), which form characters by striking an inked ribbon against the paper, and nonimpact printers (such as ink-jet and laser printers), which use a variety of techniques to produce characters without physical impact on the paper.

A further classification is based on the basic unit of printing, and categorizes printers as character printers, line printers, or page printers, according to whether they print one character, one line, or a complete page at a time.

print spooler ↝ utility program that stores information in a temporary file before sending it on to a printer. Print spoolers help computers to work efficiently, allowing the ↝ central processing unit (CPU) to carry on with other work while a document is being printed.

privacy on the Internet, generally used to mean the right to control who has access to the personal information generated by interaction with computers.

The right to privacy is one of the most hotly debated issues on the Internet, as commercial suppliers seek to gather more and more information about their customers. The most common approaches to securing the right to privacy are technological, via encryption, and legislative, via laws such as Britain's Data Protection Act. A third approach is to use services such as ↝ anonymous remailers to strip identifying information from individual messages when posting contentious or sensitive material. More Web sites are now creating privacy documents, a statement which explains to people how the Web site owner will use any information collected in the course of the visit. This is of particular concern when ↝ online shopping, where personal and financial information is likely to be entered using Web forms. This statement may be backed up by registration with a third-party trust organization, which checks the statement and issues a certificate saying that it conforms to basic rules. If the Web site is found to be breaking its own privacy rules the trust certificate can be withdrawn.

privacy enhanced mail *PEM*, Internet protocol that gives a degree of confidentiality to ↝ e-mail, using various ↝ public-key cryptography methods.

Electronic Privacy Information Center

http://www.epic.org/

Site attempting to focus public attention on privacy issues. News and information covering free speech on the Internet, freedom of information, 'censorware' and filtering programs, hacking, and related topics are included, along with practical tips on how to protect your personal information on the Internet.

WEB LINK

procedural programming programming in which programs are written as lists of instructions for the computer to obey in sequence. It closely matches the computer's own sequential operation.

procedure small part of a computer program that performs a specific task, such as clearing the screen or sorting a file. A procedural language, such as BASIC, is one in which the programmer describes a task in terms of how it is to be done, as opposed to a declarative language, such as PROLOG, in which it is described in terms of the required result. See ⮑ programming.

Careful use of procedures is an element of ⮑ structured programming. In some programming languages there is an overlap between procedures, ⮑ functions, and ⮑ subroutines.

process control automatic computerized control of a manufacturing process, such as glassmaking. The computer receives ⮑ feedback information from sensors about the performance of the machines involved, and compares this with ideal performance data stored in its control program. It then outputs instructions to adjust automatically the machines' settings.

Because the computer can monitor and reset each machine hundreds of times each minute, performance can be maintained at levels that are very close to the ideal.

processing cycle sequence of steps performed repeatedly by a computer in the execution of a program. The computer's central processing unit (CPU) continuously works through a loop, involving fetching a program instruction from memory, fetching any data it needs, operating on the data, and storing the result in the memory, before fetching another program instruction.

processor another name for the ⮑ central processing unit or ⮑ microprocessor of a computer.

program set of instructions that controls the operation of a computer. There are two main kinds: ⮑ applications programs, which carry out tasks for the benefit of the user – for example, word processing; and ⮑ systems programs, which control the internal workings of the computer. A ⮑ utility program is a systems program that carries out specific tasks for the user. Programs can be written in any of a number of ⮑ programming languages but are always translated into machine code before they can be executed by the computer.

program counter alternative name for ⮑ sequence-control register.

program documentation ⮑ documentation that provides a complete technical description of a program, built up as the software is written, and is intended to support any later maintenance or development of the program.

program files files which contain the code used by a computer program.

program flow chart type of ⮑ flow chart used to describe the flow of data through a particular computer program.

program loop part of a computer program that is repeated several times. The loop may be repeated a fixed number of times (counter-controlled loop) or until a certain condition is satisfied (condition-controlled loop). For example, a counter-controlled loop might be used to repeat an input routine until exactly ten numbers have been input; a condition-controlled loop might be used to repeat an input routine until the ∽ data terminator 'XXX' is entered.

programmer job classification for ∽ computer personnel. Programmers write the software needed for any new computer system or application.

programming writing instructions in a programming language for the control of a computer. Applications programming is for end-user programs, such as accounts programs or word-processing packages. Systems programming is for operating systems and the like, which are concerned more with the internal workings of the computer.

There are several programming styles. Procedural programming, in which programs are written as lists of instructions for the computer to obey in sequence, is by far the most popular. It is the 'natural' style, closely matching the computer's own sequential operation. Declarative programming, as used in the programming language PROLOG, does not describe how to solve a problem, but rather describes the logical structure of the problem. Running such a program is more like proving an assertion than following a procedure. Functional programming is a style based largely on the definition of functions. There are very few functional programming languages, HOPE and ML being the most widely used, though many more conventional languages (for example C) make extensive use of functions. Object-oriented programming, the most recently developed style, involves viewing a program as a collection of objects that behave in certain ways when they are passed certain 'messages'. For example, an object might be defined to represent a table of figures, which will be displayed on screen when a 'display' message is received.

programming language special notation in which instructions for controlling a computer are written. Programming languages are designed to be easy for people to write and read, but must be capable of being mechanically translated (by a ∽ compiler or an ∽ interpreter) into the ∽ machine code that the computer can execute. Programming languages may be classified as ∽ high-level languages or ∽ low-level languages. See also ∽ source language.

program trading in finance, buying and selling a group of shares using a computer program to generate orders automatically whenever there is an appreciable movement in prices.

One form in use in the USA in 1989 was index arbitrage, in which a program traded automatically whenever there was a difference between New York and Chicago prices of an equivalent number of shares. Program trading comprised some 14% of daily trading on the New York Stock Exchange by volume in September 1989, but was widely criticized for lessening market stability. It has been blamed, among other factors, for the Stock Market crashes of 1987 and 1989.

Project Gutenberg electronic 'library' containing hundreds of 'etexts' – books made freely accessible via the ⇝ World Wide Web and downloadable via ⇝ FTP. The project started in 1971 at the University of Illinois. For copyright reasons, most of the books available are classics dating from before the 20th century, but there are also some current reference books – including the current *CIA Factbook*.

PROLOG contraction of programming in logic, high-level computer programming language based on logic. Invented in 1971 at the University of Marseille, France, it did not achieve widespread use until more than ten years later. It is used mainly for ⇝ artificial intelligence programming.

PROM acronym for *programmable read-only memory*, memory device in the form of an integrated circuit (chip) that can be programmed after manufacture to hold information permanently. PROM chips are empty of information when manufactured, unlike ROM (read-only memory) chips, which have information built into them. Other memory devices are ⇝ EPROM (erasable programmable read-only memory) and ⇝ RAM (random-access memory).

prompt symbol displayed on a screen indicating that the computer is ready for input. The symbol used will vary from system to system and application to application. The current cursor position is normally next to the prompt. Generally prompts only appear in ⇝ command line interfaces.

proportional font font in which individual letters of the alphabet take up different amounts of space according to their shape.

Computer fixed fonts are designed so that each letter has the same width and takes up the same amount of space on a line. A letter 'l', however, logically is thinner than a letter 'o'. Proportional fonts allow spacing according to these differences, and are therefore easier to read. Until the advent of personal computers and font software such as Adobe ⇝ PostScript, proportional spacing was the province of professional typography, used in books, newspapers, magazines, and other commercial publishing.

protected mode operating mode of ⇝ Intel microprocessors (80286 and above), which allows multitasking and provides other features such as ⇝ extended memory and ⇝ virtual memory (above 1 Gbyte). Protected mode operation also improves ⇝ data security.

protocol agreed set of standards for the transfer of data between different devices. They cover transmission speed, format of data, and the signals required to synchronize the transfer. See also ⇝ interface.

proxy server on the ⇝ World Wide Web, a server which 'stands in' for another server, storing and forwarding files on behalf of a computer which might be slower or too busy to deal with the request itself. Many ⇝ URLs (Web addresses) redirect the enquirer to a proxy server which then supplies the requested page.

In 1996, the authorities in Singapore imposed a legal requirement on local Internet providers to filter all traffic via a government-run proxy server that can block access to various sites – the first serious government attempt to censor the Internet.

pseudonym name adopted by someone on the Internet, especially to participate in ➤ Usenet or discussions using IRC (➤ Internet Relay Chat). Pseudonyms are often jokey or witty, and are sometimes used to conceal the user's gender or identity.

PSP abbreviation for ➤ payment service provider.

PSTN abbreviation for *Public Switched Telephone Network*, telephone network used by the general public, and sometimes used as the medium to link ➤ LANs. PSTNs are minor roads which lead to the ➤ information superhighway.

public key in ➤ public-key cryptography, a string of ➤ bits that is associated with a particular person and that may be used to decrypt messages from that person or to encrypt messages to him/her.

public-key cryptography system of ➤ cryptography that allows remote users to exchange encrypted data without the need to transmit a secret digital 'key' in advance. The system was first proposed by Whitfield Diffie and Martin Hellman in a widely read and influential paper 'New Directions in Cryptography' (1976).

Several algorithms in common use apply public-key cryptography, including the ➤ RSA algorithm (published in 1977 in *Scientific American* and named after its inventors, Ronald Rivest, Adi Shamir, and Leonard Adleman) and the Skipjack algorithm used in the ➤ Clipper chip. The disadvantage is that it is extremely slow, so it is common on the Net to see ➤ Pretty Good Privacy (PGP), which uses RSA, being used to encrypt only a digest of the message generated using a ➤ hash function. This is appended to the end of the message along with a listing of the user's public key.

In public-key cryptography, each party has a personal pair of keys, one private and one public. The private key is kept secret, while the public key is distributed widely – to friends, business partners, and even to public key servers – computers which store many users' public keys so that anyone can obtain a copy. The two keys are complementary. The sender of a message may encrypt his message using the recipient's public key. This message can then only be decrypted using the recipient's private key. Using both sets of keys serves both to authenticate the message and ensure its privacy.

Public-key cryptography can also be used to create and verify a ➤ digital signature. The core framework for security for e-commerce transactions is known as ➤ public key infrastructure (PKI).

public key infrastructure *PKI*, core framework required to provide ➤ public key cryptography and ➤ digital signature services for ➤ electronic commerce transactions via the Internet. A PKI provides confidentiality (to keep information private), integrity (to prove it has not been altered), authentication (to prove the identity of a person or a computer ⮑ application), and non-repudiation (to prevent information being disowned). ⮑ SET is a form of PKI.

A PKI consists of a certification authority (CA) for the issue of ⮑ digital certificates, a certificate repository (or directory) to allow applications to obtain certificates, a certificate revocation system, a key backup and recovery system (not the same as ⮑ key escrow), support for non-repudiation of digital signatures, automatic key update, management of key histories, validation of certificates issued by another CA, and time-stamping to identify when a transaction took place, as well as software to support all of these activities.

public news server site, often provided by an institution, which provides free access to ⮑ Usenet. Public news servers offer an alternative to taking a news feed from an ⮑ Internet Service Provider (ISP).

pull-down menu list of options provided as part of a ⮑ graphical user interface. The presence of pull-down menus is normally indicated by a row of single words at the top of the screen. When the user points at a word with a ⮑ mouse, a full menu appears (is pulled down) and the user can then select the required option. Compare with ⮑ pop-up menu.

In some graphical user interfaces the menus appear from the bottom of the screen and in others they may appear at any point on the screen when a special menu button is pressed on the mouse.

push-button in a ⮑ dialog box or ⮑ toolbar, a square, oval, or oblong button which presents the user with an option. By clicking on the button, the user opts to initiate an action such as centering text or saving a file. Most programs offer keyboard ⮑ shortcuts as an alternative to using a push-button, for example one can often hit the return key instead of clicking the 'OK' button in a dialogue box. Compare ⮑ radio button.

push technology automatic transmission of information to Internet users, without their having to find it and 'pull' it to themselves. Push technology was introduced in 1996 by PointCast (now EntryPoint) and Marimba, and in 1997, ⮑ Microsoft and ⮑ Netscape built push 'channels' into their Web ⮑ browsers. The technology did not prove popular with consumers, however, as the principle was too similar to 'junk e-mail' (see ⮑ spamming). Marimba now aims its technology at large companies and ⮑ application service providers, for corporate distribution and management of software.

Quake computer game released in 1996 as a successor to ↪ *Doom* and produced by ↪ id Software. It is a strategy game using ↪ 3-D graphics.

Players navigate their way around 32 levels of mazes, uncovering secrets and combatting alien enemies. A command line console system allows players to enter ↪ source code to enhance play.

quantum computing use of particles such as atoms, ions, and photons to perform computations, initally suggested by physicist Richard Feynman in 1982. In 1985, David Deutsch of the University of Oxford described a 'universal quantum computer' that would be able to perform feats beyond the capabilities of conventional computers. No such computer has been built to date, but quantum computing is thought to show great promise in certain areas, such as cryptography.

Quantum particles obey the laws of quantum mechanics, which are different from the laws of classical physics. Where a classical bit of information can have two states (1 or 0; on or off), a qubit (quantum bit) has an infinite number of possibilities, and can at the same time be a classical 1 or 0. This is called superposition. Logical operations can be performed on qubits, but when a measurement is performed, superposition is destroyed and the state is reduced to either 1 or 0.

Quark US company founded in 1981 by Tim Gill, who wrote the first ↪ word-processing program for the ↪ Apple III computer. The company is named after the elementary particle proposed as the building block for all matter.

The QuarkXPress ↪ desktop publishing program was originally released in 1987 for the Apple ↪ Macintosh, and is also available to run under Microsoft ↪ Windows. More than a million users in over 100 countries worldwide now use QuarkXPress and Quark's other, related, publishing software.

question mark ?, wild card character standing for any single character in most operating systems. It allows a user to specify a group of files whose names differ by only one character for mass handling. Typing 'dir part?.doc' in a DOS directory would display a list of files such as part1.doc, party.doc, and so on. The letter 'x' is often used to mean the same thing.

queue backup of ↪ packets of data awaiting processing, or of ↪ e-mail waiting to be read.

QuickDraw object-based graphics display system used by the Apple ↪ Macintosh range of microcomputers. The use of QuickDraw gives most Macintosh applications the same ↪ look-and-feel.

QuickTime multimedia utility developed by Apple, initially for the ↪ Macintosh, but now also available for ↪ Windows. Allows multimedia, such as sound and video, to be embedded in other documents, including Web pages.

quoting common practice in electronic communications. When replying to an e-mail, or adding to a ↪ newsgroup ↪ thread, users quote all or part of the

Quake Perfect

http://quake.perfect.co.uk/

Central source of UK information for devotees of the computer game *Quake*. There is comprehensive news of leagues, players, latest software releases, and other related sites.

WEB LINK

original message in their response. The usual method of doing this is by preceding each quoted line with the symbol >.

QWERTY standard arrangement of keys on a UK or US typewriter or computer keyboard. Q, W, E, R, T, and Y are the first six keys on the top alphabetic line. The arrangement was made in the days of mechanical keyboards in order that the keys would not jam together. Other European countries use different arrangements, such as AZERTY and QWERTZ, which are more appropriate to the language of the country.

radio button in a ⤳ dialog box, a round button denoting an option. Users are offered a choice of radio buttons, and can choose only one.

RAID acronym for *redundant array of independent* (or *inexpensive*) *disks*, arrays of disks, each connected to a bus, that can be configured in different ways, depending on the application. RAID 1 is, for example, disk mirroring, while RAID 5 spreads every character between disks. RAID is intended to improve performance and data security.

RAM acronym for *random-access memory*, memory device in the form of a collection of integrated circuits (chips), frequently used in microcomputers. Unlike ⤳ ROM (read-only memory) chips, RAM chips can be both read from and written to by the computer, but their contents are lost when the power is switched off.

   Many modern commercial programs require a great deal of RAM to work efficiently. In 2000, most PCs were supplied with 128 megabytes (MB) of RAM.

random access alternative term for ⤳ direct access.

random number one of a series of numbers having no detectable pattern. Random numbers are used in ⤳ computer simulation and ⤳ computer games. It is impossible for an ordinary computer to generate true random numbers, but various techniques are available for obtaining pseudo-random numbers – close enough to true randomness for most purposes.

range check ⤳ validation check applied to a numerical data item to ensure that its value falls in a sensible range.

RARE abbreviation for *Réseaux Associés pour la Recherche Européenne*, association of national and international European computer networks and their users.

   It received the Best UK Developer Award in the 1998 Bafta Interactive Entertainment Awards.

raster graphics computer graphics that are stored in the computer memory by using a map to record data (such as colour and intensity) for every ⤳ pixel that makes up the image. When transformed (enlarged, rotated, stretched, and so on), raster graphics become ragged and suffer loss of picture resolution, unlike ⤳ vector graphics. Raster graphics are typically used for painting applications, which allow the user to create artwork on a computer screen much as if they were painting on paper or canvas.

raster image processor full name for printer program ⤳ RIP.

ray-tracing in computer graphics, method of rendering sharp, detailed images. Designers specify the size, shape, colour, and texture of objects and the type and location of light sources, and use a program to devise a mathematical model tracing how light rays would bounce off the surfaces. The results, complete with shading, shadows, and reflections, depict 'virtual worlds' with near-photographic clarity.

Random Number Generator

http://www.fourmilab.ch/hotbits/

Internet resource that delivers genuine random numbers, generated by radioactive decay.

WEB LINK

RBOC abbreviation for *Regional Bell Operating Company*, regional telecommunications operator formed with the US government break-up of America's giant telecommunications operator, AT&T. Since AT&T was known as *Ma Bell*, the RBOCs are sometimes known as *Baby Bells*.

RDP abbreviation for ↪ Remote Desktop Protocol.

read-only storage permanent means of storing data so that it can be read any number of times but cannot be modified. CD-ROM is a read-only storage medium; CD-ROMs come with the data already encoded on them.

RealPlayer software supplied by RealNetworks Inc. for broadcasting live or pre-recorded sound and video over the Internet. Microsoft's equivalent to RealPlayer is Windows Media Player.

real-time system program that responds to events in the world as they happen. For example, an automatic-pilot program in an aircraft must respond instantly in order to correct deviations from its course. Process control, robotics, games, and many military applications are examples of real-time systems.

record collection of related data items or fields. A record usually forms part of a ↪ file. Records may be of either fixed or variable length; variable records require a separator at the end of the field, in order that the end of the record can be detected by the computer.

recursion technique whereby a function or ↪ procedure calls itself into use in order to enable a complex problem to be broken down into simpler steps. For example, a function that finds the factorial of a number n (calculates the product of all the whole numbers between 1 and n) would obtain its result by multiplying n by the factorial of $n - 1$.

redundancy duplication of information. Redundancy is often used as a check, when an additional check digit or bit is included. See also ↪ validation.

refresh to redraw the image on a ↪ VDU. All such images are a series of frames created by a device – in the case of a cathode ray tube, an electron beam – which 'paints' the image on the screen, ↪ pixel by pixel. This process is too rapid for the human eye to detect, although a high refresh rate (number of times a screen is redrawn per second) is said to reduce eye strain.

register memory location that can be accessed rapidly; it is often built into the computer's central processing unit.

Some registers are reserved for special tasks – for example, an instruction register is used to hold the machine-code command that the computer is currently executing, while a sequence-control register keeps track of the next command to be executed. Other registers are used for holding frequently used data and for storing intermediate results.

registration informing a manufacturer that you have bought their product. For computer hardware, registration brings the consumer benefits such as on-site service and access to a free telephone helpline. Software houses also give registered customers telephone support and may supply them with upgrades and new product information.

For ⮑ shareware, registration is virtually synonymous with payment. Programs are supplied save-disabled, incomplete, or with frequent, annoying built-in reminders to register. Only by sending the small fee requested can the user obtain a code to release the program's full potential, as well as the legal right to continue using it.

Registry dedicated database used in Microsoft Windows 95, 98, and NT, to store details of how the operating system and various applications programs have been set-up for one or more users. In earlier versions of Windows, these details were kept in ini (initialization) files such as Win.ini and in configuration files such as config.sys.

Regulation of Investigatory Powers Act or *RIP Act*, UK government legislation passed in July 2000. The government's stated aim was to give the UK police and security services the same right to read ⮑ electronic mail as they currently have to read postal mail and to tap telephone messages, under warrant from a judge.

Critics of the act point to draconian clauses which reverse the normal presumption of an individual's innocence until he or she is proved guilty. Many business people feel that the act also makes nonsense of the government's stated intention of making the UK the best country in which to carry out ⮑ electronic commerce.

relational database ⮑ database in which data are viewed as a collection of linked tables. It is the most popular of the three basic database models, the others being network and hierarchical.

relative (of a value) variable and calculated from a base value. For example, a relative address is a memory location that is found by adding a variable to a base (fixed) address, and a relative cell reference locates a cell in a spreadsheet by its position relative to a base cell – perhaps directly to the left of the base cell or three columns to the right of the base cell. The opposite of relative is ⮑ absolute.

reload command which asks a ⮑ browser to reopen a currently-displayed ⮑ URL. Reloading may 'unstall' a partially loaded page or bring a faster download from a busy server.

remote access term used to describe the issue of, and the computer ⮑ hardware and ⮑ software designed to be used by, employees needing access to their company ⮑ network and data whilst away from the office, either at home or travelling. The main problems relate to security, because public networks like the ∽ Internet are often used. An industry has emerged to provide special security devices and networking equipment to make remote access secure and reliable.

Remote Desktop Protocol *RDP*, communications protocol through which servers running Microsoft's Windows NT Terminal Server software communicate with ∽ thin clients which may be running Microsoft Windows ∽ CE operating system. While Microsoft provides a Microsoft-to-Microsoft system, firms like ∽ Citrix provide connectivity with non-Microsoft systems.

remote sensing process of making observations of a planetary surface or atmosphere from far away, for example from an airplane or satellite.

With a simple aerial, receiver, and software it is possible to download images straight on to a personal computer – helping amateur meteorologists, for example, to make weather forecasts.

remote terminal terminal that communicates with a computer via a modem (or acoustic coupler) and a telephone line.

remote terminal
Remote computer terminals communicate with the central mainframe via modems and telephone lines. The controller allocates computer time to the terminals according to predetermined priority rules. The multiplexer allows more than one terminal to use the same communications link at the same time (multiplexing).

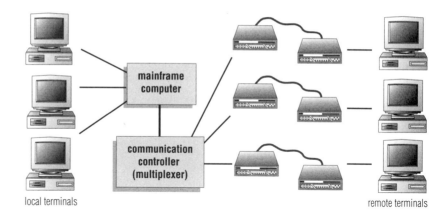

local terminals

remote terminals

TIP

repetitive strain injury

RSI can be avoided by correct posture and regular screen breaks. In particular, keyboard users should ensure that their wrists are as level as possible when inputting.

rendering using a computer to draw an image on a computer screen. In graphics, this often means using ∽ ray-tracing, ∽ phong shading, or a similar program to turn an outline sketch into a detailed image of a solid object.

repetitive strain injury *RSI*, inflammation of tendon sheaths, mainly in the hands and wrists, which may be disabling. It is found predominantly in factory workers involved in constant repetitive movements, and in those who work with computer keyboards. The symptoms include aching muscles, weak wrists, tingling fingers and in severe cases, pain and paralysis. Some victims have successfully sued their employers for damages. In 1999 RSI affected more than a million people annually in Britain and the USA.

In many RSI cases there is no actual sign of tissue damage, and some researchers are beginning to believe that the origin of the pain may be due to a problem in the brain rather than the tissues, with the brain rewiring its neurones to cope with continual repetitive movements until it loses awareness of which finger is which.

request for comments expansion of the abbreviation RFC.

reserved word word that has a meaning special to a programming language. For example, 'if' and 'for' are reserved words in most high-level languages.

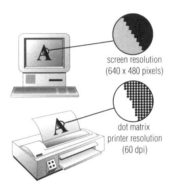

screen resolution
(640 x 480 pixels)

dot matrix
printer resolution
(60 dpi)

resolution number of dots per unit length in which an image can be reproduced on a screen or printer. A typical screen resolution for colour monitors is 75 dpi (dots per inch). A ◈ laser printer will have a printing resolution of 600 dpi upwards, and an ◈ ink-jet printer typically has a resolution of 300 dpi. Photographs in books and magazines have a resolution of 1,200 dpi or 2,400 dpi.

response time delay between entering a command and seeing its effect.

return-to-base warranty warranty on a piece of hardware that requires the owner to return it to the retailer or the factory for service. Compare ◈ on-site warranty.

reverse engineering analysing an existing piece of computer hardware or software by finding out what it does and then working out how it does it. Companies perform this process on their own products in order to iron out faults, and on their competitors' products in order to find out how they work. For example, the microchips in the first IBM PCs were reverse engineered by other computer firms to make compatible machines without infringing IBM's copyright.

reverse video alternative term for ◈ inverse video.

RFC abbreviation for *request for comments*, discussion document on the subject of standards for the Internet. RFCs start as technical proposals lodged with the Internet Architecture Board by computer engineers. The proposals are published on the Internet, where they are subject to general review. After any necessary amendments are made, RFCs become agreed procedures across the network.

resolution
An example of typical resolutions of screens and printers. The resolution of a screen image when printed can only be as high as the resolution supported by the printer itself.

RGB abbreviation of *red–green–blue*, method of connecting a colour screen to a computer, involving three separate signals: red, green, and blue. All the colours displayed by the screen can be made up from these three component colours.

rich text format file format usually abbreviated to ⟿ RTF.

right click on IBM-compatible PCs, a click on the right-hand button of the mouse that brings up a context-sensitive menu presenting a range of options relevant to the user's current activity.

RIP abbreviation for *raster image processor*, program in a laser printer (or other high-resolution printer) that converts the stream of printing instructions from a computer into the pattern of dots that make up the printed page. A separate program is required for each type of printer and for each page description language (such as ⟿ PostScript or ⟿ PCL).

RIPs are very demanding programs because of the complexity of a typical printed page. It is not unusual for RIPs to run on extremely fast and powerful ⟿ RISC ⟿ microprocessors, which are sometimes more powerful than the processor in the computer attached to the printer.

RISC acronym for *reduced instruction-set computer*, microprocessor (processor on a single chip) that carries out fewer instructions than other (⟿ CISC) microprocessors in common use in the 1990s. Because of the low number and the regularity of ⟿ machine code instructions, the processor carries out those instructions very quickly.

RISC microprocessors became commercially available in the mid-1980s and were used mainly in Unix workstations and servers. They are now widely used in games consoles and laser printers, as well as in microcomputers made by Acorn and Apple Computer.

rlogin contraction of *remote login*, ⟿ Unix program that enables users to log in on another computer via the Internet. Compare ⟿ Telnet.

rogue value another name for ⟿ data terminator.

ROM acronym for *read-only memory*, memory device in the form of a collection of integrated circuits (chips), frequently used in microcomputers. ROM chips are loaded with data and programs during manufacture and, unlike ⟿ RAM (random-access memory) chips, can subsequently only be read, not written to, by computer. However, the contents of the chips are not lost when the power is switched off, as happens in RAM.

ROM is used to form a computer's permanent store of vital information, or of programs that must be readily available but protected from accidental or deliberate change by a user. For example, a microcomputer ⟿ operating system is often held in ROM memory.

root account used by system administrators and other superusers in ↪ Unix systems. Users logged in as root (or in some systems, avatar) have permission to access and change all the files in the system.

root directory top directory in a ↪ tree-and-branch filing system. It contains all the other directories.

ROT13 contraction of *rotate by 13 characters*, simple encryption system where each of the 26 letters of the alphabet is swapped for one 13 characters along. This procedure is not meant to keep things secret, merely to hide things that not everyone may wish to see in plain text form: for example the punchline to a joke, a sports result, or whether the butler did it. Some Usenet newsreaders have ROT13 facilities built in.

router device that pushes traffic through a packet-switched network. On the Internet, traffic travels through a series of routers that relay each packet of data to its destination by the best possible route.

RS-232 interface standard type of computer ↪ interface used to connect computers to serial devices. It is used for modems, mice, screens, and serial printers.

RSA name of both an encryption ↪ algorithm and the company (RSA Inc) set up to exploit that algorithm in commercial encryption products. First described in 1977 by its inventors, Ronald Rivest, Adi Shamir, and Leonard Adelman, and published in *Scientific American*, the RSA algorithm is used in the free program ↪ Pretty Good Privacy (PGP) and in commercial products released by RSA Laboratories.

RSI abbreviation for ↪ repetitive strain injury, a condition affecting workers, such as typists, who repeatedly perform certain movements with their hands and wrists.

RSUP abbreviation for *Reliable SAP Update Protocol*, bandwidth-saving protocol for Novell networks developed by router manufacturer Cisco Systems.

RTF abbreviation for *Rich Text Format*, file format designed to facilitate the exchange of documents between different word-processing programs. RTF text files make it possible to transfer formatting such as font styles or paragraph indents from one program to another.

run-time system programs that must be stored in memory while an application is executed.

run-time version copy of a program that is provided with another application, so that the latter can be run, although it does not provide the full functionality of the program. An example is the provision of run-time versions of Microsoft ↪ Windows with Windows applications for those users who do not have the full version of Windows.

SAA abbreviation for ↝ systems application architecture.

sampling measurement of an analogue signal (such as an audio or video signal) at regular intervals. The result of the measurement can be converted into a ↝ digital signal that can be electronically enhanced, edited, or processed.

sans-serif font typeface, such as Helvetica or Gill Sans, the strokes of which terminate in plain ends. Such fonts are very clear and are often used for posters and signposts. Research into how people read text on computer monitors has shown that using sans-serif fonts can greatly improve the ease with which the text is read.

scalability ability of a software or hardware system or a network to grow without breaking down or requiring an expensive redesign. Scalable systems may thus be tested and perfected at a modest size and then expanded to meet future needs.

scalable font font that can be used at any size and any resolution, on a screen or hard-copy device, such as a laser printer or image setter. Scalable fonts are always ↝ outline fonts. Adobe, ↝ Postscript, and ↝ TrueType are scalable fonts.

scanner device that can produce a digital image of a document for input and storage in a computer. It uses technology similar to that of a photocopier. Small scanners can be passed over the document surface by hand; larger versions have a flat bed, like that of a photocopier, on which the input document is placed and scanned.

Scanners are widely used to input graphics for use in ↝ desktop publishing. If text is input with a scanner, the image captured is seen by the computer as a single digital picture rather than as separate characters. Consequently, the text cannot be processed by, for example, a word processor unless suitable optical character-recognition software is available to convert the image to its constituent characters. Scanners vary in their resolution, typical hand-held scanners ranging from 75 to 300 dpi. Types include flat-bed, drum, and overhead.

Scanners also exist to scan photographic film and transparencies. These devices are used by people who continue to take pictures with conventional cameras but then want to make a high-quality digital copy of the picture in order to manipulate the image in some way or print the image on a computer printer.

Scart socket acronym for *Syndicat des Constructeurs d'appareils Radio Récepteurs et Téléviseurs*, 21-pin audio/video connector used in consumer electronics equipment such as television sets and video recorders. Scart was defined by a group of French television manufacturers, and Scart cables are often the preferred method for connecting video games consoles to TV sets.

Schickard, Wilhelm (1592–1635) German inventor of a calculator that could perform multiplication and division by using logarithms (which enable multiplication and division to be done by addition and subtraction).

Science Learning Network group of international science museums linked via the Web, with the aim of improving science teaching in primary schools by presenting science in an informal way. The network was set up in the USA in 1995, with grants from the National Science Foundation and the computer company Unisys.

The original six US museums linked to the network are in Boston (Massachusetts), Miami (Florida), Philadelphia (Pennsylvania), Portland (Oregon), St. Paul (Minnesota), and San Francisco (California). These were joined in 1998 by seven museums around the world, in Amsterdam (the Netherlands), Helsinki (Finland), London (England), Mexico City (Mexico), Paris (France), Singapore, and Tokyo (Japan).

> **TIP**
>
> **screen dump**
>
> In Windows, pressing PrintScreen copies a screen dump to the clipboard. Alt|PrintScreen copies only the active window.

screen dump process of making a printed copy of the current VDU screen display. The screen dump is sometimes stored as a data file instead of being printed immediately.

screen grabber software which can take a snapshot of the contents of a computer screen and save it as a picture file. Screen grabbers are useful for creating the screen shots seen in many computer magazines to illustrate software reviews and instructions.

> **TIP**
>
> **screen saver**
>
> Many computers now contain energy-saving circuitry to black out idle screens, rendering screen savers superfluous.

screen saver program designed to prevent a static image from 'burning' itself into the phosphor screen of an idle computer monitor. If the user leaves the computer alone for more than a few minutes, the screen saver automatically displays a moving or changing image – perhaps a sequence of random squiggles, or an animation of flying toasters – on the screen. When the user touches any key, the computer returns to its previous state.

script in communications, a series of instructions for a computer. For example, when users log on to an ISP (Internet Service Provider) or other service, their computers follow a script containing passwords and other information to tell the ISP's server who they are.

scripting language simple programming language used to issue a set of commands (a script), often to control a particular software application. A popular scripting language commonly used on the Internet is ↩ JavaScript.

scrollback automatic scrolling of messages down the screen as they are received in ↩ Internet Relay Chat (IRC), ↩ bulletin boards, or similar forums.

scrollbar narrow box along two sides of a ↩ window, enabling users to move its contents up, down, left, or right. Each end of the scrollbar represents the same end of the document on display, and the ↩ mouse is used to move a small 'scrollbox' up and down the bar to scroll the contents or to click on the directional arrows.

scrolling action by which data displayed on a VDU screen are automatically moved upwards and out of sight as new lines of data are added at the bottom.

SCSI abbreviation for *small computer system interface*; pronounced 'scuzzy', standard method for connecting peripheral devices (such as printers, scanners and CD-ROM drives) to a computer. A group of peripherals linked in series to a single SCSI ⮎ port is called a daisy-chain.

SCSIs are common in file servers and high-performance computers. One of the main advantages of a SCSI is that devices attached to it can communicated to each other independently of the CPU. Another important feature is the ability to connect devices that are external to the main computer unit.

The latest SCSI ⮎ bus has a ⮎ bandwidth in excess of 40 megabytes.

SDK abbreviation for *software development kit*, suite of programs supplied to software developers to help them develop applications for environments such as Microsoft Windows and Microsoft Office.

SDRAM abbreviation for *synchronous dynamic random-access memory*, latest generation of ⮎ DRAM memory modules, rapidly replacing ⮎ EDO-RAM technology. SDRAM ⮎ memory chips are able to transfer data in a single clock cycle, because their operations are synchronised with the system clock.

search engine remotely accessible program to help users find information on the Internet. Commercial search engines such as ⮎ AltaVista and ⮎ Lycos comprise databases of documents, ⮎ URLs, ⮎ Usenet articles, and more, which can be searched by keying in a key word or phrase. The databases are compiled by a mixture of automated agents (⮎ spiders) and ⮎ webmasters registering their sites.

Search engine	Web address	Description
AltaVista	http://www.altavista.digital.com	funded by DEC; select word search
Infoseek	http://www.infoseek.com	powerful engine searches whole Web or focuses on 9 major topic sections; provides related sites
Lycos	http://www.lycos.com	extensive index of documents, including by words in title, headings, subheadings, and hyperlinks
UK Index	http://www.ukindex.co.uk	database of almost exclusively UK sites with vetted selection
WebCrawler	http://www.webcrawler.com	database created using spider (automated search routine)
Yahoo!	http://www.yahoo.com	search-tree offering constant refinement of choice

search engine
Major search engine programs with main functions listed.

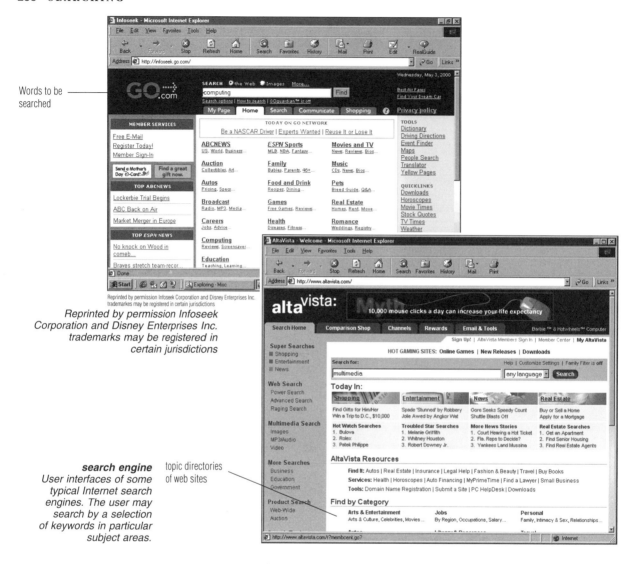

Words to be searched

Reprinted by permission Infoseek Corporation and Disney Enterprises Inc. trademarks may be registered in certain jurisdictions

Reprinted by permission Infoseek Corporation and Disney Enterprises Inc. trademarks may be registered in certain jurisdictions

search engine
User interfaces of some typical Internet search engines. The user may search by a selection of keywords in particular subject areas.

topic directories of web sites

US researchers estimate that search engines in 1999 are indexing only approximately 16% of the 800 million publicly available Web pages when used individually; when the 11 main search engines are combined to conduct a metasearch they still fail to index more than half of the Web pages. This is partly because many Web sites generate pages 'on the fly', filling in standard Web page templates with information from databases.

searching extracting a specific item from a large body of data, such as a file or table. The method used depends on how the data are organized. For example, a binary search, which requires the data to be in sequence, involves first deciding which half of the data contains the required item, then which quarter, then which eighth, and so on until the item is found.

search request structured request by a user for information from a ⮑ database. This may be a simple request for all the entries that have a single field meeting a certain condition. For example, a user searching a file of car-registration details might request a list of all the records that have 'VOLKSWAGEN' in the ⮑ field recording the make of car. In more complex examples, the user may construct a search request using operators like AND, OR, NOT, CONTAINING, and BETWEEN.

An example of a search request using all these operators is:

CAR SEARCH: registration number containing XTW and make Volkswagen and model Polo and body hatchback and colour white or black and registered between 1989 and 1991.

This search request would produce a list of all the white or black Volkswagen Polo hatchbacks registered between 1990 and 1996 that contained the letters XTW in their registration number.

SECAM acronym for *Système Electronique Couleur Avec Mémoire*, television and video standard used in France, some states in Eastern Europe, and a few other countries. It is broadly similar to the ⮑ PAL system used in most of Europe.

sector part of the magnetic structure created on a disk surface during ⮑ disk formatting so that data can be stored on it. The disk is first divided into circular tracks and then each circular track is divided into a number of sectors.

secure HTTP communications protocol that provides the basis for privacy-enhanced or encrypted communications between a Web ⮑ browser and a server. Secure HTTP enables users to send private information such as credit card numbers and addresses over the Internet.

secure socket layer *SSL*, standard protocol built into Web ⮑ browsers such as Netscape and Internet Explorer, which provides an encrypted channel for private information such as credit card numbers and passwords.

Considered a key technology to allow commerce across the World Wide Web, SSL began appearing on the Net in 1995.

security protection against loss or misuse of data; see ⮑ data security.

seek time time taken for a read-write head to reach a particular item of data on a ⮑ disk track.

Sega Japanese ⮑ games console and software manufacturer. Sega's best-known games character is 'Sonic the Hedgehog'.

In 1999 Sega launched its latest console, the Dreamcast. After the relative flop of its 1995 release, the Sega Saturn, the company has its console credibility riding on the success of this latest machine, which has 128-bit computer technology and Internet connectivity as standard, provided by BT in the UK. On its first day of launch in the USA the Dreamcast achieved sales of $1 million. The Dreamcast faces serious competition in 2000 when Sony, the

---

TIP

secure HTTP

Most web browsers will warn you if data you are about to disclose over the network will not be covered by secure HTTP.

market leader, will release its rival console, the PlayStation2, and Nintendo will release Dolphin, its latest machine.

sensor device designed to detect a physical state or measure a physical quantity, and produce an input signal for a computer. For example, a sensor may detect the fact that a printer has run out of paper or may measure the temperature in a kiln.

The signal from a sensor is usually in the form of an analogue voltage, and must therefore be converted to a digital signal, by means of an ⇝ analogue-to-digital converter, before it can be input.

sequence-control register or *program counter*, special memory location used to hold the address of the next instruction to be fetched from the immediate access memory for execution by the computer (see ⇝ fetch–execute cycle). It is located in the control unit of the ⇝ central processing unit.

sequential file file in which the records are arranged in order of a ⇝ key field and the computer can use a searching technique, like a binary search, to access a specific record. See ⇝ file access.

serial device device that communicates binary data by sending the bits that represent each character one by one along a single data line, unlike a ⇝ parallel device.

serial file file in which the records are not stored in any particular order and therefore a specific record can be accessed only by reading through all the previous records. See ⇝ file access.

serial interface ⇝ interface through which data is transmitted one bit at a time.

Serial Line Internet Protocol method of connecting a computer to the Internet; usually abbreviated to ⇝ SLIP.

serif font typeface, such as Times or Palatino, the strokes of which terminate in ornamental curves or cross-strokes. These are said to aid legibility.

server computer used as a store of software and data for use by other computers on a ⇝ network. See ⇝ file server.

SET acronym for *Secure Electronic Transfer*, form of ⇝ public key infrastructure developed by the credit card companies Visa and Mastercard. SET provides confidentiality and integrity of information, and authentication of customer and merchant, but is expensive and difficult to implement.

set-top box box containing decoding equipment for satellite or cable television broadcasts. Such boxes represent a means of linking television sets to a network such as the ⇝ Internet, enabling people to browse the ⇝ World Wide Web using their televisions as the monitor, or to view ⇝ video-on-demand.

SGML abbreviation for *Standard Generalized Markup Language*, ⮑ International Standards Organization standard describing how the structure (features such as headers, columns, margins, and tables) of a text can be identified so that it can be used, probably via ⮑ filters, in applications such as ⮑ desktop publishing and ⮑ electronic publishing. ⮑ HTML and ⮑ VRML are both types of SGML.

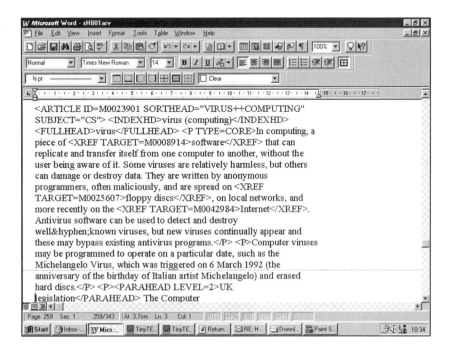

SGML
An example of an SGML source file. No on-screen formatting is used; headings and paragraphs are tagged as such and only appear in a different typeface in the final display.

shared memory bus architecture *SMBA*, system of ⮑ buses that allows parallel computers to share ⮑ RAM for greater processing power.

shareware software distributed free via the Internet or on disks given away with magazines. Users have the opportunity to test its functionality and ability to meet their requirements before paying a small registration fee directly to the author. This may bring additional functionality, documentation, and occasional upgrades. Shareware is not copyright-free. In the 1980s and early 1990s, many shareware libraries existed, but shareware has since fallen in popularity.

shell program that mediates access to a particular system or server. Microsoft Windows is a shell that interposes a ⮑ graphical user interface and other utilities between the operator and ⮑ MS-DOS. In DOS itself, the file COMMAND.COM is a shell that makes the operating system display a ⮑ prompt and enables it to interpret user instructions. Shells can also be used to improve computer security.

shell script Unix equivalent of batch files created for a program shell. Essentially, shell scripts allow users to create their own commands by creating a file that contains the sequence of commands they want to run and then designating the file as executable. Thereafter, typing the name of the file executes the sequence of commands.

Shockwave ↝ application that enables interactive and multimedia features, such as movies, sounds, and animations, to be embedded in Web pages. Unlike ↝ Java , which achieves these effects by using a special programming language, Shockwave allows developers to add items created with conventional ↝ authoring tools such as ↝ Director or Freehand.

shortcut keyboard combination or icon which activates a procedure otherwise available only through pull-down menus and ↝ dialog boxes. Most commercial software comes with built-in keyboard shortcuts and ↝ pushbuttons, and many allow users to create their own custom shortcuts. In Microsoft Windows, a shortcut is an icon that launches a program direct from the desktop.

signal processing digitizing of an ↝ analogue signal such as a voice stream.

signature or *.sig*, personal information appended to a message by the sender of an ↝ e-mail message or ↝ Usenet posting in order to add a human touch. Signatures, which are optional, usually carry the sender's real name and e-mail address, and may also include the writer's occupation, telephone number, and the ↝ URL of his or her ↝ home page. Many have a short quote, motto, or slogan, and a few incorporate ↝ ASCII art. .Sig is the name of the file in which signature information is stored on a Unix system.

silicon chip ↝ integrated circuit with microscopically small electrical components on a piece of silicon crystal only a few millimetres square.

One chip may contain more than a million components. A chip is mounted in a rectangular plastic package and linked via gold wires to metal pins, so that it can be connected to a printed circuit board for use in electronic devices, such as computers, calculators, television sets, car dashboards, and domestic appliances.

Silicon Graphics, Inc *SGI*, manufacturer of high-performance workstations and software designed primarily for graphics and image processing.

Simple Mail Transfer Protocol *SMTP*, protocol for transferring electronic mail between computers, commonly abbreviated to ↝ SMTP.

Simple Network Management Protocol *SNMP*, agreed method of managing a computer network, commonly abbreviated to ↝ SNMP.

simplex method in linear computer programming, an algorithm designed to find the optimum solution in a finite number of steps.

TIP

Shockwave

In order to experience Shockwave, you must have a browser that supports it – perhaps via an appropriate plug-in.

TIP

signature

It is considered bad netiquette to post a signature of more than four lines or so.

simulation short for ⟿ computer simulation.

Sinclair, Clive Marles (1940–) British electronics engineer. He produced the first widely available pocket calculator, pocket and wristwatch televisions, a series of home computers, and the innovative but commercially disastrous C5 personal transport (a low cyclelike three-wheeled vehicle powered by a washing-machine motor). He was knighted in 1983.

Single In-line Memory Module *SIMM*, small printed circuit board carrying multiple ⟿ memory chips. Although there are electrical contacts on both sides of the board they are electrically connected and do not function independently.

site location at which computers are used. If a company uses only ⟿ IBM computers, for example, it is known as an IBM site. The term is also used for a computer which acts as a ⟿ server for files that can be accessed via the ⟿ World Wide Web, also called a ⟿ Web site.

site licence licence issued with commercial software entitling the purchaser to install the program onto machines within a particular site or campus.

16-bit term describing the ability to process 16 ⟿ bits at a time. The Intel 286 series of microprocessors are examples of 16-bit processors.
   The term is used slightly differently to specify the quality of the sound produced by ⟿ sound cards, where it refers to digital audio resolution; the quality of sound produced by a 16-bit sound card is roughly equivalent to that produced by a compact disc.

64-bit term describing the ability to process 64 ⟿ bits simultaneously. Compaq's Alpha processor is the best known 64-bit chip. However, Intel and Hewlet-Packard are jointly developing a new 64-bit processor, named Itanium. The Itanium processor was expected to begin shipping in HP servers in July 2000. Advanced Micro Devices (AMD) plans to launch its own 64-bit chip, code-named Sledgehammer, in early 2001.

slide show in computing ⟿ presentation graphics programs, facility to display a presentation electronically instead of outputting it onto film or paper. The program displays the images ('slides') using the computer's full screen or an overhead projector. Slide shows are a versatile display method: presenters can customize timings to suit what they have to say and incorporate sound and movies into their presentations.

SLIP abbreviation for *serial line Internet protocol*, older of two standard methods for connecting a computer to the Internet via a modem and telephone line. Unlike PPP (Point-to-Point Protocol), a SLIP connection needs to have its ⟿ IP address reset every time it is used, and offers no ⟿ error detection.

Smalltalk first high-level programming language used in ⮑ object-oriented applications.

smart term for any piece of equipment that works with the help of a microprocessor: a 'smart' carburettor, for example, maintains the correct proportion of air-to-petrol vapour in a car engine by electronically monitoring engine temperature, acceleration, and other variables. Designers are incorporating smart technology into an increasing range of products, such as smart toasters, which can prevent toast from burning. Smart furniture, such as chairs with cushions that adjust themselves according to the size and weight of the person sitting in them, is a typical area of current research.

Architects are already making smart buildings, especially large office blocks and hospitals. Such buildings are wired with sensors to monitor heating, lighting, and air quality. A central computer automatically performs simple tasks such as turning lights out when there is nobody in a room, adjusting air conditioning, and even darkening photoelectric windows to counteract bright sunlight.

smart card plastic card with an embedded microprocessor and memory. It can store, for example, personal data, identification, and bank-account details, to enable it to be used as a credit or debit card. The card can be loaded with credits, which are then spent electronically, and reloaded as needed. Possible other uses range from hotel door 'keys' to passports.

The smart card was invented by French journalist Juan Moreno in 1974. Smart cards now have as much computing power as the leading personal computers of 1990.

smiley alternative term for ⮑ emoticon, named after the original smiling face :-).

SMPTE abbreviation for *Society of Motion Picture and Television Engineers*, US organization founded in 1916 to advance the theory and application of motion-imaging technology including film, television, video, computer imaging, and telecommunications.

The SMPTE has 8,500 members in 72 countries, including engineers, executives, technical directors, camerapeople, editors, and consultants. It is based in White Plains, New York, USA.

SMTP abbreviation for *simple mail transfer protocol*, basic protocol for transferring electronic mail between computers. SMTP is an agreed procedure for identifying the host, sending and receiving data, and checking e-mail addresses. It is the e-mail delivery mechanism for almost all Internet based e-mail.

SNA abbreviation for IBM's ⮑ Systems Network Architecture.

snail mail in the computing community, nickname for the conventional postal service. E-mail can deliver messages within minutes while conventional postal services take at least a day. One's postal address is therefore a 'snail mail address'.

sniffer software tool that analyses the transport data attached to ↝ packets sent across a network, used to monitor the network's efficiency and level of usage. Hackers (see ↝ hacking) also use sniffers to collect people's passwords for ↝ Telnet connections.

SNMP abbreviation for *Simple Network Management Protocol*, ↝ protocol which gathers information from ↝ network ↝ hardware to monitor its performance. An updated version of SNMP, called Remote Network Monitoring Specification (RNMS), enables network hardware devices to send alerts to network management software systems when different types of errors exceed prescribed limits.

SOAP acronym for *Simple Object Access Protocol*, method of bi-directional communication developed by ↝ Microsoft, DevlopMentor, and Userland Software. SOAP allows programs running under different operating systems to communicate with each other across ↝ firewalls using ↝ HTTP and ↝ XML as the exchange mechanisms.

SOAP is similar to the Internet Inter-Orb Protocol (IIOP), which is part of ↝ Corba, and also to ↝ Sun Microsystems' Remote Method Invocation (RMI), which allows communication between programs written in ↝ Java.

socket mechanism for creating a connection to an application on another computer. A socket combines an ↝ IP address (denoting the host computer on a network) with a port number describing the application (perhaps ↝ FTP or ↝ SMTP) the user requires.

soft-sectored disk another name for an unformatted blank disk; see ↝ disk formatting.

software collection of programs and procedures for making a computer perform a specific task, as opposed to ↝ hardware, the physical components of a computer system. Software is created by programmers and is either distributed on a suitable medium, such as the ↝ floppy disk, or built into the computer in the form of ↝ firmware. Examples of software include ↝ operating systems, ↝ compilers, and applications programs such as payrolls and word processors. No computer can function without some form of software.

To function, computers need two types of software: application software and systems software. Application software, such as a payroll system or a ↝ word processor, is designed for the benefit of the end user. Systems software performs tasks related to the operation and performance of the computer system itself. For example, a systems program might control the operation of the display screen, or control and organize backing storage.

software agent see ↝ intelligent agent

software piracy unauthorized duplication of computer software. Although some software piracy is done by companies for financial gain, most piracy is

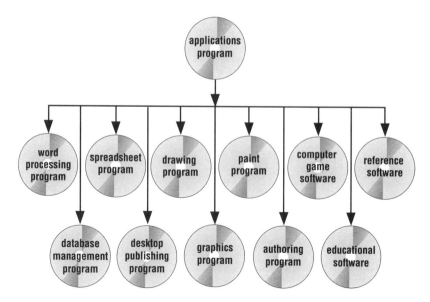

software
The various types of software application program that are available for computer systems.

done by private individuals who lend disks to friends or copy programs from the workplace to their computers at home.

Software manufacturers' attempts to protect their property – for example, by using special codes to prevent programs from being installed more than once from each set of disks – have proved unpopular with users and bypassable by determined copiers. Because computer data is so easy to duplicate, and the use of unauthorized software is so hard to detect, it appears nigh impossible to enforce anti-piracy law. The only sure way to prevent it appears to be for manufacturers to sell each copy of their software with a dongle – a coded plug that must actually be fitted to the computer for the software to function.

In the UK, unauthorized copying of software is covered by the Copyright, Designs and Patents Act 1988, which makes it a criminal offence to copy or distribute programs or to run them on more than one computer without the manufacturer's express permission in the software licence. It is also illegal to loan software to anyone else for copying, or for companies to encourage employees to make or use illegal copies of software at work. The maximum penalty is two years in prison and an unlimited fine, and offenders may also face civil prosecution for damages by the makers of the pirated software.

software project life cycle various stages of development in the writing of a major program (software), from the identification of a requirement to the installation, maintenance, and support of the finished program. The process includes ↪ systems analysis and ↪ systems design.

software suite set of complementary programs which can be bought separately, or (at a considerable saving) as a bundled package. ↪ Office suites are an especially common form of software suite.

TIP

software piracy

It is illegal to loan software to anyone else for copying, or for companies to encourage employees to make or use illegal copies of software at work.

Package	Manufacturer	Description
ClarisWorks	Claris	with word processor, spreadsheet, database, and paint and draw programs; flexible and creative document design
Microsoft Works	Microsoft	with ➲ Wizards to help create the required document; pre-installed on many new PCs
Perfect Works	Corel	includes paint and draw packages

software suite
Some major software suites with functions listed

Examples include: Adobe's graphics software which includes Photoshop (for processing photographs), Pagemaker (for page layout), and Illustrator (for creating illustrations); and Macromedia's multimedia software, which comprises Director (for creating presentations), xRes2 (for editing images), SoundEdit (for editing sound), and Extreme 3D (for 3D modelling and animation).

Solaris brand of Unix sold by ➲ Sun Microsystems. Solaris started as a version of Unix licensed from AT&T, but Sun bought out the licence from a later owner, and no longer pays royalties on sales. Although most commonly found on Sun workstations and servers, versions have been made available for the Intel 80486 and later processors.

Sony Japanese electronics company that produced the Walkman, the first easily portable cassette player with headphones, in 1980. It diversified into entertainment by the purchase of CBS Records in 1988 and Columbia Pictures in 1989. Sony made the 3.5 in disk drives for the Apple Macintosh in 1984, and also manufactures microchips and ➲ games consoles, amongst other products.

During the 1970s Sony developed the Betamax video-cassette format, which technicians rated as more advanced than the rival VHS system developed by the Matsushita Corporation, but the latter eventually triumphed in the marketplace. Sony's late former senior executive, Akio Morita, was co-author of *A Japan That Can Say No* (1989) and sequels.

In 1999 sales were 4,355 billion yen/\$27 billion, and there were about 21,000 employees.

sorting arranging data in sequence. When sorting a collection, or file, of data made up of several different ➲ fields, one must be chosen as the key field used to establish the correct sequence. For example, the data in a company's mailing list might include fields for each customer's first names, surname, address, and telephone number. For most purposes the company would wish the records to be sorted alphabetically by surname; therefore, the surname field would be chosen as the key field.

The choice of sorting method involves a compromise between running time, memory usage, and complexity. Those used include selection sorting, in which the smallest item is found and exchanged with the first item, the second smallest exchanged with the second item, and so on; bubble sorting, in which adjacent items are continually exchanged until the data are in sequence; and insertion sorting, in which each item is placed in the correct position and subsequent items moved down to make a place for it.

SoundBlaster most popular type of ↝ sound card for IBM-compatible PCs. SoundBlaster cards are made by ↝ Creative Labs.

sound card printed circuit board that, coupled with a set of speakers, enables a computer to reproduce music and sound effects.

source code original instructions written by computer programmers. Before these instructions can be understood, they must be processed by a ↝ compiler and turned into ↝ machine code.

source language language in which a program is written, as opposed to ↝ machine code, which is the form in which the program's instructions are carried out by the computer. Source languages are classified as either ↝ high-level languages or ↝ low-level languages, according to whether each notation in the source language stands for many or only one instruction in machine code.

Programs in high-level languages are translated into machine code by either a ↝ compiler or an ↝ interpreter program. Low-level programs are translated into machine code by means of an ↝ assembler program. The program, before translation, is called the source program; after translation into machine code it is called the object program.

source program program written in a ↝ source language.

spamming advertising on the ↝ Internet by broadcasting to many or all ↝ newsgroups regardless of relevance; spam is the junk e-mail received. Spamming is contrary to netiquette, the Net's conduct code, and is likely to result in the advertiser being bombarded by flames (angry messages), and 'dumping' (the downloading of large, useless files).

Sparc brand name formed from Scalable Processor Architecture to describe the design of ↝ RISC processors designed by Sun Microsystems. Sparc chips are used in computers running ↝ Solaris, Sun's version of ↝ Unix.

speech chip see ↝ DSP.

speech recognition or *voice input*, any technique by which a computer can understand ordinary speech. Spoken words are divided into 'frames', each lasting about one-thirtieth of a second, which are converted to a wave form. These are then compared with a series of stored frames to determine the most likely word. Research into speech recognition started in 1938, but the technology did not become sufficiently developed for commercial applications until the late 1980s.

TIP

soundcard

16-bit soundcards give better reproduction than 8-bit soundcards, and usually offer stereo sound.

Stop Mass Unsolicited E-mail Advertisements

http://www.coyotecom. com/stopjunk.html

Brief explanation of how to avoid getting, and how to complain about, 'spam'. Of interest to anyone who has ever been frustrated by wading through junk e-mail in their inbox.

WEB LINK

There are three types: separate word recognition for distinguishing up to several hundred separately spoken words; connected speech recognition for speech in which there is a short pause between words; and continuous speech recognition for normal but carefully articulated speech.

speech recognition software computing system that enables data to be input by voice. It includes a microphone and ⤳ sound card that plugs into the computer and converts the analogue signals of the voice to digital signals. Examples include Dragon Naturally Speaking and IBM's Via Voice.

The user must read sample sentences to the computer on first use to familiarize it with individual pronunciation. Early software was very inaccurate and slow, but by the mid-1990s speeds of 80 words per minute with 95–99% accuracy were achievable.

speech synthesis or *voice output*, computer-based technology for generating speech. A speech synthesizer is controlled by a computer, which supplies strings of codes representing basic speech sounds (phonemes); together these make up words. Speech-synthesis applications include children's toys, car and aircraft warning systems, and talking books for the blind.

spider program that combs the ⤳ Internet for new documents such as Web pages and ⤳ FTP files. Spiders start their work by retrieving a document such as a Web page and then following all the links and references contained in it. They repeat the process with the followed links, supplying all the references they find to a database that can be searched via a ⤳ search engine.

spooling process in which information to be printed is stored temporarily in a file, the printing being carried out later. It is used to prevent a relatively slow printer from holding up the system at critical times, and to enable several computers or programs to share one printer.

spreadsheet program that mimics a sheet of ruled paper, divided into columns down the page, and rows across. The user enters values into cells within the sheet, then instructs the program to perform some operation on them, such as totalling a column or finding the average of a series of numbers. Highly complex numerical analyses may be built up from these simple steps.

Columns and rows in a spreadsheet are labelled; although different programs use different methods, columns are often labelled with alpha characters, and rows with numbers. This way, each cell has its own reference, unique within that spreadsheet. For example, A5 would be the cell reference for the fifth row in the first column. Cells can also be grouped using references; the range H9:H30 groups together all the cells in column H between (and including) rows 9 and 30. Single references or cell ranges may be used when inputting formulae into cells.

When a cell containing a formula is copied and pasted within a spreadsheet, the formula is said to be relative, meaning the cell references from which it takes its values are relative to its new position. An absolute reference does not change.

The pages of a spreadsheet can be formatted to make them easier to read; the height of rows, the width of columns, and the typeface of the text may all be changed. Number formats may also be changed to display, for example, fractions as decimals or numbers as integers.

Spreadsheets are widely used in business for forecasting and financial control. The first spreadsheet program, Software Arts' VisiCalc, appeared in 1979. The best known include ⮑ Lotus 1-2-3 and Microsoft ⮑ Excel.

Software	Manufacturer	Description
1–2–3	Lotus	long-established and full-featured; able to work with e-mail programs, strong on complex analyses
Excel	Microsoft	powerful and user-friendly; with built-in functions and Wizards
Quattro Pro	Corel	extensive built-in functions; good value; provides visual representation of formulas

spreadsheet
*some major
spreadsheet programs
with functions listed.*

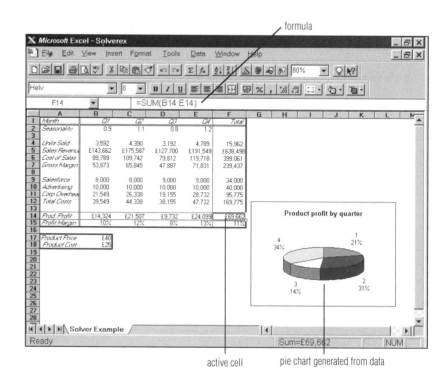

spreadsheet
*A typical spreadsheet soft-
ware package. The data it
contains may be output in
a graphical form, enabling
the production of charts
and diagrams.*

Sprint US telecommunications company supplying data and long-distance voice connections. It was founded in 1899 as the Brown Telephone Company. In October 1999, Sprint was acquired by ⬿ MCI WorldCom for $115 billion to form WorldCom, a company expected to hold about 30% of the US market.

Sprint began offering long distance service under the Sprint brand name in 1986. The company was the first to connect coast-to-coast fibreoptic transmissions.

sprite graphics object made up of a pattern of ⬿ pixels (picture elements) defined by a computer programmer. Some ⬿ high-level languages and ⬿ applications programs contain routines that allow a user to define the shape, colours, and other characteristics of individual graphics objects. These objects can then be manipulated and combined to produce animated games or graphic screen displays.

SQL abbreviation for *structured query language*, high-level computer language designed for use with ⬿ relational databases. Although it can be used by programmers in the same way as other languages, it is often used as a means for programs to communicate with each other. Typically, one program (called the 'client') uses SQL to request data from a database 'server'.

Although originally developed by IBM, SQL is now widely used on many types of computer.

SRAM acronym for *static random-access memory*, computer memory device in the form of a silicon chip used to provide ⬿ immediate access memory. SRAM is faster but more expensive than ⬿ DRAM (dynamic random-access memory), and does not require such frequent refreshing.

stack method of storing data in which the most recent item stored will be the first to be retrieved. The technique is commonly called 'last in, first out'.

Stacks are used to solve problems involving nested structures; for example, to analyse an arithmetical expression containing subexpressions in parentheses, or to work out a route between two points when there are many different paths.

stand-alone computer self-contained computer, usually a microcomputer, that is not connected to a network of computers and can be used in isolation from any other device.

standards any agreed system or protocol that helps different pieces of software or different computers to work together.

In the fast-moving area of computer technology, standards have sometimes developed haphazardly: market forces brought about de facto standards such as the ⬿ MS-DOS operating system for PCs, or the 3.5 in floppy disk. If computers are to communicate over a network, however, standards must be coordinated: the ⬿ World Wide Web, for example, works because everybody who uses it agrees to follow the same conventions, such as using ⬿ HTML to build Web documents. Other standards, like ⬿ SMTP – the procedure for sending e-mail – exist to make cross-platform communication (for example between a ↝ Unix machine and a ↝ Macintosh) possible. Bodies involved with this process include: the ↝ Internet Architecture Board, which lays down basic procedures by promulgating RFCs, the W3 Consortium, which looks after HTML, and the International Standards Organization.

start bit ↝ bit used in ↝ asynchronous communications to indicate the beginning of a piece of data.

startup screen screen displayed by a PC while it loads its ↝ operating system and other resident software. Well-known startup screens include the Windows 95 'flying window' motif and the Macintosh 'smiling face'. It is also possible to create a custom start-up screen, perhaps incorporating a favourite image or corporate logo.

static IP address abbreviation for *static Internet Protocol address*, ↝ IP address which is permanently assigned to a particular user. Most Internet Service Providers (ISPs) use ↝ dynamic IP addressing for their customers. Static IP addressing is, however, generally used by businesses or any organization running its own site and is also available for individuals from some ISPs, such as Demon Internet, allowing them to set up ↝ FTP or Web sites on their home computers. Static IP addressing also allows a higher degree of tracking an individual user's actions on the Internet.

steganography camouflaging messages in large computer files, especially those carrying audio, video, or graphics, by appropriating a small percentage of their constituent data. For example, a graphics file measuring 500 × 500 ↝ pixels, using 32 ↝ bits to represent each pixel, contains 8 million bits. A single bit of each pixel (perhaps the 1st, the 15th, or the 32nd) could be used to insert some 5,000 words of text, chopped into individual bits, without making any perceptible difference to the image. The text message itself can be encrypted using ↝ Pretty Good Privacy (PGP) for added security.

stepper motor electric motor that can be precisely controlled by signals from a computer. The motor turns through a precise angle each time it receives a signal pulse from the computer. By varying the rate at which signal pulses are produced, the motor can be run at different speeds or be turned through an exact angle and then stopped. Switching circuits can be constructed to allow the computer to reverse the direction of the motor.

By combining two or more motors, complex movement control becomes possible. For example, if stepper motors are used to power the wheels of a small vehicle, a computer can manoeuvre the vehicle in any direction.

Stepper motors are commonly used in small-scale applications where computer-controlled movement is required. They are often used inside dot-matrix and ink-jet printers, to control both the feeding of the paper and the movement of the print head across the page. In larger applications, where greater power is necessary, pneumatic or hydraulic systems are usually preferred.

Steganography

http://members.tripod.com /steganography/stego.html

Thorough guide to the technique of camouflaging messages. The contents include the history of steganography, description of various techniques, a guide to available software, and discussions of the implications of steganographic technology.

WEB LINK

stereoscopic display display which achieves a 3-dimensional (3D) image effect using only one ⇝ monitor, and a pair of special glasses. The effect is achieved by running the monitor at double the normal frame rate and arranging to show only every other frame to each eye by means of special polarising glasses which black out each eye alternately. This enables each eye to see a normal frame rate image, and the two images differ sufficiently to cause a 3D image to be seen. These kind of displays are used for industrial 3D visualisation, and in 3D cinemas.

stop bit ⇝ bit used in ⇝ asynchronous communications to indicate the end of a piece of data.

story board in film and television, technique for reviewing a particular story or scene before it is expensively filmed, animated, or scripted.

The scene is broken down into key frames or moments and sketched in varying detail onto boards with accompanying text outlining the plot's progress.

streaming sending data, for example video frames or radio broadcasts, in a steady flow over the Internet. Streaming requires data to pass through a special channel or dedicated connection; conventional ⇝ packets, which travel by a multiplicity of routes, may arrive in the wrong order or be duplicated on the way. Streaming is used in multimedia presentations, such as ⇝ RealAudio, RealVideo, RealText, and Flash animations; it enables presentations to be commenced before files are finished downloading. The data is placed in a temporary memory area until it is downloaded.

string group of characters manipulated as a single object by the computer. In its simplest form a string may consist of a single letter or word – for example, the single word SMITH might be established as a string for processing by a computer. A string can also consist of a combination of words, spaces, and numbers – for example, 33 HIGH STREET ANYTOWN ALLSHIRE could be established as a single string.

Most high-level languages have a variety of string-handling ⇝ functions. For example, functions may be provided to read a character from any given position in a string or to count automatically the number of characters in a string.

structured programming process of writing a program in small, independent parts. This makes it easier to control a program's development and to design and test its individual component parts. Structured programs are built up from units called modules, which normally correspond to single ⇝ procedures or ⇝ functions. Some programming languages, such as Pascal and Modula-2, are better suited to structured programming than others.

style sheet pre-set group of formats used in word processing, presentation graphics, and page layout programs. Style sheets impose margins, fonts, point sizes, alignments, and other criteria to give text a uniform appearance. In a page layout program, designers might use different style sheets for headings, picture captions, and main text.

subject drift tendency for postings in ↝ Usenet, and sometimes entire news-groups, to wander away from their original subject matter. As threads accumulate in response to a posting, the subject heading is retained, but the discussions can rapidly go off at a tangent. Thus a thread headed 'Re: Ice cream – favourite flavours' might actually be a long-running discussion about Napoleon.

subnotebook portable computer, usually a PC-compatible, that is smaller than a notebook computer but larger than a handheld computer. Subnotebooks often leave out features such as floppy disk and CD-ROM drives. One example is the Toshiba Libretto.

subroutine small section of a program that is executed ('called') from another part of the program. Subroutines provide a method of performing the same task at more than one point in the program, and also of separating the details of a program from its main logic. In some computer languages, subroutines are similar to ↝ functions or ↝ procedures.

substring portion of a ↝ string. In searching a text database, for example, specifying that a sequence of letters is a substring will widen the search from just matching words to other words in which that sequence of letters appears. For example, searching a database on the string 'computer' will not retrieve entries which use 'computing' or 'compute'. Searching on the substring 'comput' however, will retrieve all three. The technique adds flexibility when the exact syntax of the search term is unknown.

subsystem hardware and/or software that performs a specific function within a larger system. ↝ Silicon Graphics, for example, uses subsystems to perform the many calculations needed for computer animation.

Sun Microsystems named after the *Stanford University Network*, US-based computer manufacturer founded in 1982 with the motto 'the network is the computer'. Sun specializes in office networks, workstations, and servers running ↝ Solaris, a version of the Unix operating system. Sun pioneered the concept of open systems – technology that is available to other manufacturers – and in 1995 released Java, a platform-independent programming language.

supercomputer fastest, most powerful type of computer, capable of performing its basic operations in picoseconds (trillionths of a second), rather than nanoseconds (billionths of a second), like most other computers.

To achieve these extraordinary speeds, supercomputers use many processors working together and techniques such as cooling processors down to nearly absolute zero temperature, so that their components conduct electricity many times faster than normal. Supercomputers are used in weather forecasting, fluid dynamics, and aerodynamics. Manufacturers include Cray Research, Fujitsu, and NEC.

Of the world's 500 most powerful supercomputers, 232 are in the USA, 109 in Japan, and 140 in Europe, with 23 in the UK. In 1992 Fujitsu announced the launch of the first computer capable of performing 300 billion calculations a second. In 1996 University of Tokyo researchers presented a computer able to perform 1.08 trillion floating-point operations per second.

SuperJANET acronym for *Super Joint Academic Network*, high speed telecommunications network linking academic sites in the UK. The government-funded project, a successor to ⇝ JANET, was started in 1989. Many institutions are now linked to SuperJANET, which has ample ⇝ bandwidth to support ⇝ multimedia educational projects, such as the televisation of operations for medical students. SuperJANET has gateways to the Internet via mainland Europe and the USA. This enables all of the institutions connected to SuperJANET to have Internet access.

support particular type of hardware or software that is compatible with a relevant standard or another type of hardware or software. A given printer might, for example, support 600 dpi (dots per inch) resolution, or a particular computer system might support SVGA graphics.

support environment collection of programs (⇝ software) used to help people design and write other programs. At its simplest, this includes a ⇝ text editor (word-processing software) and a ⇝ compiler for translating programs into executable form; but it can also include interactive debuggers for helping to locate faults, data dictionaries for keeping track of the data used, and rapid prototyping tools for producing quick, experimental mock-ups of programs. Support environments are sometimes referred to as Integrated Development Environments (IDEs). Common examples are Microsoft Visual Studio (for C++ and Java) and Microfocus (for COB).

surfing exploring the ⇝ Internet. The term is derived from 'channel surfing', or flicking rapidly through the dozens of channels typically available on cable TV networks.

SVGA abbreviation for *super video graphics array*, graphic display standard providing higher resolution than ⇝ VGA. SVGA screens have resolutions of either 800×600 or $1,024 \times 768$ pixels.

swap to move segments of data in and out of memory. For fast operation as much data as possible is required in main memory, but it is generally not possible to include all data at the same time. Swapping is the operation of writing and reading from the backup store, often a special space on the disk.

switch network device which allows the interconnection of a number of computers or ⇝ local area network (LAN) segments. Switches differ from more traditional ⇝ bus devices in that when a computer on one socket of the switch needs to talk to another a dedicated path is made through the switch between the two sockets. This allows the computers to communicate at the full speed of the switch, rather than having to compete for a share of the ➾ bandwidth on the bus.

symbolic address symbol used in ➾ assembly language programming to represent the binary ➾ address of a memory location.

symbolic processor computer purpose-built to run so-called symbol-manipulation programs rather than programs involving a great deal of numerical computation. They exist principally for the ➾ artificial intelligence language ➾ LISP, although some have also been built to run ➾ PROLOG.

symmetric-key cryptography system of ➾ cryptography whereby both sender and recipient have identical digital 'keys' used to encrypt and decrypt messages. Although simpler and faster than ➾ public-key cryptography, this method depends on the secure transmission of a key to the recipient before an encrypted message can be read. The most popular example of symmetric-key cryptography is the ➾ Data Encryption Standard (DES), used by the US government.

synchronous regular. Most communication within a computer system is synchronous, controlled by the computer's own internal clock, while communication between computers is usually ➾ asynchronous. Synchronous telecommunications are, however, becoming more widely used.

system administrator or *sysadmin*, person who runs and maintains a computer system, especially a ➾ local area network (LAN). The responsibilities of a systems administrator typically include installing hardware and software, supervising system security, fixing faults, and organizing training.

system flow chart type of ➾ flow chart used to describe the flow of data through a particular computer system.

system implementation process of installing a new computer system.
　　To ensure that a system's implementation takes place as efficiently and with as little disruption as possible, a number of tasks are necessary. These include ordering and installing new equipment, ordering new stationery and storage media, training personnel, converting data files into new formats, drawing up an overall implementation plan, and preparing for a period of either ➾ parallel running or ➾ pilot running.

SYSTEM.INI abbreviation for *System Initialization*, file used by Microsoft Windows to store information about which parts of Windows to load and how to set itself up on the PC on which it is running, for example SYSTEM.INI specifies drivers for the keyboard, graphics card, and sound card, if any. Most of the settings managed by the SYSTEM.INI file have been developed so that they can be found in the Windows Registry.

system requirements minimum specification necessary in order to use a particular piece of hardware or software.

TIP

system requirements

Some system requirements err on the low side. In general, assume that performance will be slow if your system matches the minimum. Beware that many computer games will not run without a 3D graphics card installed on your system.

systems analysis investigation of a business activity or clerical procedure, with a view to deciding if and how it can be computerized. The analyst discusses the existing procedures with the people involved, observes the flow of data through the business, and draws up an outline specification of the required computer system. The next step is ↝ systems design. A recent system is Unified Modeling Language (UML), which is specifically designed for the analysis and design of ↝ object-oriented programming systems.

Systems analysis and design methodologies currently in use include Yourdon, SSADM (Structured Systems Analysis and Design Methodology), and Soft Systems Methodology.

Systems Application Architecture *SAA*, IBM model for client–server computing, introduced in 1987. SAA was a grandiose attempt to reduce the incompatibilities between IBM's many ranges of hardware, including mainframes, minicomputers, and PCs. It uses ↝ CUA (common user access) standards to ensure that commands and keystrokes are used consistently in different applications.

systems design detailed design of an ↝ applications package. The designer breaks the system down into component programs, and designs the required input forms, screen layouts, and printouts. Systems design forms a link between systems analysis and ↝ programming.

Systems Network Architecture *SNA*, set of communication protocols developed by IBM and incorporated in hardware and software implementations. See also ↝ TCP/IP and ↝ Open Systems Interconnection (OSI).

systems program program that performs a task related to the operation and performance of the computer system itself. For example, a systems program might control the operation of the display screen, or control and organize backing storage. In contrast, an ↝ applications program is designed to carry out tasks for the benefit of the computer user.

System X in communications, a modular, computer-controlled, digital switching system used in telephone exchanges.

System X was originally developed by the UK companies GEC, Plessey, and STC at the request of the Post Office, beginning in 1969. A prototype exchange was finally commissioned in 1978, and the system launched in 1980.

T1 link US term for a digital telephone line which can transfer data at 1.544 megabits per second. T1 lines are a type of ↝ Integrated Services Digital Network (ISDN) communication.

T3 US term for a digital telephone standard that transmits data at 44.736 megabits per second, widely used for ↝ Integrated Services Digital Network (ISDN) lines.

tag formatting command that tells a browser how it should display an element in a Web page or other document. In ↝ HTML, tags are separated from text by angle brackets and travel in pairs: one for *on* and one for *off*. <whisper> The same technique is used for effect in geeky e-mail </whisper>.

tape streamer backing storage device consisting of a continuous loop of magnetic tape. Tape streamers are largely used to store dumps (rapid backup copies) of important data files (see ↝ data security).

TAPI abbreviation for *Telephony Application Programming Interface*, program included in ↝ Windows 95 to enable applications to use the telephone. The TAPI standard was developed by Microsoft and Intel in 1993.

tar compression routine in common use on the Internet. Originally developed for ↝ Unix operating systems, the tar utility archives files and directories by grouping them together into one large file, which can then be compressed and stored off-line. It is often used to distribute software for Unix systems, and tar files bear the extension .tar. A file with the extension tar.Z is a tar archive that has also been compressed with the Unix compression utility.

taskbar strip at the bottom of a ↝ Windows 95, 98, 2000, or NT screen containing icons ('task buttons') of all programs launched in the current session. The taskbar makes it possible to switch between applications simply by clicking the mouse on a task button.

T-carrier high-speed communications service supplied by one of the USA's telecommunications companies. Lines with different capacities are identified by number, such as T-1, T-2, T-3, T-4, and so on.

TCO Swedish Confederation of Professional Employees, association of 18 trade unions, whose activities include the specification and management of an international quality and environmental labelling scheme for the computer industry. Their scheme covers workstation efficiency, monitors, printers, and most recently, keyboards. The scheme has been most widely used by monitor manufacturers, who display TCO92 or TCO95 labels to show their conformity with electromagnetic emissions standards.

TCP/IP abbreviation for *transport control protocol/Internet protocol*, set of network protocols, developed principally by the US Department of Defense. TCP/IP is the protocol used by the Internet, and is the technology that underpins Internet services like the ↝ World Wide Web, ↝ Internet Relay Chat, and ↝ electronic mail. TCP/IP has always been the principal networking protocol used by ↝ Unix, and is now supported by almost all types of operating system.

telco in computing slang, contraction of *telecommunications company*.

TeleAdapt company that specializes in supplying worldwide telephone and power adaptor plugs for portable computer users.

TeleAdapt is based in London, England, and has offices in San Jose, California, and Sydney, Australia.

telecommuting working from home using a telephone, fax, and ↝ modem to keep in touch with the office of the employing company. In the late 1990s, it was estimated that 11 million US workers and 1.9 million British workers were telecommuters.

Most telecommuters are self-employed, or sales people spending much of their time on the road. However, the number of part-time telecommuters, for example working one day per week at home, is growing.

telemedicine use of computer communications to improve medical practice and training. One example of its use is remote consulting, which involves a consultant using video-conferencing-type technology to examine a patient, and even to assist remotely during surgery. This kind of technology is invaluable for treating patients in far outlying areas, or in countries with limited medical resources.

Telephony Application Programming Interface Windows program, commonly abbreviated to ↝ TAPI.

teletext broadcast system of displaying information on a television screen. The information – typically about news items, entertainment, sport, and finance – is constantly updated. Teletext is a form of ↝ videotext, pioneered in Britain by the British Broadcasting Corporation (BBC) with Ceefax and by Independent Television (ITV) with Teletext.

Telnet Internet utility that enables a user to work on a remote computer as if directly connected. Telnet connections to a remote computer system are typically much cheaper than long-distance telephone calls; the user makes a local call to an Internet access provider and the rest of the connection is handled via the Internet at no additional cost. ↝ Bulletin board systems usually work via Telnet.

template file that lays down a document's format. Templates are used in word processing, spreadsheet, and other programs to specify all the styles used in a document, such as fonts, margins, macros, formulas, and so on. They are widely used to automate the production of documents such as memos, mailings, and reports, making sure that they have a uniform appearance.

**Telemedicine:
A Guide to Assessing
Telecommunications
for Health Care**

http://www.nap.edu/
readingroom/books/
telemed/summary.html

Overview of the development of telemedicine and summary of a US report into its future direction. The difficulties of evaluating telemedicine are set out.

WEB LINK

TIP

Telnet

Telnet is available via a Web browser, providing the right helper application is available.

terabyte 1,024 ↩ gigabytes, or 1,099,511,627,776 ↩ bytes.

teraflops jargon for 1 trillion floating point operations (computations) per second. Despite earlier predictions, there was still no single computer in 2000 that could boast teraflop performance. Just over one teraflop has been achieved by utilizing thousands of smaller computers, all working in parallel over the Internet.

Entropia is one of the organizations which links together many supercomputers with the aim of making new advances, such as finding very large prime numbers.

IBM expects to build a ↩ petaflop computer by the end of 2004.

terminal device consisting of a keyboard and display screen (↩ VDU) to enable the operator to communicate with the computer. The terminal may be physically attached to the computer or linked to it by a telephone line (remote terminal). A 'dumb' terminal has no processor of its own, whereas an 'intelligent' terminal has its own processor and takes some of the processing load away from the main computer.

terminal emulation communications program such as ↩ Telnet that allows a computer to emulate a terminal or workstation of a remote host. The host accepts instructions from the remote computer as if it were one of its own workstations.

terminate and stay resident *TSR*, term given to an MS-DOS program that remains in the memory – for example, a clock, calculator, or thesaurus. The program is recalled by the use of a ↩ hot key.

test data data designed to test whether a new computer program is functioning correctly. The test data are carefully chosen to ensure that all possible branches of the program are tested. The expected results of running the data are written down and are then compared with the actual results obtained using the program.

test message message in ↩ Usenet that is posted simply to make sure that one's software or network connections are working properly.

T$_E$X (pronounced 'tek') public domain text formatting and typesetting system, developed by Donald Knuth and widely used for producing mathematical and technical documents. Unlike ↩ desktop publishing applications, T$_E$X is not ↩ WYSIWYG, although in some implementations a screen preview of pages is possible.

text editor program that allows the user to edit text on the screen and to store it in a file. Text editors are similar to ↩ word processors, except that they lack the ability to format text into paragraphs and pages and to apply different typefaces and styles.

TFT display another name for ↩ active matrix LCD.

TIP

test message

It is considered bad netiquette to post test messages to ordinary newsgroups. They should be posted to one of the special newsgroups, such as alt.test, which are entirely devoted to test messages.

thin client simplified network computer or terminal. In a thin client network all the applications are executed on a central server computer, sometimes called a terminal server. All of the users' input, that is, mouse movements, clicks, and keyboard presses, are encoded using special protocols and sent to the terminal server, which then feeds them to the appropriate application. The output from the applications (for example, images and sounds) is then similarly encoded and sent back over the network to refresh the image on screen. Examples of this kind of technology are Microsoft's Windows Terminal Server, Citrix MetaFrame, and X Windows.

1394 high speed external serial ↝ bus system designed to connect computers and consumer electronics devices such as camcorders, digital television sets, DVD players, scanners, and colour printers. One 1394 port can connect up to 63 devices.

1394 is specified as a standard by an Institute of Electronic and Electrical Engineers committee, IEEE.1394. The system started life at Apple Computer as FireWire, and is called i.Link by Sony Corporation. 1394 was designed in part to replace the ↝ SCSI bus.

32-bit term describing the ability to process 32 ↝ bits at a time. The Intel 386 and 486 series of microprocessors are examples of 32-bit processors.

The term is also used to specify the quality of sound produced by ↝ sound cards, where increased speed indicates the ability to produce more fully detailed (and therefore more realistic) sound. Windows NT, OS/2, and Windows 95/98 are all examples of 32-bit operating systems.

thread subject line of electronic messages within an online topic or conference. Most online conferencing systems use some kind of threading; one advantage is that it makes it easy for readers of a particular conference or forum to skip over sections that do not interest them. Threading is an important feature of off-line readers, as otherwise it is difficult to tell how individual messages relate to one another.

3-D graphics graphics defined by width, height, and depth (in mathematical terms, x, y, and z axes). In business applications such as spreadsheets, 3-D graphics allow users to display complex relationships between several different types of data. In computer animation, animators can make films composed entirely of computer-generated 3-D graphics, such as *A Bug's Life* (1999) and *Toy Story 2* (2000).

thumbnail small version of a larger image used for reference. A ↝ PhotoCD or ↝ clip art collection might initially present images as thumbnails, while publishing programs include the facility for designers to produce thumbnail page layouts.

TIFF acronym for *tagged image file format*, ↝ graphics file format.

tiling arrangement of ↝ windows in a ↝ graphical user interface system so that they do not overlap.

time out pre-set period of time during which a computer waits for a response from a device or another computer. For example, when sending a fax, a computer will time out the telephone call if the receiving fax machine fails to answer.

time-sharing way of enabling several users to access the same computer at the same time. The computer rapidly switches between user ↪ terminals and programs, allowing each user to work as if he or she had sole use of the system.

Time-sharing was common in the 1960s and 1970s before the spread of cheaper computers, and is now making something of a comeback, with the advent of application service providers.

timestamp ↪ digital signature that 'fixes' a document in time, so that any later alterations can be readily detected.

TinyMUD one of the oldest and most popular ↪ MUDs, named for the efficiency of its program code.

TinySex cybersex on ↪ TinyMUD.

TN3270 variation of ↪ Telnet used to connect to IBM mainframes.

toggle to switch between two settings. In software a toggle is usually triggered by the same code, so it is important that this code only has two meanings. An example is the use of the same character in a text file to indicate both opening and closing quotation marks; if the same character is also used to mean an apostrophe, then conversion, via a toggle switch, for a ↪ desktop publishing system that uses different opening and closing quotation marks, will not be carried out correctly.

token ring protocol for ↪ local area networks, developed by IBM in 1985. A token ring network operates by connecting computers together with copper-based wiring to form a large ring. One or many tokens (sequences of bits) then circulate around the ring continuously. When a computer transmits data it grabs a passing token and attaches the data and the destination address behind the token. The token then continues to circulate around the ring. Every computer on the ring checks every passing token to see if any attached data is addressed to it. When a computer finds a token with data addressed to it, it copies the data, and sets a special bit in the token to say that the data has been received successfully. When the token works its way back around the ring to the originating computer, the originator removes the data and frees up the token for use again. Token ring has been largely superseded by ↪ Ethernet as a LAN protocol.

toolbar area at the top or side of a screen with ↪ push-buttons and other features to perform frequently used tasks. For example, the toolbar of a ↪ paint program might offer quick access to different brushes, spraycans, erasers, and other useful tools.

ToolBook multimedia authoring tool created by the US company Asymetrix for Microsoft Windows.

topology arrangement of devices in a ↝ network. The most common is the ↝ bus topology, where all the computers are interconnected using a single, open-ended cable. Most modern network solutions use either a ring or bus layout, but with physical characteristics that resemble a star layout.

total cost of ownership *TCO*, term introduced at the end of the 1980s by US market analysts (in particular the Gartner Group) to indicate the complete cost of owning a desktop device, including capital, technical support, administration, and end-user costs. TCO has been used to highlight the difference between the ownership costs of a ↝ personal computer, a ↝ network computer, and a ↝ Windows-based terminal.

touch screen input device allowing the user to communicate with the computer by touching a display screen with a finger. In this way, the user can point to a required ↝ menu option or item of data. Touch screens are used less widely than other pointing devices such as the ↝ mouse or ↝ joystick. A typical application is in public houses, where sales staff simply need to touch the items sold on the screen; a total is displayed for the customer, while the computing system connected to the screen calculates remaining stock levels.

Typically, the screen is able to detect the touch either because the finger presses against a sensitive membrane or because it interrupts a grid of light beams crossing the screen surface.

touch sensor in a computer-controlled robot, a device used to give the robot a sense of touch, allowing it to manipulate delicate objects or move automatically about a room. Touch sensors provide the feedback necessary for the robot to adjust the force of its movements and the pressure of its grip. The main types include the strain gauge and the microswitch.

trace method of checking that a computer program is functioning correctly by causing the changing values of all the ↝ variables involved to be displayed while the program is running. In this way it becomes possible to narrow down the search for a bug, or error, in the program to the exact instruction that causes the variables to take unexpected values.

traceroute network ↝ utility program which allows the user to find out the ↝ bang path taken by ↝ packets of data sent across the Internet. Traceroute can help to debug a network, or check how it works.

track part of the magnetic structure created on a disk surface during ↝ disk formatting so that data can be stored on it. The disk is first divided into circular tracks and then each circular track is divided into a number of sectors.

trackball ↝ input device that carries out the same function as a ↝ mouse, but remains stationary. In a trackball the ball controlling the cursor position is operated directly with the fingers.

tracking amount of space between text characters. Many word-processing and page layout programs allow users to adjust tracking for a wide-spaced or slightly condensed appearance.

traffic messages sent over a network such as the Internet.

transaction file file that contains all the additions, deletions, and amendments required during ➢ file updating to produce a new version of a master file.

transistor–transistor logic *TTL*, type of integrated circuit most commonly used in building electronic products. In TTL chips the bipolar transistors are directly connected (usually collector to base). In mass-produced items, large numbers of TTL chips are commonly replaced by a small number of ➢ uncommitted logic arrays (ULAs), or logic gate arrays.

transition way in which one image changes to another in a ➢ slide show, animation, or multimedia presentation.

Different transitions have a different effect on the viewer: slow mixes (fades) are gentler on the eye than sudden blackouts, and wipes – in which one scene replaces the next like a blind being pulled across the screen – are an especially dynamic type of transition.

translation program program that translates another program written in a high-level language or assembly language into the machine-code instructions that a computer can obey. See ➢ assembler, ➢ compiler, and ➢ interpreter.

transputer member of a family of microprocessors designed for parallel processing, developed in the UK by Inmos. In the circuits of a standard computer the processing of data takes place in sequence; in a transputer's circuits processing takes place in parallel, greatly reducing computing time for those programs that have been specifically written for it.

The transputer implements a special programming language called OCCAM, which Inmos based on CSP (communicating sequential processes), developed by C A R Hoare of Oxford University Computing Laboratory.

Though backed by the British government, Inmos was not commercially successful. It was taken over by UK company Thorn-EMI in 1984 and traded to the French–Italian electronics company SGS-Thomson in 1989.

tree-and-branch filing system filing system where all files are stored within directories, like folders in a filing cabinet. These directories may in turn be stored within further directories. The root directory contains all the other directories and may be thought of as equivalent to the filing cabinet. Another way of picturing the system is as a tree with branches from which grow smaller branches, ending in leaves (individual files).

Trinitron ➢ monitor based on a cathode-ray tube developed by ➢ Sony, designed to give a sharper image and more uniform brightness than conventional monitors.

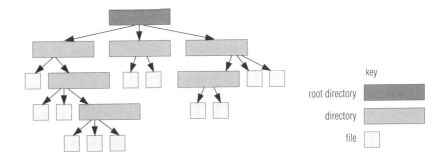

tree-and-branch filing system The directory filing structure used by computers. The structure can be likened to an upside-down tree, with the root at the top, branching downwards and outwards into sub-directories.

Trojan program that looks as though it will do something entertaining or useful but actually does something else, such as reformatting the user's hard disk. Trojans are named after the Trojan horse in Greek mythology. A virus is not a Trojan, but inserting a virus into another program – such as virus checker – would make that program a Trojan.

trolling mischievously posting a deliberately erroneous or obtuse message to a ⇝ newsgroup in order to tempt others to reply – usually in a way that makes them appear gullible, intemperate, or foolish.

TrueType scalable font system, jointly developed by Apple and Microsoft. It allows scalable fonts to be used by non-PostScript printers. Such printers are usually cheaper.

Trumpet popular shareware ⇝ TCP/IP program for Windows or ⇝ MS-DOS.

truncation error ⇝ error that occurs when a decimal result is cut off (truncated) after the maximum number of places allowed by the computer's level of accuracy.

trusted third party *TTP*, organization with which some governments would like users of encryption systems to deposit the keys to their codes, so that their electronic messages can be read without the use of enormous amounts of expensive government computer power. See ⇝ cryptography and the ⇝ Regulation of Investigatory Powers Act.

truth table in electronics, a diagram showing the effect of a particular ⇝ logic gate on every combination of inputs.

Every possible combination of inputs and outputs for a particular gate or combination of gates is described, thereby defining their action in full. When logic value 1 is written in the table, it indicates a 'high' (or 'yes') input of perhaps 5 volts; logic value 0 indicates a 'low' (or 'no') input of 0 volts.

TSR abbreviation for ⇝ terminate and stay resident.

TTL abbreviation for ⇝ transistor–transistor logic, a family of integrated circuits.

TTP abbreviation for ⇝ trusted third party.

Alan Turing Home Page

http://www.turing.org.uk/turing/

Authoritative, illustrated biography of the computer pioneer, plus links to related sites. This site contains information on his origins and his code-breaking work during World War II, as well as several works written by Turing himself.

WEB LINK

Turing, Alan Mathison (1912–1954) English mathematician and logician. In 1936 he described a 'universal computing machine' that could theoretically be programmed to solve any problem capable of solution by a specially designed machine. This concept, now called the ↝ Turing machine, foreshadowed the digital computer.

Turing is believed to have been the first to suggest (in 1950) the possibility of machine learning and artificial intelligence. His test for distinguishing between real (human) and simulated (computer) thought is known as the Turing test: with a person in one room and the machine in another, an interrogator in a third room asks questions of both to try to identify them. When the interrogator cannot distinguish between them by questioning, the machine will have reached a state of humanlike intelligence.

Turing was born in London and studied at Cambridge. During World War II he worked on the Ultra project in the team that cracked the German Enigma cipher code. After the war he worked briefly on the project to design the general computer known as the Automatic Computing Engine, or ACE, and was involved in the pioneering computer developed at Manchester University from 1948.

Turing machine abstract model of an automatic problem-solving machine, formulated by Alan Turing in 1936. It provides the theoretical basis of modern digital computing.

turnaround document output document produced by a computer that is later, after additional data has been added, used as an input document.

An example of turnaround documents are the meter-reading cards produced by gas and electricity companies. Each card is output with customer details printed in a typeface readable by OCR (optical character recognition) software and with a standard grid suitable for OMR (optical mark recognition). The meter reader inspects the customer's meter, marks the new reading on the grid, and then returns the card to the company's billing department. There, a universal document reader, capable of reading both OCR and OMR data, is used to input the new information to the computer.

turnkey system system that the user has only to switch on to have direct access to application software that is usually specific to a particular application area. Turnkey systems often use menus. The user is expected to follow instructions on the screen and to have no knowledge of how the system operates.

turtle small computer-controlled wheeled robot. The turtle's movements are determined by programs written by a computer user, typically using the high-level programming language ↝ LOGO.

TWAIN acronym for *technology without an interesting name*, software standard allowing images to be taken directly from a ↝ scanner or digital camera into any image-processing application. Before TWAIN, users were restricted to the scanners explicitly supported by their software; now, the only necessity is that both items follow the TWAIN standard.

24-bit colour term specifying that a ↝ video adapter is able to display more than 16 million colours simultaneously. The human eye processes 16 million colours with every blink, and a computer needs the same number of colours to be able to display pictures of a photographic quality. Powerful microprocessors, large amounts of ↝ RAM, and mass storage media are needed to handle the large computer files involved in holding such complex data.

2-D graphics graphics defined only by width and height (in mathematical terms, x and y axes). Examples of 2-D graphics are the graphics generated by spreadsheets or animated characters with no shading.

256-colour term specifying the number of colours that an 8-bit ↝ video adapter or ↝ VGA screen is able to display simultaneously. The earliest VGA screens could handle only 16 colours. By 1996 most new computer systems came equipped with a video adapter and display that could handle 256 colours, allowing the use of more detailed and complex graphics. The extra depth is useful for applications such as games and multimedia encyclopedias.

two's complement number system number system, based on the ↝ binary number system, that allows both positive and negative numbers to be conveniently represented for manipulation by computer.

In the two's complement system the most significant column heading (the furthest to the left) is always taken to represent a negative number.

For example, the four-column two's complement number 1101 stands for –3, since: –8 + 4 + 1 = –3.

UART abbreviation for *universal asynchronous receiver–transmitter*, integrated circuit that converts computer data into ↝ asynchronous signals suitable for transmission via a telephone line, and vice versa. UARTs combine a transmitter (parallel-to-serial converter) and a receiver (serial-to-parallel converter) to provide a 'bridge' between the parallel signals used by the computer and the serial signals used by communications networks.

UDP abbreviation for ↝ User Datagram Protocol.

UDSL abbreviation for ↝ Universal Digital Subscriber Line.

ULA abbreviation for ↝ uncommitted logic array, a type of integrated circuit.

UMTS abbreviation for *Universal Mobile Telecommunications System*, third generation (3G) of mobile cellular networks. UMTS networks are expected to arrive in Europe in 2002, with data transmission speeds of up to 2 megabits per second (mbps) per channel. ↝ Videoconferencing and ↝ video-on-demand are expected to be available over UMTS, as well as services that utilize its ability to calculate the location of a mobile phone to within a few metres.

In 2000 the UK government auctioned five 3G licences, bringing in £22.8 billion to the exchequer, a much higher sum than originally expected.

BT and Manx Telecom are working together to launch Europe's first commercial UMTS service on the Isle of Man in 2001. The service will use software developed by BT in conjunction with ↝ Microsoft and US long-distance telecommunications company AT&T, including business applications giving mobile access to corporate data and consumer programs which provide access to games, books, and music.

unbundling marketing or selling products, usually hardware and software, separately rather than as a single package.

uncommitted logic array *ULA*; or *gate array*, type of semicustomized integrated circuit in which the logic gates are laid down to a general-purpose design but are not connected to each other. The interconnections can then be set in place according to the requirements of individual manufacturers. Producing ULAs may be cheaper than using a large number of TTL (↝ transistor–transistor logic) chips or commissioning a fully customized chip.

undelete command that allows a user to reinstate deleted text or files. See also ↝ delete.

underflow error ↝ error that occurs if a number is outside the computer's range and is too small to deal with.

Unicode 16-bit character encoding system, intended to cover all characters in all languages (including Chinese and similar languages) and to be backwards compatible with ↝ ASCII.

Unlike ASCII, which is 8-bit and can therefore represent only 256 characters – insufficient for many diacritics outside the English language – Unicode can

Unicode Consortium

http://www.unicode.org/

Source of information about the emerging Unicode standard for encoding characters in computing. Discover how Unicode is being developed, read a glossary of useful terms, and find other useful related sites.

WEB LINK

represent 65,536 characters, big enough to handle almost all written languages, including Japanese, Tibetan, and the International Phonetic Alphabet (IPA). It was created in the 1980s by Apple and Xerox in the USA.

uninterruptible power supply (UPS) power supply that includes a battery, so that in the event of a power failure it is possible to continue operations. UPSs are normally used to provide time either for a system to be shut down in the usual way (so that files are not corrupted) or for an alternative power supply to be connected. For large systems these operations are usually carried out automatically.

Universal Digital Subscriber Line *UDSL*, low-cost version of xDSL having been standardized in 1998. UDSL is backed by a consortium of companies led by Compaq, Intel, and Microsoft.

Universal Serial Bus *USB*, royalty-free connector intended to replace the out-of-date COM and parallel printer ports that have been used in PCs since 1981. The USB allows up to 127 peripherals – including joysticks, scanners, printers, and keyboards – to be daisy-chained from a single socket, offering higher speeds and improved plug-and-play facilities.

The USB includes hardware and software specifications controlled by the multivendor USB-IF (Universal Serial Bus Implementors Forum) formed in March 1995. Some PC motherboards have included USB connectors since October 1996, and Release 2 of Windows 95 supports USB as long as peripherals come with their own drivers. Microsoft provided full software support for USB in Windows 98.

University for Industry *Ufi*, public–private partnership in the UK aimed at making businesses more competitive and individuals more employable. Ufi, working with businesses and education and training providers, will use computer technology to make learning available at a time and place to suit the learner. This could be at home, in the workplace, or at one of a national network of 'learndirect' learning centres. A range of 250 courses for all experience levels covers subjects such as ↬ information technology, basic skills, business and management skills, and industry-specific needs.

By summer 2000, 251 learning centres had been set up. Ufi was set for full national operation by autumn 2000, by which time the learndirect Web site would be launched, together with a further 178 centres. By spring 2001, over 1,000 learning centres were expected to be open.

Unix multiuser ↬ operating system designed for minicomputers but becoming increasingly popular on microcomputers, workstations, mainframes, and supercomputers.

Unix was developed by AT&T's Bell Laboratories in the USA during the late 1960s, using the programming language ↬ C. It could therefore run on any machine with a C compiler, so ensuring its wide portability. Its wide range of functions and flexibility, together with the fact that it was available free 1976–1983, have made it widely used by universities and in commercial software.

TIP

upgrade

In an office environment, it is important to carry out software upgrades simultaneously on all machines. Files created using upgrades can rarely be opened by those using older programs.

Beginners' Guide to URLs

http://www.ncsa.uiuc.edu/demoweb/url-primer.html

Guide to URLs describing what they do. The site differentiates between the different types of URL, covering 'file', 'partial', 'gopher', and 'news' URLs. The bottom of the page contains a link to more detailed information about URLs.

WEB LINK

In the 1990s, AT&T's Unix System Laboratories was taken over by Novell, which later sold it to the Santa Cruz Operation.

unshielded twisted pair *UTP*, form of cabling used for ↝ local area networks (LAN), now commonly used as an alternative to coaxial cable. The benefits of UTP over coaxial cables are that it is cheaper to install and can be used by a variety of LAN standards, for example ↝ Ethernet and ↝ Token Ring, as well as being used for telephone circuits.

upgrade improved version of an existing software program. Upgrades are sometimes available free or at low cost to registered owners of previous versions.

UPS abbreviation for ↝ uninterruptible power supply.

URL abbreviation for *Uniform Resource Locator*, series of letters and/or numbers specifying the location of a document on the ↝ World Wide Web. Every URL consists of a domain name, a description of the document's location within the host computer, and the name of the document itself, separated by full stops and backslashes. Thus *The Times* Web site can be found at http://www.the-times.co.uk/news/pages/home.html, and a tribute to Elvis Presley is at http:///www.mit.edu:8001/activities/41West/elvis.html. The complexity of URLs explains why bookmarks and links, which save the user from the chore of typing them in, are so popular.

USB abbreviation for ↝ Universal Serial Bus.

Usenet contraction of *users' network*, world's largest ↝ bulletin board system, which brings together people with common interests to exchange views and information. It consists of ↝ e-mail messages and articles organized into ↝ newsgroups. Usenet is uncensored and governed by the rules of ↝ netiquette.

User Datagram Protocol *UDP*, communications protocol that, like the Transmission Control Protocol (TCP), runs on top of the Internet Protocol (IP). UDP tolerates packets of information being lost or corrupted en route to their destination. This tolerance is an advantage if the message is one where drop-outs are less damaging than delays caused by attempts at error recovery, for example, when speech is broadcast across the Internet.

user-friendly term used to describe the ease of use of a computer system, particularly for those with little understanding or familiarity with computers. Even for experienced users, user-friendly programs are quicker to learn.

user ID contraction of *user identification*, name or nickname that identifies the user of a computer system or network. See also ↝ password.

user interface procedures and methods through which the user operates a program. These might include ↝ menus, input forms, error messages, and keyboard procedures. A ↝ graphical user interface (GUI or WIMP) is one that

Upgrading

Why do you need to upgrade? Most personal computers are assembled from commodity components, and frequently have unused spaces and sockets inside, allowing manufacturers to build a variety of specifications from a limited inventory.

It also gives manufacturers an additional marketing tool, because components can be added and swapped with relative ease, making almost every PC upgradable – or, in marketing parlance, 'future-proof'.

Theoretically, this is correct. Almost any part of a PC can be upgraded, from processor and memory to disks and display, and even the entire main circuit board (motherboard). And a host of extra components can be added, internally or externally.

Disadvantages Few people actually upgrade their PCs. Some upgrades are beyond the capabilities of the ordinary user. Others are costly, because the original component must be discarded, making the upgraded machine more expensive than one which had the higher specification in the first place.

Moreover, upgrading one component is seldom enough. If you wanted to convert a road car for racing, you might have to replace not only the engine, but the wheels, the brakes, the transmission, the subframe, and the windows. Similarly with a PC. Once you replace the processor, it may also be necessary to upgrade the memory, disks, disk controller, display, and graphics controller. By this time, you might as well have bought a new computer.

The older the PC, the less worthwhile the upgrade. Anything with a 286 or 386 processor is not worth upgrading, whereas a fast 486 or Pentium machine may have a couple of years of useful life left.

Upgrading memory The most worthwhile upgrade, which can often be done without affecting the other components, is adding extra memory. Windows requires at least 8 Mb of memory to run

adequately, and 16 Mb can give much improved performance. In many modern PCs, all you have to do is plug in an extra memory module.

Upgrading the processor chip is fairly straightforward, as long as the PC is quite new. But to be worthwhile, the new processor should be considerably faster than the old, such as upgrading from a 486 to a Pentium, and to get full benefit you will almost certainly have to upgrade some other components.

Modern software and data requires undreamed-of amounts of disk space, so upgrading from, say, a 200 Mb disk to a 1 Gb model can be effective. Most people prefer to install a second hard disk, rather than scrapping the old one. But a cheaper alternative is to double the capacity of the existing disk using compression software.

Rather than upgrading core components, ambitious PC owners would do better to consider adding new ones. Multimedia features (CD-ROM drive, sound card, and loudspeakers) can all be added quite cheaply, and without too much trouble. A modem (telephone adaptor) lets you hook up to the Internet, and send and receive faxes. And a tape backup unit lets you take backup copies of files.

Final checks Before you upgrade, consider all the components you may have to change and any knock-on effects, and calculate the cost (including your time); you may find it will be almost as much as buying a new PC.

Then check that the PC has physical space for the new chips, drive, or card, and make sure that you can return or exchange the new components if they turn out to be incompatible. Ask the PC manufacturer's advice, and check that you are not invalidating any warranty.

Finally, however minor the upgrade, always take back-up copies of all programs and data first. You never know!

Paul Bray

makes use of icons (small pictures) and allows the user to make menu selections with a mouse.

A command line interface is a character-based interface in which a prompt is displayed on the screen at which the user types a command, followed by

Creating a Web Site – URLs and HTML

Introduction Only four or five years ago, the Internet was a mystery to many people. Now, organizations and individuals alike want to be a part of the Internet. Nearly all Western companies have a presence on the Internet in the form of a Web site. Their site's uniform resource locator (URL – its electronic 'address') is routinely listed alongside their telephone, fax, and e-mail numbers. A Web site is simply a collection of information that is designed to be accessed in a special way. This information is held as a series of files stored on one or more computers. The term 'Web site' alludes to the World Wide Web – now usually just 'the Web' – which for most people is the Internet.

Jumping around the world The fundamental feature of the Web, and hence all Web sites, is the hypertext link. 'Hypertext' is a piece of text that is linked to some other piece of text. This text can be elsewhere on the same page, or stored thousands of kilometres away on another computer. The huge complexity of the Internet is handled by protocols – special electronic 'languages' that enable computers and computer networks to talk to each other. To these, the Web adds its own special Hypertext Transfer Protocol or HTTP (shown in Web site URLs, which usually begin http://www . . .). The information on Web sites must also be specially coded using the Hypertext Markup Language (HTML). HTTP and HTML allow text and graphics to be transferred to the visitor's computer where they are viewed using a 'browser' such as Netscape's Navigator or Microsoft's Internet Explorer. Web pages can be assembled by painstakingly keying in the codes, but it is far easier to use special editing software. The latest versions of leading word processors and desktop publishing packages can generate files in HTML form, and there are an increasing number of Web site creation tools. These software aids hide all the technical details from the user.

Getting connected There are several ways to connect a Web site to the world. The differences are largely dependent on scale. At the personal end of the Web are the 'home pages', in which individuals set out their life details, interests, hobbies, and obsessions for like-minded people to enjoy. At a larger scale are the sites of organizations, businesses, and academic institutions. These sites may carry numerous pages of information and regular publications, and files for visitors to download. Some companies – 'e-businesses' – now buy and sell products and services exclusively over the Web. E-business requires a secure means of transferring financial information such as credit card details. The home page is the cheapest and simplest option, both for private individuals and for many homeworkers or small businesses. Typically, an Internet Service Provider (ISP) offers a few megabytes of storage space as part of its ordinary Internet or e-mail service. It is easy to access and update the home page using an ordinary modem connection. When carefully planned, a home page can provide a rich and effective site, but it is not a practical option for large users. Instead, organizations and businesses may choose one of the range of larger-scale services offered by ISPs, and some share Internet connectivity with other companies. But most large organizations keep their own special computers, known as 'Web servers', permanently connected to the Internet. Simple modem connections are useless at this scale, so Web servers need at least an ISDN connection, and more probably leased lines. Medium- to large-sized organizations requiring a Web site must plan carefully and talk to a large number of ISPs before committing themselves.

Reaching the right people Anybody who sets up a Web site becomes a publisher. Every Web site is a form of publication, whether or not it offers conventional published media. It will succeed or fail for the same kinds of reasons as other publications. Web site planners must ask the following vital questions: What kind of content will the site provide? How will this content be organized? Who are the target visitors?

Structure and content The basic unit of Web site organization is the page. At its simplest, a Web site consists of one 'flat' page of information that the visitor reads from beginning to end. Pages rarely fit neatly into a single screen view, so

USER INTERFACE 293

Creating a Web Site (continued)

reading them involves scrolling, or clicking hyperlinks within the page. It is wise to sketch the probable text and graphic content first, then organize it for the visitor's convenience. Content and structure will probably develop together rather than follow purely 'top-down' or 'bottom-up' design paths. A separate title page is a good idea; it should identify the site, be inviting, and carry hyperlinks to the rest of the site. Other common features include news and information pages, contact details, and material for downloading. (Files for downloading use the File Transfer Protocol – FTP – and are often kept on another computer.) Unless the text content is very brief, it will be spread over several pages. Visitors should not be forced to scroll up and down a long single page. Navigation through the site is an important issue when there are several pages. A well-planned structure is the answer, together with hyperlinks within and between pages. At least one of the pages should be a 'contents' list; complex sites divided into separate areas may need a sublist for each area. Some site designs use a contents area or jump gate that is always on screen in a separate panel. Security is an ever-present problem, and not just for business transactions. Web site contents may have legal implications, and the Internet offers opportunities for the virus infestation of both host and client computers. Furthermore, hackers are always trying to find ways to reach the files stored on a Web server.

Keep it simple ... Unless the graphic content is particularly important, there are good reasons for avoiding animated displays, visual gimmicks, elaborate structures, and even the extensive use of graphics. These will soon use up an ISP's home page storage allocation. One prime cause of irritation to 'Web surfers' is a long delay before pages appear. A Web server can deliver an average page in about half a minute, but complex pages, large graphics files, animations, or JAVA programs add bulk to the page and increase the time considerably. Another important factor is compatibility. HTML 4.0 was introduced in November 1997 in order to overcome the possibility of customized and out-of-date browsers. The speed problem may fade with time as technology improves, but the requirements of good, legible design will not change. Most Web sites are based on text, and most of this is intended to be read for information rather than for impact. Good typography and sensible background colours are essential.

... and keep it alive Web sites need maintaining. Organizations and support companies usually appoint a 'Web master' to manage the workings of the site, receive comments, and sort out problems, and at least one person should be in charge of keeping the content up to date. Finally, the opportunity for visitor feedback – typically via a hyperlink to an e-mail address – will provide a means of assessing visitors' impressions of the site. Even home pages can incorporate a visitor counter to record site 'hits', and commercial sites often capture visitor e-mail addresses for mailings.

Stephen Ball

↪ carriage return, at which point the command, if valid, is executed. An example of a command line interface is the DOS prompt.

A menu-driven interface presents various options to the user in the form of a list, from which commands may be selected. Types of menu include the menu bar, which displays the top-level options available to the user as a single line across the top of the screen; selecting one of these options displays a pull-down menu. Programs such as Microsoft Word use menus in this way.

In a graphical user interface, programs and files appear as icons (small pictures), user options are selected from pull-down menus, and data are displayed in windows (rectangular areas), which the operator can manipulate in various ways. The operator uses a pointing device, typically a ↝ mouse, to make selections and initiate actions.

The study of the ways in which people interact with computers is a subbranch of ergonomics. It aims to make it easier for people to use computers effectively and comfortably, and has become a focus of research for many national and international programmes.

utility program systems program designed to perform a specific task related to the operation of the computer when requested to do so by the computer user. For example, a utility program might be used to complete a screen dump, format a disk, or convert the format of a data file so that it can be accessed by a different applications program.

UTP abbreviation for ↝ unshielded twisted pair.

UUCP abbreviation for *Unix to Unix Copy Program*, protocol which allows ↝ Unix users to share files, read ↝ Usenet articles, and exchange ↝ e-mail. The system is based on computers regularly 'polling' (connecting to) each other to swap data. Polling can take place via an ordinary telephone connection or over the Internet.

UUencode ↝ utility program that converts a ↝ binary file (typically, a program or graphics file) into ↝ ASCII text suitable for inclusion in ↝ e-mail or ↝ Usenet messages. The recipient then UUdecodes the text file, reconverting it from ASCII to the original binary file.

UUNET Technologies, Inc US-based provider of Internet access. UUNET was the first commercial Internet Service Provider, founded in 1987; the company now has an international network of ↝ PoPs and is a major ↝ backbone provider. It acquired ↝ PIPEX from Unipalm in 1996 (and spun it off again in 1998) and is now itself part of WorldCom Inc.

Vactor contraction of *virtual actor*, animated character moved and voiced by an actor behind the scenes using a ⇝ Waldo and dataglove to control the character.

validation process of checking input data to ensure that it is complete, accurate, and reasonable. Although it would be impossible to guarantee that only valid data are entered into a computer, a suitable combination of validation checks should ensure that most errors are detected.

vanilla slang word for any product or service that lacks extra features or enhancements but delivers the basic functionality required. The usage was derived from the ice cream market when Americans were being overwhelmed by the choice of flavours.

variable quantity that can take different values. Variables can be used to represent different items of data in the course of a program.

A computer programmer will choose a symbol to represent each variable used in a program. The computer will then automatically assign a memory location to store the current value of each variable, and use the chosen symbol to identify this location.

For example, the letter P might be chosen by a programmer to represent the price of an article. The computer would automatically reserve a memory location with the symbolic address P to store the price being currently processed.

A global variable is one that can be accessed by any program instruction; a local variable is one that can only be accessed by the instructions within a particular subroutine.

VBI abbreviation for ⇝ vertical blanking interval.

vCard abbreviation for *virtual business card*, emerging standard format through which users can exchange name and address information even if they use different and incompatible contact management programs from different companies (or sometimes programs from the same company, such as Microsoft). Users with handheld computers can *beam* cards to one another using ⇝ IrDA links. A vCard can also replace a ⇝ sig at the end of an e-mail message. If the vCard data is saved as a .vcf file, it can be loaded into a compatible program such as the address book supplied with Microsoft's Internet Explorer 4 Web browser.

VDU abbreviation for ⇝ visual display unit.

vector graphics computer graphics that are stored in the computer memory by using geometric formulas. Vector graphics can be transformed (enlarged, rotated, stretched, and so on) without loss of picture resolution. It is also possible to select and transform any of the components of a vector-graphics display because each is separately defined in the computer memory. In these respects vector graphics are superior to ⇝ raster graphics. Vector graphics are typically used for drawing applications, allowing the user to create and modify technical diagrams such as designs for houses or cars.

verification process of checking that data being input to a computer have been accurately copied from a source document.

This may be done visually, by checking the original copy of the data against the copy shown on the VDU screen. A more thorough method is to enter the data twice, using two different keyboard operators, and then to check the two sets of input copies against each other. The checking is normally carried out by the computer itself, any differences between the two copies being reported for correction by one of the keyboard operators.

Where large quantities of data have to be input, a separate machine called a verifier may be used to prepare fully verified tapes or disks for direct input to the main computer.

vertical blanking interval *VBI*, brief space between the drawing of television frames when no picture information is transmitted. The VBI may appear as black bars at the top and bottom of the screen on badly adjusted TV sets. Several systems have exploited the VBI to broadcast data signals for other purposes. Examples include ⇝ teletext pages (Ceefax, Teletext), subtitles for deaf viewers, and Intel's ⇝ Intercast.

vertical spam on ⇝ Usenet, spam which consists of many, often repetitive, messages per day posted to the same newsgroup or small set of newsgroups. The effect is to drown out other, more useful, conversation in the newsgroup.

VESA local bus hardware configuration laid down by the Video Electronics Standards Association for computers based on the ⇝ Intel 486 chip. It was rendered obsolete by the arrival of Pentium chips and the PCI bus.

VGA abbreviation for *video graphics array*, colour display system that provides either 16 colours on screen and a resolution of 640×480, or 256 colours with a resolution of 320×200. ⇝ SVGA (Super VGA) provides even higher resolution and more colours.

video accelerator card circuit board that contains a special microchip to process display data, freeing the ⇝ central processing unit (CPU) for other tasks. A video accelerator card speeds up the performance of computers running ⇝ Windows and other ⇝ graphical user interfaces (GUIs) which place a heavy demand on processors.

video adapter ⇝ expansion board that allows display of graphics and colour. Commonly used video adapters for IBM PC-based systems are Hercules, CGA, EGA, VGA, XGA, and SVGA.

video adapter card circuit board that provides the data needed to create a display on a ↝ monitor. Common adapter cards include ↝ VGA and ↝ SVGA.

video capture board ↝ expansion board for a personal computer which digitizes an incoming stream of analogue video. Video capture boards vary widely in the amount of data they can handle; the cheapest can handle only single frames, while the most expensive and full-featured can handle full-motion video. Once the video stream has been digitized, it can be stored, copied, digitally edited, or retouched on the computer.

Video CD CD-ROM that conforms to Philips' White Book standard for displaying full-motion digital video using MPEG data compression. Video CD is used to store films on CD-ROM for playback on Philips ↝ CD-I players and personal computers or consoles equipped with an MPEG decoder in hardware and/or software.

TIP

videoconferencing

Over the Internet, systems such as CU-SeeMe take advantage of low-cost Internet connections.

videoconferencing system which allows people in different locations to interact via video and audio. It is essentially multiparty telephone conferencing with pictures. Older videoconferencing systems required expensive equipment set up in a special-purpose room. By the mid-1990s, newer systems became available for desktop videoconferencing using much cheaper equipment so that videoconferencing facilities could be deployed to individual users' desks.

video file file, such as an MPEG or ↝ AVI file, that contains compressed video information.

video graphics card ↝ expansion board that gives personal computers their display capability. The video graphics card must match the display monitor in functionality.

video-on-demand *VOD*, system for transmission of video by cable where specific videos can be selected from a choice button on the remote control that brings up a menu on screen. Once a choice has been selected a set-top box sends a query to the video server where the video is stored in compressed format. The server sends the video back through the system where it is decompressed by the set-top box. In 2000, various VOD services were being readied for live operation, with transmission via ↝ ADSL or cable.

videophone telephone allowing the sending and receiving of pictures as well as speech.

videotext system in which information (text and simple pictures) is displayed on a television (video) screen. There are two basic systems, known as ↝ teletext and ↝ viewdata. In the teletext system, information is broadcast with the ordinary television signals, whereas in the viewdata system, information is relayed to the screen from a central data bank via the telephone network. Both systems require the use of a television receiver (or a connected VTR) with special decoder.

viewdata system of displaying information on a television screen in which the information is extracted from a computer data bank and transmitted via the telephone lines. It is one form of ↝ videotext. British Telecom (then part of the General Post Office) developed the first viewdata system, Prestel, 1975–79. Similar systems are used in other countries. Users have access to a large store of information, presented on the screen in the form of 'pages'.

Since viewdata uses telephone lines, it can become a two-way interactive information system, making possible, for example, home banking and shopping. In contrast, the only user input allowed by the ↝ teletext system is to select the information to be displayed.

However, viewdata systems have generally not been successful (the notable exception is France's Minitel) and interest has switched to the World Wide Web.

TIP

virtual community

The most detailed examination of virtual communities is Howard Rheingold's book *The Virtual Community* (1992).

virtual without physical existence. Most computers have ↝ virtual memory, making their immediate-access memory seem larger than it is. ↝ Virtual reality is a computer simulation of a whole physical environment.

virtual community group of people joined by using the same electronic conferencing system. The sense of virtual community can be extremely strong, going beyond simply exchanging mutually useful information to helping with real-life events such as family illnesses and financial crises.

virtual corporation company with no real-life headquarters but whose employees and/or individual contractors are linked via telecommunications.

virtual memory technique whereby a portion of the computer backing storage, or external, ↝ memory is used as an extension of its immediate-access, or internal, memory. The contents of an area of the immediate-access memory are stored on, say, a hard disk while they are not needed, and brought back into main memory when required.

The process, called paging or segmentation, is controlled by the computer ↝ operating system and is hidden from the programmer, to whom the computer's internal memory appears larger than it really is. The technique can be successfully implemented only if very fast backing store is available, so that 'pages' of memory can be rapidly switched into and out of the immediate-access memory.

virtual private network *VPN*, corporate computer network where data is routed via the Internet rather than, or as well as, via more expensive dedicated lines. There are several ways of implementing a VPN but the data will usually

Digital Future and Virtual Reality

Beginnings Computing started with numbers, and computation means calculation. Indeed, it's hard to say where the computer business started because it came out of the continuous development of calculating machines in the 1930s and 1940s. The ABC (Atanasoff–Berry Calculator), for example, was designed to solve differential equations, while the US Army's ENIAC (Electronic Numerator, Integrator, Analyzer, and Computer) was built to calculate shell trajectories for artillery firing tables. When computers were first used in business, it was usually for handling numerical tasks such as stock control and financial calculations. This was mainly because of their huge cost. No company was going to spend millions to computerize trivial tasks like word processing, which could be done cheaply with mechanical typewriters.

Developments Nonetheless, word processing – or at least, text editing – was an obvious application for the computer. The idea of letting a particular number stand for a particular letter of the alphabet or punctuation mark goes back thousands of years, but a popular electronic system had been invented by Emile Baudot in 1877 for sending messages by telex, and it is still in use today.

If a particular number in a computer's memory could stand for an alphanumeric character, it could just as easily stand for a graphical one, or for a single point on a high-resolution display screen. In other words, computers could also be used to handle line drawings for computer-aided drafting. Thus as computers became cheaper and more powerful, and as video display terminals became more sophisticated, they were used to handle more and more items digitally. Pictures and sounds were followed by moving colour pictures with synchronized sound, until today, no one finds it strange that a home computer can play back video sequences and films that have been digitally encoded on compact discs.

Compact discs As computers have become more capable of handling complex analogue data – such as music and photo-quality images – so computers have started to take over the storage and reproduction of these data. The compact disc is a digital (computerized) medium for music, and digital radio is already being broadcast in many countries. Digital cameras are now starting to replace ones based on plastic films coated with chemicals.

Digital television Digital television broadcasts are also being scheduled to replace analogue channels, though in most cases all it means is that digital encoding is being applied to the same old analogue signals. Until HDTV (High-Definition Television) becomes popular, all digital television means is more of the same old stuff, albeit often in widescreen format.

Virtual reality In computing, interest has moved on from two-dimensional to three-dimensional representations, particularly in the production of 3D games. In the late 1990s, this led to a boom in sales of 3D accelerator cards designed to speed up the graphics in games such as *Quake II* and *Tomb Raider*.

Advanced 3D graphics are also being used to create 'virtual worlds' where, for example, architects can explore a building before it is built, or where people from across the world – each represented in the virtual world by a graphical 'persona' or 'avatar' – can meet up and chat online. For increased realism, a user can put on a virtual reality (VR) headset and move around inside an artificial reality created by one or more computers. The effects are still primitive (in most, the resolution is so low you'd qualify as legally blind) but the rapid growth in processor power and tumbling memory prices will make VR worlds increasingly detailed. Some will be more realistic, though many will simply be more fantastical. Researchers are also developing feedback mechanisms and body suits that will provide some form of touch sensitivity.

The way ahead The story of computing can be seen as the digitization of more and more items, including words, images, sounds, films, and television signals. This process will certainly continue, and no one can predict where it will end.

Jack Schofield

be encrypted to prevent it from being read as it passes across the public parts of the Internet.

virtual reality advanced form of computer simulation, in which a participant has the illusion of being part of an artificial environment. The participant views the environment through two tiny television screens (one for each eye) built into a visor. Sensors detect movements of the participant's head or body, causing the apparent viewing position to change. Gloves (datagloves) fitted with sensors may be worn, which allow the participant seemingly to pick up and move objects in the environment.

The technology is still under development but is expected to have widespread applications; for example, in military and surgical training, architecture, and home entertainment.

Virtual Reality Modelling Language method of displaying three-dimensional images on a Web page, usually abbreviated to ↪ VRML.

virus piece of ↪ software that can replicate and transfer itself from one computer to another, without the user being aware of it. Some viruses are relatively harmless, but others can damage or destroy data.

Viruses are written by anonymous programmers, often maliciously, and are spread on ↪ floppy disks, CD-ROMs, and via networks and e-mail (↪ worm). On 4 May 2000, the 'I Love You' worm virus affected an estimated 45 million computers worldwide, causing around $7 billion/£4.4 billion worth of damage. The virus exploited a feature in the Microsoft Outlook e-mail program to spread itself around the world faster than had ever been seen before. It was written by Onel de Guzman, a 22-year-old computer school dropout from Manila, Philippines.

Antivirus software can be used to detect and destroy well-known viruses, but new viruses continually appear, and these may bypass existing antivirus programs.

The Computer Misuse Act of 1990 made the release of computer viruses an offence. In November 1995 Christopher Pile (known as the Black Baron) was sentenced to 18 months in prison for writing a virus, becoming the first person to be imprisoned for this offence.

vision system computer-based device for interpreting visual signals from a video camera. Computer vision is important in robotics where sensory abilities would considerably increase the flexibility and usefulness of a robot.

Visual Basic Microsoft computer language based on ↪ BASIC. Visual Basic provides a rich set of visual programming tools that allow programmers to copy and paste common ↪ Windows components on to forms, in order to build Windows applications. BASIC is the language that is used to combine all the graphical components, and to code subroutines.

What Is Virtual Reality?

http://www.cms.dmu.ac.uk/~cph/VR/whatisvr.html

Text-based introduction to virtual reality and an information resource list. The site covers all major aspects of the subject, and also provides a great many literature and Internet references for further reading.

WEB LINK

CERT Coordination Center

http://www.cert.org/

Site tracking and summarizing problems with the Internet, such as virus activity, scans, probes, and attacks. Based at the Carnegie Mellon University in the USA, the CERT Coordination Center studies vulnerabilities in Internet systems, publishes security alerts, and offers advice and training for those looking to improve security on their Web sites.

WEB LINK

visual display unit *VDU*, computer terminal consisting of a keyboard for input data and a screen for displaying output. The oldest and most popular type of VDU screen is the cathode-ray tube (CRT), which uses essentially the same technology as a television screen. Other types use plasma display technology and ⇨ liquid-crystal displays.

Screen resolution (the quality of the display) is dependent on the number of ⇨ pixels used; the smaller the pixel, the higher the resolution. Within the limits of the resolution supported by the screen itself, the display quality can be altered by the user to suit particular applications.

In the same way, the number of screen colours supported by a VDU can be selected by the user.

visualization turning numerical data into graphics. A simple example is to create a bar chart from a set of sales figures; more complex types of visualization include fractals and other forms of computer-generated art.

visual programming programming method that uses a system of graphics, instead of text, to build software.

VLSI abbreviation for *very large-scale integration*, in electronics, the early-1990s level of advanced technology in the microminiaturization of ⇨ integrated circuits, and an order of magnitude smaller than ⇨ LSI (large-scale integration).

VMS operating system created in 1978 by ⇨ DEC for its VAX minicomputers. VMS has since been rewritten for DEC Alpha-based machines, and renamed OpenVMS. OpenVMS provides a high level of availability, scalability, and data integrity, and is still a very good operating system for operations that use large volumes of data. Applications written for Windows NT can also run without difficulty in OpenVMS.

V numbers series of ⇨ protocols issued by the CCITT defining the rate at which modems transfer data. The numbers have come to designate a modem's speed: V.32 modems transmit at up to 9,600 ⇨ bits per second (bps); V.32bis at up to 14,400 bps; and V.34 at up to 28,800 bps.

voice input alternative name for ⇨ speech recognition.

voice mail ⇨ electronic mail including spoken messages and audio. Messages can also be generated electronically using ⇨ speech synthesis. In offices, voice mail systems are often included in computerized telephone switchboards.

voice modem ⇨ modem which handles voice as well as data communications, so that it can be used to add the capabilities of a ⇨ voice mail system to a personal computer.

Computer Viruses

Top ten Several of the biggest and most publicized computer failures of 1999 and 2000 were due to computer viruses. Unlike older viruses, which typically infected a single computer and spread when users shared floppy disks, these viruses spread across the world at lightning speed, infecting tens of thousands of computers even before the news hit television. Melissa and the Love Bug, the best-known of these, spread by e-mail using techniques that made them look to recipients like files sent to them by colleagues or friends they could trust. While the viruses themselves were harmless, the volume of e-mail they caused flooded some companies' communications systems to the point where they had to close down.

Several conditions conspire to make viruses so widespread and dangerous. First is the growing use of e-mail both within companies and among individuals. Second is the widespread use of standardized software, such as the Microsoft Windows operating system, the Outlook e-mail program, and the word-processing package Word. Melissa and the Love Bug, and other similar viruses, were able to play on common file formats, directory structures, and even Word's programming language to make the infected computers send out many copies of the viruses to the real-world contacts of the computers' owners. Third is the natural human instinct to trust that the people one knows are 'safe'.

Computer viruses aren't viruses in the biological sense: they are scraps of code that 'infect' the computer by attaching themselves to key pieces of software and reprogramming them. Like the biological viruses from which they take their name, computer viruses use the computer they infect to help them propagate; also like biological viruses, they have a variety of effects on their host computers, some of them extremely unpleasant. Some of the more famous ones erase the hard disks of infected computers (Concept), make letters fall down the screen into a heap on the bottom (Cascade), or send messages (Form, Stoned). One of the best-known viruses is Michelangelo, which activates itself on Michelangelo's birthday (March 6) and overwrites the computer's hard disk with zeroes.

Virus infection Viruses are transmitted from one computer to another via infected program files or files containing executable program code. They work in a variety of different ways, but essentially they attach themselves to common software and cause the computer to behave in unexpected ways. They can hide out in files or in the so-called 'boot sector' (that is, the sector that's read when the disk is first inserted when the computer is started) of a floppy or hard disk for long periods of time, only making their presence obvious after they have infected many files. The effect of the virus infection, such as the cascade of letters or hard disk erasure, is known as the 'payload'. Many viruses are harmless and started as jokes to which the infective code was added. Others, however, are extremely destructive, and even harmless viruses must be taken seriously since they may carry with them unknown, more destructive, functions. In general, virus infections should be cleaned up as soon as they are discovered, and a warning should be sent to anyone who has recently exchanged files or floppy disks with the infected system. If you suspect your computer has a virus, you should close down and turn off the machine immediately. Restart the computer from a write-protected floppy disk, and run a program known as a virus scanner to check the system. Virus scanners are available from companies such as Symantec and Network Associates; there is also a good, free virus scanner called F-Prot which is available over the Internet. Because new viruses are constantly being written and released, you should make sure you have the latest version of the scanner you use (most are updated monthly). Most scanners come with a utility to clean up if a virus infection is detected.

Virus screening Scanners use a variety of techniques to detect viruses. Checksums use known file sizes and checking techniques to find alterations to commonly infected files. Others look for common virus techniques, such as hooking into specific parts of the computer. You should set the scanner to check your computer when you start it up and to examine all files you download from the Net and all floppy and CD-ROM disks, even those from apparently

Computer Viruses (continued)

reliable sources such as commercial software companies and magazine cover disks. This may sound like overkill, but viruses have been distributed by all those means, and the nuisance of checking is significantly less than the nuisance of having your computer infected, as clean-up will include not only cleaning and checking every file on the computer but also all the back-ups as well. You should not assume that every time anything goes wrong with your computer that means it's been infected by a virus. Alarming symptoms like a hard disk crash or the appearance of unfamiliar graphics may have 'natural' – or at least, non-virus – causes. Clearer signs of infection are if a virus scanner identifies several files as being infected by the same virus, especially if that virus is one that's known to be 'in the wild' (some viruses have never been seen outside a computer lab), or if several scanners agree you have a virus, or if several .COM or .EXE files have increased in size by the same amount. The list of which viruses are most common changes regularly; in 1998 the viruses causing the most trouble were Microsoft Word macro viruses, easily moved from one machine to another when users swapped documents written using the Word program. The macro viruses copy themselves into the standard document templates in Word and thereafter (or until they are eradicated) infect every document created on the infected machine. Similar macro viruses exist for Excel (spreadsheet) and PowerPoint (presentation graphics). File and boot-sector viruses, which were the big problems in the early 1990s, have declined in popularity.

The Internet brings increased risk
You cannot 'catch' a virus by opening an e-mail message that is composed only of text. Viruses require executable files to do their stuff, which means they must be embedded in programs. Even if the text of the e-mail message is code for a program, it must be compiled into an actual executable file for a virus embedded in it to have any effect. Many people don't know this, though, and there is a hoax virus message that circulates on the Net that claims a virus called, variously, Penpal Greetings, Join The Crew, or Good Times (its original name), is at loose on the Net and that opening any e-mail message with those words in the title will unleash it to destroy your hard drive. When you receive such a message, do not circulate it further: the 'virus' is the infection of the Net with megabytes upon megabytes of this junk. However, your PC can be infected if you run an executable file attached to an e-mail message or if you open a Microsoft Word file that's infected with a macro virus, and some e-mail packages make the process of decoding and opening attached files automatic. Because of the dangers, you should turn off the automatic feature and you should ensure that you use an up-to-date anti-virus scanner to check all attached executable and word-processed files before opening them. Alternatively, convince people to send the word-processed files as plain text pasted into an e-mail message, where there's no risk and the resulting message is many times smaller.

Wendy M Grossman

Primarily aimed at small and home-based businesses, voice modems use a built-in ⮠ DSP and typically also include fax facilities.

voice output alternative name for ⮠ speech synthesis.

voice-to-MIDI converter microphone that sends human vocal input to a synthesizer. This system of singing to run a synthesizer does not work well unless the singer has perfect pitch, so it is not commonly used.

volatile memory ⮠ memory that loses its contents when the power supply to the computer is disconnected.

Von Neumann, John (1903–1957) or *Johann Von Neumann*, Hungarian-born US scientist and mathematician, a pioneer of computer design.

He designed and supervised the construction of the first computer able to use a flexible stored program (named EDVAC) at the Institute for Advanced Study at Princeton 1940–1952. This work laid the foundations for the design of all subsequent programmable computers.

VPN abbreviation for ⇨ virtual private network.

vPoP acronym for *virtual point of presence*, telephone link which enables users to connect to a distant point of presence (⇨ PoP) for the price of a local call.

VRAM acronym for *video random-access memory*, form of ⇨ RAM that allows simultaneous access by two different devices, so that graphics can be handled at the same time as data are updated. VRAM improves graphic display performance.

VR browser application that enables PC users to 'walk through' a ⇨ virtual reality scene on their monitors.

VRML abbreviation for *Virtual Reality Modelling Language*, method of displaying three-dimensional images on a ⇨ Web page. VRML, which functions as a counterpart to ⇨ HTML, is a platform-independent language that creates a ⇨ virtual reality scene which users can 'walk' through and follow links much like a conventional Web page.

It is possible to use VRML to create, for example, a virtual museum with all the elements of a real museum, including corridors, display cases, and multimedia demonstrations.

Other possibilities include a Web market containing stalls with goods that can be 'handled' using a mouse, or a virtual library of 'books' which can be taken off 'shelves'.

VT-100 type number of a simple character-based computer terminal originally supplied by ⇨ DEC (Digital Equipment Corporation). VT-100 terminal emulation is commonly provided in personal computer communications software and may be useful for logging on to minicomputers and networks via the Internet.

WAIS abbreviation for *Wide Area Information Server*, software tool for searching for and retrieving information from a range of archives on the ↪ Internet.

wait state situation when the ↪ central processing unit or a ↪ bus is idle. Wait states are necessary because system components run at different speeds.

Waldo mechanical device, such as a gripper arm, that follows the movements of a human limb. Waldos were developed by the nuclear industry in the 1940s for handling hazardous substances at a safe distance, and were named after a 1942 story by science fiction writer Robert Heinlein.

walkthrough another name for ↪ flythrough.

walled garden restricted Internet service, limited to those Web sites an ↪ Internet Service Provider deems appropriate. Many ↪ WAP-based mobile Internet services use the walled garden approach.

wallpaper design used as a background 'desktop pattern' on ↪ graphical user interfaces (GUIs), such as Microsoft ↪ Windows or Apple's Mac OS, and visible when no windows are open. Users can choose from a range of different wallpapers, including plain colours, textures, and repeating patterns, or design their own.

WAN abbreviation for wide area ↪ network.

wand in ↪ virtual reality, simple input device to allow users to interact with onscreen objects in three dimensions.

Wang, An (1920–1990) Chinese-born US engineer, founder in 1951 of Wang Laboratories, one of the world's largest computer companies in the 1970s. In 1948 he invented the computer memory core, the most common device used for storing computer data before the invention of the integrated circuit (chip).

Wang emigrated to the USA in 1945. He developed his own company with the $500,000 he received from IBM from the sale of his patent. One of his early contracts was the first electronic scoreboard, installed at New York's Shea Stadium. His company took off in 1964 with the introduction of a desktop calculator. Later, Wang switched with great success to the newly emerging market for word-processing systems based on cheap silicon chips, turning Wang Laboratories into a multibillion-dollar company. But with the advent of the personal computer, the company fell behind and had to seek protection from its creditors. It staged a comeback, doubling in size 1994-97 to achieve annual revenues of $1.3 billion.

WAP acronym for *wireless application protocol*, initiative started in the 1990s by Unwired Planet and mobile phone manufacturers Motorola, Nokia, and Ericsson to develop a standard for delivering Web-like applications on a new

WAP Forum

http://www.wapforum.org/

Official home of the Wireless Application Protocol (WAP) Forum, an industry association comprising 90% of all organizations involved in WAP technology development, and a leading source of information about WAP and telephony.

WEB LINK

generation of ⤳ mobile phones. It is possible to use WAP phones for e-mail and messaging, reading Web pages, shopping, booking tickets, and making other financial transactions, as well as for phone calls.

The WAP protocol has many similarities to Internet technologies. For instance, the Wireless Markup Language (WML) used to create WAP pages is very similar to ⤳ HTML, which is used to create Web pages. Similarly, the WMLScript is based on JavaScript. Both WML and WMLScript are adapted and designed for a wireless environment, to address issues like limited ⤳ bandwidth and limited processing power in the mobile phone.

UK retailer WHSmith launched its WAP book retailing service in 2000, making it the first bookseller to support the mobile technology. Also in 2000, Manchester United football team and Vodafone announced a £30 million sponsorship deal: WAP users will receive news and scores on their handsets, and ultimately be able to watch live footage; the Vodafone motif will appear on the team's strip.

WAP is text-based, and limited by the slow transmission speed (9.6 Kbps) of the ⤳ GSM technology currently used by mobile phones. In addition, keying in text on a standard mobile phone is a time-consuming and frustrating task. Mobile phones are therefore unlikely to replace personal computers as the most popular method of surfing the Web until faster access technologies such as ⤳ GPRS and ⤳ UMTS are established. WAP does have a role to play, however, particularly in the transmission of location-based data to the mobile phone, such as information on restaurants, cinemas, clubs, and taxi services. The four mobile network operators in the UK are all introducing WAP services.

Warwick, Kevin (1954–   ) British computer scientist, with an interest in ⤳ artificial intelligence and cybernetics.

Warwick worked for ⤳ BT for six years, before taking his first degree at Aston University. Subsequently, he gained a PhD and became a research student at Imperial College, London. He held positions at Oxford, Newcastle, and Warwick universities, before becoming Professor of Cybernetics at the University of Reading.

Warwick's work at Reading includes research into artificial intelligence, control, and robotics. He forecast in 1997 that in 10 to 50 years' time, robots would exist that were more intelligent than human beings.

Warwick had a chip implanted in his arm for nine days in 1998, linked to devices in his departmental building. In 2000 he and his wife Irena both had chips implanted into their arms, connected to an external computer. He hoped that the computer would be able to read emotions such as pain, anger, and joy, and that he and his wife would be able to communicate their thoughts to each other electronically via the Internet.

Watson, Thomas (John), Jr (1914–1993) US business executive. He was president of IBM 1952-61 and placed the company at the centre of the industry. As chairman (1961-71) he committed IBM to a new line of computers in 1962, the S/360s, which revolutionized the industry. He was chairman of the executive committee (1971-79) and remained active at IBM into the 1980s, with two years out to serve as US ambassador to the USSR (1979–81).

Born in Dayton, Ohio, the son of the founder of International Business Machines (IBM), he joined the firm in 1937, then served with the US Air Force in World War II (1941–45).

Watson, Thomas John (1874–1956) US business executive. He worked at National Cash Register (NCR) in Dayton, Ohio (1896–1911), becoming general sales manager. During that period he learned the punch-card industry. Sales became the driving force in all he did, particularly after he formed International Business Machines (IBM) by merging several other companies in 1924. By 1929, IBM controlled 20% of the punch device market.

Watson was born in Cambell, New York. A brilliant salesman, he rose through the ranks of NCR. However, as NCR monopolized the cash register business, he nearly ended up in jail; along with other NCR executives, he was convicted and fined for criminal conspiracy in restraint of trade. After being thrown out of NCR, Watson became general manager of the tiny Computing-Tabulating-Recording Company (CTR) in New York, which was heir to the tabulating machines that Herman ⤳ Hollerith had developed for the US Census Bureau. Watson used what he had learned at NCR to develop CTR – which was later renamed IBM – into one of the world's largest and most profitable industrial corporations. When computers were developed, Watson's son and successor, Thomas Watson Jr, was able to convert IBM's monopoly of data processing using punched cards into a monopoly of commercial computing, which survived until microprocessors changed the nature of the business.

WAV abbreviation of *Windows WAVeform*, audio file format for ⤳ IBM-compatible PCs, widely used to distribute sounds over the Internet. WAV files, which contain a digitized recording of a sound, bear the suffix .wav.

wavelength division multiplexing *WDM*, technique for sending multiple streams of light down a single fibre-optic cable. The different signals have slightly different wavelengths, or colours. WDM can greatly increase the capacity of existing fibre optic links and thus dramatically lower the cost of long-distance communications. BT started operating its first two WDM links in 1997 with 16 channels, which made them 16 times faster than before.

wavetable synthesizer ⤳ MIDI synthesizer that uses sampling – recordings of actual musical instruments – to create sounds. The authenticity of the sound source means that wavetable synthesizers can achieve very realistic results.

WBT abbreviation for a ⤳ Windows-Based Terminal. WBT is sometimes pronounced 'wabbit'.

WDM abbreviation for ⤳ wave division multiplexing.

wearable computers computers intended to be worn on the body, in some cases for disabled people. Wearable computers can provide easy access to data, and a note-taking facility, for mobile field-service workers and professionals, such as doctors, lawyers, and members of the emergency services.

Web authoring tool software for creating ↪ Web pages. The basic Web authoring tool is ↪ HTML, the source code that determines how a Web page is constructed and how it looks. Other programs, such as Java and ↪ VRML, can also be incorporated to enhance Web pages with animations and interactive features. Commercial authoring tools include HoTMetaL PRO, NetObjects' Fusion, and Microsoft's Front Page.

Web browser client software that allows access to the World Wide Web. See ↪ browser.

Webcam any camera connected to the Internet, usually for the purpose of displaying an image on a Web page. Webcams are trained on a wide range of famous sights such as London's Tower Bridge. They have also been placed inside birds' nesting boxes, refrigerators, strip clubs, and bedrooms. What may have been the first Webcam was aimed at a flask of coffee in the Cambridge University Computer Laboratory. An American, Jennifer Ringley, pioneered the use of Webcams to put her private life on public display with the JenniCam.

Webcast World Wide Web equivalent of a radio or television broadcast. Any service that is regularly or continuously updated – such as sports results and share price information – can be described as a Webcast, but the term is increasingly used for *live* events where sounds and images are transmitted in a format such as ↪ RealAudio or RealVideo.

Web hosting many ↪ Internet Service Providers (ISPs) host Web sites on computers in secure ↪ datacentres for both businesses and consumers. Sites can be stored on dedicated Web servers, on servers shared with other customers of the ISP, or on a company's own servers sited in the host's datacentre (known as 'co-locating').

Webmaster ↪ system administrator for a server on the ↪ World Wide Web.

Web page ↪ hypertext document on the ↪ World Wide Web.

Web site collection of ↪ Web pages belonging to the same company, organization, or individual. The first Web site page to be displayed on a ↪ browser is known as the ↪ home page. Sites designed to be a gateway to the rest of the ↪ World Wide Web are called ↪ portals. A Web site may be physically located on a local Web ↪ server or hosted by an ↪ Internet Service Provider (see ↪ Web hosting).

Web site traffic analysis shows which ↪ Web pages a visitor is viewing, for how long, and at what time. At the top end of the market, sophisticated analysis programs provide ↪ real-time ↪ electronic commerce revenue tracking. This can show revenue by product over time, reveal which visitors are browsing and which purchasing, and track revenue, differentiating between first-time and repeat buyers.

Web TV loosely, any set-top box or similar system that connects a television set to the Internet, mainly for the purpose of browsing Web pages.

WebTV Networks is a US company, founded in 1995 by Steve Perlman, Bruce Leak, and Phil Goldman, which provides Internet access via the television set. The company was bought by ⤳ Microsoft in 1997.

Webzine magazine published on the Web, instead of on paper. Notable examples include *FEED* (about culture and technology), *Slate* (a serious periodical funded by ⤳ Microsoft), and *Suck* (satire).

WELL, the acronym for *Whole Earth 'Lectronic Link*, San Francisco-based electronic conferencing system. It was founded in 1985 by Stewart Brand, with Larry Brilliant, Matthew McClure, and Kevin Kelly (later founding editor of ⤳ *Wired* magazine). The WELL includes among its 11,000 members a mix of leading journalists and writers, Grateful Dead fans, and technological inventors.

The WELL featured in the 1995 arrest of hacker Kevin ⤳ Mitnick, and was the site where the first few Computers, Freedom, and Privacy conferences (annual gatherings to discuss the future impact of technology) were planned. The WELL was bought in 1994 by Reebok founder Bruce Katz. In 1999, the WELL was acquired by the online magazine Salon.com.

whois searchable database of every registered domain and the names of their users. A special application, also called whois, is needed to search the database.

wide area network *WAN*, ⤳ network that connects computers distributed over a wide geographical area. 'Dumb' terminals or microcomputers act as workstations, which connect to remote systems via a local host computer.

WIDs acronym for ⤳ Wireless Information Devices.

Wiener, Norbert (1894–1964) US mathematician, credited with the establishment of the science of cybernetics in his book *Cybernetics* (1948). In mathematics, he laid the foundation of the study of stochastic processes (those dependent on random events), particularly Brownian motion.

Wiener was born in Columbia, Missouri, and received his PhD from Harvard at the age of 19. He then went to Europe to study under leading mathematicians (Bertrand Russell at Cambridge, England, and David Hilbert at Göttingen, Germany). From 1919 he taught at the Massachusetts Institute of Technology, becoming professor in 1932. He devoted much of his efforts to methodology, developing mathematical approaches that could usefully be applied to continuously changing processes.

During World War II, Wiener worked on the control of anti-aircraft guns (which required him to consider factors such as the machinery itself, the gunner, and the unpredictable evasive action on the part of the target's pilot), on filtering 'noise' from useful information for radar, and on coding and decoding. His investigations stimulated his interest in information transfer and processes such as information feedback.

Gif Wizard

http://www.gifwizard.com/

Essential bookmark for all devoted (or aspiring) Web writers, which offers a convenient wizard for reducing the size of GIF images, with trouble-free, instant delivery of up to 90% reductions.

WEB LINK

Wiener, Norbert

http://www-groups.dcs.st-and.ac.uk/history/Mathematicians/Wiener_Norbert.html

Site devoted to the life and contributions of Norbert Wiener. In addition to biographical information, you will find a list of references about Wiener and links to other essays in the archive that reference him.

WEB LINK

---

wild card character which represents 'any character' in a search or command. When comparing ⮑ strings, the computer does not seek a precise match for a wild card character. The most useful wildcards are ?, which matches any single character, and *, which matches any number of characters, including zero. Hence the ⮑ DOS commands DEL *.* – delete all files – and COPY *.DOC – copy all files with the filename extension 'DOC'.

Wilkes, Maurice Vincent (1913–   ) English mathematician who led the team at Cambridge University that built the EDSAC (electronic delay storage automatic calculator) in 1949, one of the earliest of the British electronic computers.

Wilkes was born in Dudley and studied at Cambridge. During World War II he became involved with the development of radar. He was director of the Cambridge Mathematical Laboratory 1946–80. In the late 1940s Wilkes and his team began to build the EDSAC. At the time, electronic computers were in their infancy. Wilkes chose the serial mode, in which the information in the computer is processed in sequence (and not several parts at once, as in the parallel type). This design incorporated mercury delay lines (developed at the Massachusetts Institute of Technology, USA) as the elements of the memory.

In May 1949 the EDSAC ran its first program and became the first delay-line computer in the world. From early 1950 it offered a regular computing facility to the members of Cambridge University, the first general-purpose computer service. Much time was spent by the research group on programming and on the compilation of a library of programs. The EDSAC was in operation until 1958.

EDSAC II came into service in 1957. This was a parallel-processing machine and the delay line was abandoned in favour of magnetic storage methods.

WIMP acronym for *windows, icons, menus, pointing device*, another name for ⮑ graphical user interface (GUI).

window rectangular area on the screen of a ⮑ graphical user interface. A window is used to display data and can be manipulated in various ways by the computer user.

Windows originally Microsoft's ⮑ graphical user interface (GUI) for IBM PCs and clones running ⮑ MS-DOS. Windows has developed into a family of operating systems that run on a wide variety of computers, from pen-operated palmtop organizers to large, multi-processor computers in corporate data centres.

Windows 95 is designed for homes and offices and retains maximum compatibility with programs written for the MS-DOS operating system and Windows 3. Windows NT is a 32-bit ⮑ multitasking operating system designed for business use, especially on workstations and server computers, where it is seen as a rival to ⮑ Unix and ⮑ Novell NetWare. PocketPC, formerly known as Windows CE, is a small, modular operating system that supports a subset of the Windows applications programming interface. It is used in handheld personal computers (HPCs), Windows-Based Terminals (WBTs), and consumer electronics products such as games consoles, DVD players, and television set-top boxes for Internet use. Windows 95 is limited to Intel and x86-compatible processors, but both NT and CE run on a variety of chips from different manufacturers. Windows 95, by far the most popular version, was revised three times, and in 1998 Microsoft launched an updated version called Windows 98. In February 2000 Microsoft launched Windows 2000, which will eventually replace Windows NT 4.0 and was designed to be used in ᔊ local area networks. It was originally intended to replace Windows 98 also, but, although the products may merge in the future, Windows 98's successor, Windows ME, is scheduled for release in late 2000.

In 1998 Microsoft estimated that worldwide there were 140 million users of Windows 95 or Windows NT.

Windows-Based Terminal *WBT*, network computer designed to display Microsoft Windows programs, such as Word and Excel, which are being run not on the local machine but on a server computer. WBTs have their own processor and memory but do not necessarily have a hard drive and usually will not have a floppy disk drive. WBTs typically use Microsoft's ᔊ RDP protocol and/or ICA, from ᔊ Citrix.

Windows Open Services Architecture *WOSA*, set of interfaces defined by Microsoft to enable Windows programs from different vendors to communicate with one another.

Windows WAVeform audio file format commonly abbreviated to ᔊ WAV.

WIN.INI acronym for *Windows Initialization*, file used by Microsoft Windows to store a range of settings that in general govern the appearance of Windows and some Windows 3 applications. Changes made via Windows 3's Control Panel program are often stored in WIN.INI. In Windows 95/98, control has been moved to the Registry.

Winsock contraction of Windows socket, program that supplies an interface between Windows software and a ᔊ TCP/IP application.

Wintel term for personal computers based on Microsoft Windows software and Intel processors. The advantage of the term is that it avoids reference to IBM compatibility, since IBM has not set standards in the PC industry since 1987.

Wintel PC standards are decided at frequent WinHEC (Windows Hardware Engineering) conferences, mainly under the direction of Microsoft, Intel, Compaq (the largest PC manufacturer), and Phoenix (a supplier of BIOS chips).

Wired US computing magazine founded in 1993 to serve as the voice of the 'digital revolution'. It is based in San Francisco.

Wired Ventures manages a number of advertising-supported sites on the Web, including *HotWired* (http://www.hotwired.com/). It also owns the satirical site *Suck* (http://www.suck.com/) and the search engine HotBot

---

Windows98 Annoyances

http://www.annoyances.org/win98/

Forum for intermediate to advanced users of Windows 95 who seek answers to annoying questions or have helpful tips they wish to share with others. Troubleshooting techniques, lost files, screen problems, bugs, and other topics are thoroughly discussed in this site.

WEB LINK

Winfiles.com

http://www.winfiles.com/

Site containing a wealth of information relating to the Windows operating system. As well as 'Tips and tricks', which include a variety of hints and shortcuts on all aspects of Windows, there is also a comprehensive drivers section.

WEB LINK

(http://www.hotbot.com/). By 1996, *Wired* had become such a strongly recommended magazine that there were a number of parodies, including *ReWired* and, on the Web, *HowTired* (http://www.howtired.com/).

wired gloves interface worn on the hands for ↝ virtual reality applications. The gloves detect the movement of the hands, enabling the user to 'touch' and 'move' objects in a virtual environment.

wire frame method of creating three-dimensional computerized animations by drawing a series of frames showing the moving image in outline, like a moving skeleton. When the designer is satisfied with the action of the wire-frame figure, he or she adds the 'skin', superimposing textures to give the final effect.

Wireless Information Devices *WIDS*, generic label for a growing class of portable systems such as mobile phones, handheld computers, digital cameras, and electronic organizers.

Wirth, Niklaus (1934–) Swiss-born developer of computer languages such as Euler, Pascal, Modula-2 and OBERON. He was born in Zürich, Switzerland, and has spent most of his life there and in California, USA. His programming languages have been designed to encourage good programming practices leading to reliability and the re-usability of code. This restrictive approach has found favour in the academic world, where Pascal is widely taught. So far, however, most commercial programmers working on personal computer software have largely ignored his languages and his advice.

wizard interactive tool developed by ↝ Microsoft that 'talks' program users through a complex operation, such as creating a ↝ template or a presentation. The wizard presents the user with a series of ↝ dialog boxes asking simple questions in ordinary language, which the user answers by choosing ↝ radio buttons, checking boxes, and entering information by keyboard.

The term wizard stems from programmers' slang, where it means an expert in a particular piece of software or hardware, capable of answering all manner of queries, fixing faults, and dealing with emergencies.

word group of bits (binary digits) that a computer's central processing unit treats as a single working unit. The size of a word varies from one computer to another and, in general, increasing the word length leads to a faster and more powerful computer. In the late 1970s and early 1980s, most microcomputers were 8-bit machines. During the 1980s 16-bit microcomputers were introduced and 32-bit microcomputers are now available. Mainframe computers may be 32-bit or 64-bit machines.

Word versatile and powerful word-processing program, developed by ↝ Microsoft for ↝ IBM-compatible and Apple ↝ Macintosh PCs. The program began its life as an ↝ MS-DOS program in 1983, and a year later it was

HomeRF

http://www.homerf.org/

Basic introduction to wireless home systems using Shared Wireless Access Protocol (SWAP). This developing technology will enable several personal computers to share a single broadband Internet connection, and swap files and drives between PCs and other electronic devices without wires, and will allow voice-activated control of home electronics.

WEB LINK

Software Applications

Start simple The Internet and multimedia may enjoy all the hype, but the most useful software programs you can buy for a personal computer are the old faithfuls of word processor, database, and spreadsheet.

Full-strength business programs are extremely powerful, but also rather complicated, and many people find they do not use all of the available features. For the novice, the best approach, and the best value, are offered by integrated packages, such as ClarisWorks or Microsoft Works. These generally combine word processing, spreadsheet, database, and drawing.

The best way to buy full-strength software, such as Microsoft's Word word processor, or Lotus's 1-2-3 spreadsheet, is in a suite, such as Microsoft Office or Lotus SmartSuite. These are more expensive and usually include word processor, spreadsheet, database, and presentation graphics software, and maybe extras like a diary/organizer.

In practice, most computer buyers do not need to purchase their basic software, because it is included with the computer. These software bundles typically include an integrated package or suite, home finance software, reference works like encyclopedias, and some educational and entertainment titles. Computer manufacturers and retailers buy the software cheaply in bulk, so it often represents excellent value. Beginners should not worry which particular package they are getting, since most of the big-name products are of similar quality.

However, it pays to examine the software bundle carefully. Some vendors cut corners by supplying inferior software, outdated versions, or editions with US spellings and voices. Sometimes they do not supply instruction manuals or the original disks, and occasionally they have copied the software illegally.

Whether software is bundled or purchased separately, it is worth registering with the publisher. You may then be notified when 'bugs' (errors) are found and when new versions are published, and you may receive discounts on other products. You will also get free telephone support, though usually only for a limited period. Most support calls relate to installation and learning, so it pays to start using the software straightaway.

Do you need to upgrade? Most major software packages are upgraded every 12–18 months. For many users this is a source of irritation rather than jubilation, and although publishers offer discounts, many people prefer to stick to the version they are familiar with rather than suffer the upheaval of upgrading – especially since the new version often requires a more powerful computer. Businesses seldom skip more than one generation of software, since support is harder to find on old versions, and it may confuse new recruits used to working on the latest releases.

Other software sources An alternative source of cheap software is shareware (programs published by independent authors, who distribute them for free and rely on people's honesty to pay a small fee if they use them). Shareware and free software are often available on magazine cover disks, and via the Internet, though anyone downloading software from the Internet should beware of viruses.

In future, the Internet may become the major medium for software distribution, and could revolutionize the way software is produced and sold. Cheap network computers may have no internal applications software, but call up small programs (applets) over the network as and when they are required, perhaps on a pay-as-you-use basis. Alternatively, conventional packaged software may still be sold, but made up of self-contained components. This component-ware will be tailored to the individual user. Computer enthusiasts may do this themselves, but most people will buy assemblages of components specially related to their profession, hobbies, or age-group.

Paul Bray

released as one of the first programs for the Macintosh. The advanced features and ease of use of Version 6.0, released in 1994, established Word as the market leader in its field.

WordPerfect word-processing program for various computers produced by US software company WordPerfect Corp. It was first released in 1982, and by 1987 was the dominant ⮑ MS-DOS word processor, rapidly eclipsing the previous leader, WordStar, by offering many more features, despite having the reputation of being difficult to learn.

WordPerfect Corp was slow to release a version of WordPerfect for ⮑ Windows, and when it did appear in 1992 it suffered in comparison with Microsoft ⮑ Word. WordPerfect Corp was taken over by ⮑ Novell, but the union was not a success, and most of its software was sold on cheaply to Corel.

word processing input, amendment, manipulation, storage, and retrieval of text. A computer system that runs such software is known as a word processor. Since word-processing programs became available to microcomputers, the method has largely replaced the typewriter for producing

Software	Manufacturer	Description
TopCopy	Top Level	professional program; provides integration with database and accounts
Word	Microsoft	market leader; powerful and easy to use with sophisticated spell checking
Word Pro	Lotus	formerly Ami Pro; good value program; strong on tabling and charting
WordPerfect	Corel	full-featured, including format and spell checking; customizable interface

word processing
Some major word processing-programs with main functions listed

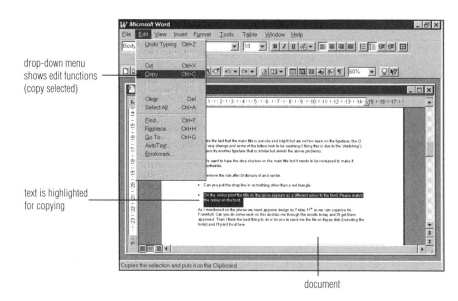

drop-down menu shows edit functions (copy selected)

text is highlighted for copying

document

word processing
A word processing software package enables text to be manipulated in a variety of ways, such as copying and pasting and changing its size and typeface.

letters or other text. Typical facilities include insert, delete, cut and paste, reformat, search and replace, copy, print, mail merge, and spelling check.

The leading word-processing programs include Microsoft Word, the market leader, Lotus WordPro, and Corel WordPerfect.

workgroup small group of computer users who need to share data and computer facilities.

workstation high-performance desktop computer with strong graphics capabilities, traditionally used for engineering (↝ CAD and ↝ CAM), scientific research, and desktop publishing. From 1985–95, workstations were frequently based on fast RISC (reduced instruction-set computer) chips running the Unix operating system. However, the market is under attack from 'Wintel' PCs with Intel Pentium processors running Microsoft Windows NT, which are cheaper and run PC software as well as workstation programs. By 1997, four of the five leading workstation manufacturers – DEC, Hewlett-Packard, IBM, and Silicon Graphics Inc, but not Sun Microsystems – had committed to supporting NT.

WorldCom international telecommunications company, founded in the USA in 1983 as Long Distance Discount Service (LDDS), a name thought up for the founders by a coffee shop employee in Hattiesburg, Mississippi. Bernie Ebbers, who was an early investor in the company, became its chief executive in 1985. The company was renamed WorldCom in 1995.

In 1996, WorldCom acquired MFS, a networking company that had already bought the ↝ Internet Service Provider ↝ UUNET Technologies, Inc. WorldCom completed the takeover of its rival ↝ MCI in 1998, becoming MCI WorldCom. In 1999, MCI WorldCom announced that it would acquire Sprint, another US telecommunications rival, whereupon the resulting company would revert to the name WorldCom. However, the takeover was abandoned in July 2000, as a result of conditions imposed by the US Department of Justice, which were not acceptable to either company.

World Intellectual Property Organization *WIPO*, specialist agency of the United Nations established 1974 to coordinate the international protection (initiated by the Paris convention 1883) of inventions, trademarks, and industrial designs, and also literary and artistic works (as initiated by the Berne convention 1886).

In December 1999, WIPO helped to put into place the Uniform Dispute Resolution Policy (UDRP), now the basis for settling trademark conflicts on the Internet. The policy was instituted after a study lasting a year by the ↝ Internet Corporation for Assigned Names and Numbers (ICANN).

World Wide Web *WWW*, ↝ hypertext system for publishing information on the ↝ Internet. World Wide Web documents ('Web pages') are text files coded using ↝ HTML to include text and graphics, and are stored on a Web server connected to the Internet. Web pages may also contain dynamic objects and

---

About the WWW

http://www.w3.org/WWW/

A good starting point for exploring the Internet as it includes 'talks' by members of the WWW Consortium team, and explains some different aspects of using the Web, as well as containing a brief history of the World Wide Web.

WEB LINK

History of the Web

http://dbhs.wvusd.k12. ca.us/Chem-History/ Hist-of-Web.html

Transcript of *Birthplace of the Web* by Eric Berger, Office of Public Affairs at FermiLab. The text covers the origins of the Web as a means of communication between scientists at CERN and at FermiLab, and describes how one person's idea in 1991 has brought about a social and cultural revolution in just a few years.

WEB LINK

Java applets for enhanced animation, video, sound, and interactivity. In 2000 it was estimated that there were over one billion pages on the Web.

The Web server can be any computer, from the simplest Apple Macintosh to the largest mainframe, if Web server software is available. Every Web page has a URL (Uniform Resource Locator) – a unique address (usually starting with http://www) which tells a browser program (such as Netscape Navigator or Microsoft Internet Explorer) where to find it. An important feature of the World Wide Web is the facility to link between documents. This enables readers to follow whatever aspects of a subject interest them most. These links may connect to different computers all over the world. Interlinked or nested Web pages belonging to a single organization are known as a Web site.

The original World Wide Web program was created in 1990 for internal use at CERN, the Geneva-based physics research centre, by Tim Berners-Lee and Robert Cailliau. The system was released on the Internet in 1991, but only caught on in 1993, following the release of Mosaic, an easy-to-use PC-compatible browser. The exponential growth of the Internet since then has been widely attributed to the popularity of the Web: from the 600-odd Web servers in existence in December 1993, the number grew to around 2,000,000 by the end of 1997.

World Wide Web Consortium *W3C*, computing industry group which seeks to promote standards and coordinate developments in the World Wide Web. Founded in 1994 and based at the Massachusetts Institute of Technology (MIT), the Consortium is directed by Tim Berners-Lee, inventor of the Web.

The W3 Consortium (W3C) is behind many initiatives, including the HTML (hypertext markup language) standard for building Web pages and the PICS content rating system. In 2000 it consisted of 57 research staff and over 400 members worldwide, including competing computing companies. Each member must sign a contract giving Berners-Lee the ultimate say in Web specifications. W3C has laboratories in France, managed by INRIA, and at Keio University, Japan.

WORM acronym for *write once read many times*, storage device, similar to a CD-ROM. The computer can write to the disk directly, but cannot later erase or overwrite the same area. WORMs are mainly used for archiving and backup copies.

worm virus designed to spread from computer to computer across a network. Worms replicate themselves while 'hiding' in a computer's memory, causing systems to 'crash' or slow down, but do not infect other programs or destroy data directly.

The most celebrated worm was the 'Internet worm' of November 1988. Released onto the Internet by Robert Morris, Jr, a graduate student at Cornell University, it infected some 6,000 systems via a loophole in Unix e-mail and finger procedures. Morris claimed that a programming bug had caused the worm to replicate far more virulently than he had intended, and took swift measures to publish an 'antidote' on the network – but by then, many machines had already been disconnected from it. Morris was later convicted, fined, and sentenced to 400 hours community service.

In June 1999 the worm virus ExploreZip overwrote files on computer systems worldwide, causing thousands of companies to close down their e-mail systems. ExploreZip reproduces by mailing itself as replies to any mails waiting in the inbox of the affected computer.

WOSA acronym for ⇨ Windows Open Services Architecture.

Wozniak, Stephen (Gary) (1950–   ) called 'Woz', US electrical engineer and computer inventor. With Steven ⇨ Jobs he formed Apple Computer in 1976 to make the Apple I.

Born in San Jose, California, the son of an engineer at Lockheed who worked on satellites, he built his first computer at the age of 13, and went on to study electrical engineering at the University of California at Berkeley in 1971. The same year he began to collaborate with Jobs in building 'blue boxes' that allowed people to make free long-distance calls. They then began to make computers out of borrowed 'chips' and, working out of a family garage, he and Jobs designed the Apple I. Wozniak was now working for Hewlett-Packard, and Apple Computer was formed when Hewlett-Packard refused to back the new computer.

In the ensuing years, Wozniak played a major role in designing the later Apple models, Lisa and Macintosh. He took several years off (it is claimed that he suffered from amnesia after a near-fatal crash in a small plane), returned to Apple in 1983, but left in 1985 after a series of disagreements with Jobs. In 1985 he started a new company, MBF, to explore new possibilities for electronics. He also became involved in other projects, including UNUSON ('unite us in song'), with its goal of eliminating international enmities by using new communication devices. In 1990 he joined Mitchell Kapor in establishing the Electronic Frontier Foundation to provide legal aid for computer hackers facing criminal prosecution and to research the legal aspects of computer communication.

write-once technology technology that allows a user to write data onto an optical disk once. After that the data are permanent and can be read any number of times.

write protection device on disks and tapes that provides ⇨ data security by allowing data to be read but not deleted, altered, or overwritten.

WYSIWYG acronym for *what you see is what you get*, program that attempts to display on the screen a faithful representation of the final printed output. For example, a WYSIWYG ⇨ word processor would show actual page layout – line widths, page breaks, and the sizes and styles of type.

World Wide Web Workbook

http://sln.fi.edu/primer/setup.html

Guide for novice Web surfers (limited to users of PCs with Windows). Topics include hypertext, graphics, hypergraphics, image maps, and thumbnails. Once the basics have been covered, users are offered a short tour with the help of Spot, the mascot 'Webdog'.

WEB LINK

x ∾ wild card character often used to describe versions of hardware or software. One might, therefore, refer to Windows 3.x (any version of Windows, from 3.0 to 3.31), or an x86 chip (any of the chips manufactured by ∾ Intel with serial numbers ending in 86).

X.25 communications protocol for sending ∾ packets of data over a network.

X.400 standard maintained by the ITU (International Telecommunications Union, formerly the ∾ CCITT) which forms the basis for a message handling system. X.400 is used as a shorthand term for a number of recommendations and standards involved in running some electronic mail systems over telecommunications lines.

X.500 directory standards for network addresses, issued by the ∾ Comité Consultatif International Téléphonique et Télégraphique (CCITT).

Xeon brand name of a type of Intel Pentium II processor designed for use in servers and high-end workstations. The Xeon processor was launched in 1998. The equivalent product designed for use in low cost personal computers is the ∾ Celeron.

Xerox PARC Xerox Corporation's Palo Alto Research Center in California. During the 1970s and 1980s, Xerox PARC spawned a series of major computing innovations, including ∾ Ethernet networks and ∾ graphical user interfaces (GUIs). Laser printing, ∾ Smalltalk, and the first (never-manufactured) personal computer were also developed there.

Xerox never capitalized on these inventions, leaving entreprenuers such as Steve ∾ Jobs and Bill ∾ Gates to bring them into the marketplace, but Xerox PARC remains at the cutting edge of computer innovations.

XGA abbreviation for *extended graphics array*, colour display system which provides either 256 colours on screen and a resolution of 1,024 × 768 ∾ pixels or 25,536 colours with a resolution of 640 × 480. This gives a much sharper image than, for example, ∾ VGA, which can display only 16 colours at 480 lines of 640 pixels.

XHTML abbreviation for *eXtensible HyperText Markup Language*, latest version of HTML to be released by the ∾ World Wide Web Consortium (W3C). Most of the markup tags that were available in HTML 4.0 are still available in XHTML. The major development is that the entire language has been rewritten in ∾ XML (eXtensible Markup Language). The design is modular, with different modules for different classes of markup tags; for example, there are separate modules for form tags, and for frame tags. This modularity means that devices that don't need all the functions of HTML can be designed to handle only the core modules. This makes their programming easier and more compact, and suits the new breed of mobile Web browsers, and devices like TV set-top boxes.

Because XML has been used to design XHTML, Web authors have to be more careful with HTML syntax and presentation; XHTML is case sensitive for example.

XML abbreviation for *eXtensible Markup Language*, simplified subset of SGML for defining languages for specific purposes or specific industries for use on the World Wide Web. XML is more powerful than HTML but less cumbersome than SGML. XML has been developed through the ↝ World Wide Web Consortium (W3 Consortium). The W3 Consortium published XML 1.0 in December 1997.

XML was used to create ↝ XHTML 1.0, the latest version of ↝ HTML from the W3 Consortium. XML also provides the last piece of technology required to develop truly portable applications. The Internet provides the global network, ↝ Java provides portable programs, and XML enables programmers to create portable data.

Xmodem ↝ FTP ↝ protocol designed to make transmitting files via telephone speedy and error-free.

XON/XOFF control commands used when two devices ↝ handshake using a modem connection. XON starts or resumes transmission of data and XOFF pauses it. XON and XOFF can be manually activated by control-Q and control-S, respectively.

X/Open multivendor computer industry body formed in 1984 to ratify and support the use of Unix as an open operating system. In February 1996, X/Open merged with the Open Software Foundation to form The Open Group.

XOR contraction of *exclusive or*, search filter meaning 'A or B, but not both'. Thus a search for 'chocolate xor biscuit' might yield 'chocolate', 'biscuit', 'chocolate cake' and 'shortbread biscuit' but never 'chocolate biscuit'. See also ↝ Boolean algebra.

X Windows networked window management system developed as part of Project Athena at the Massachusetts Institute of Technology (MIT) in 1984. It has been adopted as a standard by the Unix community but is platform-independent and versions exist for many different operating systems. X Windows enables a user to open windows into a number of different computers at the same time, either using an X Terminal or via X software running on a PC, a Unix workstation, or another computer. Although X Windows is not a graphical user interface, it provides software tools to support such interfaces: Motif is a popular Unix GUI built on X.

X got its name because it started from an earlier MIT development called W. X Window System is now a trademark of The Open Group.

Yahoo! ⌖ search engine for the ⌖ World Wide Web, based on a catalogue of indexed resources. Yahoo!, for some time the only search engine on the Web, was created at Stanford University by post-graduate students David Filo and Jerry Yang.

The name – from Swift's *Gulliver's Travels* but found by searching a dictionary – is supposed to stand for Yet Another Hierarchical Officious Oracle.

Although originally set up as a search engine, Yahoo! has been developed as a series of international ⌖ portals. Its various sites are among the most visited on the Web.

Yahoo!
The Yahoo! World Wide Web user interface, which enables the user to search for occurrences of a particular word, or to browse through selected subject areas

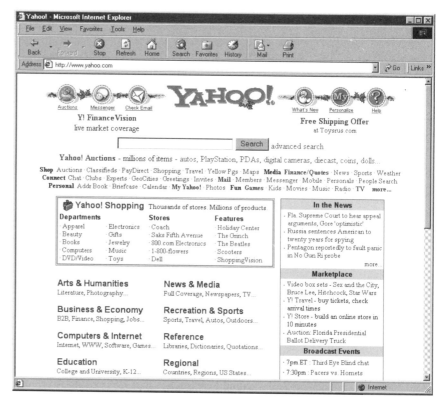

z-buffer ↝ buffer for storing depth information for displaying three-dimensional graphics. (Two-dimensional images may be displayed using x, y coordinates but the third dimension implies x, y, and z.) In a graphics card, z-buffer memory keeps track of which onscreen elements are visible and which are hidden behind other objects.

zero wait state term applied to ↝ central processing units that run without wait states – that is, without waiting for slower chips.

ZIF socket acronym for *zero insertion force socket*, socket on a computer's ↝ motherboard that enables a chip to be easily removed or inserted by use of a lever. ZIF sockets are usually only used for expensive ↝ microprocessors that are designed to be upgraded.

Zimmermann, Phil(ip) R (1955–) US security consultant and author of the encryption program ↝ Pretty Good Privacy (PGP). He was an obscure security consultant in Colorado, with an interest in cryptography until the ready availability of PGP caught the eye of the US Justice Department, which in 1993 began investigating whether Zimmermann had violated US export restrictions on strong encryption products. He consistently denied having released PGP to the Net, and in 1996 the Justice Department dropped the investigation without indicting him.

Zip drive portable disk drive manufactured by or under license from ↝ Iomega. Zip drives can store 100 ↝ megabytes (MB) or 250MB on each 3.5-in disk.

zipped file file that has been compressed using the ↝ PKZIP program.

Zmodem ↝ FTP ↝ protocol for transferring files across the ↝ Internet or other communications link. It offers the facility to use ↝ wild cards to search files and to resume interrupted transfers where they left off.

Zuse, Konrad (1910–1995) German inventor of the world's first binary digital computer. Zuse worked on building computers in Berlin, Germany, from 1935 onwards, starting in his parents' living room. He built the first binary digital computer, the Z1, in 1938, and in 1941 completed the world's first program-controlled electromechanical digital computer, the Z3.

Zuse performed astonishing feats considering that he was working almost alone during a world war. (Unlike the American military, which backed ENIAC, Germany's Nazi regime was not interested in computing.) The Z3 was destroyed in a bombing raid and the Z4 had to be moved around to protect it. After the war, the Z4 was set up as a scientific computer at the Technical University in Zürich, and, in 1949, Zuse founded a successful computer company, which was eventually taken over by Siemens.

Chronology of Computing

c. 2500 BC   The people of Mesopotamia (now Iraq) develop a positional numbering (place-value) system, in which the value of a digit depends on its position in a number.

876 BC   A symbol for zero is used for the first time, in India.

c. 190 BC   Chinese mathematicians use powers of 10 to express magnitudes.

1614   Scottish mathematician John Napier invents logarithms, which enable lengthy calculations involving multiplication and division to be carried out by addition and subtraction.

1615   William Oughtred in the UK invents the slide rule.

1623   Wilhelm Schickard in Germany invents the mechanical calculating machine.

1642   Blaise Pascal in France produces a mechanical calculating machine, the Pascaline, which uses rotating wheels to do arithmetic.

1672–74   German mathematician Gottfried Leibniz builds his first calculator, the Stepped Reckoner.

1679   Leibniz introduces binary arithmetic, in which only two symbols are used to represent all numbers.

1794   Claude Chappé in France builds a long-distance signalling system using semaphore.

1805   Joseph-Marie Jacquard in France develops an automatic loom controlled by punch cards.

1820   The first mass-produced calculator, the Arithometer, is developed by Charles Thomas de Colmar.

1823   Charles Babbage in the UK constructs a Difference Engine for calculating logarithms and trigonometric functions. Later he develops but fails to complete an Analytical Engine, which has the elements of a mechanical computer.

1839   Charles Wheatstone and William Cooke devise an electric telegraph in the UK. In the USA, Samuel F B Morse, who has developed the telegraph independently of Wheatstone and Cooke, sends the first message using the Morse code.

1854   George Boole in the UK publishes his system of symbolic logic, now called Boolean algebra.

1858   The first transatlantic telegraph cable is laid.

1876   Alexander Graham Bell in the USA invents the telephone.

1884   The first long-distance telephone line is installed, between Boston and New York.

1886   William Burroughs develops the first commercially successful mechanical adding machine.

1890   Herman Hollerith develops tabulating machines using punched cards for use in the US Census. Hollerith's company is one of the parts from which IBM (International Business Machines) is formed in 1924, and punched cards – first exploited by Joseph-Marie Jacquard in 1805 – are widely used in data processing until the 1970s.

1892   The first automatic telephone exchange is opened, at La Porte, Indiana.

1894   Guglielmo Marconi pioneers wireless telegraphy in Italy, later moving to England.

1900   Reginald Fessenden in the USA first broadcasts voice by radio.

1901   Marconi transmits the first radio signals across the Atlantic.

1904   Ambrose Fleming in the UK invents the diode valve, which allows the flow of electricity in one direction only.

1907   Charles Krumm introduces the forerunner of the teleprinter.

1924   The Computing-Tabulating-Recording Company changes its name to International Business Machines (IBM).

1936   Alan Turing in the UK develops the idea that all solvable problems can be solved using algorithms. He writes a seminal paper, 'On Computable Numbers', that influences John von Neumann and the development of computing.

1937   The first binary adding machine is constructed from telephone relays, strips of tin, bulbs, and other items by George Stibitz, an engineer at the Bell Telephone Laboratories in New Jersey, USA. He calls it the Model K because it is built on his kitchen table.

1938   Konrad Zuse, working in his parents' living room in Berlin, Germany, completes the Z1, the first binary calculating machine. Binary logic later becomes the standard method of operation for electronic computers.

1940   Stibitz and a team at Bell Laboratories, USA, complete the construction of the Complex Number Calculator, a full-scale relay calculator based on the development of his kitchen-table ideas.

1941   Zuse assembles the Z3, the first program-controlled electromechanical calculator. The German High Command rejects his proposal to build an electronic computer using valves (vacuum tubes).

1942   John Atanasoff and Clifford Berry complete the ABC or Atanasoff–Berry Calculator, one of the first electronic calculating machines. In 1973, a US Judge decides that this is enough of a computer to invalidate patents on the ENIAC, which is widely considered to be the first electronic computer.

1943   An electronic computer, Colossus, is constructed at Bletchley Park, England, to help with wartime code-breaking. Colossus is operational before ENIAC, but its development is kept secret for 32 years.
• In the USA, the Harvard University Mark I or Automatic Sequence Controlled Calculator, partly financed by IBM, becomes the first program-controlled calculator.

1944   John von Neumann and Oscar Morgenstern develop game theory in the USA.

1945   ENIAC (Electronic Numerical Integrator Analyzer And Computer) – often considered to be the first electronic computer – is completed by J Presper Eckert and John W Mauchly at the Moore School at the University of Pennsylvania. A valve-based machine, it can be reprogrammed using cables and plugboards, that is, essentially by rewiring it. However, Eckert and Mauchly have already proposed building a computer that can store and run programs: EDVAC (Electronic Discrete Variable Computer). John von Neumann's description of the project, 'First Draft of a Report on the EDVAC', is widely circulated and stimulates the building of similar machines following what becomes known as the 'von Neumann architecture'.

1946   Eckert and Mauchly leave the Moore School to found the first commercial computer company, which leads to the UNIVAC (Universal Automatic Computer) and the US mainframe computer industry.

1947   William Shockley, John Bardeen, and Walter Brattain invent the junction germanium transistor at Bell Labs.

1948   IBM's SSEC (Selective Sequence Electronic Calculator), an electromechanical system, runs a stored program on 27 January, while Manchester University's Mark I prototype runs the first stored program on an electronic computer on June 21.

1949   EDSAC (Electronic Delay Storage Automatic Calculator), the first full-scale electronic stored program computer, goes into operation at Cambridge University, England, ahead of Eckert and Mauchly's BINAC (Binary Automatic Computer), which is more than a year behind schedule.

1951   First commercially produced computers are delivered: a Ferranti Mark I going to Manchester University in February, and Eckert and Mauchly's first UNIVAC to the US Census Bureau in March.
• Whirlwind, the first real-time computer, is designed at MIT by Jay Forrester and Ken Olsen for the US air-defence system.

• Grace Murray Hopper of Remington Rand, USA, invents the first compiler computer program.

1952   EDVAC is completed at the Institute for Advanced Study, Princeton, USA, by John von Neumann and others.
• G W Dummer of the Royal Radar Establishment in the UK describes an integrated circuit that may be the first computer chip, but his prototype does not work.

1954   The silicon transistor is developed by Gordon Teal of Texas Instruments, USA.
• The first operating system is developed by Gene Amdahl for the IBM 704 computer.
• George Devol files a patent in the USA for a robotic arm controlled by programs written on punched cards.

1956   The first transatlantic telephone cable is laid.
• The computer programming language FORTRAN (Formula Translation) is devised.
• A computer chess program scores its first victory over a human being.

1957   Digital Equipment Corporation is founded by Ken Olsen.

1958   The first integrated circuit, containing five components, is built by US electrical physicist Jack Kilby of Texas Instruments.

1959   The planar transistor, which is built up in layers, or planes, is designed by Robert Noyce of Fairchild Semiconductor Corporation, USA.
• The computer programming language COBOL (Common Business-Oriented Language) is devised, having wide application in commercial computing.

1960   The first small computer, the PDP-1, is developed by Digital Equipment Corporation.

1962   Ivan Sutherland, a graduate student at MIT, USA, demonstrates Sketchpad, a program that uses a light pen to create drawings.
• Telstar pioneers transatlantic satellite communications, transmitting live TV pictures.

1963   The PDP-8, the first mass-produced minicomputer, is launched by Digital Equipment Corporation (DEC).

1964   Launch of IBM System/360, the first compatible family of computers.
• John Kemeny and Thomas Kurtz of Dartmouth College invent BASIC (Beginner's All-Purpose Symbolic Instruction Code), a computer language similar to FORTRAN.

1965   The first supercomputer, the CD6600, is developed by Seymour Cray at Control Data Corporation in the USA.
• The Advanced Research Projects Agency (ARPA) in the USA sponsors research into a 'cooperative network of time-sharing computers' which eventually becomes the Internet.
• Ted Nelson coins the term 'hypertext' and starts to imagine a global network of computers with jump-linked texts, like the World Wide Web.

1966   *Computer Weekly*, the world's first weekly computer publication, is launched in the UK.
• Charles Kao suggests using optical fibres for telecommunications.

1967   The first floppy disk drive is built at IBM.

1968   Doug Engelbart of the Stanford Research Institute, California, demonstrates the first hypertext computer system controlled by a mouse.
• Intel Corporation is founded in California by Robert Noyce and Gordon Moore to launch the first commercial 1K random access memory (RAM) chip.

1969   Researchers at four US campuses – Stanford Research Institute, the University of California at Santa Barbara and Los Angeles, and the University of Utah – link their computers to form the ARPANET, which is the starting point of the Internet.
• At Bell Labs, Ken Thomson and Dennis Ritchie begin the development of the Unix operating system.

1970   The 8-inch floppy disk drive is introduced by IBM.
• Gene Amdahl, a former IBM S/360 mainframe designer, leaves to form Amdahl Corporation to develop the first computer that is 'plug compatible' with an IBM system.

1971   The first microprocessor or 'computer on a chip', the Intel 4004, is developed by Marcian 'Ted' Hoff and others at Intel in California, USA.
• The Pascal computer language is developed by Niklaus Wirth.
• The Poketronic, the first pocket calculator, is launched in the USA.

1972   The first coin-operated video game, Pong, is installed by Nolan Bushnell, who founds Atari in California.
• Intel launches the 8008, the first 8-bit microprocessor.

1973   The first hard disk drive, code-named Winchester, is introduced by IBM.
• University College, London, and the Royal Radar Establishment in Norway become the first overseas sites connected to the ARPANET.
• Ethernet networking is developed by Bob Metcalfe, who outlines the ideas in his Harvard PhD thesis.
• The first commercial mouse-operated computer, the Alto workstation, is developed at Xerox's Palo Alto Research Center (PARC).
• Toshiba Corporation develops Japan's first microprocessor, the 12-bit TLCS-12.

1974   The C computer language is developed at Bell Labs by Brian Kernighan and Dennis Ritchie.
• CLIP-4, the first computer with a parallel architecture, is developed by John Backus at IBM.

1975   The first commercially successful personal computer, the Altair 8800, is launched in kit form by MITS in New Mexico, USA. The Altair – a name inspired by the Star Trek television series – is based on an Intel 8080 8-bit microprocessor, and uses a version of the BASIC computer language supplied by Microsoft, a company founded by William H (Bill) Gates and Paul Allen for that purpose.
• Cray Research launches the Cray 1 supercomputer, designed by Seymour Cray. The principles of RISC processing are developed by John Cocke at IBM.

1976   Apple Computer is founded in California by Steve Jobs and Steve Wozniak, who show Wozniak's Apple I computer at the Homebrew Computer Club.
• *Adventure* or *Colossal Caves*, the first adventure game, is developed by Crowther and Woods.
• The first fault-tolerant computer is launched by Tandem.

1977   The first home computers are launched in the USA for the mass market, including the Apple II, the Commodore PET (Personal Electronic Transactor), and the Tandy-Radio Shack TRS-80.
• CP/M (Control Program/Microcomputers), the first popular operating system for microcomputers, is launched by Gary Kildall of Digital Research.
• The first optical fibre communications cable is installed in California.
• Atari launches the VCS (Video Computer System), the first popular home games console.

1978   The first spreadsheet, VisiCalc, is developed by Dan Bricklin and Bob Frankston.
• *Space Invaders*, a coin-operated video game, is introduced by Taito of Japan.
• The 8086 processor – foundation of the x86 line – is launched by Intel.

1979   After several years of trials, the Prestel videotext system is launched by the UK's Post Office to deliver information to television sets via a phone line and modem.
• CompuServe and The Source, time-sharing online services, are launched in the USA.
• Ethernet local area networking is announced by Xerox, Digital Equipment Corporation, and Intel.
• The Micromodem 100 modem is introduced in the USA by Hayes Microcomputer Products.
• Usenet is set up between two US universities using UUCP, the Unix-to-Unix Copy Program.
• MUD, the first multi-user adventure game, is developed by Richard Bartle and Roy Trubshaw at the University of Essex, England.
• The Atari 400 and 800, the first home computers designed for playing games, are launched by Atari.

1980   Clive Sinclair's Sinclair Electronics enters the UK computer market with the Sinclair ZX80, the first computer for less than £100.

1981   The IBM Personal Computer or PC is launched by IBM, based on an Intel 8088 microprocessor and Microsoft's BASIC and Disk Operating System

(DOS), which IBM licenses but does not buy.
• Warner Amex, CompuServe, and Atari combine to launch the first cable TV information service in Columbus, Ohio.
• Xerox launches the Xerox Star, the first commercial computer with a graphical user interface, a mouse, an object-oriented software system, and built-in Ethernet networking.
• Adam Osborne introduces the first portable (luggable) computer, the Osborne 1: it weighs 11 kg/24 lb.
• The Teletel communications network, where small Minitel computer terminals are provided instead of printed telephone directories, is introduced in France.

1982 TCP/IP – a communications protocol proposed by Vint Cerf and Bob Kahn in 1974 – is made the standard for the ARPANET: this marks the beginning of the Internet as a network of networks.
• Compaq introduces the first portable computer compatible with the IBM PC.
• Intel announces the 80286 processor.
• The first shareware software – a communications program called PC-Talk – is distributed by Andrew Fluegelman.
• AT&T, a US telephone company, is broken up by the US Justice Department, creating the 'Baby Bells' or RBOCs (Regional Bell Operating Companies), but a long-running anti-trust case against computer giant IBM is abandoned.

1983 Apple launches Lisa, its first mouse-operated computer with a graphical user interface inspired by work at Xerox PARC.
• Microsoft, similarly inspired, announces a graphical 'interface manager' called Windows, and ships a mouse with its first word processor, Microsoft Word.
• Novell introduces the NetWare network operating system for local area networks of personal computers.
• Gavilan unveils the first portable computer with a touchpad panel that works as a mouse.
• Commodore launches the SX-64, the first portable computer with a colour screen.
• IBM announces the IBM PC Junior, a home-oriented version of the PC.

1984 Apple launches the Macintosh computer, with a built-in black and white screen, using a long television commercial created to be shown only once, during the US Superbowl football final.
• IBM launches the IBM PC AT (Advanced Technology), which sets the standard for PC-compatibility for the following decade.
• Novelist William Gibson coins the term 'cyberspace' in an influential work of science fiction, *Neuromancer*.
• The first commercial publication on CD-ROM is developed by The Library Corporation for IBM PC-compatible computers.

• Microsoft launches MSX, an 8-bit home-computer standard adopted by 14 manufacturers including Sony and Canon.

1985 The first mass-market mouse-driven 16-bit colour computers are launched in the USA by Atari (Atari ST) and Commodore (Amiga), while Microsoft ships the first version of Windows for IBM-compatible PCs. The Atari uses Digital Research's GEM (Graphical Environment Manager) interface, which is also available for IBM PCs.
• Intel announces the 386 processor.
• In the UK, Inmos announces the T414 transputer, the first off-the-shelf microprocessor for building parallel computers, and Acorn announces the ARM (Acorn RISC Machine) processor.

1986 The first Unix workstation based on a RISC processor, the PC RT or 6150, is launched by IBM. Hewlett-Packard launches the Spectrum family of RISC-based computers.

1987 IBM tries to take back control of the microcomputer industry by launching a range of PS/2 (Personal System/2) personal computers running a new OS/2 operating system developed with Microsoft. IBM's strategy, called Systems Application Architecture (SAA), also includes its proprietary mainframe computers and minicomputers.
• Apple introduces the Macintosh II line with separate system boxes and colour monitors.
• In the UK, Acorn launches the Archimedes, the first mass-market computer based on a RISC processor.

1988 Apple launches a lawsuit against Microsoft and Hewlett-Packard, arguing that their programs – Windows and NewWave – infringe copyrights on its Macintosh interface.
• The 'Gang of Nine' computer manufacturers, led by Compaq, announce the development of the EISA (Extended Industry Standard Architecture) as an alternative to the incompatible MCA (Micro Channel Architecture) used in IBM's PS/2 systems.
• NeXT unveils a cube-shaped Unix workstation, the first computer with an erasable optical disk drive replacing the floppy disk drive.

1989 Intel announces the 486 processor and its first RISC processor, the i860.
• The first pocket-sized PC-compatible computers are announced by Atari (Portfolio) and Poqet (Poqet PC).
• The first hand-held games console, the GameBoy, is launched in Japan by Nintendo.
• GRiD Systems introduces the GridPad, a large portable computer with a touch-sensitive screen, stylus, and handwriting recognition software instead of a keyboard.
• Headstart Technologies launches a PC with a built-in CD-ROM drive.

- Wafer-scale silicon memory chips, able to store 200 million characters, are announced by Anamartic.
- World chess champion Garry Kasparov beats Deep Thought, a chess-playing computer developed at Carnegie-Mellon University, in a two-game match.

1990 Microsoft releases Windows 3, a popular windowing environment for PCs.
- Dragon Systems ships Dragon Dictate, the first speech recognition system designed for personal computers.

1990–91 A prototype of the World Wide Web is developed at CERN, Europe's particle physics research centre, by Tim Berners-Lee, who posts his code on the Internet in the alt.hypertext newsgroup.

1991 PenPoint, the first operating system designed for pen-based computers, is released by Go Corporation of the USA, which is developing a handheld electronic organizer.

1992 Philips launches the CD-I (Compact-Disc Interactive) player, based on CD audio technology, to provide interactive multimedia programs for home users.

1993 Intel launches its 586 processor, but because a judge has ruled that rival manufacturers can use x86 designations, it calls it the Pentium.
- Microsoft unveils a 'New Technology' version of Windows, called Windows NT.
- Apple introduces the Newton MessagePad handheld computer, described as a 'Personal Digital Assistant' (PDA), with built-in handwriting recognition.
- Mosaic, the first graphical browser for the World Wide Web, is released free of charge by the National Centre for Supercomputing Applications (NCSA) at the University of Illinois, USA.
- Apple finally loses its five-year look-and-feel lawsuit against Microsoft and Hewlett-Packard.
- In the UK, an electronic version of the Guardian newspaper is launched for those with impaired vision. The newspaper is transmitted overnight to a PC in the user's home and printed out in Braille or spoken by a speech synthesizer.

1994 Cyberia is opened in London, England, providing coffee with Internet access: it claims to be the world's first cybercafé.

1995 Microsoft launches Windows 95 to replace Windows 3.
- Intel launches the Pentium Pro microprocessor for servers.
- Sun Microsystems releases the Java computer language.
- Sound is added to the World Wide Web when Progressive Networks releases RealAudio, an audio streaming technology.

1996 Microsoft launches the Windows CE operating systems for handheld computers and consumer electronics products.
- Matsushita Electric Industrial Co Ltd and Toshiba launch the world's first commercial DVD (Digital Video Disc, or Digital Versatile Disc) players.
- IBM's computer Deep Blue, developed from the Deep Thought chess machine, beats Russian grandmaster Garry Kasparov at chess: it is the first time a computer has beaten a human grand master in tournament play, but Kasparov wins the match 4–2.

1997 Intel introduces the Pentium II processor.
- In the USA, an attempt to bring legislation to control the Internet, intended to prevent access to obscene material, is rejected as unconstitutional.
- IBM's Deep Blue chess machine defeats grandmaster Garry Kasparov in a match by 3.5–2.5.

1998 The first tournament is held in a new league for professional players of computer games.
- Microsoft launches Windows 98, an upgrade to its Windows 95 program. It integrates its World Wide Web browser program Internet Explorer into the package, angering rival browser manufacturers, principally Netscape.

1999 Microsoft unveils Venus, whereby people in Shenzhen, China can access the Internet through their TVs.
- The Melissa virus spreads via e-mail to more than 100,000 computers around the world.
- Microsoft is forced to shut down its free e-mail service, Hotmail, when a hacker's Web page allows users to access the messages of any of its 40 million users.
- The entire Encyclopaedia Britannica, with the addition of archived news updates from current media sources, is launched on the Internet, with free access.

2000 Microsoft launches Windows 2000, a new version of its successful Windows program, but containing code that has been completely rewritten to take full advantage of advances in PC development over the past decade.
- After a long-running dispute between the US government and Microsoft over its unfair marketing of Internet Explorer, Judge Thomas Penfield Jackson recommends that the corporation be broken up into two separate companies.
- Auction of 3G mobile phone licenses brings in £22.8 billion for the UK government.
- BT Cellnet launches the first pre-pay WAP phone service.
- The Love Bug virus strikes 45 million computers worldwide, causing $10 billion worth of damage.
- BT's ADSL broadband service begins.